Plays by Early American Women, 1775–1850

Amelia Howe Kritzer,
Editor

Ann Arbor

THE UNIVERSITY OF MICHIGAN PRESS

To Bert

1998   1997   1996   1995   4   3   2   1

Plays by early American women, 1775–1850 / Amelia Howe Kritzer,
complier and editor.
    p. cm.
    Includes bibliographical references and index.
    ISBN 0-472-09598-6 (alk. paper) — ISBN 0-472-06598-X (pbk : alk. paper)
    1. American drama—Women authors.   2. American drama—19th century.
3. American drama—18th century.   4. Women—United States—Drama.
I. Kritzer, Amelia Howe, 1947–   .
PS628.W6P595   1995
812'.20809287—dc20   94-45115
                                                                          CIP

ACKNOWLEDGMENTS

I completed much of the research for this volume while I was a Fellow of the
Women's Studies Research Center at the University of Wisconsin at Madison, and
I would like to acknowledge support of the Center and its director at that time,
Cyrena Pondrom. Capable and helpful librarians in the Cairns Collection of Ameri-
can Women Writers and the Microforms Collection at the University of Wisconsin
Memorial Library facilitated the research; in this connection, I would particularly
like to thank Yvonne Schofer and Ed Duesterhoeft.

Colleagues at West Virginia University and at other institutions have offered
valuable suggestions and encouragement. My special thanks to John Whitty, Marian
Hollinger, Bernard Schultz, Bob Skloot, Rosemarie Bank, Tom Postlewait, Judith
Barlow, Kim Marra, and Brenda Murphy.

Camera-ready copy for this volume has been provided by the author.

CONTENTS

Introduction

It may come as a surprise to readers that women playwrights were actively represented on the early American stage. Standard histories of the American theatre prior to 1850 have accorded a place to only two women dramatists: Mercy Otis Warren (1728-1814), the Massachusetts Patriot best known for polemic plays that were not intended for the stage, and Anna Cora Mowatt (1819-70), whose brilliant comedy of manners, *Fashion* (1845), has become part of the American dramatic canon. These two writers, while important, do not reveal the full range and strength of dramatic work by early American women.

This collection of previously neglected but historically significant plays by early American women covers the time period bounded by the works of Warren and Mowatt—1775 to 1850. The plays in this collection are drawn from the works of approximately thirty American women whose plays were printed during this period.[1] The bibliography appended to the plays, in fact, extends to 1900, and includes a further 165 women who published plays between 1850 and 1900.

Although their plays have fallen into obscurity and been accessible for many years only on microprint and in rare book collections, several of the playwrights represented in this volume were highly successful, producing large or very popular bodies of dramatic work. Some achieved additional success in other literary genres, as performers, as educators, or as public figures. Together they offer, in their lives and plays, a sample of the range of perspectives and types of involvement early American women writers brought to the theatre.

Women playwrights of early America participated actively in theatre's project of creating a distinctive definition of the American, taking for themselves the challenge of creating both comic types and exemplary models of American womanhood. Their plays, which almost unanimously present female central characters, reveal a great deal about the ways in which the authors viewed their circumstances and defined themselves. All the earlier plays, and most of the later ones, express the nationalistic fervor that was common to the period. Many extol the freedom offered by the United States and caution audiences to use it responsibly. Because of drama's close connection with social life, relying as it does on recognizable situations, the plays point to common patterns in the day-to-day life of early America, as perceived by women. At the same time, they highlight the ideas, hopes, and aspirations of the most educated and socially active women of the new nation. One of the most remarkable aspects of these plays by early

---

[1]The printing of a play usually meant that the work had been successfully produced and/or that the author was well known.

American women is the frequency with which their action centers on a female character's interaction with and influence upon a major historical event.

Women playwrights projected their images and ideas of the American woman not only through the characters, situations, and speeches they created, but also, in a more primary way, through the act of issuing dramas for public production. When she published a play, the female playwright presented herself as a woman who made a profession of writing. Women playwrights of early America were helped in the task of constructing positive images of themselves as professional dramatists by a number of models available in English theatre. In her defense of professions for women, titled "Observations on Female Abilities," published in *Massachusetts Magazine* in 1788, Judith Sargent Murray was able to enumerate eight women dramatists of note, even though she omitted mention of the prolific women playwrights of Restoration England, as her moral outlook doubtless obliged her to do. Comedies by Susannah Centlivre (1667-1723), Hannah Parkhouse Cowley (1743-1809), and Elizabeth Inchbald (1753-1821) were among the most popular works in the early American theatrical repertoire. The comic opera *Rosina*, by Frances Moore Brooke (1724?-89), was another perennial favorite. Illustrative of the presence of women dramatists in the early American theatrical repertoire is the 1794 season of the Old American Company in Philadelphia: of the sixty plays presented between September 22 and December 4, twelve were written by women, and an additional two were creations of the French pantomimist Madame Gardie (Pollock 225-30).[2]

All of the women whose work is included in this volume registered their plays in a manner that indicated their feminine gender. Five of the playwrights—Susanna Haswell Rowson, Mary Carr (later Mary Carr Clarke), Frances Wright (later Frances Wright D'Arusmont), Charlotte Mary Sanford Barnes (later Charlotte Barnes Conner), and Louisa Medina—wrote under their own names. Mercy Otis Warren published her political satires anonymously (as was the custom for such writers of either sex) but later claimed at least *The Group* (1775), asking John Adams to verify her claim.[3] She published her tragedies under her own name. Judith Sargent Murray and Sarah Pogson (or Sarah Pogson Smith) did not use their names on the title pages of their works. Murray saw her two plays performed as the work of "An American Lady," in 1795 and 1796, but later published them under the feminine pseudonym Constantia, which was known to be her pen name. Sarah Pogson published her work as "By a

---

[2]This percentage, while certainly not high, would not be matched by many resident theatre companies today.

[3]He did so.

Lady" but registered the copyright under her own name; only through the recent rediscovery of a long-misplaced register of copyrights in South Carolina was her authorship of *The Young Carolinians* (1818) and other works established (Kable 73).

Although it appears that use of a masculine pseudonym was not common, identifying oneself as a dramatist involved special risks. The theatre was scorned, in this period, by the pious and very proper. Women who publicly associated themselves with theatre could tarnish their, and their families', reputations. Anna Cora Mowatt acknowledged this problem in her autobiography, describing the actor's position as "on the outer side of a certain conventional pale of society" (214). At the same time, many of the women playwrights expressed a concern that their work might be rejected by the male critic, who, as Rowson wrote in a preface to one book, "with lengthened visage and contemptuous smile, sits down to review the literary productions of a *woman*." He leafs through a few pages, and then, "Catching the author at some *that* or *therefore* / At once condemns her without *why* or *wherefore*" (*Mentoria* 2).

For Mowatt and Rowson, as for a number of other women playwrights, association with the theatre—usually as an actor—provided the context in which they wrote for it. In the prefaces to their works and other expository writings, these women often expressed support for theatre in defiance of strict convention as well as the hope that theatre would gain in reputation through the involvement of people with high moral values. For those women who chose to write plays in the absence of previous association with theatre, the motivations were various. In some cases financial need spurred the decision: theatre, despite its drawbacks, was one area of enterprise open to women. In other cases, the aspiring playwright wanted to use theatre's public forum to advance a particular idea or position. The desire for fame seems to have been a contributing factor in some women's choice of theatre writing. The public notice attendant on theatrical careers, of course, proved to have negative consequences for some of the playwrights—especially when that notice was not favorable. Mary Carr Clarke backhandedly castigates the "snarling critic tribe" in the introduction to *The Fair Americans* (1815), and Judith Sargent Murray engaged in a protracted dispute with a critic that expanded to include her husband and actually imperiled his career. Those who apparently did receive favorable reviews offered effusive thanks in the prefaces to their published plays.

Space, of course, limits the playwrights whose work can be included in this collection, and several women dramatists whose plays are not to be found in it are worthy of note. Ann Julia Kemble Hattan (1764-1838), a member of a well-known theatrical family, wrote the libretto for the first

American opera, *The Songs of Tammany; or, The Indian Chief* (1794; unfortunately not extant) on commission for New York's Tammany Society. In its successful first run at the John Street Theatre, this work proved so politically controversial that it inspired four days of public demonstrations (Hughes 68-69); despite this turbulent premiere, it was performed regularly in New York and other cities for several years. Margaretta V. Bleecker Faugeres (1771-1801) published her verse tragedy *Belisarius* in 1795. Elizabeth Fries Lummis Ellet (1818-77), a feminist historian of American women, wrote poetic plays that were commercially produced; best known was the tragedy *Teresa Contarini* (1835). Caroline Lee Whiting Hentz (1800-1856) won drama contests at both Philadelphia's Arch Street Theatre and New York's Park Theatre for her romantic plays *De Lara; or, The Moorish Bride* (1831) and *Werdenberg; or, The Forest League* (1832), respectively. Delia Salter Bacon (1811-59), prominent New England lecturer, associate of Harriet Beecher Stowe, and advocate of the theory that the works of Shakespeare were written by Raleigh or Bacon, published *The Bride of Fort Edwards* (1839), a drama about an incident in the Revolution. Most important of the playwrights not included is Anna Cora Mowatt (later Anna Cora Mowatt Ritchie), whose well-known play *Fashion* is available in many anthologies.

Since the plays in this volume are drawn from the dusty depths of obscurity, where they have lain for many years, and do, in fact, vary considerably in their literary and theatrical merit, the prospective reader might well wonder what they can offer of interest. This collection will, it is hoped, prove of value in four ways. First, it will offer a more complete picture of American drama in the period covered than has been available in existing theatre histories and drama anthologies that claim to be comprehensive but have tended to ignore and slight the work of women. Second, it will make available the dramatic writing of women such as Wright and Rowson, whose essays and novels, respectively, have been extensively studied. Third, it will present, through the dramatic fictions that follow (as well as in the brief biographies of the writers), fascinating representations of the lives of American women in the late eighteenth and early nineteenth centuries. Finally, it will offer for reassessment plays that have been excluded from the American dramatic canon but which, for a variety of reasons, are worthy of contemporary attention.

The Playwrights

The lives of the women whose plays are included in this collection show a varied picture of interest and involvement in drama. Mercy Otis Warren (1728-1814), probably the best known of all the women included here, played a significant part in the political and social events of the Revolutionary era. As a sister of the Patriot leader James Otis, close friend of John and Abigail Adams, and wife of a prominent Patriot who served as president of the Provincial Congress and paymaster general of Washington's army, Warren lived at the center of revolutionary activity in New England. Born the third child and first daughter of the prosperous Otis family, she grew up in Barnstable, Massachusetts, sharing the companionship and lessons of her gifted older brother, while balancing study with the domestic duties demanded of a daughter. Living at home through young adulthood, she read widely and wrote occasional poetry. Through her brother, who went on to Harvard, she encountered both the political ideas animating the American Revolution and the person she was to marry.

After an extended courtship, Mercy Otis married James Warren in 1754; she was twenty-six (an advanced age for a bride at the time) and considered an intellectual prodigy. The happiness of the Warrens' fifty-four years of marriage is documented in a large body of correspondence. The couple had five sons. In the ten years leading up to the Revolution, the Warrens' home at Plymouth served as a frequent meeting place for those interested in discussing politics. The charismatic James Otis emerged as one of the first Patriot leaders; his writings and organizational abilities laid the foundations for the successful revolution. Otis, however, became increasingly known for erratic behavior, and the head injury he received in a tavern encounter with Tory sympathizers brought about serious mental deterioration and put an end to his political career.

Perhaps prompted by the incapacitation of her brother, Warren entered the ranks of the numerous political pamphleteers and satirists on both sides of the Patriot-Tory divide in 1772, with *The Adulateur*, first published serially and anonymously in *The Massachusetts Spy*. This satire highlighted what Warren perceived to be the moral gulf between the two sides, with brave and honest Brutus (Samuel Adams) representing the Patriots and ignoble Rapatio (colonial governor Thomas Hutchinson) representing the Tories. At the urging of John Adams (who had missed the event itself because he had been visiting the Warrens), she wrote a humorous poetic tribute to the Boston Tea Party, "The Squabble of the Sea-Nymphs," in 1773. A second dramatic satire, *The Defeat*, appeared serially in the *Boston Gazette* during 1773, but is extant only in fragmentary form.

The Group, Warren's most successful dramatic satire, appeared in 1775, first by installments in the *Boston Gazette* and the *Massachusetts Spy*, then in full editions published in Philadelphia, Boston, and New York. Passionately partisan—as was most polemic literature of the period—and fired by the drama of unfolding events, *The Group* energetically satirizes the Tory governing council put in place by the British Parliament in 1774, after colonial governor Hutchinson (Rapatio) had fled to England. In the course of confidential chats among themselves, the Tory leaders reveal the base motives, cowardly fears, and petty rivalries imputed to them by Patriots. Like other work of its time, *The Group* makes continual and, to the contemporary reader, eventually wearying references to classical myth, British history, and world political figures. The wealth of these references—vivid evidence of Warren's intellect and education—doubtless increased the weight of her dramatic indictment of the Tory leadership. What truly gave the satire its bite, however, were the personal details she incorporated into her representations of the individual leaders.

Warren based her thinly disguised portraits of such notable Tories as Timothy Ruggles, who as Hateall calls for war even if it kills his own family and friends, and Daniel Leonard, who as Beau Trumps loves fine clothes and luxuries, on thorough acquaintance with her subjects. She knew very well that Ruggles was a cousin of John Adams and that Leonard dressed foppishly and was the only lawyer in Massachusetts to keep his own chariot. The fact that these men were American-born only increased the bitterness with which Warren portrayed them as traitors. Whether from this bitter viewpoint or from actual knowledge of the men she caricatured, Warren gives misogyny a prominent place in the catalog of vices displayed by the Tories: Simple Sapling disregards his wife's welfare, and Hateall boasts that he married for money and broke his wife's spirits with "the green hickory." In any case, Warren ends the play with a woman's perspective, introducing a nameless "lady, nearly connected with one of the principal actors in the group," who voices Patriot sentiments. Again, Warren writes from life: a number of her intimates, including her brother James and sister Mary, had marriages that were divided by differing political loyalties. With the remarkable confidence in the untried revolutionary forces expressed throughout the play, Warren's "lady" solemnly predicts defeat of the British.

Biographer Katherine Anthony quotes from passages in Warren's correspondence indicating that the acclaim and popularity enjoyed by *The Group* caused her to question whether satire was an appropriate vehicle for a woman writer. In a letter to John and Abigail Adams, she stated her opinion that "the particular circumstances of our unhappy times" justified "a little personal acrimony" on the part of male writers but worried that a woman who "indulges her pen to paint in the darkest shades even those whom vice and venality have rendered contemptible" might compromise her character. Both Adamses reassured her that her God-given "Powers for the Good of the World" should be exercised (95).

Two additional political satires of the Revolutionary era have been attributed to Mercy Otis Warren—*The Blockheads; or The Affrighted Officers* (1776), a caustic reply to a satirical skit titled *The Blockade of Boston* written by the British general Burgoyne; and *The Motley Assembly* (1779), a comedy lampooning the Boston's Tory-allied fashionable set. Both plays are written in prose, employing a farcical style and crude language. Warren never claimed them, but literary historians generally agree in viewing them as her work.

Among Warren's postrevolutionary writings are two historical tragedies in blank verse, written in the late 1780s and published in 1790. Though she sent these works to Adams in London, in the hope they would be produced there, the plays were never performed. Both deal with the upheaval of civil war and take as their themes the fragility of freedom and the pain caused by divided personal loyalties. *The Ladies of Castile* deals with an unsuccessful attempt at the revolutionary overthrow of a tyrant. It is notable for an unusual female character—a young mother who lays aside her maternal role to take up the sword of revolution when her husband is captured. A subplot deals with lovers who find themselves on opposing sides of the conflict. *The Sack of Rome* offers a more conventional treatment of the competing claims of love and honor, but its principal female character nonetheless displays considerable complexity.

Warren's later years brought many misfortunes, including the early deaths of three sons, estrangement from the Adamses, and financial difficulties. Nevertheless, she continued to write, publishing in 1805 her best-known nondramatic work, a three-volume history of the American Revolution.

Susanna Haswell Rowson (1762-1828), another well-known woman of her time, was born in England, but brought to America at a young age by her father, a British naval officer assigned to the customs office in Massachusetts. Susanna enjoyed a pleasant and privileged childhood, reading the books in her father's library and receiving informal tutoring from adults in the household and family friends. One such friend was James Otis, Patriot pamphleteer and brother of Mercy Otis Warren; this connection would indicate that the two women must have been acquainted, though separated by age. The outbreak of the Revolution reversed the Haswell family's fortunes. Loyal to the Crown but mindful of family ties and property in Massachusetts, Haswell attempted to remain neutral, but he and his family were detained under guard and their property confiscated. In 1778, through an exchange of prisoners, the Haswell family was sent to England. Susanna was then sixteen years old.

In England, Susanna attempted to contribute to the support of her impoverished family by working as a governess and writing. During the following eight years, she sent poems and short stories to various publications and in 1786 published her first novel, *Victoria*. This novel was dedicated to the Duchess of Devonshire, Georgiana Cavendish,[4] the "reigning queen" of London society and a writer herself, who acted as Susanna's patron, introducing her work to such notables as Samuel Adams and Mrs. Siddons and introducing Susanna herself to the Prince of Wales.

Later in 1786, Susanna Haswell married William Rowson, a London hardware merchant and trumpeter in the Royal Horse Guards. She continued to publish stories, poems, and novels. Most notable among her works during this period was *Charlotte: A Tale of Truth*, popularly known as *Charlotte Temple*, published in 1791. This novel went through innumerable editions and became "America's first best-selling novel." Brandt states that *Charlotte Temple* was the "most widely-read book" in America, "with the possible exception of Benjamin Franklin's *Autobiography*, before the appearance of Harriet Beecher Stowe's *Uncle Tom's Cabin* in 1852" (52). An indication of Rowson's interest in drama at this early stage of her writing career is provided in the long poem "A Trip to Parnassus; or The Judgment of Apollo on Dramatic Authors and Performers" (1788), a discussion in verse of the major theatre personalities of the period.

When her husband's hardware business failed in 1792, the Rowsons, with William's teenaged sister, joined an acting troupe. After touring in England and performing in Edinburgh, the Rowsons were recruited for the New American Company managed by Thomas Wignell and Alexander Reinagle. They came to the United States and performed from 1794 to 1796 with the Wignell-Reinagle company in Philadelphia's Chestnut Street Theatre as well as for shorter periods in Baltimore, Annapolis, and Washington. William served as prompter for the company, playing occasional small roles, while the young Charlotte performed minor ingenue roles and Susanna specialized in comic character acting. As was typical for performers of the period, she played thirty-five roles in her first four-and-a-half-month season in Philadelphia. Mates, in *The American Musical Stage before 1800*, states that the Rowsons also performed at the Art Pantheon, or Ricketts Amphitheatre, which opened in October of 1795, across the street from the Chestnut Street

---

[4]The aristocratic and wealthy Cavendish family was known for producing writers and literary patrons, including the essayist and dramatist Margaret Lucas Cavendish, duchess of Newcastle (1623-73).

Theatre and alternating playing nights with it. Appearing in pantomimes and farces, Susanna Rowson is said to have danced sailors' hornpipes and become the "first female Harlequin in America" (161).

The wealth of theatrical activity in Philadelphia toward the close of the eighteenth century made it a fertile environment for the aspiring actor and playwright. It is worthy of note that during their first season with the company known as the "New American Company," its competitor, known as the "Old American Company" and performing at the Southwark Theatre, introduced Ann Julia Kemble Hattan's *Tammany* to Philadelphia audiences. Similarly, the Rowsons' employment in Philadelphia overlapped with that of Mrs. Marriott, of the Old American Company, who wrote *The Chimera; or, Effusions of Fancy*, a farce afterpiece. It is possible that these women playwrights met, and, since both Rowson and Marriott were recruited from Edinburgh, they may have known each other before coming to Philadelphia.

Rowson's first known dramatic work, *Slaves in Algiers*, a comic opera for which Alexander Reinagle composed the music, premiered on June 30, 1794, at the Chestnut Street Theatre in Philadelphia (Pollock 221). Addressing itself to the capture of Americans by the Barbary Pirates, a contemporary issue of great interest, it claims the distinction of being the first of many plays on this theme (see Gallagher). It was also one of only two new American plays produced by the company in their first season (the other being of anonymous authorship). Though originally performed for the Rowsons' benefit,[5] with Rowson playing the role of Olivia, the play, following its successful premiere, immediately entered the company's repertory, appeared as one of the first presentations of the following season (Seilhamer 3:181-82), and was performed regularly thereafter. Contemporary critics have found the play notable for the overt comparison it makes between marriage and slavery and between patriarchal power and the power of a ruling despot.

Slaves in Algiers initiated a fruitful collaborative relationship between Rowson and Reinagle, in which she composed the libretti and/or lyrics and he the music for other full-length works and numerous popular songs. The company presented another Rowson-Reinagle collaboration, *The Volunteers*,[6] a "musical entertainment" based on Pennsylvania's recent Whiskey Rebellion, in January, 1795; President and Mrs. Washington apparently attended its second performance (Pollock 239). For the Rowsons' benefit

---

[5]The benefit performance was a form of compensation for actors in the eighteenth and early nineteenth centuries, in which proceeds of the evening were given to the particular actor. Married couples usually shared a benefit. The actor(s) could chose the play and the role(s) played for the benefit.

[6]None of Rowson's dramatic works except *Slaves in Algiers* are extant.

of June 19, 1795, Susanna Rowson wrote another new work, *The Female Patriot*, an adaptation of Massinger's *The Bondman* (Seilhamer 3:176, 184-85). *The American Tar*, presented for the Rowson's benefit of June 17, 1796, was also probably from her pen (Seilhamer 3:214), and she may have written the adaptation of Lessing's *Minna von Barnhelm* that was performed as *The Disbanded Officer* in 1795 (Brandt 105).

Rowson continued to write in other genres during this time, publishing a four-volume novel, *Trials of the Human Heart*, in 1795 and issuing American editions of her previously published novels. The influential publisher Matthew Carey became one of the chief promoters of Rowson's work. A "political-literary adversary of Carey," William Cobbett, a writer who "enjoyed attacking prominent figures," took the role of her chief detractor (Brandt 108). His 1795 review occasioned one of the disputes with critics that plagued the careers of several of the playwrights whose works are presented in this volume.

Cobbett, complaining that Rowson was being called the "American Sappho" and had been immodest enough to mention (in her preface to *Slaves in Algiers*) the "unbounded marks of approbation" with which her works had been greeted in America, took her to lengthy task for what he considered grammatical errors or examples of poor expression in *Slaves in Algiers* (Brandt 108-9). He went on to impugn her professed loyalty to the United States, calling attention to her father's position in the British military. He crowned his argument by ominously predicting that allowing women like Rowson freedom of expression would cause "the reformed church. . . to raze the odious word *obey* from their marriage service" and result in "our present house of Representatives [being] succeeded by members of the other sex " (qtd. in Brandt 109-10). Rowson found a defender in one such member of the U.S. House of Representatives, John Swanwick, who wrote three pamphlets rebutting Cobbett. Rowson herself answered Cobbett's most serious accusation—that of false, opportunistic patriotism—in her preface to *Trials of the Human Heart*. The Rowson biographer and critic Ellen Brandt concludes her discussion of this incident with the observation that it primarily "serves to illustrate the immediate popularity and celebrity of Susanna Rowson in America. She was discussed. She was attacked and defended. She was a woman to reckon with" (111).

At the end of the 1796 season, the Rowsons, along with seven other actors, quit the New American Company and signed contracts with John B. Williamson to act with his company at the Federal Street Theatre in Boston. There they found a theatre that insisted on strict propriety from both actors and patrons and an environment in which plays interacted significantly with the intense political debates of the time. The Rowsons were given better parts in Boston, he appearing onstage regularly and she receiving more favorable reviews of her performances. She wrote *Americans in England* for their benefit performance on April 12, 1797. It ran an additional three nights, a sign of considerable success in the theatre of the late eighteenth century, and was later produced by another company under the title *The Columbian Daughter*. Afterward the company introduced *Slaves in Algiers*; this play ran only one performance in that season, perhaps because it was not new, having continued to be regularly performed in New York and Philadelphia, sometimes under a slightly altered title, such as *Slaves Released from Algiers* or *Americans in Algiers*.

Susanna Rowson found acting a difficult sphere in which to earn a living. She complained of irresponsibility on the part of fellow actors (notwithstanding the praise she accords the company in her preface to *Slaves in Algiers*) and of the rudeness of audience members. Most troubling, however, may have been the financial instability of theatre companies. The troupe the Rowsons had joined in Boston began to founder, and at the end of the 1797 season it disbanded. After a summer engagement in Newport, Rhode Island, the Rowsons retired from the stage (Seilhamer 3:351).

Late in 1797, when she was thirty-five years old, Rowson determined to settle in Boston, where her two half-brothers lived, and start a school for girls (Brandt 129). Patronized by the Boston socialite Mrs. Samuel Smith and the influential Otis family, the academy proved an instant success, growing from one pupil to over a hundred in just one year (Brandt 129; Weil 3). Its success endured, surviving several changes of location and continuing even after Rowson's retirement. Rowson proved a popular and innovative teacher, introducing a pianoforte to the classroom and employing notable musicians to teach music to her pupils. Besides managing the school by herself (her husband having found employment with the Customs Service), she wrote and published volumes of classroom materials and textbooks, including primers in geography and spelling and collections of poetry. She continued to write novels, poetry, and songs. Her prominent position in the Boston literary establishment is indicated by the frequency with which she was asked to contribute a poem or song for the celebration of the president's birthday or some other public occasion.

In 1802 Rowson added to her activities by assuming the editorship of a new periodical, the *Boston Weekly Magazine*. The magazine was a miscellaneous compilation of essays, short stories, and poems, many offering advice and overt morals. Though Rowson herself is believed to have been the principal contributor, another writer known to have published work in the magazine is Judith Sargent Murray, whose play *The Traveller Returned* (1796) is included in this collection. Commonality of interest and physical proximity would argue for the two women knowing each other, though by that time neither was engaged in writing plays.[7] After this periodical ceased publication, Rowson became a frequent contributor to other magazines. She also volunteered in charitable work and reared an adopted daughter, a niece, and an illegitimate son fathered by her husband.

Rowson continued her full life of teaching, writing, and vigorous association with the most active people and important events of her time until 1822, when she retired from teaching. Despite failing health, she continued to write until her death in 1824, leaving behind her a thriving school, a just-finished novel to be published posthumously, and a genuinely remarkable body of writing.

Judith Sargent Murray was born in 1751, in Gloucester, Massachusetts, a coastal town with a population of about five thousand, in which both her parents and grandparents had been born. A biography by Vena Field (1931) is the authoritative source on Murray's life. The Sargent family was a prominent one in New England, having acquired its wealth through shipping and trading. Judith, who demonstrated unusual intellectual aptitude from an early age, received home tutoring, and it is probable that she shared her brother's lessons in Latin and Greek under a local minister as he prepared for Harvard. Although she often expressed regret at being denied the chance at a university education, Murray undoubtedly extended her early education on her own, since her writings show her to have been very widely read. In 1769, at the age of nineteen, Judith Sargent married the heir of another ship-owning family. A monument to that marriage still stands in Gloucester today—the Sargent-Murray-Gilman House, a historic mansion that, along with documents and mementos of the three families, contains portraits of Judith Sargent painted by Copley and Stuart. After the death of her first husband in 1786, Judith married John Murray, the founder of the Universalist sect in America. The Murrays lived in Boston for most of their married life. They had two children, but only their daughter Julia lived to maturity.

Murray's life encompassed, and was encompassed by, two concurrent revolutions. The War of Independence began in her home state and drew strong support from her very Patriot family. Her brother Winthrop Sargent served in Washington's army and later was appointed by President Adams to be the first governor of the Mississippi Territory. Both her father and her first husband were members of Gloucester's Committee of Safety,

---

[7]It furthermore seems a distinct possibility that Judith Sargent Murray's daughter Julia was a pupil at Rowson's Academy.

and her father was one of the delegates to the Massachusetts State convention for ratifying the Constitution in 1788.

The second revolution, which affected Murray's family even more intimately, was a religious one. It began in the early 1770s, when the doctrine of Universalism first came to Gloucester. As the influence of strict Calvinism declined, this sect, with its belief in universal salvation, gained a foothold in Massachusetts. In 1774, when John Murray came to America to preach Universalism, the Sargents opened their home to him and built the first Universalist meetinghouse in America. Judith married John Murray in 1787 and thereafter devoted much of her own energy to Universalism. That she and her husband met with considerable success is evident in the fact that, by 1793, John Murray had opened a large church in Boston, which became the largest congregation in that city and served as headquarters for a network of Universalists. The Murrays traveled frequently, meeting Martha Washington, Benjamin Rush, and other prominent people of the day. The happy outcome of both revolutions, from Murray's standpoint, undoubtedly inspired her with the courage to straightforwardly claim equality for women in her writing and feel some degree of confidence that the changes she called for would occur.

Judith Sargent Murray's writing career can be dated from a poem written in 1775, mourning the death of a younger sister. Murray did not, however, begin to publish until after her second marriage. From 1784 to 1794 she contributed poems and essays to various periodicals. For her poems she used the pen name Constantia. Her essays, which became a regular feature of the *Massachusetts Magazine*, were published as the works of "The Gleaner"—and as The Gleaner she used the fictional name Mr. Vigillius. These essays, it should be mentioned, were a very popular part of the *Massachusetts Magazine*, and the periodical did not survive for long after they were discontinued.

Murray's dramatic writing grew out of her intense interest in theatre and involvement in the campaign by liberal-minded Bostonians to rescind the legal prohibition of theatre and establish a playhouse in their city. In "Panegyric on the Drama," one of the "Gleaner" essays, she defended theatre as a reasonable form of amusement for an enlightened citizenry, refuting, one by one, the principal arguments—"waste of time . . . imprudent expenditures . . . encouragement of idleness . . . and relaxation of morals"—upon which "objections to theatrical amusements" were based (*Gleaner* 1:225-27). Her publications, furthermore, include prologues and epilogues to various plays performed privately in Boston before its first theatre opened in 1794.

Murray's two plays were written soon after the Federal Street Theatre had opened in Boston and probably were submitted to the theatre in response to a call for new plays by Americans. *The Medium or, Happy Tea-Party* premiered on March 2, 1795. It was the first production by an American-born writer to be presented in Boston and is the first play by an American-born woman known to have received a professional production. This distinction was not immediately apparent, however, as the play was brought out anonymously, and speculation about who the playwright might be focused on Royall Tyler, who had written *The Contrast* in 1787, and on Murray's husband, John. The play met with little enthusiasm from the audience. Charles S. Powell, the Federal Street's manager, offered to give the play a second performance, but Murray refused. Although Murray may have entered the public realm of drama with the thought that she put into the mouth of her character Harriott Montague, that "I would rather be paragraphed in the newspaper than not distinguished at all," she was reportedly quite distressed by critical comments and later blamed the acting company for *The Medium*'s poor reception, stating that the play had not been fairly "brought to the test" (*Gleaner* 3:13). The conviction that the production had obscured the play's merits—not an unfounded accusation in view of the generally low regard for the talents of the Federal Street Theatre's acting company at that time—provided one of the justifications for including *The Medium*, retitled *Virtue Triumphant*, in the 1798 collection.

The Traveller Returned, presented at the Federal Street Theatre on March 9, 1796, fared somewhat better. It ran for two nights initially, to a mostly favorable audience reception; however, the review of the play published by Robert Treat Paine in his newspaper, the *Federal Orrery*, initiated a heated exchange between newspaperman and playwright that eventually involved Murray's husband. In a reasonably favorable review, Paine suggested using a "pruning knife," on the soliloquies and expressions of patriotism. Murray replied anonymously, calling attention to errors in Paine's summary of the plot. Paine printed her letter but appended to it the sarcastic comment, "Damn not a play which has gone to that bourne whence no Traveller Returns!" (Field 38).

As the exchange continued, Paine expanded his satirical attack to include references to a John Murray caricature he named "Parson Flummery." Paine then went on to address John Murray directly, imputing to him authorship of *The Traveller Returned*, taunting him with a pronouncement that the play had "given up the ghost" without hope of "resurrection," and hinting that he had been a strolling player in Ireland before entering the ministry (Field 39). Replying in the *Orrery*'s rival paper, the *Columbian Centinel*, John Murray solemnly declared that he had never written a play, while carefully insisting on the value of plays in general and the merit of the particular one in question, and stoutly maintained that he had never been an actor, though again stressing his judgment that acting was an honorable profession (40). The controversy eventually died down, but Murray had no more plays performed, though her correspondence refers to a third, *The African*, which she was unable to get produced.

Both performed plays demonstrate a talent for comedy and present remarkable female characters who initiate action, express and argue for philosophical principles, and form a self-sufficient community in which women of various ages support and protect one another. A unique feature of both plays is the presentation of a female "rake reformed": the device of a character who strays from the path of virtue but returns to it through the action of the play, was familiar in the drama of the period, but Murray's plays may offer the only examples of female characters of this type.

In 1798, needing money, Murray collected her best writings, including the two produced plays, into a three-volume set titled *The Gleaner*, of which she sold 820 sets by subscription. She published this collection as the work of Constantia, though her personal letters soliciting subscriptions made the pen name a meaningless cover. More striking to readers was the revelation that Constantia and the Gleaner, Mr. Vigillius, were the same person. She explained her assumption of the pseudonym not only as a desire to be spared the negative prejudice against women writers but also as a need to keep her career separate from that of her husband. The difficulty, if not impossibility, of maintaining such separation after her revelation that she was the Gleaner, Mr. Vigillius, and Constantia might explain Murray's diminished output after 1798. Following the failure of her husband's health around 1800, Murray virtually ceased writing. As he became a complete invalid, she undertook not only to nurse him but to complete and edit his writings, publishing the *Letters and Sketches of Sermons* in 1813 and *The Life of John Murray* in 1816.

Murray became a widow in 1815 and spent the last few years of her life with her daughter and family on their plantation near Natchez, in the Mississippi Territory. She died in 1820. It had long been reported that Murray's papers were destroyed; however, in 1988 they were discovered, damaged but apparently salvageable, in an abandoned house on the grounds of the original plantation. The Mississippi Department of Archives and History is attempting their restoration.

Mary Carr, later Mary Carr Clarke, is one of the least known of the playwrights represented here. Most of the little available information about her is found in a long autobiographical preface to *The Memoirs of the Celebrated and Beautiful Mrs. Ann Carson, Daughter of an Officer of the U.S. Navy, and Wife of Another, Whose Life Terminated in the Philadelphia Prison* (2d ed.; 1838), an account of a coquette gone wrong ghostwritten by Clarke. The preface—which describes in detail the close but conflict-ridden relationship that developed between Clarke and Carson as the latter applied to Clarke for help writing her life story, formed a financial partnership with her, moved in with her, contributed to her anxieties about propriety, aggravated her financial difficulties in many ways, and finally cheated and robbed her—offers few basic facts about Clarke's life. She was born in Philadelphia, probably in the early 1790s, and lived there for some time, then moved to New York City in the late 1830s. Left in poverty after the illness and death of her husband, a military officer in the War of 1812, she first attempted to earn a living by starting a school but turned to writing and taking in boarders when the school had to close during an outbreak of "fever and ague."

In prefaces to both the Carson memoirs and to her play *The Benevolent Lawyers,* Clarke remarks on the many misfortunes she has experienced, specifying the loss of her husband, the betrayal by Ann Carson, and various financial reverses due to the vagaries of publishing. Between the publication of *The Fair Americans* in 1815 and that of *The Benevolent Lawyers* in 1823, she changed her name from Carr to Clarke. Based on the information offered in the preface to the Carson memoirs, it seems likely but not certain that Carr[8] was her first husband and Clarke the second. All Clarke tells us about her deceased husband is that he died "very shortly after Richard Smyth's execution,"[9] following a lengthy illness. References to children indicate that she had two sons, Alexander and William, and at least two daughters; the sons lived with her after she became a widow, while the daughters resided with her mother in a different section of Philadelphia.

Some information exists for four plays written by Clarke. Three of her plays were published, of which two, *The Fair Americans* and *The Benevolent Lawyers, or Villainy Detected,* are extant. No record of these two plays being produced has been found,[10] though handwritten names after the first four characters in the extant copy of *The Fair Americans* would seem to indicate performance,[11] and amateur productions were not common at the

---

[8]Her association with song writing and theatre prompts the speculation that Mary Carr Clarke was somehow related to Benjamin Carr, the well-known musician and composer, who worked with theatres in Philadelphia and New York during her lifetime; however, no connection has been traced.

[9]Richard Smyth, Ann Carson's lover, was executed in 1816, after being convicted of the murder of her husband.

[10]The notation in Nichols's bibliography that *The Fair Americans* was performed at the John Street Theatre in New York on November 9, 1789, cannot be correct, since the play takes as its subject the War of 1812. Ireland gives the date of this performance as November 5, 1789, but clearly it is a different play with the same name.

[11]These names are as follows: M. Nevi [Neville?] for Trueman, Mr. T. Jeffers [Jefferson] for Belford, Mr. H. Walsh for Clifford, Mr. Gough for Freelove, and an

time. It seems likely that they were produced, in spite of the lack of verification that they were, since unproduced plays were seldom printed. Furthermore, Clarke's reference, in the preface to *The Fair Americans*, to "the Snarling Critic Tribe, whose malignancy 'spares nor sex nor age,'" strongly suggests that, by the time this play was published in 1815, Clarke had undergone the experience of a negative review. James's history of Philadelphia theatre lists a production of *The Return from Camp* on January 6, 1815 (23). The end of the War of 1812 was celebrated soon afterward, on February 13. Given that the subject matter of *The Return from Camp*, as implied by the title, is similar to that of *The Fair Americans*, there is a reasonable probability that *The Fair Americans* is a revision of *The Return from Camp*. Replete with patriotic speeches, songs, and pageantry, it may have been expanded in response to the public's desire for vehicles of celebration, with the official end of the war. As the title implies, the work focuses on young women; it provides a fascinating and sometimes comic look at the way their lives were disrupted by the war and the ways in which they were able to cope with this disruption.

The Benevolent Lawyer, an early melodrama about a beautiful young mother who almost falls into the clutches of a lecherous villain when the return of her ship captain husband from a voyage is delayed, surely must have tempted some theatre manager enough to give it a production. Clarke's most successful play, *Sara Maria Cornell; or, The Fall River Murder*, a sensational treatment of the murder of a young factory worker, had a protracted run at New York's Richmond Hill Theatre and was published in 1833. In style and success. *Sara Maria Cornell* stands comparison with and perhaps paved the way for Louisa Medina's plays at the Bowery a short time later.

In addition to her known plays, Carr wrote numerous popular songs and several biographies—not only that of "the celebrated and beautiful Mrs. Ann Carson," but also *A Concise History of the Life and Amours of Thomas S. Hamblin, late manager of the Bowery Theatre. As communicated by his legal wife, Mrs. Elizabeth Hamblin* (1838?), and a nonextant biography of Edwin Forrest. The Ann Carson book made her, if briefly, a celebrity, as she reports that its first edition sold out immediately and was ordered by the president, the vice president, the governor of Pennsylvania, and many members of Congress. Unfortunately for Clarke, however, Carson's recidivism meant not only personal disappointment, since she sincerely liked Carson and wished for her reform, but also financial loss, since publishers were reluctant to issue a second edition of the memoirs of someone who

---

illegible notation for Harley. No names are given for other roles.

was, by that time, a confirmed criminal. The Hamblin book, an expose
written as a partisan of Hamblin's estranged wife, probably grew out of
Clarke's association with Elizabeth Hamblin during her management of the
Richmond Hill Theatre. Somewhat incongruously, Clarke also edited a
literary periodical, *The Intellectual Regale, or, Lady's Tea Tray*, beginning in
1815, and wrote several pamphlets dealing with a controversial schism in the
Catholic church.

Sarah Pogson (or Sarah Pogson Smith) presents another case in which
very little information can be found about her life. The entry for Smith in
American Women Writers indicates that she was born in Essex, England, and
died and is buried in Charleston, South Carolina, but gives no dates for
either birth or death. According to this entry, she was born the daughter
of a John Pogson, an English planter in the West Indies, and Ann Wood
Pogson; immigrated to Charleston in either 1788 or 1793 (the date on her
tombstone being semi-indecipherable); and married Judge Peter Smith of
New York. In later life she is said to have lived with her sister, Mrs.
William Blamyer, in Charleston.

Sarah Pogson Smith offered intriguing hints about her life, but nothing
verifiable, in a preface and occasional notes accompanying her publications.
In the preface to *Essays Religious, Moral, Dramatic, and Poetical*, in which she
included *The Young Carolinians* and two other plays, Pogson offered this
justification for publication of her writing:

To contribute to the means of extricating a Widow from embarrassed
circumstances, and declining health, occasioned by the encumbrance of
debt most painfully incurred. Her only son, when on the point of being
eligibly established, was suddenly taken ill, and after protracted suffering
for many months, died. This misfortune brought with it demands upon
her very narrow income, which it could not satisfy—her health was
deeply injured, and her eldest daughter fell sick: Again, heavy and
unavoidable expenses ensued—her life was spared—but in so delicate a
condition that it is only preserved by the tenderest care and attention to
climate and diet: Both are thus incapacitated from exertions, which their
education and abilities might render advantageous.

That Sarah Pogson Smith is, herself, the unfortunate widow referred to in
this passage seems an intriguing possibility, but information available about
Peter Smith contradicts the view of Sarah Pogson Smith as a widow with
almost grown children in 1818. The entry for Peter Smith in the *Dictionary
of American Biography* states that he married Sarah Pogson after the death
of his first wife in 1818. This entry, which draws on family papers of Peter
Smith, goes on to describe the marriage as short-lived, ending "in bitterness
and separation" as "the wife returned to South Carolina and the husband

gave himself up to the religious and personal peculiarities of his earlier years" (17:332). If this is true, then Sarah Pogson was unmarried at the time that she published *Essays*, a likelihood substantiated by the fact that she registered the copyright under the name "Miss Pogson."

The clues to Smith's life that can be gained from a perusal of the essays offer a clear picture of the type of woman she was but, again, very little factual detail. Some of the essays and poems are given a date and place, presumably of composition: they include "The Parsonage, 1802" for "Friendship and Benevolence"; "C** Grove" for "To Mrs. M"; "Sullivan's Island" (in Charleston Harbor) for "The Fairies" and "The Excursion"; and "Bluff W**, Ohio, 1812" for "Elegaic." They suggest that she may have traveled between 1807 and 1818. The dedication to Edward Pinckney and subscription to the volume by the Pinckney sisters, as well as numerous references to her goddaughter Maria Middleton and the Middleton family, indicate that Smith was on good terms with Charleston's leading families. Finally, the frequency with which she dedicated her works to religious and charitable causes—including the "education and care of the indigent deaf and dumb" (*Daughters of Eve*), the "seamen's floating church" (*The Arabians*), and various churches and other public institutions—implies that she was actively religious and that her involvement with charitable causes formed an important part of her identity. Of course, for a woman interested in presenting her writing to the public, but constrained by the fear that such action might be inappropriate for women, the various charitable causes to which her works are dedicated (including the widow to which the preface to the *Essays* refers) could have provided a necessary legitimation.

Pogson's earliest known play is *The Female Enthusiast*, which was published anonymously "by a lady" in 1807. This verse drama is about the murder of Jean Paul Marat by Charlotte Corday.[12] Romantic in style and nonfactual in its representation of the main character's family and personal circumstances, it presents Charlotte as a thoughtful, intelligent, and highly moral young woman who acts on her humanitarian ideals in spite of the expected cost to her. Subplots deal with the love dilemmas of Charlotte's more ordinary friend, Estelle, and the struggles of a poor, rural family whom Charlotte had befriended and helped. This play may have been produced in Charleston, because Placide, manager of the Charleston Theatre during the early 1800s, encouraged new plays by local writers, and because the large French community in Charleston would have had a strong interest in political events in France. Watson insists that the play would not have been performed at the Charleston Theatre under Placide's management,

---

[12]Charlotte Barnes Conner also wrote a play about Charlotte Corday (1851).

because of Placide's sympathy for the French Revolution, but Watson also misinterprets the play as "anti-French" (33). The fact that it was published singly, and that every other play included on the same copyright register (seven in all) is known to have been produced in Charleston, lends credence to the possibility that it was performed there.

Essays Religious, Moral, Dramatic and Poetical (1818) contains three plays. The Young Carolinians takes as its subject the capture of Americans by the Barbary Pirates (a practice that continued until the War of 1812) but treats the subject very differently than did Rowson in her 1794 play. The Young Carolinians is written from the distinct perspective of the Southern planter: while attempting to arouse the utmost pity for the Americans subjected to forced labor in Algiers, it places in the mouth of its one African-American character, an old slave on a South Carolina plantation, a glowing tribute to the kindness of his "Missess" and the opinion that he is better off than poor white men.[13] Its interest lies in the range of characters brought into play from different regions and social strata of South Carolina.

The two other plays included in the Essays are The Tyrants Victims and The Orphans. The Tyrant's Victims dramatizes the havoc wreaked by Agathocles, the selfish and ambitious King of Syracuse, while The Orphans is about three young women who are cheated out of an inheritance by their guardian and left to fend for themselves. The Essays was attributed to Maria Pinckney by Shaw and Shoemaker, catalogers of the microfilm collection of early American imprints. As reported by W. S. Kable, the discovery of a long-misplaced copyright ledger kept by the clerk of the District of South Carolina from 1794 to 1820, establishes Sarah Pogson as the "author and proprietor" of the Essays as well as of The Female Enthusiast. Smith wrote several nondramatic works, including Daughters of Eve (1826), Zerah, the Believing Jew (1837; 2d ed., 1857), and The Arabians (1844).

Frances Wright (also Frances Wright D'Arusmont) (1795-1852), a pathbreaker in everything she did, established an unusual relationship to dramatic literature. Immigrating from Dundee, Scotland, with her younger sister, at the age of twenty-one, Wright found Americans fascinating and the possibilities for endeavor in the United States exhilarating. She wrote and saw production of her play Altorf in 1819, during her first three-year sojourn in America. It premiered in New York on February 19, 1819, at the Park Theatre, cast with outstanding actors that included Henry Wallack, Edmund Simpson, and Mary Barnes, the mother of Charlotte Barnes

---

[13]Caroline Lee Whiting Hentz, another Southern woman who wrote plays during this period, was also an apologist for slavery (see her entry in the Dictionary of Literary Biography).

Conner and at that time the country's leading player of feminine tragic roles. Although only a moderate success initially, it was performed frequently thereafter in all the major theatre centers. The acting edition for the Philadelphia premiere of the play at the Chestnut Street Theatre in 1820, available on microfilm, shows that numerous cuts were made for that production.

Wright's early attempt at playwriting seems to have been part of her youthful sampling of the freedoms the new world could offer. The preface to *Altorf*, in which she makes a conscious gesture of affixing her name to the previously anonymous work that had been warmly received in New York, and then apologizes for the presumption of calling attention to herself, offers a clear image of the young Wright's all-embracing energy and optimistic idealism, in her plea for development of the drama in America:

America is the land of liberty. Here is the country where Truth may lift her voice without fear;—where the words of Freedom may not only be read in the closet, but heard from the stage. England pretends to an unshackled press: but there is not a stage in England from which the dramatist might breathe the sentiments of enlightened patriotism and republican liberty. In American alone might such a stage be formed; a stage that should be, like that of Greece, a school of virtue;—where all that is noble in sentiment, generous and heroic in action should speak to the hearts of a free people, and inspire each rising generation with all the better and noble feelings of human nature.

Altorf deals with the struggle of the Swiss states to overthrow the domination of Austria and establish their independence in the fourteenth century. While this subject might seem remote to the concerns of early-nineteenth-century Americans, the play's spoken prologue explicitly links it with "that liberty for which our fathers bled / When Washington their free battalions led." The central character in this tragedy is the young military hero, de Altorf, and Wright shows considerable dramatic skill, as well as an ability to delineate the abuse of patriarchal power, in her construction of the conflict between love and honor that engulfs Altorf. Interestingly, the play represents the two sides of this conflict in two women, both with claims on the central character; these women, however, actively assert their claims and insist on their own right to self-determination, rather than remaining the passive pawns in political maneuvers that their fathers expect them to be.

Wright, of course, moved far beyond the confines of the stage or its fictions in the following years. She never, as far as is known, wrote another play but continued to be active in public life and went on to become a famous and controversial figure. In 1826 she founded and lived in a utopian community in Tennessee that was intended to be a model of racial and sexual equality, including slaves who were able to purchase their freedom and eventually settle in Haiti. In 1828 she became editor of the *New Harmony Gazette*, renamed the *Free Enquirer*, founded by Robert Dale Owen at the New Harmony community in Indiana; she used this newspaper as a platform for feminism, urging women to throw off the confining conventions of femininity. She married W. P. D'Arusmont, but the marriage was not happy, and after their separation she spent years in frustrating attempts, through court actions, to recover her property and custody of their daughter from him. Throughout her life Wright wrote and lectured extensively in an attempt to move the citizens of her adopted country to more genuine patterns of equality between people of different races and sexes.

Louisa Medina (1813?-38) was one of the most successful playwrights of the nineteenth century. A 1983 study by Rosemarie K. Bank presents the basic information that can be found about Medina's life. She was born in Europe, the daughter of a Spanish businessman, and was a precocious writer who published her first work at the age of twelve. Though her father died before she reached maturity, Medina was able to acquire an extensive education that included such subjects as Latin, Greek, and algebra (usually unavailable to women) and was enriched by travel in Spain, France, and Ireland. Immigrating to the United States in 1831 or 1833 (according to different sources), she supported herself by teaching French and Spanish and began writing poems, short stories, and plays.

Medina became house playwright for the Bowery Theatre in New York, under the management of Thomas Hamblin. According to Mary Carr Clarke's *Concise History of the Life and Amours of Thomas S. Hamblin*, Medina first became an associate of Hamblin and a member of his household through employment as a governess to his young daughter. Eventually Medina became sexually involved with Hamblin, a man who had an extremely complex personal life that encompassed relationships with many different women and at one point made him a suspect in the sudden death of a young actress who had joined his household (Ireland 2:244-45). Medina may have married Hamblin in 1837 (secretly, since the divorce decree Hamblin had obtained from his first wife forbade him to remarry until after her death), and his 1836 will indicates that they had one child (Bank 65). Unlike other women theatre professionals whose plays are included in this volume, Medina never acted. Instead, she has, of all the women in the group, the earliest claim to being a professional playwright.

Most of Medina's known plays were written in the four years prior to her death in 1838. She specialized in effective dramatic adaptations of popular novels of the day, especially those that offered opportunities for impressive spectacle (for example, in *Nick of the Woods* one scene has a renegade Indian go over a waterfall in a flaming canoe). Ireland, in an unusual burst of praise for a woman playwright, states that Medina "had the happy faculty of seizing the most prominent points of a story and putting them into a dramatic shape, and while she rarely mutilated the original plot, contrived to throw a deeper interest and effect over the whole" (2:89). Her work was enormously successful. As Bank observes, her plays at the Bowery initiated the "long, uninterrupted run" for theatre productions in New York.[14] Three of her plays—*The Last Days of Pompeii* (1835), *Norman Leslie* (1836), and *Rienzi* (1836)—had runs of twenty-five days or longer, and the twenty-nine-day continuous run of *Pompeii* was the longest in New York theatre history to that date (Bank 61).

Medina is credited with writing thirty-four plays. Of these, eleven—all produced during the period of about five years during which she was associated with the Bowery—have been documented as her work. The difficulty in accurately attributing adaptations, which arises from the large number of such works in the mid nineteenth century and the fact that multiple dramatic adaptations would be made of popular novels, probably accounts for this discrepancy. Only three of Medina's plays were published. These were *The Last Days of Pompeii*, a love story set amid the banquets, entertainments, and ceremonies of ancient Pompeii and replete with seductions and betrayals, that, according to Ireland, "was put upon the stage with the greatest magnificence" (121); *Nick of the Woods* (1838), a complex adventure set in Kentucky that introduces a couple of tenderfeet to a range of colorful frontier characters, including a horse thief and a crazed Indian killer; and *Ernest Maltravers* (1838).

Interestingly, no prefaces are available for Medina's published plays, as the extant texts are in the form of commercial acting editions. Association of a woman, "Miss L. H. Medina," with such an acting edition, however, which includes specifications for scene design, costuming, and stage business, creates in itself a distinct image of a woman immersed in theatre and competent at creating not just a literary work but a show that would draw large audiences and justify its huge production costs in profits for the theatre.

Ernest Maltravers, as adapted by Medina from the Bulwer-Lytton novel, is less the story of the title character than of the young woman, Alice, who becomes his wife. It explores the question of whether class division, familial jealousies, and criminal intent can be overcome by the steadfast and virtuous

---

[14]The resident stock company, which was the dominant form of theatrical organization in the United States until the mid-1800s, presented plays in rotating repertory, and a continued run of more than three days for a new play was unusual.

love of one woman. The play is interesting as a melodrama, complete with indications that musical chords are to be played at moments of danger and suspense, that seriously grapples with real issues, such as love between members of different social classes, glossed over in other plays. While the play relies on stock situations, it presents complex characters and genuinely tragic elements that are the outcome of those character complexities.

Charlotte Mary Sanford Barnes, later Charlotte Barnes Conner (1818-1863), was born in New York City, into a well-known theatrical family, her parents being the lead actors at the Park Theatre in New York for many years. She made her unofficial stage debut at the age of three, with her mother, in *The Castle Spectre*, in 1822 (Ireland 1:399-400). Thirteen years later she made an official acting debut at the Tremont Theatre in Boston, playing an adult part in *The Castle Spectre*, but her acting career was not at first successful (2:79). Attempting to act tragic roles, she could not avoid negative comparison with her mother, who had been considered the foremost tragic actress of her time. In fact, as Ireland notes, it was not until she began to play masculine parts that Barnes came into her own as an actor, gaining recognition as Hamlet and great success as the boy Theodore in her own play, written in 1837, *Lafitte, The Pirate of the Gulf* [15] (2:80). She acted with her parents for some time, using her playwriting to advantage to produce new works for their benefits.

In 1846 Barnes married the actor-manager E. S. Conner and became the leading woman in his company at the Arch Street Theatre in Philadelphia. She continued to write and to play leading roles. In fact, her plays seemed to bring her not only success as a playwright but also more positive reviews as an actor, even in tragic feminine roles such as Octavia in *Octavia Bragaldi*, perhaps because they provided her with more interesting material than she had found in the existing repertoire.

Octavia Bragaldi, the best known of Barnes's plays, premiered at the Park Theatre in New York on November 8, 1837. It was performed for her father's benefit, with Charlotte Barnes in the title role. Ireland records that "the tragedy was successful, and has been repeated in almost every city of the Union" (2:240). It also played successfully in London and Liverpool. The play is based on a widely reported murder-suicide that had occurred in Frankfort, Kentucky, in 1825, and which had excited so much interest that closet dramas, including one by Edgar Allen Poe, had already been based on it (*Dictionary* 1:630). Using the conventions of poetic tragedy, Barnes set the play in fifteenth-century Milan and changed the original story in certain

---

[15] A play by the same name is among the works of Louisa Medina.

ways, giving the heroine total claim to innocence by making her the victim of a false report that her first husband has been killed in a military campaign, then a double victim of this man's ruthless ambition and malice after he returns. The central subject of the play is the loving relationship between Octavia and her second husband and its destruction by forces outside the control of the couple involved. The play provides its actors with many fine poetic speeches, including that of Octavia's death scene.

The Forest Princess (1848) focuses on Pocahontas, the young Indian woman who played an important role in the English settlement of Jamestown. Plays dealing with Pocahontas had already been written by John Nelson Barker (*The Indian Princess* [1808]) and George Washington Parke Custis (*Pocahontas* [1830]), but Charlotte Barnes Conner was concerned with the way in which these two plays had altered events and the character of Pocahontas. She engaged in months of research in the British Library, where the records of the Jamestown Settlement were held, before writing the play. Her aim was what today would be called a docudrama, a play largely based on fact but with time compressed and incidents of particular dramatic value heightened. The play is remarkable for its time in its respectful treatment of native Americans. Barnes refers to them as "North Americans," carefully transliterates their names for people and places--noting proper pronunciation--and uses known speeches of native Americans as the basis for some of the dialogue.

In 1848 Barnes Conner published a collection of her work in *Plays, Prose and Poetry*. Its preface reverberates with the confidence she evidently felt in the wake of the positive response to productions of her works. Although she modestly attributes part of this success to the star status of her parents, Barnes does also manage to project an image of herself as something of a literary prodigy, by identifying "*the extreme youth* of the actress and authoress" as an additional agent in its positive reception. Barnes Conner's education and literary ability are, in fact, quite evident in the volume, which was well received at the time (see Ireland 2:80). Although Barnes Conner wrote other dramas and adaptations—including her own dramatization of *The Last Days of Pompeii* (1835), *The Captive* (1850), and *Charlotte Corday* (1851)—this volume is her only published work.

Little is recorded about Barnes Conner's later years. It is known, however, that she remained with E. S. Conner for the remainder of her life, as they actively pursued theatrical careers and played opposite each other in *Octavia Bragaldi* countless times. E. S. Conner became manager of a theatre in Albany, New York, following his period in Philadelphia. Later the Conners went to California for a long-term acting engagement. (Ireland 2:58). In 1854 the billing they received for an engagement at the Bowery indicates that they had achieved star status (2:631).

Notes On Selection and Text

The plays in this collection represent the best and most successfully produced dramas written by American women in the period from 1794 to 1844. They have been selected with consideration for subject, genre (comedy or tragedy), and the region in which the author resided. Not all the playwrights whose works are included were born in America, but all of them spent the productive part of their lives in the United States.

All play texts have been edited to conform to contemporary spelling and punctuation, without altering the words of the original. It is hoped these changes will facilitate reading and performance. Where possible, archaic words or expressions and historic references have been footnoted to indicate their meaning. Dialect and English words that the playwright intended to be spoken with a foreign accent are spelled as in the original; words that might be confusing because of their nonstandard spelling are footnoted. Lists of characters are given in the same order as in the originals. Prefaces to the plays are presented unedited, to give an unretouched example of the style of the author.

Acting editions were used for two texts, the acting edition alone for *Ernest Maltravers* and together with the literary edition for *Altorf*. Where the acting edition is used, blocking directions have been omitted. For *Altorf* the scene divisions of the acting edition have been used.

Bibliography

American Women Writers: A Critical Reference Guide from Colonial Times to the Present, ed. Linda Mainiero. New York: Ungar, 1979.

Anthony, Katharine. *First Lady of the Revolution: The Life of Mercy Otis Warren*. Garden City, N.Y.: Doubleday, 1958.

Bank, Rosemarie K. "Theatre and Narrative Fiction in the Work of the Nineteenth-Century American Playwright Louisa Medina." *Theatre History Studies* 3 (1983): 55-67.

Barnes, Charlotte Mary Sanford. *Plays Prose and Poetry*. Philadelphia: E. H. Butler, 1848.

Bowen, Catherine Drinker. *John Adams and the American Revolution*. Boston: Little, Brown, 1950.

Brandt, Ellen B. *Susanna Haswell Rowson: America's First Best-Selling Novelist*. Chicago: Serbra Press, 1975.

Carr, Mary. (Also Clarke, Mary Carr.) *The Fair Americans*. Philadelphia, 1815.

Clapp, William W., Jr. *A Record of the Boston Stage*. 1853. Reprint. New York: Greenwood Press, 1969.

Clarke, Mary Carr. *A Concise History of the Life and Amours of Thomas S. Hamblin, Late Manager of the Bowery Theatre. As Communicated by his Legal Wife, Mrs. Elizabeth Hamblin, to Mrs. M. Clarke.* Philadelphia and New York, 1838(?).

Dictionary of American Biography, ed. Allen Johnson. New York: Scribner, 1928.

Dictionary of Literary Biography, vol. 37: *American Writers of the Early Republic*, ed. Emory Elliott. Detroit: Gale, 1985.

Field, Vena Bernadette. *Constantia: A Study of the Life and Works of Judith Sargent Murray, 1751-1820.* Orono: University of Maine (University of Maine Studies no. 2.17), 1931.

Gallagher, Kent G. *The Foreigner in Early American Drama.* The Hague: Mouton, 1966.

Hoole, W. Stanley. *The Ante-Bellum Charleston Theatre.* Tuscaloosa: University of Alabama Press, 1946.

Hughes, Glenn. *A History of the American Theatre, 1700-1950.* New York: French, 1951.

Ireland, Joseph N. *Records of the New York Stage from 1750 to 1860*, vols. 1-2. New York: Benjamin Blom, 1866; reissued 1966.

James, Janet. *Changing Ideas about Women in the United States, 1776-1825.* New York: Garland, 1981.

James, Reese D. *Old Drury of Philadelphia: A History of the Philadelphia Stage, 1800-1835.* 1932. Reprint. New York: Greenwood, 1968.

Kable, W. S. "South Carolina District Copyrights: 1794-1820." *Proof: The Yearbook of American Bibliographical and Textual Studies* 1 (1971).

Mates, Julian. *The American Musical Stage before 1800.* New Brunswick: Rutgers University Press, 1962.

Mowatt, Anna Cora. *The Autobiography of an Actress.* New York: Ticknor, Reed and Fields, 1854.

Murray, Judith Sargent. *The Gleaner*, vols. 1-3. Boston, 1898.

Odell, George C. D. *Annals of the New York Stage*, vols. 1-15 (Beginnings to 1894). 1927-49.

Pogson, Sarah. *Essays Religious, Moral, Dramatic and Poetical.* Charleston: V. Hoff, 1818.

Pollock, Thomas Clark. *The Philadelphia Theatre in the Eighteenth Century.* Philadelphia: University of Pennsylvania Press, 1933.

Rowson, Susanna. *Mentoria; or, The Young Lady's Friend.* Philadelphia: Samuel Harrison Smith, 1794.

———. *Slaves in Algiers; or, A Struggle for Freedom.* Philadelphia: Wrigley and Berriman, 1796.

Seilhamer, George O. *History of the American Theatre.* 1891. Reprint. Grosse Pointe, Mich.: Scholarly Press, 1968.

Taubman, Howard. *The Making of the American Theatre*. New York: Coward McCann, 1965.

Warren, Mercy Otis. *The Plays and Poems of Mercy Otis Warren*. Facsimile reproductions compiled and with an introduction by Benjamin Franklin V. Delmar. New York: Scholars' Facsimiles and Reprints, 1980.

Watson, Charles S. *Antebellum Charleston Dramatists*. Tuscaloosa: University of Alabama Press, 1976.

Weil, Dorothy. *In Defense of Women: Susanna Haswell Rowson (1762-1824)*. University Park: Pennsylvania State University Press, 1976.

THE GROUP,

As Lately Acted, and to Be Re-Acted to the Wonder of All

Superior Intelligences, Nigh Head-Quarters at Amboyne[1]

Mercy Otis Warren

1775

The author has thought proper to borrow the following spirited lines from a late celebrated poet, and to offer to the public by way of PROLOGUE, which cannot fail of pleasing at this crisis.

> *What! arm'd for virtue, and not point the pen,*
> *Brand the bold front of shameless guilty men,*
> *Dash the proud Gamester from his gilded car,*
> *Bare the mean heart which lurks beneath a star,*
>   *   *   *
> *Shall I not strip the gilding off a knave,*
> *Unplac'd, unpension'd, no man's heir or slave?*
> *I will or perish in the gen'rous cause;*
> *Hear this and tremble, ye who 'scape the laws;*
> *Yes, while I live, no rich or noble knave,*
> *Shall walk the world in credit to his grave:*
> *To virtue only, and her friends, a friend,*
> *The world beside may murmur, or commend.*[2]

Boston: Printed and sold by Edes and Gill, in Queen-Street.[3]

---

[1]Warren sent the manuscript, in scenes, to her husband, an officer in the Patriot forces, and it may have been given a dramatic reading in his camp.

[2]From Pope's "The First Satire of the Second Book of Horace, Imitated."

[3]This was the third edition of the play printed in 1775, and it was expanded beyond the original two-scene versions previously published.

DRAMATIS PERSONAE[4]

Lord Chief Justice Hazelrod
Judge Meagre
Brigadier Hateall
Hum Humbug, Esquire
Sir Sparrow Spendall
Hector Mushroom, Colonel
Beau Trumps
Dick, the Publican
Simple Sapling, Esquire
Monsieur de Francois
Crusty Crowbar, Esquire
Dupe, Secretary of State
Scriblerius Fribble
Commodore Batteau
Collateralis, a new-made Judge

Attended by a swarm of court sycophants, hungry harpies, and unprincipled danglers, collected from the neighboring villages, hovering over the stage in the shape of locusts, led by Massachusettensis[5] in the form of a basilisk[6]; the rear brought up by Proteus,[7] bearing a torch in one hand and a powder flask in the other; the whole supported by a mighty army and navy from Blunderland, for the laudable purpose of enslaving its best friends.

---

[4]These characters, who comprise "the group," were based on members of the Mandamus Council established by the British Parliament in 1774, as part of what came to be known as the Intolerable Acts. The Mandamus Councillors, appointed by the Crown, were to govern in place of the elected colonial assembly. Several attempts have been made to identify the actual persons on whom the characters were based. Arthur H. Quinn, in *A History of the American Drama from the Beginnings to the Civil War* (1943) offers this key: Hazelrod=Peter Oliver; Meagre=Foster Hutchinson; Hateall=Timothy Ruggles; Humbug=John Irving, Jr.; Sir Sparrow=William Pepperell; Hector Mushroom= Col. John Murray; Beau Trumps=Daniel Leonard; Dick=Richard Lechmere; Simple= Nathaniel Ray Thomas; De Francois=James Boutineau; Crusty=Josiah Edson; Dupe= Thomas Flucker; Scriblerius=Harrison Gray; Batteau=Joshua Loring; Collateralis= William Browne; Sylla=Gen. Thomas Gage.

[5]The pseudonym used by Tory writer Daniel Leonard, under which he carried on a war of words with John Adams (who wrote under the pseudonym Novanglus) in 1775.

[6]Monster with poisonous breath.

[7]A shape-changing god; the reference here is to turncoats.

ACT ONE
Scene One

A dark little parlor.   Guards standing at the door.   HAZELROD,
CRUSTY CROWBAR, SIMPLE SAPLING, HATEALL, and HECTOR
MUSHROOM.

SIMPLE: I know not what to think of these sad times—
The people armed, and all resolved to die
Ere they'll submit—
CRUSTY: I too am almost sick of the parade
Of honors purchased at the price of peace.
SIMPLE: Fond as I am of greatness and her charms,
Elate with prospects of my rising name,
Pushed into place—a place I ne'er expected—
My bounding heart leapt in my feeble breast,
And ecstasies entranced my slender brain.
But yet, ere this, I hoped more solid gains,
As my low purse demands a quick supply.
Poor Sylvia weeps, and urges my return
To rural peace and humble happiness,
As my ambition beggars all her babes.
CRUSTY: When first I 'listed in the desperate cause
And blindly swore obedience to his will,
So wise, so just, so good I thought Rapatio,[8]
That if salvation rested on his word,
I'd pin my faith and risk my hopes thereon.
HAZELROD: And why not now? What staggers thy belief?
CRUSTY: Himself—his perfidy appears.
It is too plain he has betrayed his country.
And we're the wretched tools by him marked out
To seal its ruins, tear up the ancient forms,
And every vestige treacherously destroy,
Nor leave a trait of freedom in the land.
Nor did I think hard fate would call me up
From drudging o'er my acres,
Treading the glade, and sweating at the plough,
To dangle at the tables of the great;

---

[8]As in Warren's earlier satire, *The Adulateur* (1773), Rapatio refers to Thomas
Hutchinson, colonial governor of Massachusetts from 1770 to 1774.

At bowls and cards to spend my frozen years;
To sell my friends, my country, and my conscience;
Profane the sacred Sabbaths of my God,
Scorned by the very men who want my aid
To spread distress o'er this devoted people.
    HAZELROD: Pho! What misgivings—why these idle qualms,
This shrinking backwards at the bugbear conscience?
In early life I heard the phantom named,
And the grave sages prate of moral sense
Presiding in the bosom of the just,
Or panting thongs about the guilty heart.
Bound by these shackles, long my laboring mind
Obscurely trod the lower walks of life,
In hopes by honesty my bread to gain;
But neither commerce or my conjuring rods,
Nor yet mechanics, or new-fangled drills,
Or all the ironmonger's curious arts
Gave me a competence of shining ore
Or gratified my itching palm for more,
Till I dismissed the bold, intruding guest
And banished conscience from my wounded breast.
    CRUSTY: Happy expedient! Could I gain the art,
Then balmy sleep might soothe my waking lids,
And rest once more refresh my weary soul.
    HAZELROD: Resolved more rapidly to gain my point,
I mounted high in justice's sacred seat,
With flowing robes and head equipped without,
A heart unfeeling and a stubborn soul—
As qualified as e'er a Jeffreys[9] was,
Save in the knotty rudiments of law—
The smallest requisite for modern times,
When wisdom, law, and justice are supplied
By swords, dragoons, and ministerial nods—
Sanctions most sacred in the pander's creed.
I sold my country for a splendid bribe.
Now let her sink, and all the dire alarms
Of war, confusion, pestilence, and blood,
And tenfold misery be her future doom.

---

[9]George Jeffreys, notoriously biased and cruel during his tenure as Lord Chief Justice of England in the late seventeenth century.

Let civil discord lift her sword on high—
Nay, sheathe its hilt e'en in my brother's blood;
It ne'er shall move the purpose of my soul.
Though once I trembled at a thought so bold,
By Philalethes's[10] arguments convinced
We may live demons, as we die like brutes,
I give my tears and conscience to the winds.

HATEALL: Curse on their coward fears and dastard souls,
Their soft compunctions and relenting qualms!
Compassion ne'er shall seize my steadfast breast,
Though blood and carnage spread through all the land,
Till streaming purple tinge the verdant turf—
Till every street shall float with human gore.
I, Nero-like, the capital in flames,
Could laugh to see her glutted sons expire,
Though much too rough my soul to touch the lyre.

SIMPLE: I fear the brave, the injured multitude.
Repeated wrongs arouse them to resent,
And every patriot like old Brutus[11] stands,
The shining steel half drawn—its glittering point
Scarce hid beneath the scabbard's friendly cell—
Resolved to die, or see their country free.

HATEALL: Then let them die! *The dogs we will keep down*
While N-----'s[12] my friend and G-----[13] approves the deed.
Though hell and all its hell-hounds should unite,
I'll not recede to save from swift perdition
My wife, my country, family or friends.
G-----'s mandamus[14] I more highly prize
Than all the mandates of the ethereal king.

HECTOR: Will our abettors in the distant towns
Support us long against the common cause,
When they shall see from Hampshire's northern bound

---

[10]Philalethes was a pseudonym used by Jonathan Sewall, a Tory lawyer and propagandist. He also used other pseudonyms.

[11]In Warren's *The Adulateur* (1773), Brutus was intended to be Patriot leader James Otis (Warren's brother), but used here with the modifier *old*, the name probably serves only as a classical reference.

[12]Lord North, Prime Minister of England during the period of the American Revolution.

[13]Generally considered to refer to Thomas Gage, Massachusetts governor and commander in chief of the British forces in America at the outbreak of the Revolution.

[14]The command from the British Parliament creating the non-elected council.

Through the wide western plains to southern shores
The whole united continent in arms?
    HATEALL: They shall—as sure as oaths can bind.
I've boldly sent my newborn brat abroad—
The association of my morbid brain,
To which each minion must affix his name.
As all our hope depends on brutal force,
On quick destruction, misery, and death,
Soon may we see dark ruin stalk around,
With murder, rapine, and inflicted pains,
Estates confiscate, slavery, and despair,
Wrecks, halters, axes, gibbeting, and chains—
All the dread ills that wait on civil war.
How I could glut my vengeful eyes to see
The weeping maid thrown helpless on the world,
Her sire cut off. Her orphan brothers stand,
While the big tear rolls down the manly cheek,
Robbed of maternal care by grief's keen shaft.
The sorrowing mother mourns her starving babes,
Her murdered lord torn guiltless from her side,
And flees for shelter to the pitying grave
To screen[15] at once from slavery and pain.
    HAZELROD: But more complete I view this scene of woe
By the incursions of a savage foe,
Of which I warned them, if they dare refuse
The badge of slaves, and bold resistance use.
Now let them suffer. I'll no pity feel.
    HATEALL: Nor I! But had I power, as I have the will,
I'd send them murmuring to the shades of hell.

ACT TWO

Scene One

*A large dining room. The table furnished with bowls, bottles, glasses, and
cards. The* GROUP *appear sitting around in a restless attitude. In one
corner of the room is discovered a small cabinet of books for the use of the
studious and contemplative, containing Hobbes's* Leviathan,[16] *Sipthrop's*

---

[15]Separate.
[16]This 1651 treatise was often cited in support of monarchial privilege.

Sermons,[17] *Hutchinson's* History,[18] Fable of the Bees,[19] *Philalethes on Philanthrop, with an appendix by Massachusettensis,*[20] *Hoyle on whist,*[21] Lives of the Stuarts, Statutes of Henry the Eighth and William the Conqueror,[22] *Wedderburn's* Speeches,[23] *and* Acts of Parliament for 1774.[24] HATEALL, HAZELROD, DE FRANCOIS, BEAU TRUMPS, SIMPLE, HUMBUG, SCRIBLERIUS, SIR SPARROW, *etc., etc.*

SCRIBLERIUS: (*To* DE FRANCOIS). Thy toast, Monsieur—
Pray, why that solemn phiz[25]?
Art thou, too, balancing 'twixt right and wrong?
Hast thou a thought so mean as to give up
Thy present good, for promise in reversion?
'Tis true hereafter has some feeble terrors;
But ere our grizzly[26] heads are wrapped in clay,
We may compound[27] and make our peace with Heaven.
DE FRANCOIS: Could I give up the dread of retribution,
The awful reckoning of some future day,
Like surly Hateall I might curse mankind
And dare the threatened vengeance of the skies.
Or, like yon apostate— (*Pointing to* HAZELROD, *who has retired to a corner to read Massachusettensis.*) —feel but slight remorse

---

[17]Moses Coit Tyler, in *The Literary History of the American Revolution* ((1897), identifies this as a jeering reference to the Reverend East Apthorp, a Church of England cleric associated with the Society for Propagation of the Gospel in Foreign Parts, a British missionary society vehemently opposed by Patriot Congregationalist ministers.

[18]Colonial governor Thomas Hutchinson wrote a two-volume history of Massachusetts. The first volume was published in 1764, the second in 1767.

[19]A defense of vice written by Bernard de Mandeville (1670-1733).

[20]Both Philalethes and Philanthrop were pseudonyms used by the Tory lawyer and polemicist, Jonathan Sewall. At the time this play was written, Warren believed the essays of Massachusettensis were also the work of Sewall; however, as was later established, Massachusettensis was the Tory politician and lawyer Daniel Leonard, satirized in the play as Beau Trumps.

[21]A card game. Puritans, who formed a strong element among New England Patriots, condemned card-playing.

[22]The Stuarts, Henry VIII, and William the Conqueror were considered to epitomize absolutism.

[23]England's Solicitor-General Alexander Wedderburn, who denounced Benjamin Franklin for publishing private letters written by the colonial governor Hutchinson in 1774.

[24]The Intolerable Acts were passed in 1774.

[25]Countenance.

[26]White-haired.

[27]Settle debts.

To sell my country for a grasp of gold,
But the impressions of my early youth,
Infixed by precepts of my pious sire,
Are stings and scorpions in my goaded breast.
Oft have I hung upon my parent's knee
And heard him tell of his escape from France.
He left the land of slaves and wooden shoes[28];
From place to place he sought a safe retreat,
Till fair Bostonia stretched her friendly arm,
And gave the refugee both bread and peace.
(*Aside.*) Shall I, ungrateful, raze the sacred bonds,
And help to clank the tyrant's iron chains
O'er these blest shores—once the sure asylum
From all the ills of arbitrary sway?
(*To* SCRIBLERIUS.) With his expiring breath, he bade his sons,
If e'er oppression reached the western world,
Resist its force and break the servile yoke.
    SCRIBLERIUS: Well, quit thy post. Go, make thy flattering court
To freedom's sons, and tell thy baby fears.
Show the soft traces in thy puny heart,
Made by the trembling tongue and quivering lip
Of an old grandsire's superstitious whims.
    DE FRANCOIS: No. I never can,
So great the itch I feel for titled place—
Some honorary post, some small distinction
To save my name from dark oblivion's jaws.
I'll hazard all, but ne'er give up my place.
For that, I'll see Rome's ancient rites restored,
And flame and faggot blaze in every street.
    BEAU TRUMPS: That's right, Monsieur,
There's nought on earth that has such tempting charms
As rank and show and pomp and glittering dress,
Save the dear counters at beloved quadrille.[29]
Viner, unsoiled, and Littleton may sleep,
And Coke lie moldering on the dusty shelf,[30]
If I by shuffling draw some lucky card

---

[28]A reference to poverty.

[29]Small pieces of metal used for keeping track of the score in quadrille, a card game with four players.

[30]Viner, Littleton, and Coke authored works on English law and jurisprudence, considered essential to the practice of law at the time.

That wins the livres or lucrative place.[31]

HUMBUG: When sly Rapatio showed his friends the scroll,
I wondered much to see thy patriot name
Among the list of rebels to the state.
I thought thee one of Rusticus's[32] sworn friends.

BEAU TRUMPS: When first I entered on the public stage,
My country groaned beneath base Brundo's[33] hand.
Virtue looked fair and beckoned to her lure;
Through truth's bright mirror I beheld her charms,
And wished to tread the patriotic path,
And wear the laurels that adorn his fame.
I walked awhile, and tasted solid peace,
With Cassius,[34] Rusticus, and good Hortensius,[35]
And many more, whose names will be revered
When you and I, and all the venal herd
Weighed in Nemesis's[36] just, impartial scale,
Are marked with infamy till time blot out
And in oblivion sink our hated names.
But 'twas a poor, unprofitable path;
Nought to be gained, save solid peace of mind.
No pensions, place, or title there I found.
I saw Rapatio's arts had struck so deep,
And given his country such a fatal wound,
None but its foes promotion could expect.
I trimmed and pimped and veered, and wavering stood,
But half resolved to show myself a knave;
Till the arch traitor, prowling 'round for aid,
Saw my suspense and bid me doubt no more.
He gently bowed and, smiling, took my hand,
And, whispering softly in my listening ear,
Showed me my name among his chosen band,
And laughed at virtue dignified by fools,
Cleared all my doubts and bid me persevere

---

[31]The livre is a French coin. The reference to "lucrative place" implies that the Tories awarded government posts to the winners of card games.

[32]A patriot--probably John Adams (at the time, a country lawyer)--who first appears in Warren's *The Defeat* (1773) as an associate of Cassius (Samuel Adams).

[33]Probably Francis Bernard, colonial governor of Massachusetts from 1760 to 1770, who was opposed by both Patriots and Tories.

[34]Samuel Adams.

[35]Perhaps John Hancock.

[36]Goddess of vengeance.

In spite of the restraints or hourly checks
Of wounded friendship and a goaded mind,
Or all the sacred ties of truth and honor.
   COLLATERALIS:
Come, 'mongst ourselves we'll e'en speak out the truth.
Can you suppose there yet is such a dupe
As still believes that wretch an honest man?
The latter strokes of his serpentine brain
Outvie the arts of Machiavel himself.
His Borgian[37] model here is realized,
And the stale tricks of politicians played
Beneath a vizard fair—
—Drawn from the heavenly form
Of blest religion weeping o'er the land
For virtue fallen, and for freedom lost.
   BEAU TRUMPS: I think with you—
—Unparalleled his effrontery,
When, by chicanery and specious art,
'Midst the distress in which he'd brought the city,[38]
He found a few, by artifice and cunning,
By much industry of his wily friend
The false Philanthrop[39]—fly, undermining tool,
Who with the siren's voice
Deals daily 'round the poison of his tongue—
To speak him fair and overlook his guilt.
They, by reiterated promise made
To stand their friend at Britain's mighty court
And vindicate his native, injured land,
Lent him their names to sanctify his deeds.
But mark the traitor. His high crimes glossed o'er
Conceals the tender feelings of the man,
The social ties that bind the human heart.
He strikes a bargain with his country's foes,
And joins to wrap America in flames;
Yet with feigned pity and Satanic grin,
As if more deep to fix the keen insult,
Or make his life a farce still more complete,

---

[37]Noble family of the Italian Renaissance with a reputation for being treacherous and vicious.
   [38]Boston, target of the Intolerable Acts.
   [39]Jonathan Sewall (see footnote 20).

He sends a groan across the broad Atlantic,
And with a phiz of crocodilian stamp
Can weep and wreathe, still hoping to deceive.[40]
He cries the gathering clouds hang thick about her,
But laughs within—then sobs,
"Alas, my country!"
    HUMBUG: Why so severe, or why exclaim at all
Against the man who made thee what thou art?
    BEAU TRUMPS: I know his guilt. I ever knew the man;
Thy father knew him ere we trod the stage.
I only speak to such as know him well.
Abroad I tell the world he is a saint.
But, as for interest, I betrayed my own
With the same views. I ranked among his friends,
But my ambition sighs for something more.
What merits has Sir Sparrow of his own?
And yet a feather graces the fool's cap,
Which did he wear for what himself achieved,
'Twould stamp some honor on his latest heir.
But I'll suspend my murmuring rays awhile.
Come, t'other glass, and try our luck at loo.[41]
And if, before the dawn, your gold I win;
Or ere bright Phoebus does his course begin,
The eastern breeze from Britain's hostile shore
Should waft her lofty, floating towers[42] o'er,
Whose waving pendants sweep the watery main,
Dip their proud beaks and dance towards the plain—
The destined plains of slaughter and distress—
Laden with troops from Hanover and Hesse,[43]
I would invigorate my sinking soul,
For then the continent we might control.
Not all the millions that she vainly boasts
Can cope with veteran barbarian hosts;
But the brave sons of Albion's[44] warlike race

---

[40]From exile in England, Thomas Hutchinson sent letters deploring developments in Massachusetts.

[41]A card game.

[42]Ships.

[43]German provinces from which England drew mercenary soldiers to bolster the British forces in America.

[44]England's.

Their arms and honors never can disgrace,
Or draw their swords in such a hated cause
In blood to seal a N——'s oppressive laws.
They'll spurn the service. Britons must recoil,
And show themselves the natives of an isle
Who fought for freedom in the worst of times,
Produced her Hampdens, Fairfaxes, and Pyms.[45]
But if by carnage we should win the game,
Perhaps by my abilities and fame
I might attain a splendid, glittering car,
And mount aloft, and fall in liquid air.
Like Phaeton, I'd then outstrip the wind,
And leave my low competitors behind.

Scene Two

COLLATERALIS, DICK THE PUBLICAN.

  DICK: This dull inaction will no longer do.
Month after month, the idle troops have lain,
Nor struck one stroke that leads us to our wish.
The trifling bickerings at the city gates
Or bold outrages of their midnight routs
Bring us no nearer to the point in view.
Though much the daily sufferings of the people—
Commerce destroyed and government unhinged—
No talk of tame submission yet I hear.
  COLLATERALIS: No——not the least——
——They're more resolved than ever.
They're firm, united, bold, undaunted, brave;
And every villa boasts their marshalled ranks.
The warlike clarion sounds through every street.
Both vigorous youth and the grey-headed sire
Bear the fusee[46] in regimental garbs,
Repairing to defend invaded right,
And, if pushed hard, by manly force repel.
And though Britannia sends her legions o'er,
To plant her daggers in her children's breast,

---

[45]Leaders of the Parliamentary forces that deposed Charles I in the English Civil War, 1642-1649.
[46]Torch.

It will rebound. New whetted, the keen point
Will find a sheath in every tyrant's heart.
    DICK: What then is to be done?
My finances too low to stand it long.
You well remember——
When stationed there to gripe the honest trader,
How much I plundered from your native town.
Under the sanctions of the laws of trade,
I the hard earnings of industry
Filched from their hands, and built my nest on high.
And on the spoils I rioted a while,
But soon the unrighteous pelf[47] slipped through my hand.
Nor longer idly could I waste my time;
A numerous flock was rising 'round my board,
Who urged to something that might give them bread.
My only game was hither to repair,
And court the proud oppressors of my country,
By the parade of pompous luxury
To win their favor and obtain a place.
That, with my limbeck,[48] might have kept me on,
But for the cursed, persevering spirit
Of freedom's sons, who triumph o'er distress,
Nor will comply with requisitions made
By haughty mandates from corrupted courts
To pay the workmen for the chains they'd forged.
    COLLATERALIS: No, though proud Britain wafts her wooden walls
O'er the broad waves and plants them 'round these coasts,
Shuts up their ports, and robs them of their bread,
They're not dismayed—nor servilely comply
To pay the hunters of the nabob[49] shores
Their high demand for India's poisonous weed,[50]
Long since a sacrifice to Thetis[51] made—
A rich regale. Now all the watery dames
May snuff[52] Souchong,[53] and sip in flowing bowls

---

[47]Booty.
[48]Distilling apparatus.
[49]Indian ruler's.
[50]Tea.
[51]A sea nymph. The tea sacrificed to her was that dumped in the Boston Tea Party.
[52]Inhale.
[53]A black tea.

The higher flavored choice Hysonian[54] stream,
And leave their nectar to old Homer's gods.
    DICK: The Group this morn were summoned to the camp.
The council early meets at Sylla's[55] tent,
But for what purpose yet I cannot learn.
    COLLATERALIS: Then let us haste. 'Tis novel to be called
By Sylla's order, summoned to attend.
So close he keeps his counsels in his breast,
Nor trusts us with the maneuvers of state,
I fear he half despises us himself;
And if he does, we cannot wonder much.
We're made the jest of every idle boy,
Most of us hunted from our rural seats,
Drove from our homes,[56] a prey to guilty fears.
When— when dare we return?
And now, shut up in this devoted city,[57]
Amidst the pestilence on either hand,
Pursued by every dreadful execration
That the bold tongue of innocence oppressed
Pours forth in anguish for a ruined state.

Scene Three

The fragments of the broken Council appear with trembling, servile gestures, showing several applications to the General from the under-tools in distant counties, begging each a guard of Myrmidons[58] to protect them from the armed multitudes (which the guilty horrors of their wounded consciences hourly presented to their frighted imaginations) approaching to take speedy vengeance on the court parasites who had fled for refuge to the camp, by immediate destruction to their pimps, panders, and sycophants left behind. SYLLA walking in great perplexity.

    SYLLA: Pray, how will it comport with my pretense

---

[54]Referring to green tea.

[55]Gen. Thomas Gage, commander of the British troops in Massachusetts in 1775.

[56]Many New England Tories were driven out of their homes and communities in the period just prior to the Revolution. Their first refuge was Boston, where the British kept a large concentration of military troops.

[57]Boston, which was devoted to the Patriot cause.

[58]Theasalian warriors portrayed in legend as unquestioning subordinates to their commander Achilles.

For building walls and shutting up the town,
Erecting fortresses and strong redoubts,
To keep my troops from any bold inroads
A brave, insulted people might attempt,
If I send out my little, scattered parties,
And the long-suffering, generous patriot's care
Prevents a skirmish?
Though they're the sport of wanton, cruel power,
And hydra-headed ills start up around,
Till the last hope of a redress cut off,
Their humane feelings urge them to forbear,
And wait some milder means to bring relief.
  HATEALL: 'Tis now the time to try their daring tempers.
Send out a few, and if they are cut off,
What are a thousand souls, sent swiftly down
To Pluto's gloomy shades, to tell in anguish?
Half their compeers shall sit pandemonic[59]
Ere we will suffer liberty to reign,
Or see her sons triumphant win the day.
I fain would push them to the last extreme,
To draw their swords against their legal king;
Then short's the process to complete destruction.
  DUPE: Be not so sanguine. The day is not our own,
And much I fear it never will be won.
Their discipline is equal to our own;
Their valor has been tried, and in a field
They're not less brave than are a Frederick's[60] troops.
Those members formidable pour along,
While virtue's banners shroud each warrior's head,
Stern justice binds the helmet on his brow,
And liberty sits perched on every shield.
But who's applied and asked the general's aid,
Or wished his peaceful villa such a curse
As posting troops beside the peasant's cot[61]?
  MEAGRE: None but the very dregs of all mankind,
The stains of nature—the blots of human race.
Yet, that's no matter; still they are our friends.
'Twill help our projects if we give them aid.

---

[59]Go to hell.
[60]Frederick the Great, king of Prussia in 1775.
[61]Cottage.

SIMPLE: Though my paternal acres are eat up,
My patrimony spent, I've yet an house
My lenient creditors let me improve.
Send up the troops; 'twill serve them well for barracks.
I somehow think 'twould bear a noble sound
To have my mansion guarded by the king.
    SYLLA: Hast thou no sons or blooming daughters there
To call up all the feelings of a father,
Lest their young minds contaminate by vice
Caught from such inmates, dangerous and vile,
Devoid of virtue, rectitude, or honor
Save what accords with military fame?
Hast thou no wife who asks thy tender care
To guard her from Bellona's[62] hardy sons
Who, when not toiling in the hostile field,
Are faithful votaries to the Cyprian queen[63]?
Or is her soul of such materials made,
Indelicate and thoughtless of her fame,
So void of either sentiment or sense
As makes her a companion fit for thee?
    SIMPLE: Sylvia's good natured, and no doubt will yield,
And take the brawny veterans to her board
When she's assured 'twill help her husband's fame.
If she complains or murmurs at the plan,
Let her solicit charity abroad.
Let her go out and seek some pitying friend
To give her shelter from the wintry blast,
Disperse her children 'round the neighboring cots,
And then—
    DICK: —Then weep thy folly and her own hard fate!
I pity Sylvia. I knew the beauteous maid
Ere she descended to become thy wife.
She silent mourns the weakness of her lord;
For she's too virtuous to approve thy deeds.
    HATEALL: Pho—what's a woman's tears,
Or all the whistlings of that trifling sex?
I never felt one tender thought towards them.
When young, indeed, I wedded nut-brown Kate—

---

[62]Goddess of war.
[63]Prostitute.

Blithe, buxom dowager,[64] the jockey's prey[65]—
But all I wished was to secure her dower.
I broke her spirits when I'd won her purse,
For which I'll give a recipe most sure
To every hen-pecked husband 'round the board.
If crabbed words or surly looks won't tame
The haughty shrew, nor bend the stubborn mind,
Then the green hickory, or the willow twig
Will prove a curse for each rebellious dame
Who dare oppose her lord's superior will.
    SYLLA: Enough of this. Ten thousand harrowing cares
Tear up my peace, and swell my anxious breast.
I see some mighty victim must appease
An injured nation, tottering on the verge
Of wide destruction, made the wanton sport
Of hungry harpies gaping for their prey.
Which, if by misadventures they should miss,
The disappointed vulture's angry fang
Will seize the lesser gudgeons[66] of the state;
And sacrificing to mad Alecto's[67] rage,
Lest the tide turning, with a rapid course,
The booming current rushes o'er their heads
And sweeps the "cawing cormorants from earth."[68]
    HATEALL: Then strike some sudden blow, and if hereafter
Dangers should rise, then set up for thyself,
And make thy name as famous in Columbia
As ever Caesar's was in ancient Gaul.
Who would such distant provinces subdue,
And then resign them to a foreign lord?
With such an armament at thy command,
Why all this cautious prudence?
    SYLLA: I only wish to serve my sovereign well,
And bring new glory to my master's crown,
Which can't be done by spreading ruin 'round
This loyal country——

---

[64]Propertied widow.
[65]One likely to be taken advantage of by a cheat.
[66]Small fish.
[67]One of the Furies.
[68]No source is given for this quotation, but one might guess Warren was using a Tory writer's words against him.

——Wrought up to madness by oppression's hand.
How much deceived my royal master is
By those he trusts! But more of this anon.
Were it consistent with my former plan,
I'd gladly send my sickly troops abroad,
Out from the stench of this infected town
To breathe some air more free from putrefaction,
To brace their nerves against approaching spring,
If my ill stars should destine a campaign
And call me forth to fight in such a cause.
To quench the generous spark, the innate love
Of glorious freedom planted in the breast
Of every man who boasts a Briton's name,
Until some base-born lust of foreign growth
Contaminate his soul, till false ambition
Or the sordid hope of swelling coffers
Poison the mind and brutalize the man.
    COLLATERALIS: I almost wish I never had engaged
To rob my country of her native rights,
Nor strove to mount on justice's solemn bench,
By mean submission cringing for a place.
How great the pain, and yet how small the purchase!
Had I been dumb, or my right hand cut off,
Ere I so servilely had held it up,
Or given my voice abjectly to rescind
The wisest step that mortal man could take
To curb the talons of tyrannic power—
Outstretched, rapacious, ready to devour
The fair possessions by our Maker given,
Confirmed by compacts, ratified by Heaven.
    SYLLA: Look o'er the annals of our virtuous sires,
And search the story of Britannia's deeds
From Caesar's ravages to Hampden's[69] fall,
From the good Hampden down to glorious Wolfe,[70]
Whose soul took wing on Abraham's fatal plain,[71]
Where the young hero fought Britannia's foes

---

[69]A leader in the English Civil War who refused to pay a tax levied by Charles I, John Hampden was killed in battle at the head of a Parliamentary regiment.
    [70]James Wolfe, a British general in the French and Indian War who led and was killed in the successful assault on Quebec in 1759.
    [71]The battle for control of Quebec took place on the Plains of Abraham.

And vanquished Bourbon's[72] dark, ferocious hosts,
Till the slaves trembled at a George's name.
'Twas love of freedom drew a Marlborough's[73] sword;
This glorious passion moved a Sidney's[74] pen,
And crowned with bays[75] a Harrington[76] and Locke.[77]
'Tis freedom wreathes the garlands o'er their tombs.
For her how oft have bleeding heroes fallen,
With the warm fluid gushing from their wounds,
Conveyed the purchase to their distant heirs!
And shall I rashly draw my guilty sword
And dip its hungry hilt in the rich blood
Of the best subjects that a Brunswick[78] boasts,
And for no cause, but that they nobly scorn
To wear the fetters of his venal slaves.
But swift time rolls, and on his rapid wheel
Bears the winged hours and the circling years.
The cloud-capped morn, the dark, short wintry day,
And the keen blasts of roughened Boreas's[79] breath
Will soon vanish, and approaching spring
Opes with the fate of empires on her wing. (*Exits.*)
    HAZELROD: (*Rising in great agitation*).
This balancing of passions ne'er will do,
And by the scale which virtue holds to reason,
Weighing the business ere he executes,
Doubting, deliberating, half resolved
To be the savior of a virtuous state,
Instead of guarding refugees and knaves—

---

[72]The French king, Louis XV.

[73]John Churchill, first duke of Marlborough, the distinguished English soldier who supported James II in the rebellion of 1685, but supported William of Orange in 1688.

[74]Algernon Sidney (1622-1683), English political leader who supported the Parliamentarians in the Civil War (despite his noble origins), but refused to participate in the trial of Charles I and later resigned his seat in Parliament to protest the assumption of monarchial power by Cromwell. Sidney, with three others, was accused of conspiring to murder Charles II; he was convicted in proceedings over which the notorious Jeffreys presided, and was executed in 1683. His writings were often cited by American Patriots.

[75]Wreaths of bay leaves, similar to wreaths of laurel.

[76]James Harrington (1611-1677) wrote political treatises supporting such ideas as voting by ballot.

[77]John Locke (1632-1704), English philosopher who argued against the divine right of kings and for rights of the individual.

[78]Prosperous area of Germany.

[79]God of the north wind.

The buzzing reptiles that crawl 'round his court
And lick his hand for some delicious crumb
Or painted plume to grace the guilty brow,
Stained with ten thousand falsities, trumped up
To injure every good and virtuous name
Who won't strike hands and be his country's foe.
I'll hasten after and stir up his soul
To dire revenge and bloody resolutions,
Or the whole fabric falls, on which we hang,
And down the pit of infamy we plunge,
Without the spoils we long have hoped to reap. (*He crosses the stage rapidly
and goes out after Sylla.* MEAGRE *and* DUPE *at the further part of the
stage.*)
    MEAGRE: As Sylla passed I marked his anxious brow.
I fear his soul is with compassion moved
For suffering virtue, wounded and betrayed;
For freedom, hunted down in this fair field—
The only soil, in these degenerate days,
In which the heavenly goddess can exist.
    DUPE: Humanity recoils; his heart relucts
To execute the black, the accursed design—
Such I must call it, though thy guilty friends,
Thy subtle brother,[80] laid the artful plan.
"And like the toad squat at the ear of Eve,"[81]
Infusing poisons by his snaky tongue,
Pushed Brundo on to tread the thorny path
And plunge his country in ten thousand woes;
Then, slyly jostling him behind the scenes,
Stepped in his place, for which he long had sighed.
    MEAGRE: Yes, all allowed he played a master game,
And dealt his cards with such peculiar skill
That every dangler about the court—
As you and I and all might well suppose—
Thought the chains fixed which Brundo only clanked.
But yet, unless some speedy method's found
To break the union, and dissolve the bonds
That bind this mighty continent so firm—
Their Congresses, their Covenants, and leagues,

---

[80]Meagre was based on Foster Hutchinson, whose brother Thomas Hutchinson
(Rapatio) was lieutenant governor under Francis Bernard (Brundo).
    [81]From Milton's *Paradise Lost.*

With their Committees[82] working in each town
With unremitting vigilance and care
To baffle every evil machination
Of all state rooks[83] who peck about the land,
If not broke up will ruin all at last.
Amidst the many scribblers of the age,
Can none be found to set their schemes afloat,
To sow dissension and distrust abroad,
Sap that cement that bears down all before it
And makes America a match for all
The hostile powers that proud Europe boasts?
    DUPE: Not all the swarms of prostituted pens
Nor hireling smatterers[84] scribbling for gain,
From the first pensioned on the northern list[85]
To bigot priests who write from southern shores,[86]
With all their phantoms, bugbears, threats, or smiles,
Will e'er persuade them to renounce their claim
To freedom, purchased with their fathers' blood.
How various are the arts already tried,
What pains unwearied to write men to sleep
Or rock them in the cradle of despair,
To doze supinely till they should believe
They'd neither eyes, nor tongues, or strength to move
But at the nod of some despotic lord!
What shifts, evasions, what delusive tales,
What poor prevarication for rash oaths,
What nightly watchings, and what daily cares
To dress up falsehood in some fair disguise
Or wrap the bantling[87] of their midnight dreams
In the soft vest of friendship, to betray,
Then send it forth in every fairy form
To stalk at noontide, giddy with fond hope
That some new gambols[88] might deceive again

---

[82]Committees of Safety were established in towns and regions to coordinate the struggle against British rule.

[83]Literally, crows; figuratively, swindlers or cheats.

[84]Gossips.

[85]Tories who escaped to Nova Scotia and received pensions or civil posts from the English government.

[86]The Episcopal Church, considered a Tory ally, was stronger in the south.

[87]Offspring.

[88]Tricks.

Men broad awake, who see through all the cheat.
    MEAGRE: There still is hope; why need we yet despair?
The doughty champion of our sinking cause,
The deep "arcana" of whose winding brain
Is fraught with dark expedients to betray,
By the long labors of his veteran quill,
By scattering scraps from every musty code
Of canon, civil, or draconian laws,
Quoting old statutes, or defining new,
Treasons, misprisions, riots, routs, cabals,
And insurrections of these stubborn times.
He'll sure prevail and terrify at last,
By bringing precedents from those blest days
When royal Stuarts Britain's scepter swayed,
And taught her sons the right divine of kings;
When pains and forfeitures an hundred fold
Were dealt to traitors puny when compared
To the bold rebels of this continent,
From Merrimac to Mississippi's banks,
Who dare resist a ministerial frown.
In spite of all the truth Novanglus[89] tells,
And his cool, reasoning argumentive style,
Or master strokes of his unrivaled pen,
They will divide, and wavering, will submit
And take the word of Massachusettensis
That men were born already bitted,[90] curbed,
And on their backs the saddles prominent,
For every upstart sycophant to mount.
    DUPE: Not Massachusettensis's oily tongue,
Or retailed nonsense of a Philarene,[91]
Nor Senex's rant, not yet dull Grotius's[92] pen
Or the whole Group of selfish, venal men,
If gathered from cold Zembla's[93] frozen shore
To the warm zone where rapid rivers roar,

---

[89]Pen name used by John Adams.
[90]With bits in their mouths, for bridles.
[91]Name applied by Warren to a Tory writer, perhaps the English satirist Soame Jenyns, whose pamphlet lampooning the Patriots was a best-seller.
[92]Senex and Grotius were evidently Tory writers. It is doubtful that Warren meant Hugo Grotius, the Dutch Renaissance scholar, since Samuel Adams admired his writing.
[93]Novaya Zemblya, a chain of islands in the Arctic Ocean explored by Hudson.

Can either coax them or the least control
The valorous purpose of their Roman souls.
    MEAGRE: Let not thy soft timidity of heart
Urge thee to terms, till the last stake is thrown.
'Tis not my temper ever to forgive,
When once resentment's kindled in my breast.
I hated Brutus[94] for his noble stand
Against the oppressors of his injured country.
I hate the leaders of these restless factions,
For all their generous efforts to be free.
I curse the senate[95] which defeats our bribes,
Who Hazelrod impeached for the same crime.[96]
I hate the people who, no longer gulled,
See through the schemes of our aspiring clan;
And from the rancor of my venomed mind,
I look askance on all the human race.
And if they're not to be appalled by fear,
I wish the earth might drink that vital stream
That warms the heart and feeds the manly glow,
The love inherent, planted in the breast,
To equal liberty, conferred on man
By him who formed the peasant and the king!
Could we erase these notions from their minds,
Then (paramount to these ideal whims,
Utopian dreams of patriotic virtue
Which long have danced in their distempered brains)
We'd smoothly glide on 'midst a race of slaves,
Nor heave one sigh, though all the human race
Were plunged in darkness, slavery, and vice.
If we could keep our foothold in the stirrup,
And, like the noble Claudia[97] of old,
Ride o'er the people if they don't give way,
Or wish their fates were all involved in one;

---

[94]James Otis.

[95]The Massachusetts Legislature.

[96]In a dramatic move, the Massachusetts Legislature impeached Chief Justice Peter Oliver (Hazelrod), in February, 1774, on the grounds that he received a salary from George III and therefore could not act independently.

[97]Roman emperor Claudius.

For I've a brother, as the Roman dame,[98]
Who would strike off the rebel neck at once.
   DUPE: No, all is o'er unless the sword decides,
Which cuts down kings, and kingdoms oft divides.
By that appeal I think we can prevail.
Their valor's great, and justice holds the scale.
They fight for freedom, while we stab the breast
Of every man who is her friend professed.
They fight in virtue's ever-sacred cause,
While we tread on divine and human laws.
Glory and victory, and lasting fame
Will crown their arms and bless each hero's name!
   MEAGRE: Away with all thy foolish, trifling cares,
And to the winds give all thy empty fears.
Let us repair and urge brave Sylla on.
I long to see the sweet revenge begun.
As fortune is a fickle, sportive dame,
She may for us the victory proclaim,
And with success our busy ploddings crown,
Though injured justice stern and solemn frown.
Then they shall smart for every bold offense.
Estates confiscated will pay the expense.
On their lost fortunes we a while will plume,
And strive to think there is no after doom. (*They exit. As they pass off the stage, the curtain draws up and discovers to the audience a* LADY *nearly connected with one of the principal actors in the group, reclined in an adjoining alcove, who in mournful accents accosts them.*)
   LADY: What painful scenes are hovering o'er the morn,
When spring again invigorates the lawn!
Instead of the gay landscape's beauteous dies[99],
Must the stained field salute our weeping eyes,
Must the green turf and all the mournful glades,
Drenched in the stream, absorb their dewy heads;
Whilst the tall oak and quivering willow bends,
To make a covert for their country's friends
Denied a grave amid the hurrying scene
Of routed armies scouring o'er the plain,

---

[98]Agrippina minor, the sister of Caligula, who was involved in many instances of intrigue and violence. Caligula wished that all his opponents shared one neck, so that he could decapitate them all with one blow.
[99]Day (Latin).

Till British troops shall to Columbia yield,
And freedom's sons are masters of the field!
Then o'er the purpled plain the victors tread,
Among the slain to seek each patriot dead,
While freedom weeps that virtue could not save,
But conquering heroes must enrich the grave.
An adamantine[100] monument they rear,
With this inscription: *Virtue's sons lie here!*

Finis

---

[100]Indestructible.

SLAVES IN ALGIERS; OR, A STRUGGLE FOR FREEDOM:

A Play, Interspersed with Songs, In Three Acts

Susanna Haswell Rowson

As Performed at the New Theatres in Philadelphia and Baltimore

1794

First performed June 30, 1794, Chestnut Street Theatre, Philadelphia. Originally printed for the author in Philadelphia by Wrigley and Berriman, 1794.

Dramatis Personae

Men: Women:
Muley Moloc, Dey[1] of Algiers   Zoriana, a Moriscan
Mustapha   Fetnah, a Moriscan
Ben Hassan, a Renegado.[2]   Selima, a Moriscan
Sebastian, a Spanish slave   Rebecca, an American
Augustus, an American captive   Olivia, an American
Frederic, an American captive
Henry, an American captive
Constant, an American captive
Sadi
Selim
Slaves, Guards, Etc.

Preface

In offering the following pages to the public, I feel myself necessitated to apologize for the errors which I am fearful will be evident to the severe eye of criticism.

The thought of writing a Dramatic Poem was hastily conceived and as hastily executed; it being not more than two months, from the first starting of the idea, to the time of its being performed.

I feel myself extremely happy in having an opportunity, thus publicly, to acknowledge my obligation to Mr. Reinagle for the attention he manifested, and the taste and genius he displayed in the composition of the music. I must also return my thanks to the Performers, who so readily accepted and so ably supported their several characters: Since it was chiefly owing to their exertions that the Play was received with such unbounded marks of approbation.

Since the first performance, I have made some alterations; and flatter myself those alterations have improved it: But of that, as well as of its merits in general, I am content to abide the decision of a candid and indulgent Public.

Some part of the plot is taken from the Story of the Captive, related by

---

[1]Governor.
[2]Traitor; in this case, to his original religion.

Cervantes, in his inimitable Romance of *Don Quixote*, the rest is entirely the offspring of fancy.

I am fully sensible of the many disadvantages under which I consequently labour from a confined education; nor do I expect my style will be thought equal in elegance or energy to the productions of those who, fortunately, from their sex, or situation in life, have been instructed in the Classics, and have reaped both pleasure and improvement by studying the Ancients in their original purity.

My chief aim has been to offer to the Public a Dramatic Entertainment, which, while it might excite a smile, or call forth the tear of sensibility, might contain no one sentiment in the least prejudicial to the moral or political principles of the government under which I live. On the contrary, it has been my endeavour to place the social virtues in the fairest point of view, and hold up to merited contempt and ridicule their opposite vices. If, in this attempt, I have been the least successful, I shall reap the reward to which I aspire, in the smiles and approbation of a Liberal Public.

Prologue
To the New Comedy of Slaves in Algiers
Written and Spoken by Mr. Fennell.

When aged Priam to Achilles' tent
To beg the captive corse of Hector went,
The silent suppliant spoke the father's fears,
His sighs his eloquence—his prayers his tears,
The noble conqueror by the sight was won,
And to the weeping sire restor'd the son.

No great Achilles holds *your* sons in chains,
No heart alive to friends' or father's pains,
No generous conqueror who is proud to show,
That valor vanquish'd is no more his foe;—
But one, whose idol, is his pilfer'd gold,
Got, or by piracy, or subjects sold.
Him no fond father's prayers nor tears can melt,
Untaught to feel for, what he never felt.

What then behoves it, they who help'd to gain,
A nation's freedom, feel the galling chain?
They, who a more than ten year's war withstood,
And stamp'd their country's honor with their blood?

Or, shall the noble Eagle see her brood,
Beneath the pirate kite's fell claw subdu'd?
View her dear sons of liberty enslaved,
Nor let them share the blessings which they sav'd?
—It must not be—each heart, each soul must rise,
Each one must listen to their distant cries;
Each hand must give, and the quick sail unfurl'd,
Must bear their ransom to the distant world.

Not *here* alone, Columbia's sons be free,
Where'er they breathe there must be liberty.
—There *must*! There *is*, for he who form'd the whole,
Entwin'd blest freedom with th' immortal *soul*.
Eternal twins, whose mutual efforts fan,
That heavenly flame that gilds the life of man,
Whose light, 'midst manacles and dungeons drear,
The sons of honor, must forever cheer.

What tyrant then the virtuous heart can bind?
'Tis vices only can enslave the mind.
Who barters country, honor, faith, to save
His life, tho' free in person, is a slave.
While he, enchain'd, imprison'd tho' he be,
Who lifts his arm for liberty, is free.

Tonight our author boldly dares to choose,
This glorious subject for her humble muse;
Tho' tyrants check the genius which they fear,
She dreads no check, nor persecution *here*;
Where safe asylums every virtue guard,
And every talent meets its just reward.

Some say the Comic muse, with watchful eye,
Should catch the reigning *vices* as they fly,
Our author boldly has reversed that plan,
The reigning *virtues* she has dar'd to scan,
And tho' a woman, pled the Rights of Man.

Thus she, with anxious hope her fate abides,
And to your care, the tender plant confides,
Convinc'd you'll cherish what to freedom's true;
She trusts its life to candor and to you.

ACT ONE

Scene One

City of Algiers. Apartment at the DEY's. FETNAH and SELIMA.

FETNAH: Well, it's all vastly pretty—the gardens, the house and these fine clothes. I like them very well, but I don't like to be confined.

SELIMA: Yet, surely, you have no reason to complain. Chosen favorite of the Dey, what can you wish for more?

FETNAH: Oh, a great many things. In the first place, I wish for liberty. Why do you talk of my being a favorite? Is the poor bird that is confined in a cage (because a favorite with its enslaver) consoled for the loss of freedom? No! Though its prison is of golden wire, its little heart still pants for liberty. Gladly would it seek the fields of air, and even perched upon a naked bough, exulting carol forth its song, nor once regret the splendid house of bondage.

SELIMA: Ah! But then our master loves you.

FETNAH: What of that? I don't love him.

SELIMA: Not love him?

FETNAH: No. He is old and ugly; then he wears such tremendous whiskers. And when he makes love, he looks so grave and stately that, I declare, if it was not for fear of his huge scimitar, I should burst out a-laughing in his face.

SELIMA: Take care you don't provoke him too far.

FETNAH: I don't care how I provoke him, if I can but make him keep his distance. You know I was brought here only a few days since. Well, yesterday, as I was amusing myself, looking at the fine things I saw everywhere about me, who should bolt into the room, but that great, ugly thing Mustapha. "What do you want?" said I!

"Most beautiful Fetnah," said he, bowing till the tip of his long, hooked nose almost touched the toe of his slipper, "Most beautiful Fetnah, our powerful and gracious master, Muley Moloc, sends me, the humblest of his slaves, to tell you he will condescend to stop in your apartment tonight, and commands you to receive the high honor with proper humility."

SELIMA: Well—and what answer did you return?

FETNAH: Lord, I was so frightened, and so provoked, I hardly know what I said; but finding the horrid-looking creature didn't move, at last I told him that if the Dey was determined to come, I supposed he must, for I could not hinder him.

SELIMA: And did he come?

FETNAH: No, but he made me go to him; and when I went trembling into the room, he twisted his whiskers and knit his great beetle brows. "Fetnah," said he, "You abuse my goodness; I have condescended to request you to love me." And then he gave me such a fierce look, as if he would say, and if you don't love me, I'll cut your head off.

SELIMA: I dare say you were finely frightened.

FETNAH: Frightened! I was provoked beyond all patience, and thinking he would certainly kill me one day or other, I thought I might as well speak my mind, and be dispatched out of the way at once.

SELIMA: You make me tremble.

FETNAH: So, mustering up as much courage as I could: "Great and powerful Muley," said I, "I am sensible I am your slave. You took me from an humble state, placed me in this fine palace, and gave me these rich clothes. You bought my person of my parents, who loved gold better than they did their child; but my affections you could not buy. I can't love you."

"How!" cried he, starting from his seat, "How, can't love me?" And he laid his hand upon his scimitar.

SELIMA: Oh, dear! Fetnah!

FETNAH: When I saw the scimitar half drawn, I caught hold of his arm. "Oh, good my lord," said I, "Pray do not kill a poor little girl like me! Send me home again, and bestow your favor on some other, who may think splendor a compensation for the loss of liberty."

"Take her away," said he. "She is beneath my anger."

SELIMA: But how is it, Fetnah, that you have conceived such an aversion to the manners of a country where you were born?

FETNAH: You are mistaken. I was not born in Algiers. I drew my first breath in England. My father, Ben Hassan, as he is now called, was a Jew. I can scarcely remember our arrival here, and have been educated in the Moorish religion, though I always had a natural antipathy to their manners.

SELIMA: Perhaps imbibed from your mother.

FETNAH: No. She has no objection to any of their customs, except that of their having a great many wives at a time. But some few months since, my father, who sends out many corsairs,[3] brought home a female captive to whom I became greatly attached. It was she who nourished in my mind the love of liberty and taught me woman was never formed to be the abject slave of man. Nature made us equal with them and gave us the

---

[3]Pirate ships, especially of the Barbary Pirates who, between 1785 and 1815, attacked American ships, seizing vessels and cargoes and taking captive crews and passengers.

power to render ourselves superior.

SELIMA: Of what nation was she?

FETNAH: She came from that land where virtue in either sex is the only mark of superiority. She was an American.

SELIMA: Where is she now?

FETNAH: She is still at my father's, waiting the arrival of her ransom, for she is a woman of fortune. And though I can no longer listen to her instructions, her precepts are engraven on my heart. I feel that I was born free, and while I have life, I will struggle to remain so.

Song:

I.

The rose just bursting into bloom,
Admired where'er 'tis seen,
Diffuses 'round a rich perfume,
The garden's pride and queen.
When gathered from its native bed,
No longer charms the eye;
Its vivid tints are quickly fled.
'Twill wither, droop, and die.

II.

So woman when by nature dressed,
In charms devoid of art
Can warm the stoic's icy breast,
Can triumph o'er each heart,
Can bid the soul to virtue rise,
To glory prompt the brave,
But sinks oppresed, and drooping dies,
When once she's made a slave. (*Exits.*)

Scene Two

BEN HASSAN's *house.*

REBECCA: (*Discovered reading*).

"The soul, secure in its existence, smiles
At the drawn dagger, and defies its point.
The stars shall fade away, the sun itself
Grow dim with age, and nature sink in years,

But thou shall flourish in immortal youth,
Unhurt, amidst the war of elements,
The wreck of matter, or the crush of worlds." (*Lays down the book.*)

Oh, blessed hope! I feel within myself that spark of intellectual heavenly fire that bids me soar above this mortal world, and all its pains or pleasures—its pleasures! Oh, long—long since I have been dead to all that bear the name! In early youth, torn from the husband of my heart's selection—the first, only object of my love. Bereft of friends, cast on an unfeeling world, with only one, poor stay on which to rest the hope of future joy. I have a son—my child! My dear Augustus, where are you now? In slavery. Grant me patience, heaven! Must a boy born in Columbia, claiming liberty as his birthright, pass all his days in slavery? How often have I gazed upon his face, and fancied I could trace his father's features; how often have I listened to his voice, and thought his father's spirit spoke within him. Oh, my adored boy! Must I no more behold his eyes beaming with youthful ardor when I have told him how his brave countrymen purchased their freedom with their blood? Alas! I see him now but seldom. And when we meet, to think that we are slaves—poor, wretched slaves, each serving different masters—my eyes overflow with tears. I have but time to protect his life, and at some future day restore his liberty.

Enter BEN HASSAN.

BEN HASSAN: How do you do, Mrs. Rebecca?

REBECCA: Well in health, Hassan, but depressed in spirit.

BEN HASSAN: Ah! Dat be very bad. Come, come, cheer up. I vants to talk vid you. You must not be so melancholy. I be your very good friend.

REBECCA: Thank you, Hassan, but if you are in reality the friend you profess to be, leave me to indulge my grief in solitude. Your intention is kind, but I would rather be alone.

BEN HASSAN: You likes mightily to be by yourself, but I must talk to you a little. I vantsh to know ven you think your ransom vil come. 'Tis a long time, Mrs Rebecca, and you knows—

REBECCA: Oh, yes, I know I am under many obligations to you, but I shall soon be able to repay them.

BEN HASSAN: That may be, but 'tis a very long time since you wrote to your friends. 'Tis above eight months. I am afraid you have deceived me.

REBECCA: Alas! Perhaps I have deceived myself.

BEN HASSAN: Vat, den you have no friends? You are not a voman's of fortune?

REBECCA: Yes, yes, I have both friends and ability, but I am afraid my letters have miscarried.

BEN HASSAN: Oh! Dat ish very likely. You may be here dish two or three years longer, perhaps all your life times.

REBECCA: Alas! I am very wretched. (*Weeps.*)

BEN HASSAN: Come, now, don't cry so. You must consider, I never suffered you to be exposed in the slave market.

REBECCA: But my son! Oh, Hassan, why did you suffer them to sell my child?

BEN HASSAN: I could not help it. I did all I could. But you knows I would not let you be sent to the Dey. I have kept you in my own house, at mine own expense— (*Aside.*) for which I have been more than doubly paid.

REBECCA: This is indeed true, but I cannot at present return your kindness.

BEN HASSAN: Ah! You be very sly rogue; you pretend not to know how I loves you.

REBECCA: (*Aside*). What means the wretch?

BEN HASSAN: You should forget your Christian friends, for I dare say they have forgot you. I vill make you my vife, I vill give you von, two, tree, slaves to vait on you.

REBECCA: Make me your wife! Why, are you not already married?

BEN HASSAN: Ish, but our law gives us great many vives. Our law gives liberty in love. You are an American and you must love liberty.

REBECCA: Hold, Hassan. Prostitute not the sacred word by applying it to licentiousness. The sons and daughters of liberty take justice, truth, and mercy, for their leaders, when they list under her glorious banners.

BEN HASSAN: Your friends will never ransom you.

REBECCA: How readily does the sordid mind judge of others by its own contracted feelings. You, who much I fear, worship no deity but gold, who could sacrifice friendship—nay, even the ties of nature at the shrine of your idolatry—think other hearts as selfish as your own. But there are souls to whom the afflicted never cry in vain—who, to dry the widow's tear or free the captive, would share their last possession. Blest spirits of philanthropy, who inhabit my native land, never will I doubt your friendship; for sure I am, you never will neglect the wretched.

BEN HASSAN: If you are not ransomed soon, I must send you to the Dey.

REBECCA: Even as you please. I cannot be more wretched than I am. But of this be assured: however depressed in fortune, however sunk in adversity, the soul secure in its own integrity will rise superior to its enemies and scorn the venal wretch who barters truth for gold. (*Exits.*)

BEN HASSAN: 'Tis a very strange voman, very strange indeed. She does not know I got her pocket-book, with bills of exchange in it. She thinks I keep her in my house out of charity, as if she was in her own country. 'Tis dev'lish hard indeed, when masters may not do what they please with their slaves. Her ransom arrived yesterday, but den she don't know it. Yesh, here is the letter: ransom for Rebecca Constant and six other Christian slaves. Vell, I vill make her write for more. She is my slave; I must get all I can by her. Oh, here comes that wild young Christian, Frederic, who ransomed himself a few days since.

Enter FREDERIC.

FREDERIC: Well, my little Israelite, what are you muttering about? Have you thought on my proposals? Will you purchase the vessel and assist us?

BEN HASSAN: Vat did you say you would give me?

FREDERIC: We can, amongst us, muster up two thousand sequins. 'Tis all we have in the world.

BEN HASSAN: You are sure you can get no more?

FREDERIC: Not a farthing more.

BEN HASSAN: Den I vill be satisfied with dat. It will in some measure reward me— (*Aside.*) for betraying you.

FREDERIC: And you will purchase the vessel.

BEN HASSAN: I will do every thing that is necessary— (*Aside.*) for my own interest.

FREDERIC: You have conveyed provision to the cavern by the sea side, where I am to conceal the captives to wait the arrival of the vessel.

BEN HASSAN: Most shartingly, I have provided for them as— (*Aside.*) as secure a prison as any in Algiers.

FREDERIC: But, are you not a most extortionate old rogue, to require so much before you will assist a parcel of poor devils to obtain their liberty?

BEN HASSAN: Oh! Mr. Frederic, if I vash not your very good friend, I could not do it for so little. The Moors are such uncharitable dogs, they never think they can get enough for their slaves. But I have a vasht deal of compassion; I feels very mush for the poor Christians. I should be very glad— (*Aside.*) to have a hundred or two of them my prisoners.

FREDERIC: You would be glad to serve us?

BEN HASSAN: Shartingly. (*Aside.*) Ven I can serve myself at the same time.

FREDERIC: Prithee, honest Hassan, how came you to put on the turban?

BEN HASSAN: I'll tell you.

Song:

Ven I vas a mighty little boy,
Heart-cakes I sold and pepper-mint drops;
Wafers and sweet chalk[4] I used for to cry,
Alacumpeine[5] and nice lolly-pops.

The next thing I sold vas the rollers[6] for the macs,[7]
To curl dere hair; 'twas very good.
Rosin I painted for[8] sealing wax,
And I forged upon it vel brand on vast hood.

Next to try my luck in the alley I vent,[9]
But of dat I soon grew tired and wiser.
Monies I lent out at fifty per cent,
And my name was I. H. in the Public Advertiser.

The next thing I did was a spirited prank,
Which at one stroke my fortune was made;
I wrote so very like the cashiers at the bank,
The clerks did not know the difference, and the monies was paid.

So, having cheated the Gentiles, as Moses commanded,
Oh, I began to tremble at every gibbet that I saw!
But I got on board a ship, and here was safely landed,
In spite of the judges, counsellors, attorneys, and law.[10]

FREDERIC: And so, to complete the whole, you turned Mohammedan.
BEN HASSAN: Oh, 'twas the safest way.
FREDERIC: But Hassan, as you are so fond of cheating the gentiles, perhaps you may cheat us.

---

[4]Chalky clay was eaten by pregnant women and others with pica. Perhaps the confection referred to was sweetened white clay.

[5]Elecampane, the wild "horse-heel" plant used as a remedy for various ills.

[6]Probably refers to curl papers.

[7]May refer to Scottish people.

[8]To resemble.

[9]Probably refers to gambling.

[10]This song was not written by Mrs. Rowson.

BEN HASSAN: Oh, no! I swear by Mohammed.

FREDERIC: No swearing, old Trimmer. If you are true to us, you will be amply rewarded. Should you betray us, (*Sternly.*) by heaven, you shall not live an hour after. Go, look for a vessel. Make every necessary preparation; and remember, instant death shall await the least appearance of treachery.

BEN HASSAN: But I have not got monies.

FREDERIC: Go, you are a hypocrite. You are rich enough to purchase an hundred vessels, and if the Dey knew of your wealth—

BEN HASSAN: Oh! Dear Mr. Frederic, I am very poor, but I vill do all you desire, and you vill pay me afterwards. (*Aside.*) Oh, I wish I could get you well paid with the bastinado.[11] (*Exits.*)

FREDERIC: I will trust this fellow no farther. I am afraid he will play us false. But should he, we have yet one resource: we can but die, and to die in a struggle for freedom is better far than to live in ignominious bondage. (*Exits.*)

Scene Three

Another apartment at the DEY*'s.* ZORIANA *and* OLIVIA.

ZORIANA: Alas, it was pitiful. Pray proceed.

OLIVIA: My father's ill health obliging him to visit Lisbon, we embarked for that place, leaving my betrothed lover to follow us. But ere we reached our destined port, we were captured by an Algerine corsair, and I was immediately sent to the Dey, your father.

ZORIANA: I was then in the country, but I was told he became enamored of you.

OLIVIA: Unfortunately he did. But my being a Christian has hitherto preserved me from improper solicitations, though I am frequently pressed to abjure my religion.

ZORIANA: Were you not once near making your escape?

OLIVIA: We were. My father, by means of some jewels which he had concealed in his clothes, bribed one of the guards to procure false keys to the apartments. But on the very night when we meant to put our plan in execution, the Dey, coming suddenly into the room, surprised my father in my arms.

ZORIANA: Was not his anger dreadful?

OLIVIA: Past description. My dear father was torn from me and,

---

[11]A stick used to inflict beatings, usually on the soles of the feet.

loaded with chains, thrown into a dungeon, where he still remains. Secluded from the cheering light of heaven—no resting place but on the cold, damp ground—the daily portion of his food so poor and scanty, it hardly serves to eke out an existence lingering as it is forlorn.

ZORIANA: And where are the false keys?

OLIVIA: I have them still, for I was not known to possess them.

ZORIANA: Then banish all your sorrow. If you have still the keys, tomorrow night shall set us all at liberty.

OLIVIA: Madam!

ZORIANA: Be not alarmed, sweet Olivia. I am a Christian in my heart, and I love a Christian slave, to whom I have conveyed money and jewels sufficient to ransom himself and several others. I will appoint him to be in the garden this evening. You shall go with me and speak to him.

OLIVIA: But how can we release my father?

ZORIANA: Every method shall be tried to gain admittance to his prison. The Christian has many friends, and if all other means fail, they can force the door.

OLIVIA: Oh, heavens, could I but see him once more at liberty, how gladly would I sacrifice my own life to secure his!

ZORIANA: The keys you have will let us out of the house when all are locked in the embraces of sleep. Our Christian friends will be ready to receive us, and before morning we shall be in a place of safety. In the mean time, let hope support your sinking spirits.

Song:

Sweet cherub clad in robes of white,
Descend celestial Hope;
And on thy pinions, soft, and light,
Oh bear thy votary up.
'Tis thou can soothe the troubled breath,
The tear of sorrow dry;
Can'st lull each doubt and fear to rest,
And check the rising sigh.
      Sweet cherub &c. (*They exit.*)

Scene Four

A garden outside of a house, with small, high lattices. HENRY *and* FREDERIC.

FREDERIC: Fearing the old fellow would pocket our cash and betray us afterwards, I changed my plan, and have entrusted the money with a Spaniard, who will make the best bargain he can for us. Have you tried our friends? Will they be staunch?

HENRY: To a man. The hope of liberty, like an electric spark, ran instantly through every heart, kindling a flame of patriotic ardor. Nay, even those whom interest or fear have hitherto kept silent, now openly avowed their hatred of the Dey and swore to assist our purpose.

FREDERIC: Those whose freedom we have already purchased have concerted proper measures for liberating many others, and by twelve o'clock tomorrow night we shall have a party large enough to surround the palace of the Dey and convey from thence in safety the fair Zoriana. (*Window opens and a white handkerchief is waved.*)

HENRY: Soft! Behold the signal of love and peace.

FREDERIC: I'll catch it as it falls. (*He approaches; it is drawn back.*)

HENRY: 'Tis not designed for you. Stand aside. (HENRY *approaches. The handkerchief is let fall, a hand waved, and then the lattice shut.*) 'Tis a wealthy fall, and worth receiving.

FREDERIC: What says the fair Mohammedan?

HENRY: Can I believe my eyes? Here are English characters, and, but I think 'tis impossible, I should say this was my Olivia's writing.

FREDERIC: This is always the way with you happy fellows who are favorites with the women; you slight the willing fair one, and dote on those who are only to be obtained with difficulty.

HENRY: I wish the lovely Moor had fixed her affections on you instead of me.

FREDERIC: I wish she had with all my soul—Moor or Christian, slave or free woman. 'Tis no matter; if she was but young, and in love with me, I'd kneel down and worship her. But I'm a poor, miserable dog; the women never say civil things to me.

HENRY: But do you think it can be possible that my adorable Olivia is a captive here?

FREDERIC: Prithee, man, don't stand musing and wondering, but remember this is the time for action. If chance has made your Olivia a captive, why, we must make a bold attempt to set her at liberty, and then I suppose you will turn over the fair Moriscan to me. But what says the letter?

HENRY: (*Reads*). "As you have now the means of freedom in your power, be at the north garden gate at ten o'clock, and when you hear me sing, you will be sure all is safe, and that you may enter without danger. Do not fail to come. I have some pleasant intelligence to communicate." Yes, I will go and acquaint her with the real state of my heart.

FREDERIC: And so make her our enemy.

HENRY: It would be barbarous to impose on her generous nature. What, avail myself of her liberality to obtain my own freedom, take her from her country and friends, and then sacrifice her a victim to ingratitude and disappointed love?

FREDERIC: 'Tush, man, women's hearts are not so easily broken. We may, perhaps, give them a slight wound now and then, but they are seldom or never incurable.

HENRY: I see our master coming this way. Begone to our friends. Encourage them to go through with our enterprise. The moment I am released I will join you.

FREDERIC: 'Till when adieu. (*They exit in different directions.*)

ACT TWO

Scene One

Moonlight. A Garden. ZORIANA *and* OLIVIA.

ZORIANA: Sweet Olivia, chide me not; for though I'm fixed to leave this place and embrace Christianity, I cannot but weep when I think what my poor father will suffer. Methinks I should stay to console him for the loss of you.

OLIVIA: He will soon forget me. Has he not already a number of beautiful slaves, who have been purchased to banish me from his remembrance?

ZORIANA: True, but he slights them all. You, only, are the mistress of his heart.

OLIVIA: Hark, did you not hear a footstep?

ZORIANA: Perhaps it is the young Christian. He waits the appointed signal. I think all is safe. He may approach.

Song:

Wrapped in the evening's soft and pensive shade,
When passing zephyrs scarce the herbage moves,
Here waits a trembling, fond, and anxious maid,
Expecting to behold the youth she loves.
Though Philomela on a neighboring tree
Melodious warbles forth her nightly strain,

Thy accents would be sweeter far to me,
Would from my bosom banish doubt and pain.

Then come, dear youth, come haste away,
Haste to this silent grove;
The signal's given, you must obey,
'Tis liberty and love.

Enter HENRY.

HENRY: Lovely and benevolent lady, permit me thus humbly to thank you for my freedom.

OLIVIA: Oh Heavens, that voice!

ZORIANA: Gentle Christian, perhaps I have overstepped the bounds prescribed my sex. I was early taught a love of Christianity, but I must now confess my actions are impelled by a tenderer passion.

HENRY: That passion which you have so generally avowed has excited my utmost gratitude, and I only wish for power to convince you how much you have bound me to your service.

OLIVIA: Oh! (*Faints.*)

ZORIANA: What ails my friend? Help me to support her. She is an amiable creature, and will accompany us in our flight. She revives. How are you? Speak, my Olivia.

HENRY: Olivia, did you say?

OLIVIA: Yes, Henry, your forsaken Olivia.

HENRY: Oh, my beloved! Is it possible that I see you here in bondage? Where is your father?

OLIVIA: In bondage too. But Henry, you had forgot me. You could not renounce your vows and wed another.

HENRY: Oh, no! Never for one moment have my thoughts strayed from my Olivia. I never regretted slavery but as it deprived me of your sweet converse, nor wished for freedom but to ratify my vows to you.

ZORIANA: (*Aside*). How? Mutual lovers! My disappointed heart beats high with resentment, but in vain. I wish to be a Christian, and I will, though my heart breaks, perform a Christian's duty.

HENRY: Pardon, beauteous lady, an involuntary error. I have long loved this Christian maid; we are betrothed to each other. This evening I obeyed your summons to inform you that grateful thanks and fervent prayers were all the return I could make for the unmerited kindness you have shown me.

OLIVIA: Generous Zoriana, blame not my Henry.

ZORIANA: Think not so meanly of me as to suppose I live but for myself. That I loved your Henry I can without a blush avow, but 'twas a love so pure that to see him happy will gratify my utmost wish. I still rejoice that I've procured his liberty. You shall, with him, embrace the opportunity, and be henceforth as blest— (*Aside.*) as I am wretched.

HENRY: You will go with us.

ZORIANA: Perhaps I may—but let us now separate. Tomorrow, from the lattice, you shall receive instructions how to proceed. In the meantime, here is more gold and jewels. I never knew their value till I found they could ransom *you* from slavery.

HENRY: Words are poor.

ZORIANA: Leave us. My heart's oppressed. I wish to be alone. Doubt not the safety of your Olivia; she must be safe with me, for she is dear to you. (HENRY *kisses her hand, bows, and exits. They stand some time without speaking.*)

ZORIANA: Olivia!

OLIVIA: Madam!

ZORIANA: Why are you silent? Do you doubt my sincerity?

OLIVIA: Oh, no. . . but I was thinking: if we should fail in our attempt—if we should be taken—

ZORIANA: Gracious heaven forbid!

OLIVIA: Who then could deprecate your father's wrath? Yourself, my Henry, and my dearest father—all, all, would fall a sacrifice.

ZORIANA: These are groundless fears.

OLIVIA: Perhaps they are; but yet, I am resolved to stay behind.

ZORIANA: Do not think of it.

OLIVIA: Forgive me. I am determined, and that so firmly, it will be in vain to oppose me. If you escape, the Power who protects you will also give to me the means of following. Should you be taken, I may perhaps move the Dey to forgive you, and even should my prayers and tears have no effect, my life shall pay the forfeiture of yours.

ZORIANA: I will not go.

OLIVIA: Yes, gentle lady, yes. You must go with them. Perhaps you think it will be a painful task to meet your father's anger, but indeed it will not. The thought of standing forth the preserver of the dear author of my being, of the man who loves me next to heaven, of the friend who could sacrifice her own happiness to mine, would fill my soul with such delight that even death, in its most horrid shape, could not disturb its tranquility.

ZORIANA: But can you suppose your father, and your lover—

OLIVIA: You must assist my design. You must tell them I am already at liberty and in a place of safety. When they discover the deception, be it your task, my gentle Zoriana, to wipe the tear of sorrow from their eyes. Be a daughter to my poor father. Comfort his age; be kind and tender to him. Let him not feel the loss of his Olivia. Be to my Henry—oh, my bursting heart—a friend, to soothe him in his deep affliction. Pour consolative on his wounded mind, and love him, if you can, as I have done. (*Exits.*)

Scene Two

Dawn of day.   Another part of the garden, with an alcove.   Enter FREDERIC.

FREDERIC: What a poor, unfortunate dog I am. Last night I slipped into the garden behind Henry, in hopes I should find some distressed damsel who wanted a knight-errant to deliver her from captivity, and here have I wandered through windings, turnings, alleys, and labyrinths, till the devil himself could not find the way out again. Someone approaches. . . by all that's lovely, 'tis a woman—young, and handsome too. Health glows upon her cheek, and good humor sparkles in her eye. I'll conceal myself, that I may not alarm her. (*Exits into the alcove.*)

Enter FETNAH.

Song:

Aurora, lovely blooming fair,
Unbarred the eastern skies,
While many a soft pellucid tear.
Ran trickling from her eyes.
Onward she came, with heart-felt glee,
Leading the dancing hours;
For though she wept, she smiled to see
Her tears refresh the flowers.
Phoebus, who long her charms admired,
With bright refulgent ray
Came forth, and as the maid retired,
He kiss'd her tears away.

FETNAH: What a sweet morning. I could not sleep, so the moment the doors were open, I came out to try and amuse myself. 'Tis a delightful garden, but I believe I should hate the finest place in the world, if I was obliged to stay in it whether I would or no. If I am forced to remain here much longer, I shall fret myself as old and as ugly as the Mustapha. That's no matter; there's nobody here to look at one but great, black, goggle-eyed creatures, that are posted here and there to watch us. And when one speaks to them, they shake their frightful heads, and make such a horrid noise. Lord, I wish I could run away, but that's impossible. There is no getting over these nasty high walls. I do wish some dear, sweet, Christian man would fall in love with me, break open the garden gates, and carry me off.

FREDERIC: (*Stealing out*). Say you so, my charmer? Then I'm your man.

FETNAH: And take me to that charming place where there are no bolts and bars, no mutes and guards, no bowstrings[12] and scimitars. Oh, it must be a dear, delightful country, where women do just what they please!

FREDERIC: I'm sure you are a dear, delightful creature.

FETNAH: (*Turning, sees him, and shrieks*).

FREDERIC: Hush, my sweet little infidel, or we shall be discovered.

FETNAH: Why, who are you, and how came you here?

FREDERIC: I am a poor, forlorn creature, over head and ears in love with you, and I came here to tell you how much I adore you.

FETNAH: (*Aside*). Oh, dear, what a charming man! I do wish he would run away with me.

FREDERIC: Perhaps this is the lady who wrote to Henry. She looks like a woman of quality, if I may judge from her dress. I'll ask her. You wish to leave this country, lovely Moor?

FETNAH: Lord, I'm not a Moriscan. I hate 'em all. There is nothing I wish so much as to get away from them.

FREDERIC: Your letters said so.

FETNAH: Letters!

FREDERIC: Yes, the letters you dropped from the window upon the terrace.

FETNAH: (*Aside*). He takes me for some other. I'll not undeceive him, and maybe he'll carry off. Yes, sir—yes, I did write to you.

FREDERIC: To me!

FETNAH: To be sure. Did you think it was to anybody else?

FREDERIC: Why, there has been a small mistake.

FETNAH: (*Aside*). And there's like to be a greater if you knew all.

FREDERIC: And do you indeed love me?

FETNAH: Yes, I do, better than anybody I ever saw in my life.

FREDERIC: And if I can get you out of the palace, you will go away with me?

FETNAH: To be sure, I will. That's the very thing I wish.

FREDERIC: Oh, thou sweet, bewitching little— (*Catching her in his arms.*)

---

[12]A bowstring is a garrote, or cord for strangling.

MULEY MOLOC: (*Without*). Tell him Fetnah shall be sent home to him immediately.

FETNAH: Oh, lord, what will become of us? That's my lord the Dey! You'll certainly be taken.

FREDERIC: Yes, I feel the bowstring round my neck already. What shall I do? Where shall I hide?

FETNAH: Stay, don't be frightened. I'll bring you off. Catch me in your arms again. (*She throws herself in his arms as though fainting.*)

Enter MULEY MOLOC *and* MUSTAPHA.

MULEY MOLOC: I tell thee, Mustapha, I cannot banish the beautiful Christian one moment from my thoughts. The women seem all determined to perplex me. I was pleased with the beauty of Fetnah, but her childish caprice—

MUSTAPHA: Behold, my lord, the fair slave you mention, in the arms of a stranger.

FREDERIC: (*Aside*). Now, goodbye to poor pilgarlic.[13]

FETNAH: (*Pretending to recover*). Are they gone, and am I safe? Oh! Courteous stranger, when the Dey my master knows—

MULEY MOLOC: What's the matter, Fetnah? Who is this slave?

FETNAH: (*Kneeling*). Oh, mighty prince, this stranger has preserved me from the greatest outrage.

MULEY MOLOC: What outrage?

FETNAH: Now, do not look angry at your poor little slave who, knowing she had offended you, could not rest, and came early into the garden to lament her folly.

FREDERIC: (*Aside*). Well said, woman.

MULEY MOLOC: Rise, Fetnah. We have forgot your rashness. Proceed.

FETNAH: So, as I was sitting, melancholy and sad, in the alcove, I heard a great noise, and presently four or five Turks leaped over the wall and began to plunder the garden. I screamed. Did not you hear me, Mustapha?

FREDERIC: (*Aside*). Well said, again.

FETNAH: But the moment they saw me, they seized me and would have forced me away, had not this gallant stranger run to my assistance. They, thinking they were pursued by many, relinquished their hold and left me fainting in the stranger's arms.

---

[13]A bald man (literally, peeled garlic).

MULEY MOLOC: 'Tis well.

MUSTAPHA: But, gracious sir, how came the stranger here?

FREDERIC: (*Aside*). Oh, confound your inquisitive tongue!

MULEY MOLOC: Aye, Christian, how came you in this garden?

FETNAH: He came from my father. Did not you say my father sent you here?

FREDERIC: (*Bows*). (*Aside*). Now, who the devil is her father?

FETNAH: He came to beg leave to gather some herbs for a salad, while they were still fresh with morning dew.

FREDERIC: (*Aside*). Heaven bless her invention!

MULEY MOLOC: Go to your apartment.

FETNAH: Oh, dear! If he should ask him any questions when I am gone, what will become of him? (*Exits.*)

MULEY MOLOC: Christian, gather the herbs you came for, and depart in peace. Mustapha, go to my daughter Zoriana. Tell her I'll visit her some two hours hence, till when I'll walk in the refreshing morning air.

(*Exit* MULEY *and* MUSTAPHA.)

FREDERIC: Thanks to dear little infidel's ready wit, I breathe again. Good Mr. Whiskers, I am obliged by your dismission of me. I will depart as fast as I can, and yet I cannot but regret leaving my lovely little Moor behind. Who comes here? The apostate Hassan! Now could I swear some mischief was afoot. I'll keep out of sight and try to learn his business. (*Retires.*)

Enter BEN HASSAN *and* MUSTAPHA.

BEN HASSAN: Indeed, I am vashtly sorry that my daughter has offended my good lord the Dey, but if he will admit me to his sublime presence, I can give him intelligence of so important a nature as, I makes no doubt, will incline him to pardon her for my sake.

MUSTAPHA: I will tell him you wait his leisure. (*Exits.*)

FREDERIC: The traitor is on the point of betraying us. I must, if possible, prevent his seeing the Dey. (*Runs to* BEN HASSAN *with all the appearance of violent terror.*) Oh! My dear friend Hassan, for heaven's sake, what brought you here? Don't you know the Dey is so highly offended with you that he vows to have you impaled alive?

BEN HASSAN: Oh, dear! Mr. Frederic, how did you know?

FREDERIC: It was by the luckiest chance in the world! I happened to be in this garden, when I overheard a slave of yours informing the Dey that you had not only amassed immense riches, which you intended to carry out of his territories, but that you had many valuable slaves which you kept concealed from him, that you might reap the benefit of their ransom.

BEN HASSAN: Oh! What will become of me? But come, come, Mr. Frederic, you only say this to frighten me.

FREDERIC: Well, you'll see that; for I heard him command his guards to be ready to seize you when he gave the signal, as he expected you here every moment.

BEN HASSAN: Oh! What shall I do?

FREDERIC: If you stay here, you will certainly be *bastinadoed—impaled—burnt*!

BEN HASSAN: Oh, dear! Oh, dear!

FREDERIC: Make haste, my dear friend. Run home as fast as possible! Hide your treasure and keep out of the way.

BEN HASSAN: Oh dear! I wish I was safe in Duke's Place. (*Exits.*)

Scene Three

FETNAH's *Apartment.* FETNAH *and* SELIMA.

FETNAH: Now will you pretend to say you are happy here, and that you love the Dey?

SELIMA: I have been here many years. The Dey has been very good to me, and my chief employment has been to wait on his daughter, Zoriana, till I was appointed to attend you. To you, perhaps, he may be an object of disgust. But looking up to him, as a kind and generous master, to me he appears amiable.

FETNAH: Oh, to be sure, he is a most amiable creature! I think I see him now, seated on his cushion, a bowl of sherbet by his side, and a long pipe in his mouth. Oh, how charmingly the tobacco must perfume his whiskers. "Here, Mustapha," says he, "Go, bid the slave Selima come to me." Well it does not signify. That word slave does so stick in my throat. I wonder how any woman of spirit can gulp it down.

SELIMA: We are accustomed to it.

FETNAH: The more's the pity; for how sadly depressed must the soul be, to whom custom has rendered bondage supportable.

SELIMA: Then, if opportunity offered, you would leave Algiers?

FETNAH: That I would, most cheerfully.

SELIMA: And, perhaps, bestow your affections on some young Christian?

FETNAH: That you may be sure of. For say what you will, I am sure the woman must be blind and stupid who would not prefer a young, handsome, good-humored Christian to an old, ugly, ill- natured Turk.

Enter SADI, with robe, turban, &c.

FETNAH: Well, what's your business?

SADI: I—I—I—I'm afraid I'm wrong.

SELIMA: Who sent you here?

SADI: I was told to take these to our master's son, young Soliman. But somehow, in the turnings and windings in this great house, I believe I have lost myself.

SELIMA: You have mistaken—

FETNAH: Mistaken? No, he is very right. Here, give me the clothes. I'll take care of them. (*Takes them.*) There, there, go about your business. It's all very well. (*Exit* SADI.) Now, Selima, I'll tell you what I'll do. I'll put these on, go to the Dey, and see if he will know me.

SELIMA: He'll be angry.

FETNAH: Pshaw! You're so fearful of his anger. If you let the men see you are afraid, they'll hector and domineer finely. No, no, let them think you don't care whether they are pleased or no, and then they'll be as condescending and humble. Go, go. Take the clothes into the next apartment. (*Exit* SELIMA.) Now, if by means of these clothes, I can get out of the palace, I'll seek the charming young Christian I saw this morning. We'll get my dear instructress from my father's and fly, together, from this land of captivity to the regions of peace and liberty.

ACT THREE

Scene One

A kind of grotto. FREDERIC, HENRY, SEBASTIAN, *and* SLAVES.

SEBASTIAN: Now, if you had trusted me at first, I'll answer for it, I had got you all safe out. Aye, and that dear, sweet creature, madam Zoriana, too! What a pity it is she's Mohammedan. Your true-bred Mohammedans never drink any wine. Now, for my part, I like a drop of good liquor. It makes a body feel so comfortable—so. . . so. . . I don't know howish, as if they were friends with all the world. I always keep a friend or two hid here. (*Takes out some bottles.*) Mum. Don't be afraid. They are no tell-tales—only when they are trusted too far.

FREDERIC: Well, Sebastian, don't be too unguarded in trusting these very good friends tonight.

SEBASTIAN: Never fear me. Did not I tell you I'd show you a place of safety? Well, haven't I performed my promise? When I first discovered this cave, or cavern, or grotto, or cell, or whatever your fine-spoken folks may call it, "This," said I, "Would be a good place to hide people in." So I never told my master.

HENRY: This fellow will do some mischief with his nonsensical prate.

FREDERIC: I don't fear him. He has an honest heart, hid under an appearance of ignorance. It grows duskish, Sebastian. Have we good sentinels placed at the entrance of the cell?

SEBASTIAN: Good sentinels! Why, do you suppose I would trust any with that post but those I could depend on?

HENRY: Two hours past midnight we must invest[14] the garden of the Dey. I have here a letter from Zoriana which says she will at that time be ready to join us, and lead us to the prison of my Olivia's father. Olivia is by some means already at liberty.

SENTINEL: (*Without*). You must not pass.

FETNAH: No, but I must. I have business.

SEBASTIAN: What, what, what's all this? (*Exits.*)

FETNAH: Nay, for pity's sake, don't kill me! (*Re-enter* SEBASTIAN, *forcing in* FETNAH *habited like a boy.*)

SEBASTIAN: No, no, we won't kill you. We'll only make you a slave, and you know that's nothing.

FETNAH: (*Aside*). There is my dear Christian, but I won't discover myself till I try if he will know me.

HENRY: Who are you, young man, and for what purpose were you loitering about this place?

FETNAH: I am Soliman, son to the Dey, and I heard by chance that a band of slaves had laid a plot to invest the palace, and so I traced some of them to this cell and was just going—

FIRST SLAVE: To betray us.

SECOND SLAVE: Let us dispatch him and instantly disperse till the appointed hour.

SEVERAL SLAVES: Aye, let us kill him.

HENRY: Hold! Why should we harm this innocent youth?

FIRST SLAVE: He would be the means of our suffering most cruel tortures.

HENRY: True, but he is now in our power—young, innocent, and unprotected. Oh, my friends, let us not, on this auspicious night, when we hope to emancipate ourselves from slavery, tinge the bright standard of liberty with blood.

SLAVES: 'Tis necessary. Our safety demands it. (*They rush on* FETNAH. *In her struggle, her turban falls off. She breaks from them and*

---

[14]Surround.

runs to FREDERIC.)

FETNAH: Save me, dear Christian! It's only poor little Fetnah.

FREDERIC: Save you, my sweet little infidel? Why, I'll impale the wretch who should move but a finger against you.

SEBASTIAN: Oh, oh! A mighty pretty boy, to be sure.

FREDERIC: But tell me how got you out of the palace, and how did you discover us?

FETNAH: I have not time now, but this I will assure you: I came with a full intention to go with you, if you will take me, the whole world over.

FREDERIC: Can you doubt—

FETNAH: Doubt? No, to be sure, I don't; but you must comply with one request before we depart.

FREDERIC: Name it.

FETNAH: I have a dear friend who is a captive at my father's. She must be released, or Fetnah cannot be happy, even with the man she loves. (*Draws aside, and confers with* HENRY.)

SEBASTIAN: Well, here am I, Sebastian, who have been a slave two years, six months, a fortnight, and three days; and have all that time worked in the garden of the Alcaide,[15] who has twelve wives, thirty concubines, and two pretty daughters. And yet not one of the insensible hussies ever took a fancy to me. 'Tis dev'lish hard, that when I go home I can't say to my honored father, the barber, and to my reverend mother, the laundress, "This is the beautiful princess who fell in love with me, jumped over the garden wall of his serene holiness her father, and ran away with your dutiful son, Sebastian." Then, falling on my knees, thus—

HENRY: What's the matter, Sebastian? There is no danger. Don't be afraid, man.

FREDERIC: Sebastian, you must take a party of our friends, go to the house of Ben Hassan, and bring from thence an American lady. I have good reason to think you will meet with no opposition. She may be at first unwilling to come, but tell her friends and countrymen await her here.

FETNAH: Tell her, her own Fetnah expects her.

FREDERIC: Treat her with all imaginable respect. Go, my good Sebastian. Be diligent, silent, and expeditious. You, my dear Fetnah, I will place in an inner part of the grotto, where you will be safe, while we effect the escape of Olivia's father.

FETNAH: What, shut me up? Do you take me for a coward?

HENRY: We respect you as a woman, and would shield you from danger.

---

[15]Commander of a fortress or warden of a prison.

FETNAH: A woman! Why, so I am. But in the cause of love or friendship, a woman can face danger with as much spirit, and as little fear, as the bravest man amongst you. Do you lead the way; I'll follow to the end. (*Exit* FETNAH, FREDERIC, HENRY, &c.)

SEBASTIAN: Bravo! Excellent! Bravissimo! Why, 'tis a little body, but, ecod, she's a devil of a spirit. It's a fine thing to meet with a woman that has a little fire in her composition. I never much liked your milk-and-water ladies. To be sure, they are easily managed, but your spirited lasses require taming; they make a man look about him. Dear, sweet, angry creatures: here's their health. This is the summmum-bonum of all good. If they are kind, this, this, makes them appear angels and goddesses. If they are saucy, why then, here—here, in this we'll drown the remembrance of the bewitching, froward little devils. In all kind of difficulties and vexations, nothing helps the invention or cheers the courage like a drop from the jorum.[16]

Song:

When I was a poor, little, innocent boy,
About fifteen or eighteen years old,
At Susan and Marian I cast a sheep's eye,
But Susan was saucy and Marian was shy;
So I flirted with Flora, with Cecily and Di.

But they, too, were frumpish and cold.
Says Diego, one day, what ails you I pray?
I fetched a deep sigh. Diego, says I,
Women hate me. Oh, how I adore 'em.
Pho; nonsense, said he, never mind it, my lad.
Hate you, then hate them boy. Come, never be sad.
Here, take a good sup of the jorum.

If they're foolish and mulish, refuse you, abuse you,
   No longer pursue,
   They'll soon buckle too,
   When they find they're neglected,
   Old maids, unprotected,
   Ah, then 'tis their turn to woo;
But bid them defiance, and form an alliance
With the mirth-giving, care-killing jorum.

---

[16]Large drinking bowl; also, the liquor contained in such a bowl.

I took his advice, but was sent to the war,
And soon I was called out to battle.
I heard the drums beat. Oh, how great was my fear.
I wished my self sticking, aye up to each ear
In a horse pond, and skulked away to the rear.

When the cannon and bombs 'gan to rattle,
Said I to myself, you're a damned foolish elf,
Sebastian, keep up. Then I took a good sup.
Turkish villains, shall we fly before 'em;
What, give it up tamely and yield ourselves slaves
To a pack of rapscallions, vile infidel knaves?
Then I kissed the sweet lips of my jorum.

No, hang 'em, we'll bang 'em, and rout 'em, and scout 'em.
    If we but pursue
    They must buckle too.
    Ah, then without wonder,
    I heard the loud thunder
    Of cannon and musketry too.
But bid them defiance, being firm in alliance
With the courage-inspiring jorum. (*Exits.*)

Scene Two

BEN HASSAN's *house.* REBECCA *and* AUGUSTUS.

AUGUSTUS: Dear Mother, don't look so sorrowful. My master is not very hard with me. Do, pray, be happy.

REBECCA: Alas! My dear Augustus, can I be happy while you are a slave? My own bondage is nothing. But you, my child—

AUGUSTUS: Nay, Mother, don't mind it. I am but a boy, you know. If I was a man—

REBECCA: What would you do, my love?

AUGUSTUS: I'd stamp beneath my feet the wretch that would enslave my mother.

REBECCA: There burst forth the sacred flame which heaven itself fixed in the human mind. Oh, my brave boy! (*Embracing him.*) Ever may you preserve that independent spirit, that dares assert the rights of the oppressed—by power unawed, unchecked by servile fear.

AUGUSTUS: Fear, mother? What should I be afraid of? Ain't I an

American, and I am sure you have often told me, in a right cause the Americans did not fear anything.

Enter HASSAN.

HASSAN: So, here's a piece of work. I'se be like to have fine deal of troubles on your account. Oh, that ever I should run the risk of my life by keeping you concealed from the Dey!

REBECCA: If I am trouble to you, if my being here endangers your life, why do you not send me away?

BEN HASSAN: There be no ships here for you to go in. Besides, who will pay me?

REBECCA: Indeed, if you will send me to my native land, I will faithfully remit to you my ransom—aye, double what you have required.

BEN HASSAN: If I thought I could depend—

Enter SERVANT.

SERVANT: Sir, your house is surrounded by armed men.

BEN HASSAN: What, Turks?

SERVANT: Slaves, sir, many of whom I have seen in the train of the Dey.

BEN HASSAN: Vhat do they vant?

SERVANT: One of my companions asked them, and received for answer, they would show us presently.

SEBASTIAN: (*Without*). Stand away, fellow. I will search the house.

REBECCA: Oh, heavens! What will become of me?

BEN HASSAN: What will become of me? Oh! I shall be impaled, burnt, bastinadoed, murdered! Where shall I hide? How shall I escape them? (*Runs through a door, as though into another apartment.*)

SEBASTIAN: (*Without*). This way, friends. This way.

REBECCA: Oh, my child, we are lost!

AUGUSTUS: Don't be frightened, Mother. Through this door is a way into the garden. If I had but a sword, boy as I am, I'd fight for you till I died. (*Exits with* REBECCA.)

Enter SEBASTIAN &c.

SEBASTIAN: I thought I heared voices this way. Now, my friends, the lady we seek is a most lovely, amiable creature, whom we must accost with respect and convey hence in safety. She is a woman of family and fortune, and is highly pleased with my person and abilities. Let us, therefore, search every cranny of the house till we find her. She may not recollect me directly, but never mind. We will carry her away first, and assure her of her safety afterwards. Go, search the rooms in that wing. I will, myself, investigate the apartments on this side. (*Exit* SLAVES.) Well, I have made these comrades of mine believe I am a favored lover in pursuit of a kind mistress. That's something for them to talk of, and I believe many a fine gentleman is talked of for love affairs, that has as little foundation. And so one is but talked of as a brave or gallant man, what signifies whether there is any foundation for it or no? And yet, hang it, who knows but I may prove it a reality. If I release this lady from captivity, she may cast an eye of affection. . . may—why, I dare say she will. I am but poor Sebastian, the barber of Cordova's son, 'tis true, but I am well made—very well made. My leg is not amiss: then I can make a graceful bow. And as to polite compliments, let me just find her, and I'll show them what it is to have a pretty person, a graceful air, and a smooth tongue. But I must search this apartment. (*Exits.*)

Scene Three

Another apartment. Enter BEN HASSAN, *with a petticoat and robe on, a bonnet and deep veil in his hand.*

BEN HASSAN: I think now, they vill hardly know me in my vife's clothes. I could not find a turban, but this headdress of Rebecca's vill do better, because it vill hide my face. But how shall I hide my monies? I've got a vasht deal, in bills of exchange and all kinds of paper. If I can but get safe off with this book in my pocket, I shall have enough to keep me easy as long as I live. (*Puts it in his pocket and drops it.*) Oh, this is a judgment fallen upon me for betraying the Christians! (*Noise without.*) Oh, lord! Here they come. (*Ties on the bonnet and retires into one corner of the apartment.*)

Enter SEBASTIAN &c.

SEBASTIAN: There she is. I thought I traced the sweep of her train this way. Don't mind her struggles or entreaties, but bring her away. Don't be alarmed, madam. You will meet with every attention. You will be treated with the greatest respect, and let me whisper to you there is more happiness in store for you than you can possibly imagine. Friends, convey her gently to the appointed place. (*They take up* HASSAN *and carry him off.*)

BEN HASSAN: Oh—o—o—oh! (*Exits.*)

Enter AUGUSTUS *and* REBECCA.

AUGUSTUS: See, my dear Mother, there is no one here. They are all gone. It was not you they came to take away.

REBECCA: It is for you I fear, more than for myself. I do not think you are safe with me. Go, my beloved; return to your master.

AUGUSTUS: What, go and leave my mother without a protector?

REBECCA: Alas, my love, you are not able to protect yourself. And your staying here only adds to my distress. Leave me for the present. I hope the period is not far off when we shall never be separated.

AUGUSTUS: Mother! Dear Mother! My heart is so big it almost chokes me. Oh, how I wish I was a man! (*Exits.*)

REBECCA: Heaven guard my precious child! I cannot think him quite safe anywhere, but with me his danger would be imminent. The emotions of his heart hang on his tongue, and the least outrage offered to his mother he would resent at peril of his life. My spirits are oppressed. I have a thousand fears for him and for myself. The house appears deserted. All is silent. What's this? (*Takes up the pocket book.*) Oh! Heaven! Is it possible? Bills, to the amount of my own ransom and many others—transporting thought! My son, my darling boy, this would soon emancipate you! Here's a letter addressed to me. The money is my own. Oh, joy beyond expression! My child will soon be free. I have also the means of cheering many children of affliction with the blest sound of liberty. Hassan, you have dealt unjustly by me, but I forgive you; for while my own heart overflows with gratitude for this unexpected blessing, I will wish every human being as happy as I am this moment. (*Exits.*)

Scene Four

Dey's garden.

ZORIANA: How vain are the resolves, how treacherous the heart of a woman in love. But a few hours since, I thought I could have cheerfully relinquished the hope of having my tenderness returned, and found a relief from my own sorrow in reflecting on the happiness of Henry and Olivia. Then why does this selfish heart beat with transport at the thought of their separation? Poor Olivia—how deep must be her affliction. Ye silent shades, scenes of content and peace, how sad would you appear to the poor wretch who wandered here the victim of despair. But the fond heart, glowing with all the joys of mutual love, delighted views the beauties scattered round, thinks every flower is sweet and every prospect gay.

Song:

In lowly cot or mossy cell,
With harmless nymphs and rural swains,
'Tis there contentment loves to dwell;
'Tis there soft peace and pleasure reigns.
But even there, the heart may prove
The pangs of disappointed love.

But softly, hope persuading,
Forbids me long to mourn;
My tender heart pervading,
Portends my love's return.
Ah, then how bright and gay
Appears the rural scene;
More radiant breaks the day;
The night is more serene.

Enter HENRY.

HENRY: Be not alarmed, madam. I have ventured here earlier than I intended to inquire how my Olivia effected her escape.

ZORIANA: This letter will inform you. But, early as it is, the palace is wrapped in silence. My father is retired to rest. Follow me, and I will conduct you to the old man's prison.

HENRY: Have you the keys?

ZORIANA: I have. Follow in silence. The least alarm would be fatal to our purpose. (*They exit.*)

Scene Five

The grotto again. SEBASTIAN, *leading in* BEN HASSAN.

SEBASTIAN: Beautiful creature, don't be uneasy. I have risked my life to procure your liberty, and will, at the utmost hazard, convey you to your desired home. But, oh, most amiable—most divine—most delicate lady, suffer me thus humbly on my knees to confess my adoration of you, to solicit your pity, and—

BEN HASSAN: (*In a feigned tone*). I pray, tell me why you brought me from the house of the good Ben Hassan, and where you deign to take me.

SEBASTIAN: Oh, thou adorable, be not offended at my presumption;

but having an opportunity of leaving this place of captivity, I was determined to take you with me, and prevent your falling into the power of the Dey, who would, no doubt, be in raptures should he behold your exquisite beauty. Sweet, innocent charmer, permit your slave to remove the envious curtain that shades your enchanting visage.

BEN HASSAN: Oh, no! Not for the world. I have, in consideration of many past offenses, resolved to take the veil and hide myself from mankind forever.

SEBASTIAN: That, my dear, sweet creature, would be the highest offense you could commit. Women were never made, with all their prettiness and softness and bewitching ways, to be hid from us men, who came into the world for no other purpose than to see, admire, love, and protect them. Come, I must have a peep under that curtain. I long to see your dear little sparkling eyes, your lovely blooming cheeks—and I am resolved to taste your cherry lips. (As SEBASTIAN *struggles to kiss* HASSAN, *the bonnet falls off.*) Why, what in the devil's name have we here?

BEN HASSAN: Only a poor old woman who has been in captivity—

SEBASTIAN: These fifty years at least, by the length of your beard.

FREDERIC: (*Without*). Sebastian, bring the lady to the waterside and wait till we join you.

BEN HASSAN: I wish I was in any safe place.

SEBASTIAN: Oh, ma'am you are in no danger anywhere. Come, make haste.

BEN HASSAN: But give me my veil again. If anyone saw my face, it would shock me.

SEBASTIAN: And damme, but I think it would shock them. Here, take your curtain, though I think to be perfectly safe you had best go barefaced.

BEN HASSAN: If you hurry me I shall faint. Consider the delicacy of my nerves.

SEBASTIAN: Come along; there's no time for fainting now.

BEN HASSAN: The respect due—

SEBASTIAN: To old age—I consider it all—you are very respectable. Oh, Sebastian what a cursed ninny you were to make so much fuss about a woman old enough to be your grandmother. (*They exit.*)

Scene Six

Inside the palace. MULEY MOLOC *and* MUSTAPHA

MULEY MOLOC: Fetnah gone, Zoriana gone. . . and the fair slave Olivia?

MUSTAPHA: All, dread sir.

MULEY MOLOC: Send instantly to the prison of the slave Constant. 'Tis he who has again plotted to rob me of Olivia. (*Exit* MUSTAPHA.) My daughter, too, he has seduced from her duty. But he shall not escape my vengeance.

Re-enter MUSTAPHA.

MUSTAPHA: Some of the fugitives are overtaken, and wait in chains without.

MULEY MOLOC: Is Zoriana taken?

MUSTAPHA: Your daughter is safe. The old man, too, is taken, but Fetnah and Olivia have escaped.

MULEY MOLOC: Bring in the wretches. (HENRY, CONSTANT, *and several* SLAVES *brought in, chained.*) Rash old man, how have you dared to tempt your fate again? Do you not know the torments that await the Christian who attempts to rob the harem of a Musselman?

CONSTANT: I know you have the power to end my being, but that's a period I more wish than fear.

MULEY MOLOC: Where is Olivia?

CONSTANT: Safe, I hope, beyond your power. Oh, gracious heaven, protect my darling from this tyrant, and let my life pay the dear purchase of her freedom.

MULEY MOLOC: Bear them to the torture. Who and what am I, that a vile slave dares brave me to my face?

HENRY: Hold off! We know that we must die, and we are prepared to meet our fate like men. Impotent, vain boaster, call us not slaves. You are a slave indeed, to rude, ungoverned passion, to pride, to avarice and lawless love. Exhaust your cruelty in finding tortures for us, and we will smiling tell you the blow that ends our lives strikes off our chains and sets our souls at liberty.

MULEY MOLOC: Hence! Take them from my sight. (CAPTIVES *taken off.*) Devise each means of torture. Let them linger months, years, ages, in their misery.

Enter OLIVIA.

OLIVIA: Stay, Muley, stay. Recall your cruel sentence.

MULEY MOLOC: Olivia here; is it possible?

OLIVIA: I have never left the palace. Those men are innocent. So is your daughter. It is I alone deserve your anger; then on me only let it fall. It was I procured false keys to the apartments; it was I seduced your daughter to our interest. I bribed the guards and with entreaty won the young Christian to attempt to free my father. Then, since I was the cause of their offenses, it is fit my life should pay the forfeiture of theirs.

MULEY MOLOC: Why did you not accompany them?

OLIVIA: Fearing what has happened, I remained, in hopes, by tears and supplications, to move you to forgive my father. Oh, Muley, save his life! Save all his friends, and if you must have blood to appease your vengeance, let me alone be the sacrifice.

MULEY MOLOC: (Aside). How her softness melts me. (To OLIVIA.) Rise, Olivia. You may on easier terms give them both life and freedom.

OLIVIA: No. Here I kneel till you recall your orders. Haste, or it may be too late.

MULEY MOLOC: Mustapha, go bid them delay the execution. (Exit MUSTAPHA.)

OLIVIA: Now teach me to secure their lives and freedom, and my last breath shall bless you.

MULEY MOLOC: Renounce your faith. Consent to be my wife. Nay, if you hesitate—

OLIVIA: I do not. Give me but an hour to think.

MULEY MOLOC: Not a moment. Determine instantly. Your answer gives them liberty or death.

OLIVIA: Then I am resolved. Swear to me, by Mohammed—an oath I know you Musselmen never violate—that the moment I become your wife my father and his friends are free.

MULEY: By Mohammed I swear, not only to give them life and freedom, but safe conveyance to their desired home.

OLIVIA: I am satisfied. Now leave me to myself a few short moments, that I may calm my agitated spirits and prepare to meet you in the mosque.

MULEY MOLOC: Henceforth I live but to obey you. (Exits.)

OLIVIA: On what a fearful precipice I stand. To go forward is ruin, shame and infamy; to recede is to pronounce sentence of death upon my father and my adored Henry. Oh, insupportable! There is one way, and only one, by which I can fulfill my promise to the Dey, preserve my friends, and not abjure my faith. Source of my being, Thou canst read the heart which Thou hast been pleased to try in the school of adversity. Pardon the weakness of an erring mortal, if, rather than behold a father perish—if, rather than devote his friends to death, I cut the thread of my existence and rush unbidden to Thy presence. Yes, I will to the mosque, perform my promise, preserve the valued lives of those I love, then sink at once into the silent grave and bury all my sorrow in oblivion. (*Exits.*)

Scene Seven

Another apartment. Enter OLIVIA *and* MULEY MOLOC.

MULEY MOLOC: Yes, on my life, they are free. In a few moments they will be here.
OLIVIA: Spare me the trial. For the whole world, I would not see them now; nor would I have them know at what price I have secured their freedom.

Enter HENRY *and* CONSTANT.

CONSTANT: My child—
HENRY: My love—
OLIVIA: My Henry! Oh, my dear father? Pray excuse these tears.

Enter MUSTAPHA.

MUSTAPHA: Great sir, the mosque is prepared, and the priest waits your pleasure.
MULEY MOLOC: Come, my Olivia.
HENRY: The mosque—the priest— What dreadful sacrifice is then intended?
OLIVIA: Be not alarmed. I must needs attend a solemn rite which gratitude requires. Go, my dear father. Dearest Henry, leave me, and be assured when next you see Olivia she will be wholly free.

Enter REBECCA.

REBECCA: Hold for a moment.
MULEY MOLOC: What means this bold intrusion?
REBECCA: Muley, you see before you a woman unused to forms of state, despising titles. I come to offer ransom for six Christian slaves. Waiting your leisure, I was informed a Christian maid, to save her father's life, meant to devote herself a sacrifice to your embraces. I have the means: make your demand of ransom, and set the maid, with those she loves, at liberty.
MULEY MOLOC: Her friends are free already, but for herself she

voluntarily remains with me.

REBECCA: Can you, unmoved, behold her anguish? Release her, Muley. Name but the sum that will pay her ransom. 'Tis yours.

MULEY MOLOC: Woman, the wealth of Golconda[17] could not pay her ransom. Can you imagine that I, whose slave she is—I, who could force her obedience to my will and yet gave life and freedom to those Christians to purchase her compliance—would now relinquish her for paltry gold? Contemptible idea. Olivia, I spare you some few moments to your father. Take leave of him, and as you part, remember: his life and liberty depend on you. (*Exits.*)

REBECCA: Poor girl, what can I do to mitigate your sufferings?

OLIVIA: Nothing. My fate, alas, is fixed. But, generous lady, by what name shall we remember you? What nation are you of?

REBECCA: I am an American; but while I only claim kinship with the afflicted, it is of little consequence where I first drew my breath.

CONSTANT: An American? From what state?

REBECCA: New York is my native place. There did I spend the dear, delightful days of childhood; and there, alas, I drained the cup of deep affliction to the very dregs.

CONSTANT: My heart is strangely interested. Dearest lady, will you impart to us your tale of sorrow, that we may mourn with one who feels so much for us?

REBECCA: Early in life, while my brave countrymen were struggling for their freedom, it was my fate to love and be beloved by a young British officer to whom, though strictly forbid by my father, I was privately married.

CONSTANT: Married! Say you?

REBECCA: My father soon discovered our union. Enraged, he spurned me from him, discarded, cursed me; and for four years I followed my husband's fortune. At length, my father relented; on a sickbed he sent for me to attend him. I went, taking with me an infant son, leaving my husband and a lovely girl, then scarcely three years old. Oh, heavens! What sorrows have I known from that unhappy hour. During my absence the armies met; my husband fell. My daughter was torn from me. What then availed the wealth my dying father had bequeathed me? Long—long did I lose all sense of my misery, and returning reason showed me the world only one universal blank. The voice of my darling boy first called me to myself. For him I strove to mitigate my sorrow; for his dear sake I have endured life.

---

[17]A city of ancient India noted for its diamond trade.

CONSTANT: Pray proceed.

REBECCA: About a year since, I heard a rumor that my husband was still alive. Full of the fond hope of again beholding him, I, with my son, embarked for England; but before we reached the coast we were captured by an Algerine.

CONSTANT: Do you think you should recollect your husband?

REBECCA: I think I should, but fourteen years of deep affliction have impaired my memory and may have changed his features.

CONSTANT: What was his name? Oh, speak it quickly!

REBECCA: His name was Constant; but wherefore—

CONSTANT: It was. It was. Rebecca, don't you know me?

REBECCA: Alas, how you are altered. Oh, Constant, why have you forsaken me so long?

CONSTANT: In the battle you mention, I was indeed severely wounded—nay, left for dead in the field. There my faithful servant found me, when some remaining signs of life encouraged him to attempt my recovery; and by his unremitting care I was at length restored. My first returning thought was fixed on my Rebecca, but after repeated inquiries, all I could hear was that your father was dead and yourself and child removed farther from the seat of war. Soon after, I was told you had fallen a martyr to grief for my supposed loss. But see, my love, our daughter, our dear Olivia. Heaven preserved her to be my comforter.

OLIVIA: (*Kneeling and kissing* REBECCA). My mother, blessed word! Oh, do I live to say I have a mother.

REBECCA: Bless you, my child, my charming, duteous girl; but tell me by what sad chance you became captives.

CONSTANT: After peace was proclaimed with America, my duty called me to India, from whence I returned with a ruined constitution. Being advised to try the air of Lisbon, we sailed for that place, but heaven ordained that here in the land of captivity I should recover a blessing which will amply repay me for all my past sufferings.

Enter MULEY MOLOC.

MULEY MOLOC: Christians, you trifle with me. Accept your freedom, go in peace, and leave Olivia to perform her promise. For should she waver or draw back, on you I will wreak my vengeance.

REBECCA: Then let your vengeance fall. We will die together; for never shall Olivia, a daughter of Columbia, and a Christian, tarnish her name by apostasy or live the slave of a despotic tyrant.

MULEY MOLOC: Then take your wish. Who's there?

Enter MUSTAPHA *hastily.*

MUSTAPHA: Arm, mighty sir! The slaves throughout Algiers have mutinied. They bear down all before them. This way they come. They say if all the Christian slaves are not immediately released, they'll raze the city.

REBECCA: Now! Bounteous heaven, protect my darling boy, and aid the cause of freedom!

MULEY MOLOC: Bear them to instant death.

MUSTAPHA: Dread sir, consider.

MULEY MOLOC: Vile, abject slave, obey me and be silent! What, have I power over these Christian dogs, and shall I not exert it? Dispatch, I say! (*Huzza and clash of swords without.*) Why am I not obeyed? (*Clash again; confused noise; several huzza's.*)

AUGUSTUS: (*Without*). Where is my mother? Save, oh, save my mother.

FREDERIC: (*Speaking*). Shut up the palace gates. Secure the guards, and at your peril suffer none to pass.

AUGUSTUS: (*Entering*). Oh, Mother, are you safe?

CONSTANT: Bounteous heaven! And am I then restored to more—much more than life—my Rebecca? My children? Oh, this joy is more than I can bear.

Enter FREDERIC, FETNAH, SEBASTIAN, BEN HASSAN, SLAVES, &c.

SEBASTIAN: Great and mighty Ottoman, suffer my friends to show you what pretty bracelets these are. Oh, you old dog, we'll give you the bastinado presently.

FREDERIC: Forbear, Sebastian. Muley Moloc, though your power over us is at end, we neither mean to enslave your person, or put a period to your existence. We are free men, and while we assert the rights of men, we dare not infringe the privileges of a fellow creature.

SEBASTIAN: By the law of retaliation, he should be a slave.

REBECCA: By the Christian law, no man should be a slave. It is a word so abject that to speak it dyes the cheek with crimson. Let us assert our own prerogative, be free ourselves, but let us not throw on another's neck the chains we scorn to wear.

SEBASTIAN: But what must we do with this old gentlewoman?

BEN HASSAN: Oh, pray, send me home to Duke's Place.

FREDERIC: Ben Hassan, your avarice, treachery, and cruelty should be severely punished; for, if anyone deserves slavery, it is he who could raise his own fortune on the miseries of others.

BEN HASSAN: Oh, that I was but crying old clothes in the dirtiest alley in London!

FETNAH: So, you'll leave that poor old man behind?

FREDERIC: Yes, we leave him to learn humanity.

FETNAH: Very well. Goodbye, Frederic. Goodbye, dear Rebecca. While my father was rich and had friends, I did not much think about my duty; but now he is poor and forsaken, I know it too well to leave him alone in his affliction.

MULEY MOLOC: Stay, Fetnah. Hassan, stay. I fear from following the steps of my ancestors, I have greatly erred. Teach me, then, you who so well know how to practice what is right, how to amend my faults.

CONSTANT: Open your prison doors. Give freedom to your people. Sink the name of subject in the endearing epithet of fellow citizen. Then you will be loved and reverenced; then will you find, in promoting the happiness of others, you have secured your own.

MULEY: Henceforward, then, I will reject all power but such as my united friends shall think me incapable of abusing. Hassan, you are free. To you, my generous conquerors, what can I say?

HENRY: Nothing, but let your future conduct prove how much you value the welfare of your fellow creatures. Tomorrow we shall leave your capital and return to our native land, where liberty has established her court—where the warlike Eagle extends his glittering pinions in the sunshine of prosperity.

OLIVIA: Long, long, may that prosperity continue. May freedom spread her benign influence through every nation, till the bright Eagle, mixed with the dove and olive branch, waves high, the acknowledged standard of the world.

THE END

EPILOGUE
Written and spoken by Mrs. Rowson.

PROMPTER: (*Behind*). Come, Mrs. Rowson! Come! Why don't you hurry?

MRS. ROWSON: (*Behind*). Sir I am here—but I'm in such a flurry,
Do let me stop a moment just for breath! (*Enters.*)
Bless me! I'm almost terrified to death.
Yet sure, I had no real cause for fear,
Since none but liberal, generous friends are here.
Say, will you kindly overlook my errors?

You smile. Then to the winds I give my terrors.
Well, ladies, tell me: how d'ye like my play?
"The creature has some sense," methinks you say;
"She says that we should have supreme dominion,
"And in good truth, we're all of her opinion.
"Women were born for universal sway;
"Men to adore, be silent, and obey."

True, ladies: beauteous nature made us fair
To strew sweet roses round the bed of care.
A parent's heart of sorrow to beguile,
Cheer an afflicted husband by a smile.
To bind the truant that's inclined to roam,
Good humor makes a paradise at home.
To raise the fallen, to pity and forgive:
This is our noblest, best prerogative.
By these, pursuing nature's gentle plan,
We hold in silken chains the lordly tyrant man.

But pray, forgive this flippancy. Indeed,
Of all your clemency I stand in need.
To own the truth, the scenes this night displayed
Are only fictions drawn by fancy's aid.
'Tis what I wish. But we have cause to fear
No ray of comfort the sad bosoms cheer
Of many a Christian, shut from light and day,
In bondage languishing their lives away.

Say, you who feel humanity's soft glow,
What rapt'uous joy must the poor captive know,
Who, freed from slavery's ignominious chain,
Views his dear, native land and friends again?

If there's a sense more exquisitely fine,
A joy more elevated, more divine,
'Tis felt by these whose liberal minds conceived
The generous plan by which he was relieved.

When first this glorious universe began,
And heaven to punish disobedient man
Sent to attend him, through life's dreary shade,
Affliction—poor dejected, weeping maid,

Then came Benevolence, by all revered.
He dried the mourner's tears; her heart he cheered.
He wooed her to his breast, made her his own,
And Gratitude appeared, their first-born son.
Since when, the father and the son have joined,
To shed their influence o'er the human mind;
And in the heart where either deign to rest,
Rise transports difficult to be expressed.
Such, as within your generous bosoms glow,
Who feel returned the blessings you bestow.
Oh, ever may you taste those joys divine,
While Gratitude—sweet Gratitude—is mine.

THE TRAVELLER RETURNED

Judith Sargent Murray

1796

First performed at the Federal Street Theatre, Boston, March 9, 1796. Originally published as No. LXXX-LXXXIV (pp. 116-163) in The Gleaner, vol. 3, by Judith Sargent Murray [pseud. Constantia] (Boston, 1798).

Prefatory Material in <u>The Gleaner</u>:

Perhaps 'tis well with lenient eye to view
Those errors that from inexper'ence grew—
To shield the germ that may perchance expand,
If by the airs of soft indulgence fann'd.

To the Author of the Gleaner.
Sir,
Your prompt attention to "Virtue Triumphant" induces me to forward
you *The Traveller Returned.* It is the second Dramatic production of the
same Author, and is, perhaps, as worthy to supply a few numbers for the
Gleaner as the first. I am, Sir, with due respect, your most obedient
humble servant.
                    Philo Americanus.

Persons of the Drama

Men: Women:

Mr. Rambleton   Mrs. Montague
Major Camden   Harriot Montague
Mr. Stanhope   Emily Lovegrove
Alberto Stanhope   Mrs. Vansittart
Mr. Vansittart   Bridget
Patrick O'Neal
Obadiah
Members of the Committee of Public Safety
Officers, Soldiers, Sailors, and Servants

ACT FIRST

Scene: A parade.[1] Sea prospect. Ship discovered at a distance.

Enter MR. RAMBLETON.

RAMBLETON: 'Tis well. Auspicious morn, I hail thy gladsome rays. Once more I breathe again my native air. Once more I tread that earth, now doubly dear for having given birth to such a race of heroes as Rome, in all her pride of greatness, could never boast. (*Hallooing without.*)

Enter PATRICK, *with* SAILORS *bearing trunks.*

PATRICK: Ow, may I never see my own, sweet country again, if I did not think this land of America had been all salt water, d'ye see, we were so long in finding it. Arrah now, while we are standing here, by my soul, we may as well be looking after a place to rest ourselves in, so we may.

RAMBLETON: Here, friends, deposit your burdens in this niche. Your ship is under sail; it will be prudent for you to get on board as soon as possible. Farewell, comrades. (*Gives them money.*)

SAILORS: (*All vociferate*). God bless your honor. You are a gentleman. God bless your honor! (*Exit* SAILORS.)

RAMBLETON: Now, Patrick, you must keep guard here, while I proceed to reconnoiter.

PATRICK: Ow, that I shall, master. But did you not say, now, that you should be after taking your land tacks on board?

RAMBLETON: I did, Patrick. Twelve miles from this city, nineteen years since, I left my family.

PATRICK: Twelve miles, do you say? Ow then, that is but a trifle, my dear. It is only six miles apiece, master; and who would grudge that, I wonder, for the sake of seeing the sweet faces of wife and children. But did not you say, now, how that you had written them word you was dead, or the like of that?

RAMBLETON: I said, Patrick, that they probably supposed me dead, for they have not heard from me since I left them. A friend whom I commissioned for that purpose has informed me in general terms of their welfare. I forbade particulars.

PATRICK: Arrah, is not that strange, now?

---

[1]Parade ground.

RAMBLETON: I have very powerful reasons for my conduct; and remember, Patrick, you must be secret.

PATRICK: Ow, never fear Patrick O'Neal, sir. An Irishman shall hang, drown, and quarter for you, sir, and afterwards serve you every bit as well as if nothing at all, at all had happened.

RAMBLETON: I had an estate in this city. I am not sure that I shall not find my family here, but my present purpose is to take lodgings.

PATRICK: Arrah, get out with that, now. If Patrick O'Neal was three thousand miles separated from his bit of an Irish girl, he shall swing his hammock close along side of her for all that, honey. Give me lave to say, sir, would it not be better if you went right home to your own wife, now?

RAMBLETON: All in good time, Patrick. But, hist, who have we here? Stand at one side.

Enter MAJOR CAMDEN.

CAMDEN: This sea breeze is very refreshing during this sultry season. I will enjoy it a little. Hah, a ship under sail, and without colors, too! This looks suspicious. Bless me, a stranger of dignified mien and prepossessing aspect. I will accost him. It is a divine morning, sir.

RAMBLETON: It is so, young man, and I feel enough interested in you to wish you may enjoy it.

CAMDEN: Thank you, sir. Can you tell from whence came yonder ship, that now crowds every sail to quit our coast?

RAMBLETON; I can, sir. You wear your country's uniform, and it is a fair presumption that you will emulate her virtues. That ship, sir, is British property, hired by me to transport myself, my baggage, and my servant across the vast Atlantic.

CAMDEN: But are you not apprised that our guardian legislators have recommended to the good people of the United States a suspension of all intercourse with the subjects of his Britannic majesty during the war?

RAMBLETON: Yes, sir, but I presume they have not proscribed the true-born sons of America?

CAMDEN: Certainly not, sir.

RAMBLETON: Well, sir, in this land of liberty I commenced my being. Some years previous to the present struggle, private motives induced me to quit it; and, perhaps, I should not yet have returned had not fame's shrill clarion, so loudly sounding my country's honors, have given to ambition the fleetest wings, and thus accelerated my suspended purpose.

CAMDEN: Your words involve conviction. And yet, perhaps, I should not trust.

RAMBLETON: The morn of life is seldom found suspicious. I come prepared to aid a struggling people. My purse, my counsel, they shall both be theirs; and, if need be, my sword shall fight their battles.

CAMDEN: (*Pausing*). What is the line of conduct which Camden should pursue?

RAMBLETON: (*Aside*). Camden! Hah, that name awakens in my soul the strongest passions! (*To* CAMDEN.) If you have doubts, examine well my baggage—my person. I dare the strictest scrutiny.

CAMDEN: Pshaw, I disdain suspicion and venerate your frankness.

RAMBLETON: Only direct me for a single night to some convenient lodging.

CAMDEN: I am at present here on duty. Will you accept apartments under the same roof with me?

RAMBLETON: Most gladly.

CAMDEN: Then, sir, I will conduct you.

RAMBLETON: I will speak to my servant and accompany you immediately. Here, Patrick— (PATRICK *comes forward*.)

PATRICK: Sir.

RAMBLETON: I shall send persons who will assist in conveying my trunks to my lodgings.

PATRICK: So do then—and, by the body of St. Patrick, my shelf shall be able to carry them like nothing at all, at all. (*Exit*.)

Scene changes to an apartment in an inn. MR. *and* MRS. VANSITTART *at breakfast*.

MRS. VANSITTART: Why, husband, at this rate we shall certainly starve!

VANSITTART: Vife! Vife! I to vish you voult eat your preat ant putter, and let that content you at this present time.

MRS. VANSITTART: Content me? Lord, how can I be contented? No jonteel people are contented. Besides, are we not over head and ears in debt, and not a single dollar to help ourselves? I thought, when I married a Dutchman, who they say, can make land out of water, that I should at least have been above so low a thing as poverty.

VANSITTART: Lort, Lort! Mrs. Vansittart, you are quite unreasonaple now. Have I not tolt you a thousant times, that I coult not vork without tools? Suppose I pe a Tutchman—vhy my creat ancestor, Van Tromp himself, coult never fleet his ships vithout vater. You are as pat as the Egyptian task-masters, for you are alvays expecting prick[2] vithout shtraw.

---

[2]Brick. The speech refers to the Biblical Egyptian Pharoah who increased the labor of the Hebrew slaves by making them gather straw for the bricks they made, without

MRS. VANSITTART: I say, husband, there is straw enough, and you miss many a jonteel opportunity. Major Camden, for instance: he could not appear so alegunt without a power of money. I warrant you, his trunks contain many a good pound; and, as he is in such haste to get rid of his cash as to part with it to every shameless beggar, no one could say it would not be doing a perlite thing to assist him in the disposal of it.

VANSITTART: Torothy, Torothy! How are we to come at it, at this present time?

MRS. VANSITTART: Get everything in readiness, force the trunks, make off before we are discovered, and thus give all our creditors the slip at once. (*They rise from table.*)

VANSITTART: Mercy on us! Mercy on us!

MRS. VANSITTART: In the general confusion into which the great people are thrown, it would be easy to retire indignantly with our money, and nobody would be the wiser.

VANSITTART: Torothy, Torothy! Tost thou never reflect? (*Screams in her ear.*) Tost never think of the callows, chilt? Cot a' mercy! It voult make my very ploot chill, to see my poor tear Torothy swinging in the air! (*Affects to weep ludicrously.*)

MRS. VANSITTART: Lord! Mr. Vansittart, how could you fright a body so? (*Knocking at the door.*) I shan't get the odious figure out of my head today. You are as unperlite as a Heartentot.[3] (*Knocking at the door repeated.*) Do see who is at the door. For pity's sake, how came it fastened? (VANSITTART *opens the door.*)

Enter MAJOR CAMDEN, *introducing* MR. RAMBLETON.

CAMDEN: Landlord, I have brought you a new lodger, and I recommend him to your best attention.

VANSITTART: (*Bowing*). Ve shalt pe prout to vait on the shentleman, at this present time.

CAMDEN: Mrs. Vansittart, be so obliging as to order breakfast in your little parlor.

MRS. VANSITTART; (*Affectedly*). You shall be obeyed, sir.

CAMDEN: I will show you into the parlor, Mr. Rambleton. (*Exit* MAJOR CAMDEN *and* MR. RAMBLETON.)

MRS. VANSITTART: Rambleton—Rambleton. Who can this same Rambleton be?

---

decreasing their quota of bricks per day (*Exodus* 5:6-19.)

[3]Hottentot; barbarian.

VANSITTART: Rampleton, Rampleton—and vat the plague is that to you? Now vhy ton't you set apout getting preakfast for the shentlemen, I say?

MRS. VANSITTART: Lord, man, it is already got. I have only to order it in. (*Exit* MRS. VANSITTART.)

VANSITTART: Vicket jate! Vicket jate! It vill pe a vonter if she toes not prink me to shame. Ant yet, Cot knows, I have creat occasions. If I coult safely come at a coot hantsome rount sum, I pelieves I shoult not stick at pocketing it, any more than poor Torothy. (*Loud knocking at the door.* MRS. VANSITTART *passes hastily over the stage, and throws open the door.*)

Enter PATRICK, *with* PORTERS *bearing trunks.*

PATRICK: Arrah now, good people, can you tell me if one Mr. Rambleton has cast anchor hereabouts?

MRS. VANSITTART: Oh, yes, sir, and he is now at breakfast in the parlor.

PATRICK: Arrah, then, Patrick O'Neal did not care if my shelf had a little of that same breakfast, after Master Rambleton has eaten it, honey. By my soul, I am quite wary[4]—so I am—and if you shall be after showing me where I will stow this rich cargo, I will be for stepping into your cabin a bit and trating myself with breakfast, dinner and supper, all at one meal—so I shall.

MRS. VANSITTART: Here, Mr. Patrick, this way—this way, if you please. I will show you Mr. Rambleton's chamber.

PATRICK: Mr. Patrick! How the jeuce could the sweet crature find out my name, now?

(PATRICK *and* PORTERS *follow* MRS. VANSITTART *with the baggage.*)

VANSITTART: So, so. Mrs. Vansittart is likely to get into pusiness, I fint, at this present time. (*Exits.*)

SCENE: *A parlor in the inn.* MR. RAMBLETON *and* MAJOR CAMDEN *just rising from the breakfast table.*

RAMBLETON: Well, I would travel many a rood[5] to see this wonder of a man. I have never doubted his intrepid valor and inborn patriotism, but are his military talents so great as you describe?

CAMDEN: I hold them to be unequalled, sir. Having the happiness to

---

[4]Weary.
[5]English measure of length.

be born in the neighborhood of Mount Vernon, I have enjoyed the patronage of the General, and I have been an eyewitness of the most glorious achievements.

RAMBLETON: Cannot you furnish me with some examples? I should dwell with singular pleasure on a recital so interesting.

CAMDEN: Fame early marked the steps of the youthful Warrior; and his political address, undaunted bravery, and military talents were all evinced in his journey from Winchester, his defense of Fort Necessity, and his judicious arrangements after Braddock's defeat.[6]

RAMBLETON: His conduct would indeed have done honor to a veteran.

CAMDEN: And, sir, were there no other proof of his uncommon military abilities but the victorious actions of Trenton and Princeton[7] (both of which were the result of his superintending genius), they were alone sufficient to place him on the highest summit of martial glory!

RAMBLETON: Young man, I admire thy generous warmth.

CAMDEN: Oh, sir, had you seen him in an hour of the greatest public depression—his noble bosom torn with apprehensions for his oppressed country—hazarding his person in front of the enemy's line—animating his followers by example, as well as precept—and, with intrepid valor, pressing on to death or victory!

RAMBLETON: May eternal blessings crown his honored head!

CAMDEN: Various are the scenes which have witnessed his undaunted bravery, while his unyielding fortitude and equanimity, under the pressure of complicated evils, authorize the most elevated ideas of the firmness and magnanimity of his mind.

RAMBLETON: It is hardly possible to reverence his virtues too highly; and yet, the ignominious death of Major Andre[8] has taught some people to question his sensibility.

CAMDEN: Gracious God! Had they witnessed the struggles which the case of that interesting, brave, and truly accomplished man occasioned in the bosom of the Warrior, they would have learned to venerate the sorrows of a martial spirit. But, sir, there are periods when sacrifices on the altar of public opinion become absolutely indispensable.

RAMBLETON: Undoubtedly there are.

CAMDEN: Question his sensibility, sir! He deeply laments the

---

[6]The events referred to occurred during the French and Indian War, 1754-1763.

[7]The capture of those two cities after the famous crossing of the Delaware River on Christmas night, 1776.

[8]The execution, in 1780, of British army officer Major John Andre for spying caused considerable controversy.

calamities of the war! And, while his soul bleeds for his country, the delicacy of his feelings acknowledges a suitable sympathy with the unfortunate of every description.

RAMBLETON: This finishing of his character gives me inexpressible satisfaction.

CAMDEN: I glory in my country, sir. And, while I do reverence to warriors, philosophers and statesmen whose fame shall reach the utmost verge of polished humanity, I forget not to estimate as they deserve the merits of those matchless soldiers whose hardships have been incredible—who have withstood the most splendid offers of the enemy, when, at the same moment, their footsteps over the frozen ground were tracked by their blood!

RAMBLETON: Heroic men! They merit more than language can express! How long have you served in this unequalled army, sir?

CAMDEN: My father had designed me for mercantile life; but, on the commencement of hostilities, he received letters from a friend abroad which determined him to arm me in my country's cause.

RAMBLETON: (*Aside*). Little does he suspect the hand which penned those letters; but, though my bounding heart would leap into his bosom, I will not yet disclose myself. (*To* CAMDEN.) To bear arms in defense of the invaded Rights of Man is truly honorable, sir.

CAMDEN: It is so, sir, and many brave citizens have lately joined our standards. Some hours hence, the noble volunteers will rendezvous on that parade where first we met. Should your curiosity lead you thither, you may observe a specimen of that spirit which animates the bosoms of FREE AMERICANS!

RAMBLETON: I will not lose the opportunity, sir.

CAMDEN: Engagements unavoidable command me hence.

RAMBLETON: Do not hesitate. We are both at home. (*Exit* MAJOR CAMDEN.) I will attend to my baggage and then prepare for observation. (*Exits.*)

SCENE: *A bedchamber in the inn. Enter* MR. RAMBLETON, *preceded by* PATRICK.

RAMBLETON: Patrick, I have business abroad, and I wish you to tarry within during my absence.

PATRICK: Juring your absence? Ow, that I shall, sir, and, although I wander all over the city, I shall not stir a bit. Never fear Patrick O'Neal, sir.

RAMBLETON: Well, good Patrick, leave me for the present.

PATRICK: Ow, that I shall, now, with the biggest pleasure in life.

(*Exit* PATRICK.)

RAMBLETON: So far [all] is well. (*Takes out a box, from which he produces a miniature picture, richly set, on which he gazes impassioned.*) Angelic loveliness! And could such a form become the receptacle of deliberate vice? Yet she was grossly wanting, both to herself and me, if not absolutely guilty, and this day must decide whether the portrait or the original shall ever again resume their seat in my bosom. (*Puts up the miniature in the box and places it on the toilette.*) My agitation, so near the scene of action, is extreme. Perhaps—but I'll think no more. It is full time that I commence my operations. (*Exits.*)

ACT SECOND

SCENE: An apartment in MRS. MONTAGUE's *house.* EMILY LOVEGROVE *is seated in a contemplative attitude. She rises and advances forward.*

EMILY: Misfortune upon misfortune! The loss of my dear and tender parents! My patrimony reduced by the ruinous paper currency almost to nothing. And, as if these repeated strokes were not sufficient, I am no sooner adopted by the sister of my mother, from whom I receive even maternal tenderness, than my wayward heart becomes ungratefully attached to the very man who is on the point of marriage with her daughter! Gracious Heaven! Was ever unfortunate girl so cruelly circumstanced! But here comes my unsuspecting cousin, as happy as youth, innocence and vivacity can render her.

Enter HARRIOT MONTAGUE.

HARRIOT: Dear Emily, where have you hid yourself? Why, I have had the most divine ramble imaginable, and have been searching the house over to make you a partaker of my felicity. But tell me, dear, has not this straw hat and lilac ribbons a most fascinating effect? Oh, I have been so enchantingly flattered— But, I protest, you look as if you had been in tears! You are melancholy, my dear.

EMILY: No, Harriot, not melancholy—only tranquil. But where have you been, my love?

HARRIOT: Been! Why, you shall hear: I just looked in on Mrs. Fallacy and found her exercising her talents at ridicule by describing to neighbor Chitchat, in a manner truly ludicrous, the party she last night entertained in such a high style of elegance, and with such apparent affection—ha, ha, ha!

EMILY: And could this give you pleasure, Harriot? It has, I assure you, a contrary effect on me. I shall henceforth never enjoy myself in her society.

HARRIOT: Never enjoy yourself in her society, Emily? Why, she is the most sprightly and agreeable woman in the world.

EMILY: It may be so; but I should be confident that I, in my turn, should be served up as the subject of her unwarrantable mirth. And, indeed, Harriot, it is an eternal truth that whoever will divert you at the expense of anyone with whom they are apparently in the habits of friendship, will not hesitate to sacrifice you, whenever occasion offers.

HARRIOT: Ah, this may do well enough for you plodding, sentimental girls; but I, who resolve to enjoy the present moment, am determined to laugh where I can, and not be so grossly absurd as to throw myself into the horrors by anticipated evil—ha, ha, ha! Laughing, my dear, is absolutely necessary to any existence—ha, ha, ha.

EMILY: You are a happy girl, cousin.

HARRIOT: Why, so I think, Emily; for who should I meet at Mrs. Fallacy's but Miss Worthy, Arrabella Clermond, and Eliza Meanwell. So, gallanted by Alberto Stanhope, away we scampered, and had the most delectably romantic promenade that can be conceived of.

EMILY: Had Major Camden been of the party, the pleasure you seem to have derived therefrom might have been accounted for.

HARRIOT: For pity's sake, Emily, be quiet, or you will absolutely make me as melancholy as yourself.

EMILY: Will the name of Major Camden make you melancholy, cousin?

HARRIOT: Oh, yes, it is a perfect antidote to every mirthful idea.

EMILY: Amazing! I had thought you regarded him as your future husband.

HARRIOT: So mamma would have me, Emily; but if ever I do marry, child, it will be a distant day, and I pray heaven that Major Camden may not be the man.

EMILY: What can be your objection to Major Camden? He is young, rich, handsome, gay, generous, informed, and polished.

HARRIOT: Bless me, Emily! Why, you have given him qualities enough for a line of high-sounding Alexandrine measure; and, if you had but arranged them musically, I should have set you down as a most excellent poet. Could you not transpose them, my dear?

EMILY: How agreeably a heart at ease can trifle.

HARRIOT: Well then, my dear girl, seriously, and in your own way, I allow Major Camden every attribute which you have so liberally bestowed upon him. I sincerely esteem him; but for love, (*Curtseying humorously.*) I must beg your pardon for that, my dear.

EMILY: Is my aunt acquainted with your sentiments?

HARRIOT: Why, child, I do not often keep secrets from my mother. She has the most contemptible idea of love, but, *entre nous*, I believe she has been cruelly wounded by the little archer. This, however, is conjecture; for there is a mystery in the story of my good mother which, although my curiosity is wound up to the highest pitch, I could never yet unravel.

EMILY: But it is strange she should wish you to enter into engagements at which your heart relucts.

HARRIOT: It is not more strange than true, Emily. Major Camden commenced his acquaintance with my mother by saving her from imminent danger. She was taking an airing on a very rough road. Her horses took fright; the driver was thrown from his seat. A precipice was in view, and her destruction had been inevitable had not Providence sent Camden to her assistance, who saved her life at the risk of his own!

EMILY: I shudder at her danger. It was indeed an heroic action.

HARRIOT: The gratitude of my mother was unbounded. Mine also was powerfully engaged. For a time it deceived me. Camden declared himself my lover; but although I have long since understood the situation of my own heart, I am not permitted to deal explicitly with Major Camden.

EMILY: But on what principle can my aunt proceed?

HARRIOT: She has a most exalted opinion of Major Camden, tenderly loves her daughter, and thinks the passions should always be under the government of reason.

EMILY: Heigh ho!

HARRIOT: And heigh ho say I! But, hang it, your glooms are contagious, I believe. I'll never stir a single step in pursuit of cross accidents, I'm resolved. (*Hums a tune.*) "The world, my dear Mira, is full of deceit."[9] (*Swims gracefully in a minuet, strikes suddenly into a cotillion step, and warbles a gay air.*)

EMILY: Amiable vivacity!

HARRIOT: I protest, Emily, you shall not be so grave. I have half persuaded my mother to consent to our hop this evening, and if you will join me, I shall be sure of success. Come, let us renew our petition in concert. (*She chants a sprightly air and runs off with* EMILY.)

Enter OBADIAH, *followed by* BRIDGET. OBADIAH *making a clamorous outcry.*

---

[9]No source is given for this line.

OBADIAH: Ouns! Blood and thunder! What will become of poor Obadiah?

BRIDGET: What's the matter, Obadiah?

OBADIAH: Oh, the maple log—the maple log was in me![10] Oh, oh, oh! What shall I do? What shall I do?

BRIDGET: What is the matter, I say, Obadiah?

OBADIAH: Oh, tarnation, tarnation, tarnation!

BRIDGET; Are you mad? (*Shaking him violently.*) Tell me what ails you, I say!

OBADIAH: I have broke—I have broke—I can't speak it—

BRIDGET: Broke what?

OBADIAH: I have broke—I have broke th—th—the—what d'ye call it—I have broke th—th—the—what d'ye call it.

BRIDGET: Th—th—the—what d'ye call it? Now what the plague do you mean, Obadiah?

OBADIAH: Why that there glass thing, Bridget, by which folks finds out when we should be cold and when we should be warm.

BRIDGET: I'll be hanged, Obadiah, if you don't mean the thermometer.

OBADIAH: Yes, Bridget, it is the mormeter, the mormeter— the worse luck mine! Yes, yes, it is the mormeter sure enough—oh, oh, oh!

BRIDGET: Why, don't take on so, man. My mistress is a good, kind lady, and never faults people for trifles and accidents, and the like of that.

OBADIAH: Does not she, Bridget? Ha, ha, ha! (*Jumps about upon the stage.*) Ha, ha, ha! Well. . . but, Bridget, I'll tell you a story, Bridget. I once lived with a lady; she looked as mild as a lamb, and she was not bigger than a good, stout yearling, but, for all that, she had spurrits to the backbone, as a body may zay. And zo, as I was saying, I lived with she, and I only broke a china teacup—it is true it belonged to a zet—but my little mistress was in such a bloody passion that she flew at me, tooth and nail, as a body may zay; and I swamp it, if she did not fetch blood of me, Bridget.

BRIDGET: Well, well, we are no boxers here; and so do you go along about your business and ask your mistress what we shall get for dinner. (*Exit* BRIDGET *and* OBADIAH.)

SCENE: *A library table covered with books.* MRS. MONTAGUE *making extracts.*[11] *She rises and moves forward.*

---

[10]Perhaps a reference to the fastening of a heavy log to a person or animal to impede movement.

[11]Copying passages.

MRS. MONTAGUE: I often think in this life of solitude to which my errors have condemned me, it is a very fortunate circumstance that I am able to turn my attention to pursuits which are at once replete with amusement and instruction. But what says my extracts? (*Reads a paper on which she has been writing.*) "Some modern philosophers are of opinion that the sun is the great fountain from which the earth and other planets derive all the phlogiston—"

Enter HARRIOT *and* EMILY.

HARRIOT: Do, dear Mamma, consent to the violin and dancing this evening, and I will be the best girl in the world.

MRS. MONTAGUE: Daughter, my commands were that I would not be interrupted. Let me see. . . where did I leave off? Oh, here it is— (*Reads.*) "Which they possess, and that this is formed from the combination of the solar rays"—

HARRIOT: Oh, Mamma, what a combination of reasons I shall have to love and honor you, if you will but oblige me. It will amuse my cousin Emily too.

MRS. MONTAGUE: Peace, Harriot. Your cousin has not expressed a wish of this kind. (*Reads.*) —"With all the opaque bodies, but particularly with the leaves of vegetables, which they suppose to be organs adapted to absorb them, and that as animals receive their nourishment from vegetables, they also obtain in a secondary manner their phlogiston from the sun"—

HARRIOT; Dear Mamma, exercise is as necessary for girls as phlogiston is for vegetables. You are our sun, Mamma, and pray now beam forth thy sweet consenting rays, and we shall be the most grateful creatures in the universe.

MRS. MONTAGUE: (*Smiling*). Why don't you speak, Emily?

EMILY: Madam, my wishes are in unison with those of my cousin.

MRS. MONTAGUE: You know, girls, that I am not fond of these convivial parties. My time of life and situation render them improper for me. But for this once, I will indulge you.

HARRIOT: (*Curtseying low*). Dear Mamma, we thank you. Emily, we will be as gay as—as—but hang it, I'll not study for a simile.

EMILY: You are perfectly right, cousin. We will express our gratitude by our hilarity rather than our wit. (HARRIOT *and* EMILY *seem to confer apart.*)

MRS. MONTAGUE: (*Resumes her reading*). "And lastly, as great masses of the mineral kingdom, which have been found in the crust of the earth, which human nature has penetrated, has evidently been formed from the recrements of animal and vegetable bodies. . . ."

HARRIOT: May I send to Mrs. Shapely to put the silver trimmings upon my white satin, Mamma?

MRS. MONTAGUE: Yes, child. (*Reads.*) "These also are supposed thus to have derived their phlogiston from the sun."

Enter OBADIAH.

OBADIAH There's Mr. Major Camden zays how that he wants Miss Montague.

MRS. MONTAGUE: Go, my dear.

HARRIOT; Heigh ho! Will you go, cousin?

EMILY: I will join you presently, my dear. (*Exit* HARRIOT.)

MRS. MONTAGUE: (*Reads*). "Another opinion concerning the sun's rays is that they are not luminous till they arrive at our atmosphere, and that there uniting with some part of the air, they produce combustion." Be so good, my dear Miss Lovegrove, to step and desire Major Camden to tarry and dine with us.

EMILY: I obey you with pleasure, madam. (*Exit* EMILY.)

MRS. MONTAGUE: (*Reads*). "And light is emitted, and that an ethereal acid, yet undiscovered, is formed from this combustion. The more probable opinion, perhaps, is that the sun is a phlogistic mass of matter whose surface is in a state of combustion, which, like other burning bodies, emits light"—

Enter OBADIAH.

OBADIAH: Bridget wants to know as how, madam, would you have the partridges roasted, with the pudding?

MRS. MONTAGUE; Yes, Obadiah. (*Exit* OBADIAH.) (*Reads.*) "With immense velocity in all directions so that these rays of light act upon all opaque bodies; and, combining with them, either displace or produce their elementary heat, and become chemically combined with the phlogistic part of them. For light is given out when phlogistic bodies unite with the oxygenous principle of the air, as in combustion or in the reduction of metallic calxes. Thus in presenting to the flame of a candle a letter wafer, if it be colored with red lead, at the time the red lead becomes a metallic drop, a flash of light is perceived. Doctor Alexander Wilson"—

Enter OBADIAH.

OBADIAH: There is a dreadful accident come to pass, madam! (*Looks rueful.*)

MRS. MONTAGUE: For pity's sake, what is it?

OBADIAH: Fraid to zay, ma'am.

MRS. MONTAGUE: I command you to speak.

OBADIAH: Won't you be angry, though?

MRS. MONTAGUE: You will make me more angry if you disobey me.

OBADIAH: Well, then— Adds rat me if I can speak.

MRS. MONTAGUE: I order you, as you value my favor, to tell what is the matter.

OBADIAH: Well, then, if I must speak, matter enow of conscience, why, I thinks everything is going to ruin! Wauns! I does not think you'll stand it long, but, ods bodikins, I was not to blame for this neither, for the matter of that, as a body may zay.

MRS. MONTAGUE; You would weary even patience itself, Obadiah. Come to the point immediately.

OBADIAH: Well, well, point enough, in conscience. Why, you must know, ma'am, that the cook has left open the door of the larder, and the gray cat has helped herzelf to the partridges. There, ma'am, there is point enough, zaving your presence.

MRS. MONTAGUE: Is that all, Obadiah? Well, I rejoice that it is no worse. Here, take this bill, and see what dispatch you can make in furnishing more.

OBADIAH: Yes, that I will, mistress. (*Aside.*) Ho, ho, ho! I swamp it, a good milk's cow this. (*Exit* OBADIAH.)

MRS. MONTAGUE: (*Reads*). "Doctor Alexander Wilson ingeniously endeavors to prove that the sun is only in a state of combustion on its surface, and that the dark spots seen on its disk are excavations, or caverns, through the luminous crust, some of which are four thousand miles in diameter." (*Throws the paper on the table.*) One is really lost in the immensity of these speculations. Perhaps books engross too much of my time. I thought my daughter sighed deeply at the name of Camden. Indeed, she has lately given me to understand that she can never be his! If I cannot reward the deserving Camden by her hand, I shall regard the disappointment as the seal of my misfortunes. (*Exits.*)

SCENE: *A parlor.* MAJOR CAMDEN *and* MISS MONTAGUE *seated.*

HARRIOT: Why, Major, you always make me grave. You are too serious—a great deal too serious for me.

CAMDEN: I have long, madam, been fully convinced that it is out of my power to render myself agreeable to you.

HARRIOT: Ha, ha, ha! That collected countenance becomes you infinitely, I protest. Look always thus captivating, and I shall be half mad with love.

CAMDEN: If you knew my heart, Miss Montague—

HARRIOT: Oh, for heaven's sake, Camden, throw aside that lullaby tone, or I shall absolutely— (*Yawns.*) Or I shall absolutely fall asleep.

CAMDEN: Madam, madam, you do not use me well. (*Rising.*) You would not use Stanhope thus.

HARRIOT: (*Aside.*) How well he reads my heart. (*To* CAMDEN.) Stanhope is as gay as a butterfly. We have laughed in concert a full hour. I protest, I think we were made for each other. But here comes my sentimental cousin; she is always to your taste, Major.

Enter EMILY LOVEGROVE.

EMILY: My aunt, sir, requests you would dine with her today.

CAMDEN: She does me honor, Miss Lovegrove, and I am infinitely obliged to her charming messenger.

HARRIOT: Well, I see by your features you are disposed to be charming company; and so, I'll take the opportunity of giving orders to Shapely respecting my dress for the evening. (*Exit* HARRIOT.)

CAMDEN: Say, Miss Lovegrove, is not extreme gaiety and uninterrupted frivolity strong marks of indifference?

EMILY: My cousin has a fund of vivacity, sir; but, as it never transgresses the bounds of discretion, it would be criminal even to wish it lessened.

CAMDEN: Would that she could combine those rational and sentimental charms which so eminently distinguish Miss Lovegrove.

EMILY: Sir, Miss Montague is amiable and good, and innocence and gaiety are frequently associates.

CAMDEN: Would I had known Miss Lovegrove sooner!

EMILY: (*Hesitating and alarmed*). Sir, you may assure yourself that my interest in the heart of Miss Montague shall be wholly employed in your favor.

CAMDEN: In the heart of Miss Montague! (*Takes her hand.*) Charming Emily! But what am I about? I stand on a precipice, down which a single movement may plunge me! Oh, Miss Lovegrove, could you witness the conflict in this devoted bosom, your heavenly sensibility, enchanting woman, would extort from your mild eye the tear of gentle pity.

EMILY: (*Blushing and trembling*). Sir, you are in full possession of all my commiseration. My most arduous efforts shall be wholly yours! And I will this moment seek my cousin, and endeavor to persuade her to become everything a man of honor can desire. (*Exits precipitously.*)

CAMDEN: She either affects ignorance, or she does not understand me.

Were I more explicit, I should be a villain. I esteem Harriot Montague; but Emily Lovegrove enchants my reason and triumphs over my dearest sentiments! Yet, the accusation of broken faith shall not entwine a soldier's laurels. Indeed, these struggles do not well suit with my profession. America, now weeping over her desolated plains and warriors slain in battle, should be my sovereign lady. It is not thus her heroes—it is not thus that WASHINGTON inglorious wastes his hours! Well, well—I'll haste to yon parade, and there forget my weakness. (*Exits.*)

ACT THIRD

SCENE: The parade; sea prospect. MR. RAMBLETON *discovered at a corner of the stage, in a convenient position for viewing the recruits.* MAJOR CAMDEN *enters, followed by* SOLDIERS *clad in the American uniform, drums beating, fifes playing, and colors flying. They perform military evolutions, marching and counter-marching, after which* MAJOR CAMDEN *addresses them.*

CAMDEN: Well, my brave fellow soldiers, it is a glorious cause in which we have engaged. My glowing spirit, with congenial ardors, marks your glad alacrity. Your promptness and your order far exceed my utmost expectations! But liberty can animate to deeds that far exceed all common credibility! The Rights of Man, my friends—auspicious liberty: these are our objects!

SOLDIERS: Huzzah for liberty! Huzzah for liberty!

CAMDEN: We have a leader, my brave friends—the patriot WASHINGTON—who, for the rights of free men, hazards his valued life and all his dearest hopes, greatly refusing every compensation!

SOLDIERS: Long live the glorious WASHINGTON! Long live our noble General! Huzzah for WASHINGTON and liberty!

CAMDEN: When power oppressive shall be crushed before him, and independence on firm base established, then will our General, like another Quintus, gladly put off the robes of power and seek, amid his loved Vernonian haunts, those calm enjoyments which attend on virtue!

SOLDIERS: Huzzah for WASHINGTON and independence!

CAMDEN: Frenchmen espouse our cause. Frenchmen have joined our battles; and, fighting by our side, the brave Fayette their leader, they will augment our triumphs!

SOLDIERS: Long live the gallant French!

CAMDEN: Our guardian legislators issue their wise decrees. Their utmost efforts ardently combining, up to their best abilities they will reward us. The Congress, fellow soldiers, are our protecting fathers!

SOLDIERS: (*Throw up their hats*). God protect the Congress! We will fight and die for the Congress!

CAMDEN: Lastly, my friends, remember, though 'tis an arduous struggle, yet your best interests are all at stake: your wives, your children, your liberties—THE PEOPLE OF AMERICA! If we are subjugated, we are no more a nation!

SOLDIERS: We will defend our liberties! We will defend the people! Long live America! Long live the free-born nation! (*Drums beat; fifes play "Washington's March." Soldiers form a procession and, headed by* MAJOR CAMDEN, *pass off the stage.*)

MR. RAMBLETON *comes forward.*

RAMBLETON: My soul is wrought up to a degree of ecstasy! My brave, brave boy! I glory in my son! How regular the movements of the soldiers! Their evolutions would have done honor to the best disciplined troops in Europe! Thank heaven, my inquiries relative to Louise have hitherto proved very satisfactory, and I hasten to complete my investigation. (*Exits.*)

SCENE: *A parlor at* MRS. MONTAGUE's. *Enter* HARRIOT, *followed by* OBADIAH.

HARRIOT: Well, Obadiah, and how did you manage?

OBADIAH: Odds flesh! Why, I thought as how I should never have found un, miss.

HARRIOT: You should have gone directly to Mr. Stanhope's.

OBADIAH: Adds wauns, Miss Harriot, and zo I did! But you zaid I must zee un myself, and zo I could na find un, adds rabbit it, if I did not chase all over the town.

HARRIOT: And so, then, you have not seen Mr. Stanhope?

OBADIAH: Oh, yes, miss—yes, yes, I have zeed un.

HARRIOT: And you told him I would comply with his request?

OBADIAH: Yes, miss, but a murrain deal of trouble I had first, though.

HARRIOT: Well—and come, what did he say?

OBADIAH: Wauns, miss, he was 'nation glad.

HARRIOT: But what did he say?

OBADIAH: Why, miss, he zaid—he zaid—why, he did not zay nothing, miss.

HARRIOT: Said nothing?

OBADIAH: No, miss, nothing—he, he, he!

HARRIOT: What do you laugh at, impertinence?

OBADIAH: Don't be angry, Miss Harriot, but I canna help laughing. Zee! He gave me all this money for my good news, and something else for somebody else, besides all this here.

HARRIOT: What is it, in the name of goodness!

OBADIAH: But won't mistress blame I, now, Miss Harriot?

HARRIOT: Fear nothing, Obadiah.

OBADIAH: But I fears mortally.

HARRIOT: Fiddlestick! Obadiah, I will take care you shall not be blamed, and if you have anything further to say, prithee let's have it.

OBADIAH: I have nothing to zay, miss, but if I was sure I should not be turned out of doors. . . (*Takes a letter, with gestures expressive of awkward fear, from his pocket.*) I would give you this here letter.

HARRIOT: (*Snatches the paper and reads*). Um, um, um!

OBADIAH: Addsnigggers! Miss Harriot, you are 'nation strong.

HARRIOT: You have acquitted yourself admirably, Obadiah. Reach me my scarf. Do you be secret, (*Gives him money.*) and expect my future favor.

OBADIAH: All this for me, Miss Harriot? What a power of money it is! Adds rabbit me, if I blab—he, he, he! Well, I vows, now, I'll zee the panorama, and the lion, and all the wild beasts—aye, and I'll zee a play too.

HARRIOT: You may go, Obadiah. Remember your word.

OBADIAH: Yes, that I wull. (*Looks at the money.*) Why, what a lucky house I have got into! Wauns! What a marvelous lucky whelp I be! (*Exits, bowing and scraping his feet.*)

HARRIOT: That I am not, strictly speaking, within the line of discretion, I am fully sensible. Alberto himself will set me down as a mad girl, although I do but comply with his pressing entreaties. But what with mothers and cousins, there is no such thing as getting a moment to oneself here; and so, for this once, I'll e'en sally forth. (*Exit HARRIOT.*)

SCENE: *The inn.* MR. *and* MRS. VANSITTART. MRS. VANSITTART *discovered holding a miniature picture.*

MRS. VANSITTART: Oh, the dear, pretty creature! Set all round with rose diamonds of the first water! I vow, husband, it is the jonteelest thing I ever saw.

VANSITTART: Rose tiamonts of the first vater! I say, Torothy, you hat petter put it on the shentleman's toilette again. You petter not pe metteling. I tell you, Torothy, you petter not pe metteling.

MRS. VANSITTART: Why, Mr. Vansittart, I would not do an unperlite thing, any more than another, but this Mr. Rambleton is most pertinaciously a spyington from the British. You see he has not a paper dollar in the world! Nothing but good, hard English crowns and guineas. His Irish servant has his pockets lined with money, and he says that his master's trunks are as rich as the mines of Poteldo.[12]

VANSITTART: Vel, and vat then?

MRS. VANSITTART: Why, as sure as you are alive, Major Camden is his accomplishment.

VANSITTART: Vel, and vat then?

MRS. VANSITTART: Why, then, it is just such another case as Arnold and Andre.[13]

VANSITTART: Vel, and vat then?

MRS. VANSITTART: Why, then, it would be doing a jonteel thing, and a patrolitical thing, to inform against them to the Committee of Safety.[14]

VANSITTART: And vat shoult ve get py that?

MRS. VANSITTART: Everything, husband; for, while our gentlemen were had before the Committee, we could ply the Irishman with his favorite liquor, and when he was secured, break open the locks, seize the cash, and make the best of our way to New York, which is at no great distance, and there remain concealed until opportunity offered to quit this Freetonian land altogether.

VANSITTART: Cot a' mercy! I smell a rat, at this present time.

MRS. VANSITTART: And then no one could say, black is the white of our eye, for we have but served ourselves at the expense of abomination Tories, and thus done a jonteel thing for our country.

VANSITTART: Why, Torothy, Torothy! Thou hast creat vistoms, ant I have creat occasions, at this present time.

MRS. VANSITTART: Well, husband, do you give information instantly, and as soon as his Toryship is secured, you shall take this picture to the jeweler's and pretend that it belonged to one of the rich relations of which you have so often boasted, and that you are obliged to part with it. And thus we shall find money to supply ourselves with cloaks, masks, &c &c., in which we shall be so disguised that our own natural-born fathers

---

[12]Probably a comically incorrect reference to Eldorado, the legendary land of riches.

[13]Benedict Arnold, a general in the American Revolutionary army, turned traitor and arranged with Major John Andre, a British officer, to surrender the forces under his command at West Point in 1780. When the plot was uncovered, Arnold escaped, but Andre was executed for spying.

[14]Committees of Safety were established in towns and regions at the outset of the American Revolution to coordinate the struggle against British rule. They became the *de facto* local government during the war.

would not know us.

VANSITTART: Vel, vel, Torothy—put I tremple all over like an aspen leaf, ant I have creat fears ve shall pring ourselves to shame!

MRS. VANSITTART: What ails you, husband? The goods of a Tory are free plunder! Why, we are doing the most handsomest thing in the world, and as we shall not break the trunks until the last moment, we are perfectly secure. Away to the Committee of Safety—away I say. (*Pushing him off.*)

VANSITTART: Oh, mercy on us! Mercy on us! I to think there pe creat tangers and creat tifficulties. (*Exits.*)

SCENE: A sequestered walk, beautifully shaded. ALBERTO STANHOPE *and* HARRIOT MONTAGUE *are discovered, sitting on the turfed seats and engaged in close conversation.*

HARRIOT: Well, Alberto, I can only repeat that I do most sincerely regret this clandestine intercourse. In compliance with your importunities, I have given you this meeting. The world considers me as a gay, unthinking girl; yet I have my moments of reflection. My preference of you I will not deny, but the, if possible, augmented indulgence of my mother hath roused to action every proper sentiment and the highest sense of the duty which I owe her.

STANHOPE: Perhaps, Harriot, your heart now decides in favor of Camden! But let him take care— (*They rise.*)

HARRIOT: Pshaw, pshaw! Stanhope, this is exactly in his style. (*Throws herself into a fencing attitude.*) Yet, don't put yourself into a passion, man; for, I protest, I begin to think he has absolutely thrown off his allegiance and that he is, at this very moment, fomenting a rebellion against his sovereign lady!

STANHOPE: What means my Harriot?

HARRIOT: Why, *entre nous*, I suspect he has conceived a most violent *penchant* for Emily Lovegrove.

STANHOPE: Heaven grant it.

HARRIOT: It would be delectable! They would make the most charming sentimental pair in the world! And I take every opportunity of leaving them together, not doubting but their private interviews will wonderfully increase their *tendresse*.

STANHOPE: Does my Harriot draw this conclusion from her own experience?

HARRIOT: (*Striking the powder out of his hair with her fan.*) Yes, villain, and hence she resolves to make no more assignations.

STANHOPE: Charming vivacity! (*Seizing her hand.*)

HARRIOT: Unhand me, wretch!

STANHOPE: But what are we to do, my angel?

HARRIOT: Do? Why, sit down, like the babes in the wood, and cry ourselves to sleep, and see what little robin red-breast will prepare our leafy covering.

STANHOPE: Prithee, do not thus trifle with my feelings. You have forbid my application to your mother.

HARRIOT: Because I knew it would be ineffectual.

STANHOPE: (*Again taking her hand*). In the name of heaven, how shall I proceed? Shall I engage my father to intercede for me?

HARRIOT: Why, ah! These managing people understand each other best, and it is as well to proceed in the good old-fashioned way. (*Looks at her watch.*) But it is time for me to scamper. Adieu. You will make one of our dancers this evening?

STANHOPE: Enchanting girl! I shall attend you with rapture!

SCENE: *An apartment at* MRS. MONTAGUE's. *Enter* MRS. MONTAGUE *and* EMILY.

MRS. MONTAGUE: Emily, where is Harriot?

EMILY: I Cannot tell, Madam; but she is fond of walking, and, I suppose, is improving this fine day by indulging in her favorite exercise.

MRS. MONTAGUE: Emily, young people generally understand each other. There was a time when I conceived the heart of my girl entirely devoted to Major Camden, but she has of late given me reason to regard her attachment as problematical. Am I to impute this apparent change to caprice, or to a growing disgust?

EMILY: (*Confused and hesitating*). Why, really, madam, it is not for me to say.

MRS. MONTAGUE: Your looks, Emily, and your manner, convince me that you could say a great deal! I am engaged in gratitude, in honor, to Major Camden. My promise is irrevocable. I had the full consent of Harriot, and the world expects their speedy union. Tell me, Emily, if you know aught which can militate against my plans?

EMILY: (*Trembling and blushing excessively*). Pray, madam, excuse me! Pray do!

Enter HARRIOT.

EMILY: (*Aside*). What a fortunate relief.

MRS. MONTAGUE: Harriot, where have you been rambling?

HARRIOT: Rambling, sure enough, Mamma! Why, half the town

over, and I am so delightfully fatigued—

MRS. MONTAGUE: Well, my love, take off your scarf, and let us have a little serious chit-chat.

EMILY: Have I your leave to retire, madam?

MRS. MONTAGUE: Go, my good girl. (*Exit* EMILY.) Tell me, Harriot, have you ceased to love Major Camden?

HARRIOT: To love him, Mamma! Why, that is a business I have never yet begun.

MRS. MONTAGUE: My dear Harriot, I am serious.

HARRIOT: Well then, Mamma, seriously, although I esteem Major Camden, I can never marry him; for I can never love him, Mamma.

MRS. MONTAGUE: If you esteem him, dear, it is sufficient.

HARRIOT: God bless you, madam! You would not surely insist that my hand should be a solitary gift?

MRS. MONTAGUE: Love, my dear, is a chimera which has undone your mother!

HARRIOT: Madam!

MRS. MONTAGUE: For your advantage, Harriot, I will sketch some particulars of my life which I had intended to keep forever from your knowledge.

HARRIOT: If you please, Mamma.

MRS. MONTAGUE: When I married your father, although I regarded him as the first of men, yet I felt not for him what is called love.

HARRIOT: (*Archly*). And was you very happy with my father, madam?

MRS. MONTAGUE: I understand you, Harriot. I engaged in a round of dissipation. I continued the most censurable pursuits, and at length imagined myself tenderly attached to a person who was every way the inferior of your father.

HARRIOT: Well, madam.

MRS. MONTAGUE: Your father continued his forbearance until convinced, by circumstances, that he had a rival in my affections, when, leaving me at our country seat, without a single remonstrance, and taking with him your brother, then only four years old, he departed this city, leading me to expect he would return with the coming day! (*Weeps.*)

HARRIOT: Dear madam, proceed!

MRS. MONTAGUE: You were then but two months old. The first post brought me a letter in which he informed me that, as he was convinced I was unalterably attached to another, he should bid me an eternal adieu; that he took with him our son, as the only solace of his exile; that he left me the uninterrupted possession of his town and country house, with a sufficient income to support myself and daughter—and he concluded by wishing me, with the man of my heart, all that felicity on which he supposed my fond imagination had calculated.

HARRIOT: For God's sake, madam, proceed!

MRS. MONTAGUE: I came immediately to town, but he had embarked on board a ship bound to some part of Europe! From season to season, for a long time, I encouraged hope; but, although nineteen years have since revolved, not a single syllable, either respecting himself or my son, hath ever blest my ears!

HARRIOT: Gracious Heaven! Both my father and my brother may be yet alive!

MRS. MONTAGUE: Alas! No— I feel it is impossible! My wounds bleed afresh at this recital! They have long since bid adieu to a world to which I am chained a miserable captive! (*Weeps agonizedly.*)

HARRIOT: Forbear! Best of mothers, forbear these tears! Surely, surely, your experience does not decide in favor of an Hymen unblessed by love?

MRS. MONTAGUE; Observe me, girl. Although I was indiscreet, I was never criminal; and the moment of your father's departure convinced me of my error. The charm was broke. I detested the author of my sufferings. I never after saw him; and, to my great satisfaction, I learned that he immediately quitted the continent. I dwelt with unutterable admiration on your father's virtues; and had I possessed worlds, I would have parted with them all to have purchased his return!

HARRIOT: Ah! Madam, your story is indeed instructive, but—

MRS. MONTAGUE: But what, my love? I am indebted to Major Camden for my life. You have received him with approbation. He is every way worthy, and, next to yourself, Harriot, he is now the dearest object of my affections! But alas, my love, you are ill! My woe-fraught narrative has been too oppressive! Heaven guard my child! Let me lead you to your chamber. (*Exit* MRS. MONTAGUE, *supporting* HARRIOT.)

ACT FOURTH

SCENE: An apartment in the inn. Enter PATRICK.

PATRICK: Ow, if ever I got into such a place before now—by my soul, the mistress of this same tavern, d'ye see, is the prettiest bit of a crature, as a body may say, that ever a man set eyes on; and, may I never see

Killmallock again, if she is not better than a shipload of peraters[15] just
landed from the county of Cork! But here comes my master, now.

Enter MR. RAMBLETON.

RAMBLETON: Well, Patrick, how wears the day, and what sort of a
house have we got into?

PATRICK: Ow, as to the day, I don't bodder myself about that, at all,
at all; for, d'ye see, I don't matter[16] time three skips of a grasshopper. But
as for the house, ow, if I was in my own, sweet Killmallock, in the county
of Limerick, in dear Ireland itshelf, my own born mother could not be
better to me. Why, they have already given me three breakfasts and as
many dinners; and, as to drink, my dear honey, ow, let me alone for that,
master.

RAMBLETON: Why, I believe, indeed, thou hast taken a plentiful
portion of the good creature. (*Loud knocking without*). But see if thou
canst open the door. (PATRICK *opens the door*. OFFICER *enters and gives*
RAMBLETON *a letter*.)

RAMBLETON: Hah! Where can I have picked up a scribbling
acquaintance already? (*Reads.*)

"Mr. Rambleton: By virtue of the power delegated to us by the people,
we summon you to appear before us, the Select Committee of Public Safety
for the City of ——. Information has been lodged against you as a spy
employed by the British government, and we have authorized the bearer of
this notification to bring you before us for the purpose of examination.

Arthur Vigilant, Secretary of the Committee of Public Safety"

RAMBLETON: (*Appears much agitated*). Can you inform me from
what source this officious interference originated?

OFFICER: Sir, my orders are to attend you to the honorable
Committee without answering any questions, but you may depend on
receiving every indulgence that the nature of the case and the circumstances
of our country will admit.

RAMBLETON: Thank you, sir. (*Aside.*) Gracious God! If Harry
Camden is the informer, my hopes of happiness will, indeed, prove the
dream of the moment! (*Walks about, agitated and distressed.*)

PATRICK: Ow, then, if it is not a shame now, to be after boddering
a stranger in his own country. I say, now, little honey, cannot you be
taking your shelf off a bit, my dear, and lave my poor master all alone with

---

[15]Probably a mispronunciation of *potatoes*.
[16]Care about.

his own faithful Patrick O'Neal, d'ye see?

OFFICER: I do but my duty, friend.

PATRICK: Your juty, do you call it! Ow, by my soul, Mr. Tipstaff, this is the first time I ever heard say it was a juty to bodder a man in his own country after he had got into foreign parts[17]! Hark'ye, little honey! Will I put a remembrance upon you, now? Suppose you and I should take a bit of a knock for love, my dear?

RAMBLETON: Patrick, you have nothing to do in this business. Sir, I attend you.

PATRICK: Arrah, my dear, now, it will never be said that Patrick O'Neal suffered his master to get into the limboes[18] alone, and so I will be after going with you, that, if we will both be taken prisoners, we may rescue one another.

RAMBLETON: Patrick, I have nothing to fear. I have valuable articles in this house, and I entrust them to your care.

PATRICK: Arrah, now, my dear, let them same articles take care of themselves. I shall be after going with your worship, d'ye see.

RAMBLETON: Patrick, I command you not to quit the house.

PATRICK: Arrah, then, I shall stay behind, for he that is willian[19] enough not to plase[20] a man in distress ought to have been assassinated twenty years before he was born, so he had. (*Exit* OFFICER *and* RAMBLETON.)

PATRICK: Ow, if I was but in dear Ireland now, in the borough of Killmallock, in the county of Limerick, maybe I'd soon see the white boys[21] about me—maybe I would. And then my shelf would be taking my poor master out of jurance—so I would. But a wet sorrow is better than a dry one, as the saying is, and so I'll be after another little sip of comfort, so I will. (*Exits.*)

SCENE: *An apartment in* MRS. MONTAGUE's *house. Enter* OBADIAH, *picking his teeth.*

OBADIAH: Well, I'll swamp it, now I have made as good a dinner as if I had eaten baked beans and pudding. Ouns, I could not fare better in

---

[17]Traveled abroad.

[18]*Limbo* was a colloquial term for prison.

[19]Villain.

[20]Please.

[21]Members of an agrarian association, known by the white shirts they wore in their night-time attacks, formed by Irish peasants in 1761, to redress their grievances against landlords.

Natick.

Enter MR. STANHOPE SENIOR.

STANHOPE SENIOR: Is your mistress at home, Obadiah?
OBADIAH: At hume, zir? He, he, he, I can't say, zir! I'll ax her if she chooses to be at hume, zir. (*Exit* OBADIAH.)
STANHOPE SENIOR: May I never take the field, but this is a fine musical[22] custom which our new-formed States have adopted: we are not always in a disposition to see our best friends, and we have a right to be at home just when we please.

Enter OBADIAH.

OBADIAH: Yes, zir, you may zee mistress. Walk after me, zir, walk after me. (*Exit* STANHOPE SENIOR, *following* OBADIAH.)

SCENE: A parlor. MRS. MONTAGUE *seated. Enter* OBADIAH, *introducing* STANHOPE SENIOR. (*Exit* OBADIAH.)

STANHOPE SENIOR; Good morrow, fair lady.
MRS. MONTAGUE: Your most obedient, Mr. Stanhope. I hope you are in health, sir?
STANHOPE: Yes, madam, partly; and yet I am not as young as I was fifty years ago, neither.
MRS. MONTAGUE: Time, sir, imprints its footsteps upon everything visible.
STANHOPE SENIOR: And yet, madam, may I never take the field, if I do not think you look as young as you did twenty years ago.
MRS. MONTAGUE: Oh, dear sir!
STANHOPE: Yes you do, yes you do; and if I was twenty years younger, madam, I do assure you I should feel strongly inclined to strike about myself.
MRS. MONTAGUE: Strike about, sir!
STANHOPE SENIOR: Yes, widow, I would make my bow, squeeze your ladyship's hand, whisper soft things in your ear, hint indirectly at marriage, and publish the bans in less time than you could finish your wedding cap.

---

[22]Murray footnoted the original thus: *Musical*, a term used in many of the interior parts of the New England States to express everything convenient, excellent or elegant; thus, they say a musical horse, day, garment, &c. &c.

MRS. MONTAGUE: You are disposed to be pleasant, sir! But as this is a subject on which I never jest, I beg leave to say that had you the faculty of renewing your youth, and were to advance with the most serious proposals, I should not hesitate in putting my negative thereon.

STANHOPE SENIOR: Indeed! Well, I profess this is somewhat surprising, but mayhap I am not to your taste. Do you not hold matrimony to be a musical thing?

MRS. MONTAGUE: Oh, yes, musical enough; but I am principled against second marriages, sir.

STANHOPE SENIOR: Oh, is that all? Well, then, I hope my son may succeed.

MRS. MONTAGUE: Your son, sir?

STANHOPE SENIOR: Yes, madam, my son has taken a violent fancy to a good, handsome young woman of whom you have the disposal. I perfectly approve his choice, and have waited on you to endeavor to obtain your consent.

MRS. MONTAGUE: (*Aside*). Can my niece have made a conquest of such importance already? (*To* STANHOPE SENIOR.) Why, sir, the young woman you mention is calculated, both in mind and person, to command affection as well as esteem. Had her father lived, her consequence would doubtless have been augmented; but I shall make every effort in my power which I can suppose will be for her advantage.

STANHOPE SENIOR: Madam, she cannot stand in need of proper aid, under your care.

MRS. MONTAGUE: Sir, it is my wish to discharge the duty of a mother.

STANHOPE SENIOR: I never heard anything more musical in my life. Madam, may I inform my son that he has your approbation?

MRS. MONTAGUE: Sir, if your son can render the young lady propitious, he shall have my best wishes.

STANHOPE SENIOR: Madam, I was made to believe that you were not favorably inclined in this affair, but the best are liable to mistakes. You have done me a very particular kindness, madam! Alberto will run mad with joy, and I will make all possible dispatch to inform him of his happiness. Sweet lady, I take my leave, and shall ever be your most obedient, humble servant.

MRS. MONTAGUE: Sir, your most obedient. (*Exit* STANHOPE SENIOR.) Quite a whimsical old gentleman, on my word! His way of thinking, too, is rather singular; for Emily's fortune is a mere trifle, and Alberto, accomplished as he is, might form the most aspiring expectations. I will take the earliest opportunity of sounding my niece, and govern myself by her wishes.

SCENE: Another apartment. HARRIOT *and* EMILY *seated on a sofa.*

HARRIOT: Well, Emily, although I have confided to you that this little heart of mine beats only for Alberto Stanhope, yet you still remain as profound as a pedant who studies obscurity, or as close as Olivia in the *Good Natur'd Man*[23]. Come, child, you had better make a confession.

EMILY: Dear Harriot, permit me to be a miser of my woes! I would slide through life performing my little part without observation, and—

HARRIOT: (*Humorously putting her hand on* EMILY's *mouth*). For heaven's sake, Emily, be not thus humble! Without observation, say you! Why, I would rather be paragraphed in the newspaper than not distinguished at all.

EMILY: Paragraphed in the newspaper!

HARRIOT: Yes, my dear, although said paragraph should hold me up in the most ridiculous point of view!

EMILY: I cannot conceive of this!

HARRIOT: Why child, a single scribbler, scratching his malicious noddle, may fabricate his abuse, and the cynic has only to preface his invidious production by the little comprehensive monosyllable *we* think and *we* wish, while he thus hands my name to thousands, who would not otherwise have known that I had an existence.

EMILY: Well, but with the knowledge of your existence, they would at the same time receive an impression that would not be to your honor.

HARRIOT: Yes, Emily, but their curiosity would be called into action—it would impel them to inquire. I should come out an innocent sufferer, be allowed my full share of merit, and acquire a prodigious deal of consequence. Ha! Ha! Ha! I protest, the very idea is enchanting.

EMILY: Mad girl! But however you may divert yourself, I still insist that were I to be publicly traduced, I should never enjoy peace afterward!

HARRIOT: Then you would be very irrational, my dear, for envy is a powerful stimulus to the misanthropic mind, and merit is ever the mark at which it aims its most envenomed shafts. But we have strangely wandered from our subject. I am positive, Emily, that my friend Camden is not indifferent to you.

EMILY: Dear Harriot, spare me. (*Enter* BRIDGET, *who presents a billet to* HARRIOT. *Exit* BRIDGET.)

HARRIOT: (*Reads*).   Raptures—um, um, um—   Eternal obligations—um, um, um! Duty—um, um, um! Reverence—oh, Emily! I am in a delirium of joy! My mamma has sanctioned my wishes! She

---

[23]Play by Oliver Goldsmith, 1768.

consents to my union with Alberto Stanhope! Camden shall be yours. Adored parent! But I will go this instant, and on my bended knees I will thank her for her unparalleled goodness. (*Exit* HARRIOT, *agitated.*)

EMILY: Well, this is passing strange! My aunt is indeed the noblest of human beings; yet, that she should thus easily relinquish the favorite wish of her soul— But I will await the issue in my chamber.

SCENE: The Library. MRS. MONTAGUE *is discovered with a book in her hand.* HARRIOT *rushes in and throws herself on her knees at the feet of her mother.*

HARRIOT: Oh, my angelic parent! May ten thousand blessings crown your honored head! You have indeed made me the happiest of human beings!

MRS. MONTAGUE: Gracious Heaven! My poor child has lost her reason!

HARRIOT: No, madam, reason at this moment imprints on my heart duty, gratitude and love, to the most condescending parent that ever bore that revered name.

MRS. MONTAGUE: Rise then, my daughter, and let me know what has discomposed you?

HARRIOT: (*Rising*). Here, madam. (*Presenting the billet she had received from Stanhope.*) These ecstatic lines, penned by my Alberto, inform me that, forgoing your former wishes, you now consent to crown our youthful hopes by your maternal approbation.

MRS. MONTAGUE: (*Taking the billet*). His ecstasies should have been addressed to Emily Lovegrove.

HARRIOT: (*Aside*). To Emily Lovegrove!

MRS. MONTAGUE: (*After reading the billet*). You have, child, acted very reprehensibly in concealing your inclinations thus long from your mother.

HARRIOT: I had hoped to have conquered them, madam, and to have bent me to my duty.

MRS. MONTAGUE: I am disposed to think the best, Harriot. I had thought the father of Alberto solicited me for my niece, and I consented that his son should address Miss Lovegrove. Imagining that you were already regarded as the wife of Camden, I could not expect to receive proposals for you.

HARRIOT: (*Weeping*). Oh, madam, how cruel is my situation!

MRS. MONTAGUE: To say truth, child, I pity you, and I lament my own embarrassments. I cannot break the heart of Harry Camden! He interests me more and more every time I behold him! I have thought,

Harriot, that he bears a strong resemblance to your father! But compose yourself, my love. Enjoy, with your accustomed vivacity, your evening's entertainment. With the coming day, I will converse with Camden, and in the meantime hope everything from the indulgence of your mother. (*They exit.*)

ACT FIFTH

SCENE: The inn. Enter PATRICK, *tipsy, with a mug in his hand. (He hiccoughs and sings.)*

> Ow! Patrick's not drunk, to be sure,
> Although in the liquor quite drowned; (*Drinks.*)
> The wine in his stomach secure,
> His head for pure joy it runs round. (*Drinks.*)
>   Tol de re lol. Tol de re lol,
> I'll stand by my master all night,
> And sleep in his hammock all day;
> And Patrick, though dead in a fright,
> Shall never be running away. (*Drinks.*)
>   Tol de re lol. Tol de re lol.
> My shelf shall be fighting for him;
> I'll follow, although I stand still.
> Ow, if I am drowned I can swim.
> The world it runs round like a mill. (*Drinks.*)
>   Tol de re lol. Tol de re lol.

Well, now, if Mistress Van—Van—jeuce take me, if I have not forgot— If she was to see me, she would be after taking me off— Don't they call it taking off? Well, now, if Master Rambleton should get out of the limboes, himshelf would be apt to think I was a little the worse for the good crature, or so. And so I'll e'en turn in; and after taking a nap, maybe I would be sober again. Here's good luck to us, Master Rambleton. (*Drinks. Exits, staggering.*)

Enter VANSITTART.

VANSITTART: Cot a' mercy! Where can Torothy pe, at this present time? I have creat occasions for manhoot. It is a polt untertaking, and I treamt all last night of coffins, cross pones and the callows. Oh, tear! I am all over of a colt sweat.

MRS. VANSITTART, *having forced the trunks, enters, followed by two servants bearing bags of money. (She slips her foot, falls head foremost into the parlor, and, in her fall, overturns a large screen.)*

VANSITTART: (*Roars out*). Cot a' mercy! Cot a' mercy!

MRS. VANSITTART: Why, husband, what ails you? I am sure you are an unmannerly fellow, to leave me sprawling thus.

VANSITTART: (*Trembling excessively*). Torothy, Torothy! Vat shall ve to, Torothy?

MRS. VANSITTART: Do! Why, put on this here mask and this cloak. (*She helps him on with the cloak.*)

VANSITTART: (*Still trembling and terrified*). Oh! Torothy, Torothy! Let me tie teat,[24] if I have not creat occasions to tislike this pusiness. It has creat tangers!

MRS. VANSITTART: Well, well, never mind. Come, let's away. (*They all mask.*) We will take the road to New York, through the woods and over the mountains. (*Exit, bearing the treasure*, VANSITTART *still agitated.*)

SCENE: A genteel parlor at MRS. MONTAGUE*'s.* MRS. MONTAGUE, &c.&c., *all in full dress.* (STANHOPE *and* HARRIOT *dancing a minuet; all the rest of the company sitting.* OBADIAH *enters and presents a folded parcel to* MRS. MONTAGUE, *who reads and, after unfolding another paper, exclaims.*)

MRS. MONTAGUE: Gracious God! My own picture! The very miniature which the man I so deeply injured was accustomed to wear next his heart! Oh, Harriot, Harriot! I am now, indeed, undone! Some villain has murdered your father!

HARRIOT: For heaven's sake, madam, explain.

MRS. MONTAGUE: Read that paper, my dear. Read it aloud, and advise me, my friends, what step I am to take.

HARRIOT: (*Reads*). "Madam: Vansittart the innkeeper, some hours since, parted with the enclosed miniature for a sum of money by no means adequate to its value. As the picture was set by me, I could not but recognize it. If you think it necessary to take any steps respecting it, you must be speedy; for I shrewdly suspect Vansittart is on the point of decamping. I have the honor to be, madam,

Your most obedient, humble servant, Jeremy Trueworth."

CAMDEN: Madam, Vansittart is my landlord. I will fly instantly and

---

[24]Die dead.

force him to confess by what means he obtained this picture.

MRS. MONTAGUE; Do, dear Harry! But before you go, it is necessary you should know I am ignorant of the fate of my husband, and that this picture was in his possession when he left me. (*Weeps.*)

STANHOPE: Camden, permit me to be the companion of your enterprise.

CAMDEN: With all my heart, Stanhope. (*Exit* CAMDEN *and* STANHOPE.)

MRS. MONTAGUE: Oh, my children! My very soul seems to die within me!

HARRIOT: Dear Emily, assist me to bear my mother to her apartment. (HARRIOT *and* EMILY *bear off* MRS. MONTAGUE, *and the scene closes.*)

SCENE: The inn. Enter PATRICK, *who is supposed to have slept off the effects of his liquor, and who raves and stamps about outrageously.*

PATRICK: Murder! Hanging! Drowning and quartering! Why, everything which ever happened in this beggarly, rascally world! Ow, it was every bit of it no more than the skip of a flea to this! The trunks are all wide open! There is not a soul left in the house, and nobody that I meet can give me a bit of an answer! My poor master clapped up, and Patrick O'Neal in a strange, outlandish country! Maybe the Indian savages shall take my shelf prisoner too, maybe they shall. Ow! What had I to do, to be after running such a wild-goose chase? But here is someone coming. I'll give um a little bit of a taste, so I will. Ow! Murder! Robbery! Bloodshed! Fire and thunder!

Enter MAJOR CAMDEN, ALBERTO STANHOPE, OFFICER, *and* SOLDIERS.

CAMDEN: Patrick, for heaven's sake, what is the matter? Where is Mr. Vansittart?

PATRICK: Ow, Master Camden, Methuselah himshelf could not tell that, I believe!

CAMDEN: What do you mean, Patrick? Is he not in the house?

PATRICK: Ow! I have searched the house from garret to cellar, and the jeuce bit of a human soul, except the cat, is there to be found! And what is more, they have broken open all my master's trunks, and boddered him out of a million guineas more than he had, my dear.

CAMDEN: Good God! Is it possible? Robbed the trunks! Where was you, Patrick?

PATRICK: Ow, you may say that—shame burn my cheek! My master, d'ye see, had gotten into the limboes; and so, to make my shelf asy, I took a drop, or so, and fell fast asleep; and then, before I was awake, the deed was done.

CAMDEN: But what do you mean by your master's being in the limboes, Patrick?

PATRICK: Why, Master Tipstaff here—isn't it Tipstaff ye call him—kidnapped him; that's all, honey.

OFFICER: Information was given to the Committee of Public Safety against Mr. Rambleton, and I had the honor of attending him before them, sir.

CAMDEN: Good heavens! I must hasten to his assistance. Mr. Stanhope, I may want your aid. The probability is that the villainous plunderers have taken the road to New York; and, by the assistance of these soldiers, sir, (*speaking to the* OFFICER) you may surprise and bring them back. Their booty will retard their flight. Patrick, you will accompany the officer; you can best designate your master's property.

PATRICK: Ow, that I shall, with the biggest pleasure in life, sir!

CAMDEN: Mr. Stanhope, we must away to the Committee. (*They exit in opposite directions.*)

SCENE: An apartment in another public house. MR. RAMBLETON *and the* MEMBERS *of the Committee of Safety seated round the table.*

RAMBLETON: Gentlemen, you have detained me many hours. I could clear up all your doubts, but I have private reasons for wishing to remain concealed at present. Yet, however you may be disposed to call my veracity in question, you have so highly obliged me by assuring me that you received no intelligence respecting me from Major Camden, that I shall not easily take offense.

FIRST MEMBER: Your attachment to Major Camden would almost induce us to suspect the fidelity of that young soldier.

SECOND MEMBER: Major Camden is a brave, a gallant officer, but so was General Arnold!

THIRD MEMBER: The defection of Arnold has rendered us abundantly more wary; we have everything at stake, sir.

RAMBLETON: I commend your caution, gentlemen. I have already narrated my accidental meeting with Major Camden, but perhaps it might be agreeable to summon the Major, and we will submit to cross-examination.

FIRST MEMBER: This, in my opinion, gentlemen, is a proper motion.

Enter a SERVANT.

SERVANT: Major Camden and Mr. Stanhope crave admittance, gentlemen.

SECOND MEMBER: Let them enter immediately. (*Exit* SERVANT.)

THIRD MEMBER: This looks well.

Enter MAJOR CAMDEN *and* MR. STANHOPE.

CAMDEN: May it please this honorable body, Mr. Stanhope and myself wait on you to offer our joint bonds for the release of Mr. Rambleton. His affairs stand in immediate need of his presence.

RAMBLETON: What mean you, sir?

CAMDEN: The villain Vansittart, having robbed you of every article of value, hath absconded!

MEMBERS OF THE COMMITTEE: (*All exclaim*). Vansittart! The very man who lodged the information!

RAMBLETON: The picture of my Louisa, then, is ravished from me!

CAMDEN: The picture, sir! (*Pauses.*) Yes—it is possible! Vansittart sold the picture to a jeweler, and it is now in the hands of Mrs. Montague, whose soul is harrowed up by agonizing fears for him whose property it was.

RAMBLETON: Oh! Give me way, and let me fly, the messenger of peace!

CAMDEN: Explain yourself, Mr. Rambleton.

RAMBLETON: If she can feel so deeply, disguises are no longer necessary. My real name is Montague, the husband of the lady whom you mention!

CAMDEN: Good heavens! What a discovery!

RAMBLETON: Having reason to call in question the tenderness of my wife, I meant this very evening to have learned her sentiments, under a disguise which should have veiled me from her knowledge; and even now I must insist on being myself the bearer of the tidings of my return. In her emotions I mean to read my fate.

CAMDEN: Upon the truth and firm affection of Mrs. Montague, I'd stake my hopes of happiness.

RAMBLETON: With the good leave of this most honorable committee, we go to make the experiment.

FIRST MEMBER: We can no longer doubt.

SECOND MEMBER: Or if we do, these gentlemen will become responsible.

CAMDEN: Most certainly. What say you, Stanhope?

STANHOPE: Ah, to the utmost farthing I can call my own! (COMMITTEE *rises. All exit.*)

SCENE: A mountain and adjacent wood. Enter VANSITTART *and* MRS.
VANSITTART, *with* SERVANTS, MRS. VANSITTART *weary.*

MRS. VANSITTART: Oh! I cannot go another step. Was ever woman
so completely fatigued? This wood will clandictedly conceal us. It would
not be doing the thing jonteelly to go any further tonight.

VANSITTART: Shenteelly! Why, who ever thought of shenteelly, at
this present time? Come along, vife—come along, Torothy, I say. (*He pulls
her after him.*)

MRS. VANSITTART: (*Struggling*). Dear Mr. Vansittart, you have no
alegunt idears.

VANSITTART: Elegant itears! Cot a' mercy! Torothy, you vould
provoke a saint!

MRS. VANSITTART: I will not proceed. I insist in sitting down.
(*They lay down their booty, and seat themselves.*)

VANSITTART: Vell, if you must pe opeyt, you must; put vife, vife, I
tell you no coot vill come of our expetition.

Enter PATRICK, OFFICER, *and* SOLDIERS, *in different directions.* (*They
all rise up, shriek, and endeavor to make their escape, but are severally seized
by their pursuers.* VANSITTART *falls flat on his face and roars tremendously.*
PATRICK *raises him.*)

VANSITTART: Oh, tear, plesset Mr. Patrick! I have creat occasions
for mercy at this present time, ant so, if you vill pe so coot as to parton me,
I vill take my piple oath that I vill never commit another roppery, as long
as I to live in this here vorlt.

PATRICK: Why, look'ye, my dear, it's none of my affair, d'ye see; but,
as you are taken prisoner, or the like of that, my shelf shall be after making
a promise that if ye cry *pecavia*[25], Mr. Rambleton shall never knock your
words down your throat. He never bodders a poor fellow who can't help
himshelf, honey.

MRS. VANSITTART: What's that you say, husband? I desire you
would behave jonteelly. I say it is an alegunt thing to take the property of
a vile Tory, and our country will thank us for it.

VANSITTART: Holt your tongue, Torothy. Holt your vicket tongue,
I say.

PATRICK: Ow, lave off your palavering, woman! You had better be
after coming along. Ow! I wish I had the white boys here, for your sake.

---

[25]Cry peccavi, i.e., confess guilt.

I would have you fairly trounced, so I would, and after that you might be carried before the justice. But humsomever, d'ye see, these same goods are all Master Rambleton's; and so, Master Tipstaff, you may do your juty again, if you plase.
(*Exit, with* OFFICER *and* SOLDIERS, *bearing the booty, and pushing the delinquents before them.*)

SCENE: A parlor in MRS. MONTAGUE's *house. Enter* HARRIOT *and* EMILY.

HARRIOT: My mamma, thank heaven, has reasoned herself into a degree of composure.

Enter MR. RAMBLETON, MAJOR CAMDEN, STANHOPE SENIOR, *and* STANHOPE.

CAMDEN: Miss Montague, this stranger (RAMBLETON *bows.*) has some knowledge of the picture which he will communicate only to your mother.
HARRIOT: I will inform my mamma immediately, sir. (*Exit* HARRIOT, *accompanied by* EMILY.)
RAMBLETON: Exquisite beauty! A perfect transcript of her mother! It was with difficulty I could forbear folding her to my bosom.
STANHOPE: Miss Montague's mind is a fit accompaniment for her exterior. It is strange, sir, (*Speaking to his father.*) that you should so immediately recognize Mr. Rambleton.
STANHOPE SENIOR: Body on me, why he was my old school-fellow! Ah, and a musical boy he was, too. Why, neighbor Montague, my name is not Stanhope if I do not mightily rejoice to see thee.

Enter MRS. MONTAGUE, *led by* HARRIOT *and* EMILY.

MRS. MONTAGUE: (*She starts back, draws away her hands, clasps them in an ecstasy of joy, and exclaims.*) Oh, all ye saints and angels! It is my husband! My long lost, highly injured, and dear, lamented husband! (*Rushing forward, she is on the point of falling, but is saved in the arms of* RAMBLETON.)
RAMBLETON: Oh, my Louisa, this one luxurious moment is a vast, an ample compensation for every evil which I ever suffered!
MRS. MONTAGUE: (*Kneeling*). Can you forgive me, Edward? My heart was never in fault. Each day since your departure has been marked by suffering, and every passing hour hath witnessed my regrets!

RAMBLETON: (*Raising her*). No more, my love. I have been too severe! But rigid honor demanded much, and I was not apprised how deeply you were wounded! (MRS. MONTAGUE *leans on* EMILY. HARRIOT *comes forward and kneels.*)

HARRIOT: And is there yet in store for Harriot Montague a father's benediction?

RAMBLETON: (*Clasping her to his bosom*). Come, my sweet cherub, thy father's heart is open to receive thee, and thou art far dearer to his soul than the lifeblood which warms him to existence.

MRS. MONTAGUE: Edward, one fond impatient question yet trembles on my tongue. Our son—

RAMBLETON: Loved Louisa, he is doubly yours, by virtue and by nature! Camden, come to my bosom! My love, behold our son!

CAMDEN: What say you, sir?

MRS. MONTAGUE: Harry Camden? Astonishing!

RAMBLETON: Yes, my soul's treasure. Behold the boy whom you so oft have pressed to that maternal bosom! Ere I became a voluntary exile, sojourning in Virginia, I left our son with Mr. Camden, a man in whom my soul confided. And 'twas from me, my son, that your supposed father received the letters that placed you in the military line.

CAMDEN: I do remember something of mystery about those letters; and with duteous veneration I kneel to such a father. (*Kneels.*)

RAMBLETON: Rise, my brave boy. Cato himself might glory in such a son!

CAMDEN: (*Bowing on the hand of* MRS. MONTAGUE). Madam, I tender never-ending duty! My elevation shall be marked by filial affection!

MRS. MONTAGUE: Harry, no words can speak the strong sensations which mingle in my bosom!

CAMDEN: Sister. . . . (*To* HARRIOT.) Thou art now everything a fond, transported brother can desire.

HARRIOT: I glory in my brother, sir.

STANHOPE SENIOR: A good, musical discovery this! (*Aside.*) And may I never dance at Alberto's wedding, if I do not think it is best to strike while the iron is hot. (*To* RAMBLETON.) My son, neighbor, has, I assure you, a very warm heart for Miss Harriot; and I cannot but hope that you will not stand in the way of the young people.

RAMBLETON: It shall be my care to break no tender ties, sir. If he wins my daughter's love, he shall have my approbation.

STANHOPE: To gain that blissful summit, my most arduous efforts shall not be wanting.

CAMDEN: (*Introducing* EMILY LOVEGROVE). Your beauteous niece, Miss Lovegrove, sir, to whose superior virtues your son would fain do justice.

RAMBLETON: (*Taking the hand of* EMILY). I understand you, Harry, but what says our daughter Emily?

EMILY: That while she blesses heaven for your return, she marks, with glowing admiration, your brave, heroic son.

RAMBLETON: Well said, my good girl! I congratulate you, Harry! A father's approbation shall not be wanting to crown the wishes of his children.

CAMDEN: (*Bowing impassioned on the hand of* EMILY). Now I am truly blest!

HARRIOT: (*Addressing her mother*). How is my dear and tender mother?

MRS. MONTAGUE: Ah, my daughter, I shudder at the precipice on which I stood! Had the marriage I so ardently desired taken place— Why, my Edward, our children have been on the point of exchanging the nuptial vow! A brother and a sister wedded! How wide the evils which, but for interposing heaven, my fatal indiscretion might have originated!

RAMBLETON: Forget them, dear Louisa, and hail thy opening prospects! Now Rambleton no more—thy Edward Montague—thy Traveller Returned, wedded to love and thee.

MRS. MONTAGUE: My enraptured spirit lowly prostrates to Edward and to heaven.

HARRIOT: This evening, sir, we had devoted to a private party—lovers of mirth, who dance away the hours—girls, like thy Harriot and her chosen friends. Even now, they grace the ballroom, glad at thy return; and, sure, convivial joys should mark this happy era!

RAMBLETON: Thank you, sweet cherub! Quick, bid the dancers enter.

(*Music plays. Scene draws and discovers the company, which immediately joins in the dance, after which the curtain drops.*)

END OF THE COMEDY

THE FEMALE ENTHUSIAST:

A Tragedy in Five Acts

Sarah Pogson[1]

1807

Charleston: Printed for the author, by J. Hoff, No. 6 Broad-Street

---

[1]Later Sarah Pogson Smith; sometimes listed as Sarah Smith Pogson.

Characters

Corday, father of Charlotte and Henry
Duval, father of Estelle
Marat
Chabot, friend of Marat
Henry, son of Corday
Belcour, Henry's friend
De Vernueil, engaged to Charlotte
Le Brun, formerly Henry's tutor, much attached to him
Old Bertrand, a blind cottager
Little boys, Bertrand's grandchildren
Jaques, Henry's servant

Charlotte Corday
Estelle
Susette, Bertrand's granddaughter
Annette, Charlotte's maid

Officers, Soldiers, Guards, Mob

Scene: *Sometimes at Caen; sometimes Paris.*

ACT I

The garden of CORDAY's *house.   Enter* JAQUES *in a soldier's undress
uniform, a cockade in his hat, a small bird cage in his hand with a bird in
it.   Sun rises.*

JAQUES: Where is Annette? She wakes not with the lark
To meet me, and how many miles I've been
To get this little bird for her. (*Looks at the bird.*)
                    When I'm gone,
Remind her of poor Jaques; but I think Annette
Cannot forget me. She often tells me so,
And then she says she hates this fine cockade! Strange,
For 'tis my pride—and though I love her well,
Can't consent to let another wear it;
Cannot stay behind my brave young master.
No—if he should lead me to the world's end—

It never shall be said Jaques deserted,
Even for the love of pretty Annette
Or the dread certainty of a bullet.
Where is she? Only one more morning left,
And yet not here! She thinks I'm not returned;
I'll go and place this songster at her window. (*Goes off.*)

Enter CHARLOTTE. *She walks thoughtfully across the stage.*

CHARLOTTE: Pure and refreshing is the morning air,
And sweet the melody of birds. My voice
Responds not now to the cheerful chorus;
Its only breathing is a fond adieu
To every dear and cherished object!
Oh, could the happy time again return
When blooming nature, all attractive, was
"The world's first spring"[2] to my delighted eyes.
Abroad creation charmed. Its wondrous beauty
Wrapped every sense; and while I gazed and thought,
Adoring praise sprung from my soul to that
Creative Power who placed me in a world
So fair—so rich in all that could delight!
Had any voice then sounded in my ear,
That 'midst this scene of harmony divine,
Vice poisoned bliss; wickedness was sanctioned;
That cruel man destroyed without offense
His fellow creature man, I should have turned
Incredulous away, and to my home's
Dear circle pointed. There simplicity
Had imaged the true picture of mankind. (*Pauses.*)

Re-enter JAQUES, *takes off his hat.*

JAQUES: My mistress rises with the sun's first beam,
But she has bent too low o'er some sweet flower;
I see a glistening dew drop on her cheek.
CHARLOTTE: Alas, Jaques, it is a *tear* of anguish.
JAQUES: Tears, my young lady? Oh, let those sorrow
Who have some crime to mourn! Thy gentle heart

---

[2]No source is given for this quotation.

Should rejoice in gladness, for it is kind,
And ever feels for poor folks when they suffer.
    CHARLOTTE: Too sensibly it feels for its own peace.
    JAQUES: Ah, were the Chevalier de Vernueil here,
Instead of Jaques, those tears had changed to smiles.
But duty called him hence, as now it does
Him, who soon will prove as brave a soldier. (*Adjusts himself.*)
Ah, ma'mselle, were the Chevalier Henry
To see those tears, perhaps a soldier's eye,
Which still is moistened by the dews of nature,
Would glisten also. And maybe his kind breast
Might grieve so much to see thee sad that he
Would be too loath to go—though duty calls.
(*Drum beats at a distance.*)
Hark! I must to mine. (JAQUES *bows hastily and goes off.*)
    CHARLOTTE: Had duty never called De Vernueil hence,
Here had I stayed in peaceful ignorance—
That duty which led me first to ask of wars,
And governments, and other scenes than those
Enfolding sweet domestic harmony.
Then to a wider field my views were opened.
Simplicity retired, but my heart throbbed
With keenest sensibility—alive
To virtue and humanity. Doth it not
Loathe a foe to either—mourn that on earth
Such foes exist, to wound mankind's repose?
Repose? If that were all! But oppression
Stalks abroad, and stains even the peaceful
Paths of life with blood! Merciless ferocity
Sways, with an uncontrolled dominion!
A monster spreads destruction! And while he
Desolates, calls out aloud, "'Tis liberty"!
Why do his black deeds remain unpunished?
Is there not one avenging hand to strike?

Enter ESTELLE.

    ESTELLE: Charlotte! Why this trembling agitation?
Oh, tell me, what alarms? What hast thou seen,
Or heard, or thought to fix an impression
So very strong on that dear countenance?
    CHARLOTTE: Oh, my Estelle! Do not ask.

(*Puts her hand to her heart.*) Here swells. . .what
Even the disclosing tongue of friendship
Must conceal. A foreign sentiment is here—
Nor can the power of language speak its force!
    ESTELLE: (*Looks at her and pauses.*) What dost thou mean?
Give to my heart whatever dwells in thine.
    CHARLOTTE: Has thou not always shared my joys and griefs?
When childhood's sports amused our infant fancies,
And since, in riper years, my thoughts and hopes
Have to thy ear, Estelle, been all unfolded,
And must thou ask my confidence in vain?
Oh, do not press me now! Some other time. (*Falls on her neck.*)
    ESTELLE: Be it then some other time, my Charlotte.
Oh, could I see thy cheerful looks return!
Why this deep dejection? De Vernueil lives,
And fair renown approves his gallant name.
Let then the youthful bosom's transport hope
Again resume its power! De Vernueil
Will return in safety to his Charlotte.
Oh, then, once more let smiles adorn thy face;
In them thy venerable father lives.
Soon, on thy tenderness a double claim
Will spring, for Henry must, alas, be gone.
    CHARLOTTE: The chord of harmony is broke forever.
Since the blest spirit of my mother fled
To join the blissful choristers of heaven,
Peace fled with her—and discord sprang in France.
Ah, Estelle, where are our transient pleasures?
Too pure to last, they all departed with her.
Changed is the face of all things in our country.
One universal overthrow of peace—
Proved from the glittering palace to the cot;
The hamlet totters, and the palace falls.
The private bosom from the public chaos
Convulsive rends, while dearest ties are torn.
Thus, my loved father loses, gem by gem,
Of all his heart's possessions. Henry goes,
And I— Ah! Like a vision of the night,
Bless his glad eyes a little space, and vanish!
    ESTELLE: Charlotte, art thou ill?

Enter ANNETTE *with a basket on her arm.*

ANNETTE: Madam, I've prepared
Everything ordered for the cottage—
    CHARLOTTE: Come, let us walk. Old Bertrand's children will
Enjoy this treat, and their pleased looks disperse
The heaviness that weighs my spirits down. (*They exit.*)

Enter HENRY.

    HENRY: The time draws near when I must quit these scenes—
These native scenes, this dear and happy home—
To join the standard of bright liberty—
High-sounding word, filling each warm breast
With sacred ardor's animating power.
Each eye, each tongue must speak in its defense;
Each arm extend to scatter wide its foes.
Yet, would I serve it in another field
Than that of carnage. But I will obey
The wishes of the tenderest father—
May he not stand in need of my support!
My Charlotte's gentle assiduities,
With tenfold kindness, will supply my place.
But, oh, she droops! That sweet vivacity,
Delighting all, gives place to deepest gloom.
In vain the ray of cheerfulness would pierce
This cloud of care—its beams, alas, too faint!
Not e'en the sympathy of those she loves
Dispels the secret gathering of thought.
Even Estelle's friendship's unavailing!
Estelle's friendship? Rich—rich possession—
Balm for all anguish—oh, transporting thought!
Is not that friendship mine? Yet more—her love!
How shall I go? How tear myself away?
My truant thoughts would wander to these scenes;
Glory have but half a willing votary.

Enter BELCOUR.

    BELCOUR: Thy meditation's serious, Henry.
One might suppose thou had'st just cheated
Thy reverend confessor, keeping back
Some great and grievous sin, which now torments
For being left without companions.

Thine is the first sad countenance I've met.
Where is the *warrior's* animated glow?
How many gallant youths in pride of heart
Would wear thy envied crest with ecstasy!
For shame! Fire at the mention of tomorrow,
When thou wilt head these candidates for fame—
These youthful patriots lead to victory!
Could friendship envy—by all that's sacred,
I should envy thee such early honors.
    HENRY: Could those, my friend, who at this moment wish
My lot was theirs—if any such there are—
Of my heart's feelings take a real view,
I think, indeed, they would reject the change;
For, oh, my Belcour, I am not happy!
    BELCOUR: And why not happy, Henry? What has chilled
Thy glowing ardor and eye-speaking joy?
Sure thou'rt not a school boy, whining to stay
A little longer by thy father's side,
When all thy comrades burn to try the field?
    HENRY: They no doubt consider me devoted
To the pursuit of arms and fair renown.
They know not that the bias of my mind
Fondly inclines to sweet domestic life;
But principle, love of true liberty,
And my torn country's welfare all prompt me
To every action that may evince
My zeal for each. Reproach would wound my breast
Worse than a thousand swords, if it could shrink
From any danger which the profession
My father has chosen for me can present.
Belcour, I could die to serve my country!
And, had my years permitted, would have been
Among the first brave repellers of its
Foreign enemies. My day is now come
To meet our foes, and my hope is glory!
Yet, were I left a choice, I should prefer
Glory of another kind—that renown
Not gained 'midst battles, blood, and victories!
Thou and I, Belcour, should have changed fortunes.
    BELCOUR: So much—so plain—thou never said'st before;
Yet what avails it now? The line is traced.
The road to laureled honor courts thy step.

And when we parted, fame was thy mistress.
HENRY: Ha! My bosom had not then unfolded
All its interests to their full extent.
But I will give thee its most secret thoughts.
True, I could face a cannon undismayed;
Yet I do not desire the dangerous honor,
And would rather be the generous statesman
Planning the happiness, prosperity,
And peace of my countrymen than leading
To battle—even like a Julius Caesar!
Could I so far be dictator, as to
Re-establish tranquility and heal
The wounds of bleeding France—by foreign swords
Less injured than by internal discord—
Remove those vultures who devour our peace,
Then should I, indeed, attain true glory.
But enough. My destiny is fixed.
BELCOUR: That destiny will lead to fairest honors.
Thy father's patriotic breast warms with
The glowing hope of seeing thee a soldier
Well approved. Thou wilt not disappoint him.
HENRY: Various circumstances now combine
To break the feeble bond 'twixt me and arms.
Charlotte droops. Some anguish preys upon her.
My father marks it with concern, and though
He longs to see me head my brave companions,
Yet would postpone the day of separation.
Oh, Belcour, they both may need my support
When too far distant even to know it.
BELCOUR: Never, Henry, shall they want a friend.
A son—a brother—will thy Belcour be.
Let this suffice, and set thy mind at ease,
Secure in all that friendship has to offer.
HENRY: Best of friends! How deep my obligation.
BELCOUR: Name not obligation! Friends know it not.
To serve a friend is but to serve oneself.
Thy sister feels the absence of De Vernueil;
That intelligent countenance cannot
Conceal her bosom's fond anxiety.
But hope will again blossom on her cheek
And sparkle in her eye. De Vernueil will return,
And with him thy Charlotte's peace and happiness.

HENRY: And when will mine, Belcour? Oh, I have sought
This moment, when all my situation
Should be unfolded to that kind bosom!
Say wilt thou, then, increase my debt, and with
Another kindness swell my gratitude?
BELCOUR: Command me every way to serve thee.
Judge by thine own heart how willing mine is
To serve its friend. In turn I have somewhat
To communicate—so interesting,
So flattering to all my hopes of bliss
That thou wilt rejoice in my bright prospects.
But I am impatient. Speak, Henry,
Every wish, and be assured of my zeal.
HENRY: May all thy prospects be crowned with possession;
That generous mind never have to exert
Its manly strength in bearing up against
Misfortune's storms, blighting disappointment,
Or the pang of being separated
From all it fondly dotes on. Oh, Estelle! (BELCOUR *starts.*)

Enter CORDAY. *He advances, bows to* BELCOUR, *then puts his hand upon* HENRY'*s shoulder affectionately.*

CORDAY: Good morning, Belcour. Good morning, my son.
I must interrupt ye for a while—
Some business requires Henry's attention.
HENRY: For the present, adieu! I will return. (*Exit* CORDAY *and* HENRY. BELCOUR *stands in amazement, having scarcely noticed the salutation of* CORDAY. *He repeats the exclamation of* HENRY.)
BELCOUR: "Oh, Estelle"! What, Henry dote on Estelle?
It cannot, must not be. Henry, I dote—
All! All but this, of fortune and of fame,
I could yield to thee! But Estelle never!
She is entwined with every thought and nerve,
And I could as soon change the course of day's
Refulgent orb as remove from my hopes
Their brightest object—my adored Estelle!
Why did I not to Henry long ago
Declare my intentions? But there no blame
Attaches to my silence, more than his.
Alas! That hateful journey sealed my lips;
Nor would I trust my pen. He was doubtless

By the same cause restrained—our separation.
And thus, while gaining trash to fill my purse,
The nobler treasure of my heart is lost! (*Exits.*)

ACT II

Scene One

A wood. Enter CHARLOTTE *and* ANNETTE.

CHARLOTTE: Annette, why were my orders disobeyed?
ANNETTE: My mistress knows I never disobey.
Dumont promised to be here at this hour. (ANNETTE *goes towards the
road.* CHARLOTTE *walks backwards and forwards in expecting agitation.*
ANNETTE *returns.*)
ANNETTE: The chaise is now in sight, ma'mselle.
But I am a poor guard. The road is bad.
Would it not be better could Jaques—or—
CHARLOTTE: This time, Annette, I mean to go alone.
Return home, and remember the cottage;
Inform Estelle. If Colin is not better,
She will do all that's needful while I am gone.
ANNETTE: But, ma'mselle, is it safe to go alone?
CHARLOTTE: Why not, good girl? 'Tis but a little way.
Dumont is careful, and the road now good.
No clouds are threatening to obscure the day.
Go, Annette. Give this letter to Estelle. (*Gives a letter.* ANNETTE *takes
it with great surprise.*)
ANNETTE: Strange fears alarm me. Why? I cannot tell.
I don't know how to go. Why this letter?
Oh, pardon my boldness; but, dear ma'mselle,
Pray, oh, pray take me! I shall neither sleep,
Nor eat, nor drink for very anxiousness.
CHARLOTTE: Let no anxiety disturb thee, Annette.
Danger awaits me at a greater distance.
Leave me, kind Annette. I wish to be alone.
ANNETTE: Indeed, indeed, I cannot. Oh, take me!
CHARLOTTE: Do not thus distress me by persisting
To ask what I must refuse. Convince me
Of real affection by obedience.
I shall speedily return, when, Annette,

Thou wilt laugh at these unnecessary fears.

ANNETTE: Ah! Some evil will surely come of this. (*She looks mournfully at her mistress, then at the letter, and goes off slowly.*)

CHARLOTTE: (*After she walks about once or twice*).
Strong are thy claims, O nature! Now do I
Feel them with an iron force grasp my heart—
Unlike their former tender pressures but
As if some cruel power was tearing from
My bosom its *vitality*, while nature,
Unwilling to forego its long abode,
Struggles with rude, convulsing violence.
Let me, then, whisper that foul name: Marat,
And the last conflict end. The monster's name
Steals every thought, and female weakness flies.
With strength I'm armed, and mighty energy
To crush the murderer and defy the scaffold.
Let but the deed be done. For it, *I'll die.*
For it, I sacrifice—I quit—myself
And all the softness of a woman's name,
Leave a venerable, doting father!
But, ah! Might not the fangs of fierce Marat
Seize on his hoary locks? For who escapes?
May not my brother raise his arm in vain
To save his aged parent and himself?
And to the countless list of victims, add
Their precious lives? No! My hand shall save them.
The innocent again shall walk in safety.
Thousands shall bless the blow by which he falls.
(*Pauses.*) And when, again,
Fond parental arms with joy enfold me,
And love and friendship spring to meet my heart,
All—all my present feelings will be lost
In the tumultuous overflow of bliss.
But, ah! What keeps me longer here? I linger
Amidst these shades; to quit them seems as the soul
Forced from the clinging and reluctant body.
That bench, those trees are eloquent. De Vernueil,
My Estelle, Henry—there have we listened
To the pure converse of the purest minds. (*Thunder is heard.*)
Hark! I must no longer stay. Oh, farewell! (*Looks around.*)
On all the past, oblivion cast thy veil.
Let no fond recollections hold my thoughts

From vengeance and Marat. (*Exits.*)

Scene Two

In another part of the wood, a cottage. Before the door, SUSETTE *is sitting at work, with a* LITTLE BOY *resting his head on her lap.*

SUSETTE: Why do I wish to see Jaques here again?
For he never looks at simple Susette.
Oh! When I think he loves some blooming maid,
I wish there was no other maid but me!
And is he going, too, to fight and die,
Like my poor father, on the bloody field?
Why do men fight, and leave their peaceful homes,
When they can laugh, and work, and play, and sing,
And "make tomorrow happy as today"?[3]
Now all our village maidens sigh like me.
(JAQUES *and* ANNETTE *approach. He is supporting her tenderly.*)
How kind he looks. Why do I tremble so?
    ANNETTE: I feel quite faint.
    JAQUES: Lean upon me, Annette.
    SUSETTE: What has happened?
    ANNETTE: Oh! My ankle is sprained.
    SUSETTE: I have a remedy will soon give ease. (SUSETTE *takes the child in her arms.* JAQUES *seats* ANNETTE *and supports her.* SUSETTE *turns around at the door, looks at them, and exits with the child.*)
    JAQUES: I wish the accident had befallen me.
    ANNETTE: Yes, Jaques, if it would keep thee from the war.
I dread to think, tomorrow is the day
When from his Annette her dear Jaques must go.
The tears that come into my aching eyes
Quite dim my sight. And now this new distress—
My mistress gone. Oh, Jaques, where is she gone?
    JAQUES: Thou art made up of very fearfulness.
Where e'er thy gentle mistress is, she's safe.
I think it strange she should have gone alone;
But we are told that God protects the good.
And, as for me, why, ever think of Jaques

---

[3]No source is given for the quotation.

As a lad that seeks an halberd⁴—not death.
So, though I would surely scorn to run away,
I should not rush into the thickest battle.
For Annette's sake, Jaques will try to live.
I love thee, Annette, better than myself. (*As* JAQUES *speaks,* SUSETTE
enters and drops a bottle she held.)
    SUSETTE: Ah! How unlucky! It was all we had.
    JAQUES: Why, my pretty Susette, one would suppose
It was thy little heart that thou had'st broke.
    SUSETTE: (*Turning away from* JAQUES).
Is it not best to come into the house
And rest awhile upon my bed, Annette?
    ANNETTE: Oh, no! I have a letter to deliver,
And must now hasten home as speedily
As my lame steps can bear me.
    JAQUES: Adieu, Susette. (JAQUES *and* ANNETTE *exit slowly.*)
    SUSETTE: And what is this that swells within my heart?
I seem to hate Annette. Hate Annette?
What, when I am taught to love my enemies,
Shall I towards my friends with anger burn,
Because my fate is not so blest as hers?
Yet, I cannot bear to think Jaques loves her.
Oh! I will seek our curate, and confess
This great offense, and pray to be forgiven. (*Exits.*)

Scene Three

An apartment in CORDAY*'s house. Enter* ESTELLE.

    ESTELLE: Charlotte's deep inquietude alarms me.
While anxious for her repose, I almost
Forget my own distress, till solitude
Awakens it. Alas, what mingled sighs
From such contending feelings rend my heart.
Oh, my Henry! How shall I tell thee all?

Enter HENRY.

    HENRY: Oh, tell me, dearest Estelle, that I am

---

⁴Weapon.

As welcome to thy sight as thou to mine
Most precious. Let us prize each moment
Of happiness. Soon I must be absent
From the treasure of my soul, but like the
Veriest parsimonious miser, shall
Forever turn to it in anxious thought.

    ESTELLE: Happiness, Henry! Oh, 'tis a meteor—
A transient vision that eludes our grasp!
Even when we see it close within our reach,
It flits away and leaves us in pursuit.
Shall we, then, think to possess a reality
That exists not under Heaven?

    HENRY: Estelle!
Thy looks are chilling as indifference.
Thou did'st not meet me thus when last we met!
Then, as now, our approaching separation
Thou knewest, yet did'st look with other eyes.
Those lips spoke words of comfort—hope—and talked
Of happiness when Henry should return
And bring his laurels home, to change them for
A wreath of love entwining.

    ESTELLE: I have now no words of comfort; no hope to bid me
Smile, and think of thy return.

    HENRY: (*Much agitated*). In pity,
Estelle, explain. Art thou changed? My heart is
Pierced with doubt. Speak, am I not dear to thee?

    ESTELLE: Cruel question, so dear Henry, that next
To duty's claim, thyself—thy happiness—
Occupy my thoughts and hopes. Changed! Indifferent!
No, Henry, thy worth and generous affection
Will live, while I live, engraved on my heart
In lasting characters, through every change
And chance of this varying existence.
After this assurance, thou need'st not doubt
My faithful love. But an unlooked-for bar
To our future union interposes.
Even, should all thy sanguine prospects
Of a quick return meet with full success,
Thy hope to move my father in our favor
Will be vain.

    HENRY: Say not so. He shall consent.

    ESTELLE: Hear me with composure, and be assured.

HENRY: Heavens! This is torture! What will follow!
ESTELLE: What sometimes thou hast anticipated.
My father designs to establish me.
HENRY: Oh, stop! Thou wilt destroy me. Yet go on—
ESTELLE: If not more thyself, I dare not—will not.
Remember what I have so often vowed.
HENRY: Oh! It shall be a shield, defending me
From every wound thy father or the world
Can inflict. To know I live in thy esteem—
In thy affection—will make all evils light.
ESTELLE: My father put two letters in my hand:
One of them sought that hand; the other spoke
Immediate, unreserved compliance.
In agitation, I returned them both,
While in my looks he plainly read rejection.
With faltering timidity, I asked
If such an answer he indeed would send.
"Why not?" he sternly said; what objection
Could I in reason make to such a man
Every way unexceptionable?
Ah! Dear Henry! Belcour—
HENRY: (*In astonishment*). Belcour! Belcour!
Then happiness is indeed a vision!
Belcour my rival? Did that letter go?
ESTELLE: It did, for entreaties availed me not.
My tears fell on his hand, but did not soften
The inflexible purpose of his will.
I threw myself in anguish at his feet—
On the point to confess our attachment,
When, alas, the strong remembrance of his
Singular prejudice, so lately known—
His strange, solemn vow never to consent
To his daughter's marrying a soldier—
Suspended the words upon my lips, and
Clasping his hand, I could only breathe out,
"Oh! Do not, my Father, make me wretched."
But the letter went, and Belcour came.
HENRY: (*Walking about in great agitation*).
I dread thy father's obstinacy;
'Tis implacable and violent.
Estelle, thou hast never yet opposed it;
But is he right, even as a parent,

To force thee to accept of any man
Repugnant to thy own free will and choice?
But, oh how winning, how good is Belcour!
May not his worth erase my humbler merit?
    ESTELLE: My Henry's merit must secure my love.
    HENRY: Ah! Had Belcour known of my attachment,
And that it was returned—what had he done?
    ESTELLE: Resigned my hand to his deserving friend.
    HENRY: Sensible of thy father's prejudices,
He would never have resigned thee, knowing
A soldier's hand would be disdained by him.
Estelle, I abhor disobedience, but
I also despise narrow prejudice,
And hoped, till now, thy father might have been
Induced to overcome the force of his.
But, ah! The hope is void; he never will.
Such singularity is culpable,
And, in some instances, to oppose it
Cannot be deemed a breach of duty.
Are we to be thrown into a state
Inimical to our happiness?
And with the rod of prejudice be scourged?
Oh, no! Consent to be mine; let this hour
Unite our destiny, beyond the power
Of earthly authority to sever. (*Takes her hand.*)
Near the cloister's walls, I left old Ronville;
Let us hasten to him, for tomorrow
I must leave thee. No, I will not leave thee
Till thou art mine by every sacred tie.
    ESTELLE: Henry, forbear; yet let me once more say
The strongest earthly power shall not prevail
To make me break my plighted faith to thee.
I must not listen to thy fond request.
I must not marry with a father's curse!
Oh, leave me Henry, and employ thyself
In noblest acts of valor. We are young.
Go, convince my father that a soldier
Is worthy of his daughter, and his love.
    HENRY: A cruel prospect is painted for me,
In the dark coloring of disappointment.
Will then thy resolution support thee
Against the firm command of a parent?

Thou dost not love, Estelle. Such cold reasoning,
Such acquiescence to future changes
Ill accord with my feelings towards thee.
I dare not trust to the uncertain future;
But as thy will directs, so I must obey.
And thy stern father, too, will be obeyed.
This heart, that fondly sues, will cease to beat;
This ardent eye shall never more meet thine!
But Belcour's will; he, thy fond protector,
Shall strew thy path with flowers. I strew but thorns,
And thou art wise to choose the path without them.
(*Waves his hand, appears to be going.*)
    ESTELLE: Stay, too hasty young man. Stay, my Henry—
    HENRY: Forgive, my sweet Estelle, oh, forgive me.
Heaven knows, if I beheld one ray of hope,
I would not urge thee against thy duty;
But I am now, as certain thou wilt be
Compelled to marry Belcour, as if I—
    ESTELLE: Henry, hast thou no confidence in me?
Oh, persuade me not to do what will impose
Deep anguish, and indeed strew my path with thorns.
    HENRY: Cold prudence is thy only sentiment.
Farewell forever! (*As he is hurrying off, enter* ANNETTE.)
Why this intrusion?
    ANNETTE: Oh, sir! My mistress!
    ESTELLE: What of thy mistress?
    ANNETTE: Oh, ma'mselle, I've been everywhere to search.
At the cottage I thought to have found you.
But here's the letter; my mistress is gone—(*Gives the letter.*)
Whither I know not. (ESTELLE *reads, in great alarm.*)
    HENRY: Gone? What does this mean?
    ESTELLE: Henry, what will become of thy sister?
(*Gives him the letter; he reads.*)
How long, good girl, since thy mistress went?
    ANNETTE: A great while, ma'mselle. I should have been
Here long ago but for an ugly accident;
But the pain I feel is nothing, to that
In my heart. Oh! Where is my mistress gone?
    ESTELLE: Go, Annette. Thy mistress will soon return.
(ANNETTE *limps off.*)

HENRY: This is wonderful[5]! Charlotte, thou art lost.
Enthusiastic[6] girl, these sentiments
Are worthy of a Roman, yet are vain.
Oh, could I save thee! But take the vengeance
Thy grieved spirit meditates—how grateful
To my soul. Life is now of no value,
But as a barrier 'twixt thee and death—
For death awaits thy deed. But I will strive
To save her. Now I no longer persist
In my request, oh my adored Estelle.
I would not leave thee a mourning bride. No,
Forget me, and obey thy father's will.
Soon I shall overtake my Charlotte,
And the sure weapon of destruction
Shall be guided by a stronger hand.
Oh, Estelle! Bid me a last adieu!
Bless me with one more kind look of love.
    ESTELLE: Ah, Henry, I am indeed overcome!
These circumstances weigh far heavier
Than all thy fond and pleading arguments.
I see thy rash design. Impetuous,
Thou wilt plunge thyself into destruction—
Not save thy sister. I—I will consent
To blend my life with thine this hour, Henry.
Then thou wilt endeavor to preserve it.
    HENRY: Thus only could'st thou save me and thy friend.
Hasten, my love. Oh, Estelle, let us fly!

As he is leading her off, enter BELCOUR.

    BELCOUR: Ha! Henry! Proceed not, sir! That lady—
    HENRY: (*As he turns his head*).
I have much to say; meet me at the hotel. (*Exit* HENRY *and* ESTELLE.)
    BELCOUR: Hold, Henry! (BELCOUR *rushes on after them. As he is going out, enter* LE BRUN, *who gently takes his arm.* BELCOUR *turns round angrily.*)
    BELCOUR: Villain, whence this insolence?
Did thy master bid thee watch me? Coward—

---

[5]Amazing.
[6]Fanatical.

LE BRUN: Pardon me sir, but what hath Henry done?
How long since in thine eye he looked a coward?
BELCOUR: Away! By heaven, he answers with his life
For this base conduct. Estelle! Oh, Estelle! (BELCOUR *again endeavors to pass.* LE BRUN *interposes himself.*)
LE BRUN: While with passion wild, I must detain thee.
Why should'st thou seek the life of such a friend?
A duel was the first of my errors.
Oh, spare thyself remorse and endless woe!
BELCOUR: Spare thy lectures, old man. Leave me, leave me.
LE BRUN: Never shalt thou pass to injure Henry.
BELCOUR: Not another moment dare to keep me. (BELCOUR *pushes* LE BRUN *from him and exits.*)
LE BRUN: Some demon seems to hover over France,
Infusing rancor in the gentlest breasts.
World of tribulation, I'm weary of thee.
Thy storms destroy; thy calms are voids we fly from.
Nothing satisfies the ever-restless soul:
It boils, or stagnates in cold apathy.
Few, few, blessed spirits taste the balmy sweets
Of that supreme and only true delight
Springing from a mind well regulated—
Enjoying wisely, feeling sensibly,
Yet commanding those tempestuous passions
That whirl the blood in eddies of distraction. (*Exits.*)

ACT III

Scene One

MARAT *discovered, sitting meanly dressed with his hat on, surrounded by a motley crew.* CHABOT *at his right hand.* MARAT *rises and comes forward.*

MARAT: Citizens! These difficulties shall cease,
And the head of each base conspirator—
Each foe to liberty and equality
Shall roll beneath us, an abject football.
My countrymen, enlightened sons of France:
Ye—ye, who comprehend *true* freedom!
Boldly trample on the groveling hearts

Of those who still adhere to kings—and priests.
Free as the air, and equal as its surface,
Citizens! Patriots! Spill your bravest blood;
Raise high the pile of slaughtered sycophants!
Exterminate all those who dare presume
To check this radiant dawn of liberty,
Which soon shall blaze a full meridian sun
Too bright for despots and their cringing slaves
To look on! Dazzled by its brilliancy,
Unable to behold the great, resplendent,
Full-orbed, mighty, glorious, liberty,
Their narrow hearts will sink within their breasts
Ignobly chained to proud nobility—
To treacherous crowns—and wily priestcraft!
Not daring to complain—much less redress
The most oppressive burdens—meanly they
Drag on existence in debasing bonds—
In bonds which ye great, deserving Frenchmen
Have so gloriously burst asunder.
By yourselves ye are emancipated.
Live! Live to triumph in the enjoyment
Of reason and its rights. Never suffer
Those dear rights again to be invaded.
Let no ambitious, traitorous, haughty despot
Chain your minds or bodies more—but be free!
Frenchmen! Countrymen! My brethren! Be free.
Stain your swords with the purple tide flowing
From dying conspirators. Let the foes
Of our liberty bleed. They are vipers.
Let not bread which should nourish true Frenchmen
Be wasted on them! No! Destroy—destroy!
Justice calls aloud, destroy! Well ye know
Whose blood to spill—and whose to spare—without
The tedious mockeries of courts and judges.
Judge for yourselves—and quickly execute.

Enter a MAN *who whispers to* MARAT. MARAT *replies aloud.*

MARAT: Tell the person business detained me.
I received her note, and will speak with her. (*Exit* MAN.)
Citizens! A person waits, well informed
Of circumstances highly important.

Delay is ever dangerous, and now
It would be culpable; therefore, I go
To hear what I trust will aid our cause.
My whole ambition is to serve it
With all my powers of mind and body.
This arm will not spare one aristocrat.
This breast harbors eternal enmity
To each opposer of its sentiments—
The sentiments of pure republicanism—
While ardor in its cause gives force and tone
To all my energies—even to my steps.
I feel a demigod— (*Struts about.*) How ennobled
By the boundless confidence of such men— (*Points to them.*)
Fellow citizens! I live to serve you. (*Exit* MARAT.)
    CHABOT: (*Advances*). We, to support the champion of freedom,
And unanimous in defense of him—
We swear to stand or fall with great Marat
The people's friend. (*Exit all.*)

Scene Two

CHARLOTTE *discovered in an antechamber.*

    CHARLOTTE: A few short moments, and his doom is fixed.
My heart that sickened if an insect died,
My bosom nursed in softest tenderness
Burn to destroy—feel a powerful impulse
Strengthening every nerve, compressing
Every thought to one keen point—revenge!
Enthusiastic fervor bears me on,
And gentler passions fly before its power!
No other hand will rise. No other eye
Will throw death's fiat on the subtle serpent.
No more shall guileless innocence be stung
By his envenomed tongue and thirst of blood;
Nor shall those brave men his savage sword condemns
Add to the mound of butchered victims.
Oh, no! No! No! He dies.

Scene Three

Back scene opens to discover MARAT *in his chamber, dressed in a loose*

bathing gown and slippers. At the farthest end of the room stands his bath.
MARAT *comes forward.*

MARAT: I have too long detained thee, young woman.
Now let me have the promised information.
    CHARLOTTE: Citizen, my errand is important.
Thy civism[7] leads thee to destroy whatever
Is prejudicial to *true* liberty,
And to the welfare of France. I am come
To point out the *deadliest* foe to *both*,
And a sure way to rid our country of him.
(Gives a packet. MARAT prepares to open it.)
Here in this packet is full information
Of a well planned and deep conspiracy;
But ere thou dost examine the contents,
Suffer me to ask, what will be the fate
Of those conspirators who fled to Normandy,[8]
And of such people as conceal the traitors—
Adopting, too, their dangerous opinions,
Which threaten ruin to the noble cause
Espoused by every true-born son of freedom?
    MARAT: Ha! Would'st thou, then, know what will be their fate?
I tell thee, girl, that they, and many more
Who think themselves secure—their heads quite safe,
Will feel the sharp axe of the guillotine.
(He looks down on the packet to open it.)
    CHARLOTTE: First—feel this sharper weapon! Die, monster!
(Stabs him. MARAT falls.) There is an end to thy destructive course!
Thou *ignis fatuus*[9] that deceived the simple;
Murderer of prisoners—of priests defenseless—
Of helpless women—die! The innocent
Shall live. Now art thou death's prisoner.

    MARAT: In sin's lowest depths, alas, I perish!
Thy friends, young woman, are too well avenged.
How did'st thou find this courage? Oh, great God!
God? Ha! That sacred name should not proceed
From my polluted lips. I dare not pray;

---

[7]Devotion to the French Revolution.
[8]A group of Girondists, political foes of Marat.
[9]Delusion.

My prayers would be but impious mockery.
The sighs of others never reached my ear;
Can those from my remorseless heart e'er reach
The mighty throne omnipotent? Oh! Oh! (*Groans loudly.*)

CHABOT *enters. He starts, then rushes up to* MARAT, *whom he supports.*

MARAT: (*Faintly*). Is it thou, Chabot? Ah! Could I but live—
But no, I die—I die. The light recedes.
My eyes are closing. . .open! Open them! (*In agony.*)
Oh, save me from that yawning gulf! Save me!
Oh! Save me! Save— (*Springs, convulsed, from the support of* CHABOT *and
dies.* CHABOT *seizes the poignard and grasps the arm of* CHARLOTTE
fiercely. She looks composedly at him.)
    CHABOT: Girl! What hast thou done? Did madness seize thee?
Tremble for the consequence of this crime.
A public expiation waits the deed;
Or my hand should now destroy, with the same
Destructive weapon, so well directed.
What instigated thee to such an act? (*Lets her go, and drops the poignard.*)
    CHARLOTTE: The cause of virtue. The world contained not,
In all its wide circumference, so black
A traitor to its peace and liberty
As base Marat. My soul is satisfied.
A woman's arm, when nerved in such a cause,
Is as the arm of the avenging angel.
Think not I am a foe to liberty!
My father is a real patriot;
My brother, at this moment, joins the friends,
Soldiers of liberty! Not assassins.
They should sink beside that fallen enemy
To all but anarchy and cruelty. (*Points to* MARAT.)
To know that, by his death, thousands are free
Fully repays the danger I incur!
Lead me to prison, if thy conscience bids;
But if one spark of heavenly liberty—
Of generous love towards thy country—
Glows within that bosom, then wilt thou say
Depart in safety. But I see thy purpose.
    CHABOT: Yes, I'll bid thee depart— Ho! Assistance!
(*Enter several* MEN.) To prison with her—where this heroism
Will soon be humbled, and that beautiful head

Bend lower than it deigns to do at present.
Away with her! (*They exit.*)

Scene Four

An apartment in DUVAL's *house.* DUVAL *is seated, looking over the
contents of a pocketbook. Enter* ESTELLE. *He looks at her.*

DUVAL: Still this dejected look, my dear Estelle?
I fear thy tender health will suffer, child.
Remember, while we sympathize with others,
Their sorrows must not leave too deep a trace,
Must not be made entirely our own.
But I will say no more; the subject wounds.
    ESTELLE: Alas! It does—
    DUVAL: And where we cannot heal,
Discussion only gives a keener pang.
'Tis not all anguish that can be partaken.
Yet, would thy father take thy every grief,
And bid that mouth forever wear a smile. (*Embraces her.*)
    ESTELLE: My kind—my dear Father!
    DUVAL: Tell me, my child,
Hast thou considered the request I made—
With deep attention weighed the matter well?
Thou know'st I cannot bear opposition.
'Twas wrong to set thy father's will at naught.
Thou canst not disappoint his darling hope.
    ESTELLE: Disappoint thy darling hope, my Father? (*In agitation.*)
    DUVAL: That were impossible. It was surprise:
Thou had'st not thought of leaving me, Estelle.
But, alas, I am in the vale of years;
Thy mother is no more—and heaven knows
That thou, my child, wilt need the fostering care
Of one whose love can ward off every ill.
Single—exposed! What—what might be thy fate
Amidst these desolating, factious times,
Sparing nor age nor sex? Ah! When I'm gone,
Virtue will be thy only legacy;
And that, if unprotected, often falls
A victim to designing villainy;
Or, vainly struggling against the dark stream
Of poverty, is overwhelmed and sinks.

ESTELLE: Oh, far, far distant be the mournful day
That deprives me of so dear a parent!
But, my Father, when it pleases *Him* who gives,
And who resumes, to take thy precious life,
Paint not the future in so deep a shade.
Virtuous industry, my dearest sir,
Is always rewarded with competence.[10]
　DUVAL: There *is* a land where such indeed's the case—
Not *thine*, my child. It is America.
There, in the conjugal or single state—
In affluence or pale-cheeked poverty—
Each female who respects herself is safe.
Each walks the path of life secure from insult,
As strongly guarded by a virtuous mind
As she who's in a gilded chariot borne,
Surrounded by an host of glittering arms.
But here, the mind adorned with every grace,
Compelled to stoop and share the body's toil,
In gloomy, isolated poverty,
Too often droops—or if it makes a stand,
Its tones are blunted by adversity.
And though it springs to pierce this earthly veil,
And catch a vision of its future state,
Where virtue will surely be rewarded
And patient merit there receive its prize;
Yet, in this life, acts an imperfect part,
Unlike the scene of wedded excellence.
Fulfilling woman's dear and sacred duties,
Scattering sweets to all within its influence,
It shines the brightest gem in nature's works.
Then, let this lovely part be thine, Estelle.
Oh, make thy own happiness—and Belcour's!
　ESTELLE: Forgive me, sir, but Belcour's happiness
Can never blend with mine. Oh, forgive me!
Look not so sternly.
　DUVAL:　　　What, still reject him?
Ungrateful girl! Know I will be obeyed.
Some puppy, sure, hath pleased thy silly eye;
Some gaudy, trifling soldier stole thy heart.

---

[10]A modest livelihood.

ESTELLE: Are there, then, no good men, or brave, or great
Among our country's valiant defenders?
From whence arose so strong a prejudice?
    DUVAL: I would sooner follow thee to thy grave,
Than ever see thee, child, a soldier's wife.
Tinsel dolls, or savages—I hate them.
Even the very best I ever knew,
De Vernueil, I cannot entirely approve.
    ESTELLE: Where is there a fault in his noble nature?
    DUVAL: What, hath he not in his letters said
That Beaurepere acted a great man's part
By terminating his own existence
When unable, at the siege of Verdun,
To make his gallant defense successful?
Soldiers used to be Christians; not so now.
They cease to consider religious duties,
And much I fear that even De Vernueil
Would desert the post assigned him on earth,
Braving the danger of offended heaven,
Than endure disgrace before his fellow man,
Or bear the slighter evils that assail.
But, I hear Belcour. Be wise and happy.
I have promised thy hand; refuse it not,
Or my blessing is refused forever. (*Exit* DUVAL.)

Enter BELCOUR.

    BELCOUR: Pardon, if I intrude. Think not, Estelle,
Presumption brings me here. 'Tis sympathy.
We feel alike the sorrows of our friends,
With deep anxiety. Yet, let us hope.
    ESTELLE: A succession of painful circumstances
Depress me almost beyond the reach of hope.
    BELCOUR: Estelle, I cannot bear to see thee thus.
Oh, how willingly would I endure the
Weight of anguish that now oppresses thee!
    ESTELLE: If thou dost, indeed, feel for my distress,
Then leave me, I beseech thee.
    BELCOUR: First, hear me.
With thy father's approbation I am come.
Oh, give me but the most distant hope, Estelle,
And I will sigh a thousand miles away,

Till the blest hour when thou shall say return.
ESTELLE: Desist, for I can never bid thee hope.
If thou dost love me, create my happiness.
BELCOUR: If I love thee? Oh, thou more precious far
Than even love's most eloquent language
Could portray, know that my fate hangs on thee,
My all of happiness! Oh, blast[11] not, then,
Its blooming hopes forever! (*Kneels.*)
ESTELLE: Rise, Belcour.
For an instant I will not deceive thee.
No length of time can change my sentiments.
BELCOUR: (*Rises in anger*).
I am despised—because thou lov'st another. (*Turns away.*)
DUVAL: Ha! Ungrateful girl, thou shalt not treat him thus.
Hence with this disobedience! Give thy hand. (*Forcibly takes her hand.*)
ESTELLE: (*Looks mournfully at her father*).
No, my Father. It cannot, cannot be.
BELCOUR: Estelle, never will I cause thy misery.
ESTELLE: I am ill. Oh, suffer me to withdraw! (DUVAL *lets her hand
fall. She retires.*)
BELCOUR: Forbear all violence. To take an hand
Without an heart would bring me wretchedness.
Time in my favor may produce a change.
DUVAL: Time, sir? 'Tis time she should be dutiful;
But this hated, monstrous revolution
Seems to extend its baleful influence
Even to the hearts of individuals,
Making our children as disobedient
To the natural government of parents
As to the good old regime of France.
But, I'll be obeyed. (*Exit* DUVAL.)
BELCOUR: (*Pauses*). She shall not hate me;
Sooner would I linger on the rack.
But can I exist without Estelle?
Oh, Henry, art thou indeed a rival?
Was I but sure he met return of love,
Could I, then, resign the sweet girl to him?
Perhaps she treats him, too, with cold disdain—
Disdain, which now destroys my peace. Ah! No,

---

[11]Destroy.

That interesting scene betrayed the truth.
Yet, it might have been Charlotte's departure
Was the sole subject of their conference,
Which then I knew not. So Henry may love
With hopeless fervor, like myself, in vain.
No sparkling hope shot from his languid eye
When last we were together—yes, one look,
One glance, declared it, when he named Estelle.
Oh! That interruption—but it is past—
Would that I had gone instead of written.
Now, meet when we will—we meet enemies.

ACT IV

Scene One

CORDAY's *house.* CORDAY *appears. He is seated with folded arms. He rises suddenly.*

CORDAY: Thus shall I finish the career of life—
When, in the arms of children, age should rest
Safe from the world's alarms, encircled there!
What! Here alone? No portion left but tears,
Of all my fair possessions. My daughter—
Oh, sweetest, best of children—my delight!
And thou, my Henry, where—where are ye now?
Oh, Thou, that dwellest in yon realms above—
That dost behold afflictions's downcast eye—
Pour into my soul, meek in resignation.
Bid me look up, then to Thy mandates bow.
Yet, let—oh, let Thy servant once embrace
The blessings Thou did'st give! But no. Never—
Never shall these streaming eyes again behold
Their joy—their overflowing joy—my children!
Ah! What can save my poor, deluded girl
But Thy protecting mercy? Oh, shield her!

Enter DE VERNUEIL *in a horseman's uniform.* CORDAY *gazes at him.*

DE VERNUEIL: My friend, my Father!
(*Embraces* CORDAY.)   Where is my Charlotte?

Where is Henry? He is not gone, I hope.
I bring dispatches from the army,
Making this my route to snatch the bliss
Of seeing those I love.
    CORDAY: (*Mournfully*). Ah! De Vernueil!
    DE VERNUEIL: What mean these looks of anguish?
    CORDAY: My daughter!
    DE VERNUEIL: What—what! Is she dead? Oh, in mercy speak.
(*Takes hold of* CORDAY's *hand with trembling agitation.*)
    CORDAY: (*Looking at him with pity and speaking fearfully*).
Not yet. Oh, fly! Fly and save thy Charlotte!

Enter a MOB. *They cry out,* "A la lanterne! A la lanterne!* [12] *He shall not live! Marat, the people's friend is assassinated by Corday's daughter. Seize him—seize him.*" DE VERNUEIL *snatches a sword from one of the mob, which he puts into* CORDAY's *hand, then draws his own broadsword and places himself before* CORDAY.

    DE VERNUEIL: My friend! Endeavor to defend thyself.
    CORDAY: Dear youth, my weak defense will not avail.
    DE VERNUEIL: And is it thus ye treat this good old man?
Behold the veteran's scars! Your soldier,
Whose age these threatening arms should now defend!
(MOB *rushes on, exclaiming,* "Marat! Vengeance!")
    DE VERNUEIL: Through my heart, your swords shall only pierce him.
(*After a struggle, in which the* MOB *are kept off, one goes behind* CORDAY *and stabs him. He falls instantly.* DE VERNUEIL *turns around and kills the man.*)

Enter BELCOUR, OFFICER, *and* SOLDIERS.

    OFFICER: Disperse—disperse! Away. (SOLDIERS *drive the* MOB *off.*
DE VERNUEIL *kneels down, raising* CORDAY's *head in his arms.*)
    CORDAY: De Vernueil, where art thou? Oh, De Vernueil!
Tell my beloved children we shall meet
Where cruelty shall wound no more. Farewell!
Ah! My children! (*Dies.*)
    BELCOUR: Alas, we come too late.
Dear De Vernueil, my heart bleeds with thine!

---

[12]To the street lamp, presumably to be hanged.

Why, oh, why was I not here to save?
Rise, rise my friend. Thou must not longer stay;
Thy life's in danger. Hasten far from here.
(DE VERNUEIL *still leans over the body. He gently rests the head down.*)
    DE VERNUEIL: Gone! Gone! Oh, that some pitying angel
Would pour the balm of life into these wounds!
What does this horror mean? (*Rises up in great agitation.*)
    BELCOUR: Here, De Vernueil,
It is impossible to explain. Go—
Estelle will unfold the dreadful story. (DE VERNUEIL *casts a lingering look at CORDAY, then around the apartment; clasps his hands; and exits.*)

Scene Two

A prison. CHARLOTTE *discovered.*

    CHARLOTTE: While the soul ranges through the boundless scope
Of never dying thought, and views at ease
Each object cherished by its mortal ties,
What are the body's bonds? Mere spider threads.
Yet when we long to clasp a father's hand;
To meet a brother's eye, a friend's caress;
To hear the accents of the voice we love—
How strains the eye, how bends the listening ear!
The arms extend—but, ah, extend in vain!
The visions fade, and the sick heart is void. (*Pauses.*)
In blest reality we yet shall meet!
Oh, may my tongue defend its noble cause,
Convincing, with triumphant energy,
That vice should be destroyed and virtue live—
That he has perished who was most its foe,
And justly fell a victim at its shrine.

Enter CHABOT *and* SOLDIERS.

    CHABOT: Charlotte Corday! Thou art now summoned
To appear and answer to the charge
Of assassination.
    CHARLOTTE: I am prepared
To stand the charge, as one whose act was just,
And for the welfare of my suffering country,
Whose gratitude and justice will proclaim me

A benefactor—not an assassin.

CHABOT: Thou art mistaken, mad enthusiast!
France will condemn thee to the guillotine—

CHARLOTTE: If such my doom, France is the fettered slave
Of factious, criminal, blood-thirsty men—
And soon will fall beneath a *weight of crimes.*

CHABOT: Lead on! (CHARLOTTE *walks out with dignity.* CHABOT *follows.*)

Scene Three

The inside of the cottage.   BERTRAND *and his* GRANDCHILDREN
discovered as SUSETTE *is feeding the blind old man.   Two or three little*
BOYS *play around them.*

BERTRAND: Can it be, Susette, that our young lady
Is gone from her father's house—none knows where?
I listened all this morn to hear her voice,
And to feel her soft hand on my shoulder,
So kind—so gentle. Take my dinner, child;
I cannot swallow. (*Leans upon the little table.*)

SUSETTE: Oh, do try, Papa.
She will no doubt return. (BERTRAND *shakes his head. The* BOYS *look anxiously at the plate.*)

BERTRAND: I cannot eat.
Give it to the children. But don't forget
Thyself, my Susette, and little—

Enter DE VERNUEIL. *A little* BOY *older than the rest has hold of his hand, appearing quite delighted. The* CHILDREN *run up to him.* SUSETTE *curtsies.*

DE VERNUEIL: Oh, this scene! Could I behold its ornament,
My Charlotte—the blessing of this family!
Old Bertrand, thy son knew me as I passed.
I spare one moment from my *precious* time
To ask, how fares it with thee, good old man?

BERTRAND: Ill, young gentleman—nor shall I be well
Till the voice we love again shall greet us.

DE VERNUEIL: Heaven bless me with "its silver tones" again

Farewell! Farewell! (DE VERNUEIL *puts a purse on the table and exits.*)

Enter ANNETTE *at the opposite door.*

ANNETTE: The poor old gentleman!
(ANNETTE *rests her arm on the table, discovers the purse.*)
What is this Susette? 'Tis an heavy purse!

BERTRAND: A purse, Annette? Generous De Vernueil!
Just like our lovely mistress—good and kind.

ANNETTE: Alas, Bertrand, 'tis said she'll ne'er return!
My sweet mistress is accused of murder!
Ah, 'tis a sad story.

BERTRAND: Of murder, girl?
She is a very lamb, and could not kill
The gnat that stung her tender, lily hand.

ANNETTE: My dear—my kind old master, too, is gone,
Killed by ruffians who were deaf to pity!
Nor could De Vernueil save the good old man. (*Loud tumult is heard.*)

SUSETTE: Hark! Where is that noise? 'Tis coming near us.
(*Looks.*) Annette—Annette. Look at those angry men.

BERTRAND: Be calm, my children. They seek De Vernueil,
But he is gone, and we have naught to fear.
Should they ask us questions, my little boys,
Deny not that De Vernueil has been here;
For to take refuge in a lie is base.
But ye all have courage to be silent.

Enter a MOB, *the same ruffians who killed Corday.*

MAN: Where is De Vernueil?
BERTRAND: Friends! He is not here.
(*A* MAN *goes up to* BERTRAND *and seizes him roughly by the arm.*)
MAN: 'Tis false! He is hid within the cottage.
BERTRAND: I tell no falsehood. De Vernueil is not here.
LITTLE BOY: Rude man, let go Papa. You will hurt him.
MAN: Yes I will, if he don't now give up

The young villain who murdered my brother.
Tell me, old man, where is that De Vernueil?
Speak, or thou shalt quickly be made to tell.
(*Shakes his arm roughly and holds a cutlass up in a menacing way.*
ANNETTE *and* SUSETTE *take hold of his upraised arm.* SUSETTE *appears
in the utmost terror.*)
    ANNETTE: Oh, believe me! De Vernueil is not here.
Search the cottage, but be not so cruel
As to hurt a defenseless, blind old man.
    MAN: Where is De Vernueil gone? For he was here.
    ANNETTE: We know not.
    LITTLE BOY: And if we did, would not tell!
    MAN: Ah! Is it so? Take a lesson for that. (*Cuts the* BOY *down, who
falls. The other* CHILDREN *scream out.* SUSETTE *falls into the arms of*
ANNETTE.) Tell where he's gone, or all shall have the same.
    BERTRAND: (*In great agitation*). What has the man done?
Oh, speak, Annette! Susette!
Children, tell me. I cannot, cannot see—(*Clasps his hands in agony and rises.*)
    MAN: Given an example of what is due
To insolence and to obstinacy.
Now let us have the truth from some of ye.
(SUSETTE *kneels at the feet of the* MAN, *and grasps his knee.*)
    SUSETTE: De Vernueil was here for a little while,
But mounted his horse and rode full speed away.
Oh, spare—spare my grandpapa, our only friend—
But if we must all die, take my life first. (*Points to her bosom and looks in
his face.*)
    MAN: Well. . .stand aside. Let us search the cottage. (*As* MOB *enters
the inner room,* ONE *of the men steals the purse from the table.*)

Scene Four

HENRY's *lodgings at Paris.* JAQUES *walking backwards and forwards.*

    JAQUES: And is this Paris, that I longed to see?
Oh, that we were a thousand leagues away!
Better to front the furious cannon ball,
Than here be waiting for the guillotine.
I am sick enough of what is called the world,
If shedding blood is all I am to view.
Ah, Annette, if we ever meet again,
I think I'll rather dig for daily bread,

Than labor on the road to fame or wealth
Through blood, or knavery to make me great—(*Walks about impatiently.*)
Fear, at last, has seized upon my heart;
Yet 'tis not for myself. That I do feel
These terrors that unman my firmest thoughts—
'Tis for thee, my hapless mistress, and thou
For whom I'd freely give my worthless life:
The kindest master heaven ever made.
Why does he stay? Alas! Perhaps he's dragged
By some fierce bloodhound, and condemned to die!
The good Le Brun—ah! He will perish too,
While on a fruitless errand I have been.
Oh! I will know their fate, or die myself,
Should I not find them here when I return,
Or meet them near that horrid prison's wall. (*Exits.*)

Enter HENRY *and* LE BRUN.

    HENRY: Jaques not arrived?
But all will not do, Le Brun. And she is lost
Irrevocably. Oh that I could devise
Some happy plan for her escape! Oh, help
Point out a way to save this dear sister.
    LE BRUN: Would a father do more to save his child?
But, ah, how impotent are our attempts
Against the strong, ungovernable rage
Of deluded, revengeful multitudes—
Against the sanguinary friends of Marat!
(*Tumult heard. "Ca ira! Ca ira!"[13] sung loudly.*)
Hark! Some new bloody deed is celebrating.
Heaven! Shall these horrors go unpunished?
    HENRY: My blood scarcely circulates. These dread sounds,
Oh my Charlotte, are heralds of thy doom!
A span but separates thee from that hour
When these savages will proclaim thy death.
Le Brun, I cannot wait an instant here.
My sister's execution shall not glut
Their brutal animosity. I will die,
Or rescue her from ignominy—

---

[13]Phrase from the "Marseillaise" and rallying cry of the revolution.

LE BRUN: I follow thee, Henry.
Jaques sure will join us at the appointed place,
When he finds we do not meet him here. (*They exit.*)

Scene Five

An apartment in DUVAL's *house.*

ESTELLE: Sorrow pursues me. 'Tis vain I fly
To hope's deceptive, treacherous promises.
They will deceive me—not restore my friends.
Ah! Could I serve them, this terrible suspense—
This torturing distress—would be relieved;
But I can only think, and fear, and think,
Till every sense with terror's palsied.
My Charlotte! My companion! Where art thou?
Oh, if false justice should demand thy life,
De Vernueil will defend it with his own!
And thou, my Henry, thou wilt not spare thine. (*Pauses.*)
But if they save thee—where is thy father?
Gone! Gone forever to the silent grave.
His fond arms will never more enfold thee.
Thine eyes, so full of sweet intelligence,
Will never dwell on that revered face,
To mark the movements of the noblest soul. (*Pauses again.*)
And is it possible such energy
Strung the meek fibers of my Charlotte's mind
To such a cord as mine could not have borne?
My spirit never could have soared so high.
Virtue I love, and hate its opposite;
But I leave to heaven's avenging hand
To punish, as its sovereign will directs—
A public scourge or individual foe.

Enter BELCOUR.

BELCOUR: Still a prisoner to this apartment?
ESTELLE: Liberty, to me, is not desirable.
Had I permission to go where I pleased,
This room would still retain its prisoner.
When real sorrow doth afflict the heart,
It will naturally seek solitude.

BELCOUR: Sorrow is relieved when participated.
Let me, then, bear away thy every grief,
So double anguish shall consume me quite.
But far hence be every selfish thought,
Till brighter prospects for thy friends arise!
ESTELLE: And are they not thy friends also, Belcour?
(BELCOUR *looks earnestly at her. She appears confused.*)
BELCOUR: These unconscious looks are daggers to my heart.
Henry's not unfortunate—not hopeless.
Estelle, dost thou not love Henry Corday?
(BELCOUR *turns away his head, as if afraid to hear the reply.*)
ESTELLE: I will never deceive thee. I do love—
BELCOUR: Ha! Beware, I cannot bear to hear it.
What would I not give to obtain that love?
The world's wide range would be a paltry step;
Its farthest verge my willing feet should find
To serve thee—blessed pilgrimage to me
If, when I returned, thy welcome smile,
Thy dear loved hand the rich, too rich reward.
And must I never hope again?
ESTELLE: Never!
BELCOUR: I must. It is my sole existence.
I cannot part with hope! No, Estelle!
No, never—till thou art another's.
ESTELLE: Not. . .if my happiness required it?
Oh, let me prove the generosity
Which once declared that thou would'st sacrifice
Thy heart's best interest to secure my peace!
BELCOUR: Name the sacrifice. Behold me ready.
Oh, bid me say—do—think—live or expire—
And, though it would be torture to resign thee,
Bid me again despair! I will say adieu! (*Looks anxiously at* ESTELLE.)
ESTELLE: Ah! Wilt thou, then, receive my confidence?
And, though I create a pang in that heart
Where I would ever fix content and peace,
Yet there is an act of duty which I owe
Both to myself and thee. It is to impart
A secret most important—
BELCOUR: Oh, proceed—
ESTELLE: I am married—
BELCOUR: Married! Married, Estelle?
ESTELLE: Heaven knows I am the wife of Henry.

Soften that angry look. He is thy friend!

BELCOUR: Thou'rt not married. I dare not believe it.

ESTELLE: Would I impose a falsehood on thee?
Good Belcour, be our friend—our brother.

BELCOUR: Thy friend? Thy brother?

ESTELLE: Alas! Our Henry,
Too, too soon he may be taken from us.
How critical his present situation!
If his father was not spared even here—
So distant from the fatal scenes at Paris—
How very poor the hope of his escape
From the fury of Marat's associates.
Oh, could'st thou behold the upraised arm
Preparing cruel execution—
The blow impending, that would bear away
A precious friend forever from thy sight—
No, no, Belcour, thy nature is more kind.
Thou could'st not endure the heart-rending scene,
Much less thine own arm raise against the youth,
Who was—who is thy friend! (BELCOUR *stands as if motionless for a time.*
At length, he approaches ESTELLE *and respectfully takes her hand.*)

BELCOUR: And still shall be.
Great was the effort, but 'tis conqueror now.
Surely thou wilt forgive, and Henry too.
I could not bear to see him lead thee off.
Then, the mean supposition that Le Brun
Was stationed there to watch me stung my soul;
And mad with rage, revenge, jealousy,
I sunk the prey of stormy passions.
But no more. All my endeavors shall be
To promote thy happiness. Allow me
Still to visit here, till by slow degrees
Thy father is weaned from his present plans.
Oh, farewell! (*Exit* BELCOUR.)

ESTELLE: Heaven give thee full reward! (*Curtain falls.*)

ACT V

Scene One

A prison darkened. CHARLOTTE *is seated in a melancholy attitude. Enter* HENRY *disguised in an old surtout[14] and slouched hat. A* GUARD *attends him with a small lantern.*

HENRY: Retire for a moment. (*Takes the lantern.*)
GUARD: Remember, sir,
My life's the forfeit of discovery. (GUARD *retires.*)
CHARLOTTE: (*Rises*). Ha! What light is that? Say, who approaches?
HENRY: (*Puts the lantern on the table*).
My sister! My Charlotte, 'tis thy brother. (*He goes up to embrace her, but she withdraws, fearfully looking around.*)
CHARLOTTE: My kind brother! Too generous Henry!
Stay not here. Leave me—leave me, or that life—
That valued life—in my misfortune dies.
Oh, fly from danger, thou best of brothers.
HENRY: Ah! Could I, then, leave thee here to perish
After obtaining, through peril and disguise,
This ardently desired meeting? No,
One way remains by which thou shalt escape.
CHARLOTTE: Escape, Henry? Ah, thou canst not save me.
HENRY: Oh, that the wretch had died by other means,
Some other heart had felt the zeal of thine,
Still had'st thou been our tender father's joy!
The darling comfort of his closing days;
His prop while duty called me from his side,
From that domestic scene of tranquil ease
Which each revolving sun gilded anew.
(CHARLOTTE *lays her hand on his arm.*)
And did this hand perform so rough a deed?
When for that deed, the sentence was pronounced—
The fatal sentence which decreed thy death—
Oh, when I beheld thy sudden paleness,
Then the swift blood remount into thy cheek,
Saw the fixing of all eyes upon thee,
While, through a blush, thy lips spoke words of gold,

---

[14]Long overcoat.

And patriotism must have gained its meed
But for the bloody villain who presided,
I could have rushed through the gazing crowd,
With melting tenderness clasped thee to my breast!
And then—then as now—have died to save thee! (*He embraces her. She falls upon his neck, but suddenly raises her head and speaks solemnly.*)

    CHARLOTTE: Those hours of delight we both have tasted
Can never be renewed again to me,
But I would not step back into the scene
To let that scourge of France remain unpunished.
I waited, looked in vain to see some arm
Hold forth the glittering sword of vengeance,
And from the face of earth exterminate
Its pestilence, Marat. No sword appeared.
The people bled; not ceased the copious stream.
My heart bled for them, while its keen feelings,
Bursting the bands which mark the female course,
Called on revenge and dared to act the Roman!
Think not I fear death! No, on the scaffold
I'll expiate what now is called a crime—

    HENRY: Name not the scaffold! Oh, why would'st thou die?

    CHARLOTTE: 'Tis but the body's death; my fame shall live,
And to my memory a tomb arise
On which all France will read and venerate
The act for which it now ordains my death.
For now, as when my steps shall mount the scaffold,
I feel the strong conviction that I bleed
For the benefit of my poor country;
And should the demon of carnage present
Another fiend as murderous as Marat,
May he soon share that horrid monster's fate,
And the true patriot who dares cut him off
Find in his country's gratitude reward.
Delusion now blinds the rude multitude,
And the worst enemy is called a friend,
While their best friends must meet a *traitor's* doom.

    HENRY: Never— If thou wilt be guided by me—

    CHARLOTTE: No effort now, my Henry, can save me.
I yield myself a victim to the times.
Draw me not back with hope's delusive hand;
For I have banished every living thought.
Yet, once more I'll think of those loved objects,

Which I shall never more on earth behold!
Bear my last adieu to our dear parent,
My Henry—what a dying child would say.
Speak for thy sister to her suffering father.
Embrace Estelle, and to my loved De Vernueil,
Oh, be a soothing guardian angel!
Watch over him, and save him from himself.
Thou know'st his passions have no medium,
For in their whelming stream his reason sinks,
When no kind voice sustains their rapid force.
And now, farewell! I conjure thee, go—
Or thou art lost with me for ever!
    HENRY: 'Tis thou must go. Oh, my sister, hear me:
We both may live. Hasten—take this disguise,
And in it, thou may'st instantly escape.
When discovered, I shall be liberated,
As not the guilty person, and unknown.
    CHARLOTTE: Such cannot be thy real expectation.
No, my beloved brother, our enemies
Would, with tenfold rage, seize on thy life
When disappointed of their *idol's* victim!
    HENRY: But thou shalt be preserved. (*Unbuttons his surtout as if to take it off, when a note drops from his bosom.*) Ha! what is this?
(*Picks up the note.*) Oh, may it bring some cheering ray of hope!
Just as I followed my conductor here,
Jaques gave this note with trembling eagerness,
And in my haste I thrust it in my bosom.
(*Opens it, stoops to the lamp and reads.*)
"In a state of mind not to be described, I arrived in Paris a few minutes ago, and had the good fortune to meet Jaques. I am hurrying on to deliver my dispatches, then obtain my adored Charlotte's release, or die. My influence is considerable, and hope supports me. . . . Alas, I have to write what I could not utter, a terrible calamity! Oh, that I could soften its horrors. Summon your fortitude. *Your* father, Henry, fell a victim to some furious partisans of Marat, and—" (HENRY *drops the note.* CHARLOTTE *leans in dumb despair against the wall.*)
Gracious heaven! He is killed!
The meek, defenseless, good old man—murdered.
My father! My father!
    CHARLOTTE: (*In a tone of agony*). My father killed?
(*She faints in* HENRY's *arms.*)
    HENRY: Wretched Charlotte.

(CHARLOTTE *revives. She puts her hands to her head.*)
CHARLOTTE: Was it some horrid dream?
Henry, did'st thou say our father was killed?
And I, who would have died for him, the cause?
Where is he? Oh, say not dead, my brother!

GUARD *rushes in.*

GUARD: Unfortunate young man, thou'st stayed too long.
The messenger of death now approaches.
We both are lost—

Enter CHABOT *with* OFFICER *and* GUARDS.

CHABOT: (*To the* GUARD). Villain! Who is that man?
CHARLOTTE: That man is my lover, yet innocent—
Admitted here by him, whose kind compassion
Could not resist the pleading voice of anguish;
Could not refuse his wretched fellow creatures
A mournful meeting and a last adieu!
This soldier was not bribed. He is a Christian!
HENRY: Noble Charlotte, I will save his life. Hear! (HENRY *takes hold of* CHABOT'*s arm, who repulses him and speaks to the* GUARD.)
CHABOT: A guard once a traitor offends no more.
We must have faithful servants. Take thy reward. (*Stabs the* GUARD, *who falls.* CHARLOTTE *turns away in horror.*)
Young man, away! But that this woman's deeds
Bespeak a soul above mean falsehood's art,
I should suppose that thou wert her accomplice.
She says thou'rt innocent, and I believe her.
Hence!
Soldiers, now conduct the prisoner!
HENRY: Oh, stop! I kneel! In mercy, let me speak. (*Kneels and takes hold of* CHABOT'*s arm.*)
CHARLOTTE: Henry! Obey my *last* request. Oh, *leave* me.
Remember what claims demand thy safe return.
Henry, dear Henry, remember *Estelle!*
HENRY: (*Rises and clasps his hands*).
This—this is too much for me to endure.
CHABOT: I can no longer wait. (*Drums beat outside the prison, and tumult heard: they cry, "To the guillotine! To the guillotine!"*)
HENRY: Oh, my sister! (HENRY *holds* CHARLOTTE *to his bosom.*)

CHABOT: Sister?

CHARLOTTE: Sister of his *heart*! Beloved youth,
A last farewell! But we shall meet above. (*She looks up.*)

CHABOT: Proceed! (CHARLOTTE *turns and looks at* HENRY *with tenderness. Drums beat louder. Cry heard: "To the guillotine! To the guillotine!" They go off, and* HENRY, *with horror in his countenance, follows.*)

Scene Two

HENRY's *lodgings. Enter* DE VERNUEIL. *He takes off his helmet and passes his hand over his forehead.*

DE VERNUEIL: Tired nature can no longer support me.
Each nerve is tortured by this harassed mind.
While the blood rushes through my burning veins,
Distracting terror maddens all my thoughts!
But I will see thee once again, my love,
Even if I perish with ten thousand wounds.
Ah! If my interest fails, and she is lost!
Wait! Must I wait? And if in vain? Hark! Hark!
The execution—heavens, what a word— (*With horror.*)
Cannot take place until tomorrow.
There is hope. One day—one day remains.

Enter LE BRUN *and* HENRY, *followed by two* MEN *bearing Charlotte's coffin.* HENRY *still disguised;* JAQUES *assisting.*

HENRY: Rest your burden. I need no further service.
Jaques, guard the door. Ah, De Vernueil! De Vernueil. (*Exit* JAQUES *and* MEN. DE VERNUEIL, *not knowing what or whom approached, had retired to the end of the room, standing, from the first entrance of the coffin, with his hands clasped, from which his helmet drops. He advances, strikes his bosom, again in a frantic manner clasps his hands, and in agony speaks.*)

DE VERNUEIL: Why do I breathe? My Charlotte, art thou there?
Where thou dost repose, there will De Vernueil.
Barbarians, have ye then murdered her?
Oh, false, vile treachery that deceived me!
But her soul thou could'st not murder! Oh, stay,
Angelic spirit! Rest on thy radiant wing,
And I will join thy flight to realms of perfect bliss. (*Draws a pocket-pistol, and before* HENRY *can prevent, shoots himself and falls.* HENRY *catches his*

arm as it drops.)

HENRY: Oh, De Vernueil, spare—

(HENRY *stoops to recover him.*) Too late! He is dead.
Wretched sight! Le Brun, support me. I sink.
Where's fortitude? Alas, it is not here. (*Strikes his breast.*)
I sink amidst this crush of happiness. (*Leans on* LE BRUN's *shoulder, then rises and stands in a desponding attitude.*)

LE BRUN: Dear boy, look up! There is a firm support.
Misfortunes prove our pious trust in Him
Who doth direct events, nor will afflict
Dependent man beyond his power to bear.
Exert thyself to rise above this storm,
To stem the torrent of affliction's stream.
So shall the mercy of approving heaven
Calm all thy sorrows and restore thy peace.
(HENRY *still looks down, wrapped in gloom.*)
Ah! Henry, thou dost not hear thy friend.
Wilt thou quite destroy thy old Le Brun? (*Takes his hand.*)
Hast thou lost Estelle? Think how she suffers.
Wilt thou not live for her? Oh, quit this house—
(HENRY *starts, then looks wildly at the coffin and* DE VERNUEIL.)

HENRY: I cannot go
Till I have seen these loved remains entombed,
Beyond the power of further injury.

LE BRUN: Thy Estelle also must not be entombed!
Leave to my care the last sad office here.
Quit Paris. Thou art beset with dangers,
Already hast by miracle escaped.
Here we are ill secured. I dread each sound.
I charge thee, go.

HENRY: No, no, I must remain.
Order Jaques to procure what is needful.
Le Brun, indulge me; do this one kind act.
Here will I watch and weep. (*Seats himself.*)

LE BRUN: May heaven guard thee! (*Exits.*)

Scene Three

DUVAL's *house. Enter* BELCOUR.

BELCOUR: Of all the passions in our nature wove,
Love is the ligature that binds the whole.

Ambition bows, casts off his crested helm
Dissolves his iron sword in beauty's tears;
And the loud trumpet calls in vain to arms,
While the young hero is a slave to love!
In vain the statesman views the height of power—
Its portal open—and the wreath of fame;
His eager step no longer climbs the ascent,
For love's allurements draw him to the vale.
And does not honor—mighty honor—tremble,
Even to the base of holy virtue's seat,
When tyrant love opposes all his wiles
To wrest a generous impulse from the heart!
Still in my breast this passion's unsubdued,
Breaks the weak bond that reason has imposed,
While hopes arise which almost overwhelm
Virtue and honor, friendship, and my peace.
Away! Away! Her Henry will return.
Vile, selfish, despicable thoughts—away!

Enter ESTELLE *at one door. As she approaches* BELCOUR, LE BRUN *enters at the opposite.* ESTELLE *rushes up to him and grasps his hand, unable to speak.*

    BELCOUR: Alone, Le Brun? (*In agitation.*)
    LE BRUN: Alas! I am alone.
    ESTELLE: And Henry! Henry Corday! Where is he?
    LE BRUN: (*With compassion*). In defense of his sister's loved remains
The gallant youth was killed. Our aid was vain.

Enter DUVAL.

    ESTELLE: Henry! My husband!
(*Falls on* LE BRUN, *who supports her.*)
    DUVAL: Henry! Thy husband?

Enter HENRY *in his own dress, followed by* JAQUES *and* ANNETTE.
HENRY *takes* ESTELLE *in his arms.*

    HENRY: Do I again enfold thee, my Estelle? (*She revives.*)
    ESTELLE: My Henry! (*They kneel at* DUVAL's *feet.*)
    HENRY: Forgive!
    DUVAL: Oh, never! Never!

Thou hast stolen my child. Hence from my sight!

BELCOUR: Dear sir, pardon!

DUVAL: Not while I live, Belcour. (*Exit* DUVAL.

HENRY *and* ESTELLE *rise. She looks after her father in evident distress, follows him almost to the door, then turns towards* HENRY, *who embraces her.*)

LE BRUN: Glad amazement makes me think I dream!
What, is my Henry here? Alive! Unhurt?
I saw thee fall. I sought thee long, dear boy,
Convinced at last the blow that felled thee down
Was fatal. But he lives! My Henry lives! (*Embraces* HENRY.)

HENRY: Stunned by a ruffian's savage blow, I fell.
They thought me dead and left me on the ground.
To him, (*Points to* JAQUES.) my faithful Jaques, I owe my life.
For, soon as the murderous riot ceased,
He bore me to a place of safety,
From whence I flew to seek my all of peace,
The only balms to heal my wounded soul—
Love and true friendship! My friend! My Belcour!
Am I in thy heart? (*Goes up affectionately to* BELCOUR.)

BELCOUR: Live ever in it! (*They embrace.*)

HENRY: But we must part, and cross the Atlantic wave—
Seek that repose we cannot here possess.
Ah, my Estelle! France and thy father frown—

JAQUES: (*Takes* ANNETTE's *hand.*)
But let them frown or smile. Jaques and Annette
Will not leave their generous benefactors.

HENRY: Come then, ye faithful servants. Good Le Brun,
I cannot leave thee. Come where quiet reigns.
Under the protection of America,
Domestic ease securely reposes.
There, we may yet enjoy tranquility;
And, 'midst the sons of true-born liberty,
Taste the pure blessings that from freedom flow.
Thy father, my Estelle, shall yet relent.
Belcour will charm each angry thought away,
And in our peaceful cot, he'll bless our union.

Finis

THE FAIR AMERICANS: A PLAY OF THE WAR OF 1812

An Original Comedy in Five Acts

Mary Carr[1]

1815

To candour, taste and justice is consign'd
This trembling offspring of a feeble mind.

Philadelphia: Printed and published by Mrs. Carr,   No. 5 Hartung's Alley, and may be had at Mrs. Neale's Library, No. 201 Chestnut Street and at Mrs. Phillip's Library, No. 119 South Third Street.

---

[1]Later Mary Carr Clarke.

To Apollo.

Sir,
Receive as the grateful effusion of a mind that fully appreciates your talents, and a heart that estimates your friendship, this simple phantom of imagination: It is the day dream of a few solitary hours, and has served to beguile its Author of a small part of the many griefs fate has portioned out for her in this life; that it will please the world she hopes, but
"Cribb'd, confin'd and harassed still,
"With trembling doubts and fears,"[2]
She lightly leans on hope's anchor, which the bright goddess but feebly supports; that it has met the approbation of some, on whose judgment and candour she places implicit confidence, she proudly boasts, and if
Apollo smiles, sure all will not condemn,
and my *"Fair Americans,"* will, I trust, when consigned to your gallantry, (which insures them one protector) travel through their native country without danger or insult except from the Snarling Critic Tribe, whose malignancy "spares nor sex nor age," and when you select a "Fair American" as a companion for life, that you may gain one whose strength of mind, purity of heart, magnanimity of soul, sweetness of temper and domestic virtues, may equal the national female character here drawn, is the sincere wish of your admirer and friend.   M.C.

Prologue
Written by a friend.

A Lady asks the efforts of my Muse:
Could I refuse her? say, could you refuse?
Could you resist, where honour bids obey?
Or shrink where female courage leads the way?
Could you recede, nor blush in crimson'd shame
When stern misfortunes urge their strongest claim?
Could you unmoved, an helpless woman see,
Thrown on the tempest of adversity,
Yet feel not all your souls within you rise,
To snatch the victim from the threat'ning skies?

---

[2]No source is given for this quotation.

Could you, capricious, thro' proud Europe roam
In search of genius, which you slight at home,
Grasp at the ignis fatuus as it flies
While your kind taper in its socket dies!
Shall foreign flow'rs transplanted in our soil
Receive your culture, and enjoy your smile,
Hugg'd to your hearts, exult o'er prostrate time,
And bloom unrivalled in a stranger clime!
Yet a poor native bud a *look* might save
Despis'd, neglected, sink into the grave,
Without one sigh to mourn its timeless doom,
Without one tear to glitter on its tomb!
Is this your patriot boast—no notes of mine,
Nor all the magic of this tuneful nine,
Could teach your hearts, those stubborn hearts of steel,
For human woes—for human ills to feel!
But no—Columbia's children shall revere
The....[illegible].[3]

---

[3]A note prefaced to the Early American Imprints microprint states that the only available text of the play is imperfect.

Dramatis Personae

Men:
General Trueman, an American officer
Captain Belford, an English officer
Major Clifford, his friend
Ensign Freelove
Harley, a farmer
Charles, his son, a lawyer
Fairfield, a farmer
Edward, a doctor, Fairfield's son
William, another son of Fairfield
Sergeant Dash, a recruiting officer
Dermot, an Irishman, servant to Fairfield

Women:
Mrs. Fairfield
Sophia, daughter of Mrs. Fairfield
Maria, another daughter of Mrs. Fairfield
Anna Harley
Hetty, maid to Fairfield

Soldiers, Sailors, Indians and Village Girls

ACT ONE

Scene One

On the banks of Lake Erie. A view of the lake. The water, clear and transparent, reflects the scenery around, which is beautifully romantic. The villagers rich and happy. Time: sunrise. Enter SOPHIA *and* ANNA.

SOPHIA: Come, my dear Anna. Haste. My mother's impatience is such, she thinks every minute an hour when I am absent.
ANNA: Ha, ha. Well, let her think. Her impatient spirit hurts only herself, and the morning is so delightful that I really must prolong our walk for another half hour.
SOPHIA: Nay, but dear girl, think how she will fret and scold.
ANNA: Pshaw, nonsense. I am resolved. (*Takes* SOPHIA's *arm and*

exits with her. The sound of drums and fifes heard. The girls run back, SOPHIA *frightened,* ANNA *pleased, though alarmed.)*

SOPHIA: Dear Anna, let us go home instantly. The noise draws nearer every moment. (*Offers to go.* ANNA *detains her.*)

ANNA: What can you fear? Are we not almost at home? Besides, why should we fear those whose duty it is to protect us? (*Sings.*)

> A soldier is a lady's man,
> He loves and fights whene'er he can.
> He still abounds with flames and darts,
> This from the cannon,
> But that to the heart.
> At beauty's shrine he's doomed to bow,
> To honor true, you well do know.
> But hark they come; see they are here,
> As I live, a band of volunteers! (*While she is singing, the sound*

approaches.)

Oh, my poor heart! (*Laughs.*)

Enter Sergeant DASH, *with five men. (The* GIRLS *hide and look through the bushes at them.)*

DASH: Well, my gallant lads, this is glorious going to war. Nothing but green fields, clear roads, trees blooming, birds singing, plenty to eat and drink, and sound sleep to refresh you. I am damned glad we are at war.

FIRST SOLDIER: So be's I, Sergeant, so as we be'ant to fight.

SECOND SOLDIER: Nay, for the matter of that, I shouldn't much mind coming in at the end of a battle, when the victory is gained. I should like to have share of the booty.

DASH: Booty? Oh, dam'me, we shall all get plenty of booty. Before the war is half over, our fortunes will be made.

THIRD SOLDIER: You don't say so.

FOURTH SOLDIER: Why, I knowed it all along, that when we had peace there was plenty for everybody.

DASH: Damn peace! I love war. Honor and fame, that's the word.

FIFTH SOLDIER: Mr. Sergeant, what is honor?

DASH: Why, don't you know?

SOLDIERS: Not I. Do tell us.

DASH: Why, honor is—is—dam'me, if I can tell you what it is, only she is my mistress.

SOLDIER: Oh, ho, some pretty girl, I suppose. (ANNA *laughs.* ALL *start and look frightened.*)

DASH: Who goes there? Advance and give the countersign, or you're dead men. (GIRLS *come from behind the bushes and laugh.*)

ANNA: Honor! Ha! Ha! Ha!

DASH: Two girls. So, so, rural damsels. What, my pretty lasses, do you attack in ambuscade? (*Goes to salute them. The* GIRLS *repulse them.*)

ANNA: Keep your distance, Sergeant, and tell us what means this talk of war.

DASH: What, a'nt the news got here yet?

ANNA: No.

DASH: Why, poor devils, don't you know we are going to be masters of all Canada, out of revenge to England for plundering our ships at sea?

ANNA: Oh, ho! So, so, the fruit is ripened at last. Its growth has been slow.

SOPHIA: And sorrow, sure, Anna. Oh, how many horrors does my imagination present to chill the soul: friends to combat with friends, or be deemed their country's foe. This, dire ambition, is thy work.

DASH: No, no, 'tis the works of England, and Congress can't help it now.

ANNA: Come Sophia. (*Turns.*) Well, Sergeant, I bid you good morning and thank you for your information. But when are we to expect the rest of the army?

DASH: They are just by. We are going round the country to recruit.

ANNA: And who is your commanding officer?

DASH: General Trueman. (*Sound of drums.*) There they come. (ANNA *and* SOPHIA *exit on one side,* SOLDIERS *on the other.*)

Scene Two

Inside FAIRFIELD's *house. Enter* MRS. FAIRFIELD *and* MARIA.

MRS FAIRFIELD: Not come home yet! Sun half an hour high, and not one wheel going in the house! Cows to milk, breakfast to get, bread to bake, beer to brew, butter to churn, cheese to press—everything to do, and nothing doing! Sophia gadding, Mary reading, and Hetty—oh, she, I dare say, is courting with that Irishman! Call her directly—but, no, no, go to your wheel.

MARIA: I thought I was to clean Edward's room.

MRS. FAIRFIELD: No, I will do that. You shan't go there again among them poison books; they make you good for nothing. To your wheel, I say. (MARIA *sits down to spin.*) Why, you, Hetty! (*Calls very loud.*) Dermot! I say, you, Hetty and Dermot! I daresay you are together somewhere. Why, Hetty!

HETTY: (*Without*). Coming, ma'am.

MRS. FAIRFIELD: "Coming, ma'am"! So is Christmas. Well, why don't you come, you creeping slut?[4]

Enter HETTY *with the hogs' tub in her hand.*

HETTY: Here I am, ma'am.

MRS. FAIRFIELD: Here you are, ma'am, and where was you when I called so long?

HETTY: Feeding the pigs, ma'am.

MRS. FAIRFIELD: And surely that should have been done half an hour ago. (*Turns to* MARIA.) Is the poultry fed, miss?

MARIA: No, madam.

MRS. FAIRFIELD: "No, madam," and why ain't they? There I shall have all the turkey poultry die of hunger; and the geese and ducks, not an ounce of fat will be on them this summer. (*Turns to* HETTY.) Go, milk the cows, hussy.[5] (*To* MARIA.) Go feed the poultry, you slut.

HETTY: Must I milk the cows before the pigs are fed?

MRS FAIRFIELD: To be sure, not. Here, Dermot—why, Dermot. Where can Miss Sophy stay? All wrong! Everything out of sorts. (*Calls.*) Why, Dermot!

Enter FAIRFIELD.

FAIRFIELD: Good morning, my dear wife and daughter! (*Kisses* MARIA *and then offers to salute* MRS. FAIRFIELD.)

MRS. FAIRFIELD: Pooh, nonsense! Where's that lazy Irishman gone, do you know?

FAIRFIELD: He has been at plough since daybreak, my dear. But what's the matter?

MRS. FAIRFIELD: Matter enough! Everything at sixes and sevens. (*Sees the* GIRLS.) Why an't you two doing as I bid you? Go! Begone! (*Exit* HETTY *and* MARIA.) Here's Sophy out walking, and Miss Maria's nose and knees together reading, while everything is standing.

FAIRFIELD: Well, my dear, whose fault is it? Why don't you be more methodical with your business? Set a proper time for everything. Allow the girls some hours of relaxation, and, take my word, things will go on better. But you are always in a bustle, and do no more than your neighbors

---

[4]In nineteenth-century usage, the term was used most often to denote a woman with careless, dirty habits.

[5]Bold or forward woman.

afterwards.

MRS. FAIRFIELD: Ha, ha! I like that, indeed! I always in a bustle—I, that have the most obedient, industrious family in the village! Did not I get four hundred yards wove last year, all spun in the house; and ha'nt I the best dairy, the fattest pigs, and finest breed of poultry in the country? Don't *I* make more butter and cheese than any woman in the village? Indeed! Do no more than my neighbors—ha, ha.

FAIRFIELD: Then why scold the girls so, my good wife, and murmur if they seek a little recreation? You loved amusement when you were a girl, so do not deny what you enjoyed at their age. We are blessed with good children, sons like their father.

MRS. FAIRFIELD: And daughters like their mother.

FAIRFIELD: Even so: good, industrious, obedient, and beautiful. (MRS. FAIRFIELD *much pleased.*)

Enter SOPHIA *and* ANNA.

SOPHIA: Oh, my dear father, such dreadful news!

MR. *and* MRS. FAIRFIELD: What? Speak!

ANNA: Only what we have so long feared: war is declared between England and America, and part of the army is just at the village. We met the recruiting party in our walk this morning.

FAIRFIELD: War said you? Once more must our fields be deluged with the best blood in the country; once more must carnage stalk abroad in the form of hostile Indians, and our flourishing villages be laid in ruins—our smoking hamlets serve but to light their distressed inhabitants in their flight. Again "must mothers weep their husbands lost, their infants slain."[6] Oh, my too prophetic heart! Long have I dreaded this resource, yet now it comes like a thunderstroke.

MRS. FAIRFIELD: But what have we to fear? We are rich, so none of our children will be compelled to fight. But don't let us sit idle here complaining when we have so much to do. (ANNA *smiles.*)

ANNA: Well, my dear godmother, good morning. I must hasten home to attend to my business. (*Exits.*)

Scene Three

Outside HARLEY's *house with a view of the village. Enter* HARLEY.

---

[6]No source is given for the quotation.

HARLEY: Where can my rattle-headed girl stay this morning? Something extraordinary detains her. Oh, there she comes, to cheer her father's heart with her smiles.

Enter ANNA. *(She runs to kiss him.)*

ANNA: My dear father, good morning.

HARLEY: Good morning to my darling child. Where did you ramble so long?

ANNA: Oh, Papa, I have dreadful news! War is declared, and preparations are making to invade Canada. A detachment from the army are encamped about three miles off. We met the recruiting party in our walk this morning.

HARLEY: War, said you, between England and America? This is what I long have dreaded. But whence comes the declaration? England has, I well know, been the aggressor; but does she to insult and injury add a thirst for human blood? If so, spirit of our forefathers reanimate our bosoms; banish from our favored nation faction and disunity. Oh, give us but one heart, one voice, one arm, and one will; but let these be for independence, free trade, and the rights of nature governed by the law of nations.

Enter CHARLES HARLEY.

CHARLES: Why, my dear father, what has thus aroused your martial spirit? You look as if preparing to encounter a host of foes.

HARLEY: And so I am. England has broke the treaty of amity and commerce made by our glorious Washington. The spirit of seventy-six is aroused, and no longer shall our Eagle crouch to their proud Lion, who may rule the plain but not the main.

CHARLES: Huzzah, huzzah! Glory and fame to the American name! Adieu to Coke upon Lyttleton. Farewell to quibbles, long court speeches with John Doe and Richard Roe. Welcome the unerring rifle and the shrill bugle. *(Going.)*

HARLEY: *(Alarmed).* Why, Charles, my son— *(Trembling.)*

CHARLES: What means my father? You surely cannot desire me to remain at home, inactive, in this hour of danger.

ANNA: *(Fondly).* But, dear brother, there is yet no danger, and sure it is time enough to quit your home and safety when called for.

CHARLES: Heard I indeed aright? Could my sister, the daughter of Edward Harley, who, in the ever-remembered revolution of '76, braved danger, even at the cannon's mouth, and followed our heroic Montgomery to the walls of Quebec—can she desire her brother and lover not to take the field (ANNA *starts.*) till danger compels them, or, in another word, to prove themselves cowards?

HARLEY and ANNA: (*Heroically*). Never, oh never, be the name of Harley or Fairfield branded by the epithet of cowardice; nor ever be female influence exerted to the dishonor of their friends, family, or country.

CHARLES: Bravo. (*Sings.*)

Come blow the shrill bugle, the loud drum awaken,
The dread rifle seize. Let the cannon loud roar.
Shall mothers, wives, daughters, and sisters left weeping,
Insulted by ruffians be drove to despair?
Ah, no, from the hills the proud Eagle comes sweeping,
And waves to the brave American Star.

The spirits of Washington, Warren, Montgomery,
Looks down from on high, with aspect serene.
We will give them a sign, and a tear to their memory.
Oh, make us as valiant as they all have been.
See children, affrighted, cling close to their mothers,
The youth grasp the sword and for battle prepare;
While beauty weeps (*pointing to* ANNA) fathers, and lovers, and brothers,
Who rush to display the American Star.

(*During the song* ANNA *weeps; then, suppressing her tears, comes to the front of the stage.*)

Yet, oh, when dire war o'er the country is raging,
And, horrid to tell, the loud cannon does roar,
When slaughter and famine and terror is slaying
Our friends and our foes, then must woman deplore;
And yet when for conquest, each bosom is burning,
And victory still hovering, from both stand afar,
Then in that hour, remember you are human,
Let mercy then beam from the American Star.

HARLEY: No, go, my son. The father's weakness is lost in the citizen's patriotism. Go, and emulate our brave departed heroes. Be like Washington, calm amidst danger, fatigue, and famine; and as Montgomery, daring and resolute through unheard-of sufferings.

CHARLES: There spoke the spirit of an American father. (ANNA *weeping.*) But what says my sister?

ANNA: Oh, Charles, go—dear, dear brother—but in the hour of battle, when the dread Indian shall have hurled the tomahawk or aimed the unerring rifle, think of your sorrowing friends and shrink, if possible, from the death blow. (*Sobs, then suppressing her feeling continues.*) Go. But, oh, William, I well know, has but the spirit of yourself. Let then the brother guard the lover, for his sister, as will that faithful lover, in the hour of danger, shield the brother for the sister's sake. (*Exits.*)

HARLEY and CHARLES: Noble girl! For such a woman what dare not man do? (*Sound of drums. They exit.*)

ACT TWO

Scene One

A camp. Soldiers pitching their tents, women cooking and preparing breakfast. Enter General TRUEMAN *and Ensign* FREELOVE.

FREELOVE: A pretty fatiguing march, gen.

TRUEMAN: Fatiguing, said you? If you complain already, when do you think to reach Quebec? We have known neither danger nor delay, secure in our own territory. It has as yet but the semblance of war.

FREELOVE: Why, ha'ant we marched ten whole days, beneath the sun's heat, on dirty roads, and been obliged to sleep three nights in our tents on straw?

TRUEMAN: Ha ha ha! Why, Freelove, you had better return, before you die with terror. Three nights on good clean straw, in the middle of summer, under a tent—poor fellow. (*Smiles.*)

FREELOVE: Look'ye, gen, to you it may be a good joke, but dam'me, if my bones don't ache most cursedly. (*Yawns.*) I am afraid I have caught cold, for *I* never slept out of a feather bed before. And if my poor mother only knew the hardships her son has encountered, they would make her heart ache.

TRUEMAN: Pshaw, Freelove! Cease these boyish repinings. I never thought you were a coward; therefore, re-assume the man till the war is ended. Canada once ours, and Britain will coincide to any terms.

FREELOVE: Oh, a few months will make us masters of all that; for the inhabitants will, of course, flock to our standard by thousands, and we shall only have to take possession. I wonder if the girls in Canada are as handsome as in America. (*Drum beats for breakfast. Soldiers run. Camp in confusion. Exit* TRUEMAN *and* FREELOVE.)

Scene Two

The village. Enter the RECRUITING PARTY, *several* COUNTRYMEN, WOMEN AND CHILDREN. *(Colors planted.)*

DASH: Come, my brave countrymen. Congress invites you, by me, to join their army and rescue Canada from British slavery. Think how glorious it will be to aid slaves in gaining their freedom, and by that ensuring their obedience and friendship forever—besides humbling the pride of England, and making them know we an't to be put upon. Come, who is willing to enter the United States Army, for only during the war? 'Tis but a few months' service. What, not one? Oh, what a set of cowardly rascals.

FIRST COUNTRYMAN: No, Mr. Sergeant, we are not cowards; but we don't want to go as enemies among those who, for many years, we have lived in friendship with. My son's wife came from Canada, and think you I will risk killing her father or brother? No, no. In the revolution of '76, I followed the brave Montgomery to the Plains of Abram, but now I won't fight till I know what for.

SECOND COUNTRYMAN: Nor I.

THIRD COUNTRYMAN: And I belong to Captain Harley's Riflemen. I am a gentleman volunteer and as good a man as my Captain. But when he leads, only will I follow.

FOURTH COUNTRYMAN: Look'ye, Mr. Sergeant, you called us cowards because we don't list. Every man in the village, and for miles round, are volunteers; and when we see occasion, we will show you the difference between a battle and a review. So goodbye. (*Exit* COUNTRY PEOPLE.)

DASH: (*Whistles*). Whew, by Gad, this is rare recruiting! Not a fellow to be had for miles round. All volunteers, but not fight till forced. Droll going to war without men.

FIRST SOLDIER: All the better for them that stay; the more booty.

DASH: March. (They *exit.*)

Scene Three

FAIRFIELD'*s garden. Enter* WILLIAM *and* EDWARD.

WILLIAM: Why, it's true, Edward, I cannot see the justice of invading Canada by way of reprisal for the depredations of England on our commerce. I think it would be better to protect the trade than invade our friends; yet, as war is declared, why it is the duty of every man to espouse his country's cause. Therefore, adieu the fertile fields, the rural ball, the soft sigh, the tender smile; and welcome the tented field, the martial shield, and all the horrors of almost civil war.

For Love shall yield
To Mars the field,
"The fife and drum
Invite to come."[7]
I will poise the spear and shield.

EDWARD: Well, so be it. I can say no more. For me, my resolution is taken never to raise an arm against the country that contains my Matilda; therefore, I remain neutral.

Enter CHARLES HARLEY *in rifle uniform.*

CHARLES: Well, William, the day is come to prove whose obedience to and affection for the laws of their country is most prompt, or warmest. But why are you not in uniform? We must welcome this advanced corps. The place of rendezvous is Sackett's Harbor. Our village has affronted the recruiting sergeant of the party; and as perfect amity ought to subsist among both officers and men, I will immediately order out the company to greet them in friendship and to show them our method of bush fighting.

Enter SOPHIA *and* MARIA.

MARIA: Oh, sight of horror!

SOPHIA: Surely, William, you do not mean to engage in this unnatural contest.

WILLIAM: Sophy, it is not for girls to condemn the rulers of a nation. We have chosen these men to act for the welfare of the country; they are citizens as well as we. Certainly, then, what they decree must be for the true interest and honor of America. *(Exits.)*

(CHARLES *and* MARIA *converse apart.)*

SOPHIA: And you, Edward?

EDWARD: Stand neuter.

MARIA: Thank heaven, all do not mean to forsake us.

CHARLES: My dear Maria, why that reproach? Sooner would I resign life than forsake you; but shall I, who have been honored by my country with a commission, dastardly resign it when danger approaches? Even you, Maria, would despise me for such pusillanimous conduct.

MARIA: *(After a severe struggle).* Well, be it so, go my dear Charles.

---

[7]No source given for quote.

Be to my brother what he will be to you, a shield to every danger. The conflict has been severe, but it is over, and I submit to fate.

MRS. FAIRFIELD: (*Without*). Why, Sophy and Maria, where are you?

MARIA: Hark, my mother calls. Come Sophia. (*Exit* GIRLS.)

Enter DERMOT, *running.*

DERMOT: Ah, may, the devil's mother fly away with me if I wouldn't rather be shot ten times a day than live with such an ould scolding devil as you are, so here goes to list. (*Going.*)

EDWARD: Hold, Dermot.

DERMOT: (*Turns*). Oh, and is it yourself, Mr. Edward, and Captain Harley? Maybe your honor's self Captain, will be after the listing me; for dam'me if a camp can be worse than this house.

EDWARD: But Dermot, do you know that the English give no quarters to any of their subjects taken in arms against them? So, if you list and are taken, you will be hung.

DERMOT: Hung, say you? Sure there's never an Irishman fears that death when he has a good musket on his shoulder; and any death is better than living with two scolding women. So goodbye, your honor. (*Exits.*)

Enter WILLIAM *in uniform.*

WILLIAM: Now, Charles, have with you. *Allons*[8]. (*Drums beat. Exit.*)

Scene Four

The camp. The troops drawn up. Drum beats. Enter CHARLES, *at the head of his company of riflemen. (They exchange salutes, march round the stage, then exit.)* *Enter* CHARLES, *General* TRUEMAN, *and* FAIRFIELD.

FAIRFIELD: My house, General, I hope you will consider as headquarters during your stay.

TRUEMAN: I thank you, worthy sir, but my undisciplined troops require the most unremitting vigilance on my part, to break them to proper military duty. I must therefore decline your generous invitation.

CHARLES: I suppose, General, you will permit me to pitch my tent among you this evening. I long for some instruction. I am also of the

---

[8]Come on (French).

opinion that private friendship promotes cooperation in the field.

TRUEMAN: (*Shakes him heartily by the hand*). You speak my very sentiments, young man, and I shall expect you. (*Exit CHARLES and FAIRFIELD.*)

Enter DERMOT.

DERMOT: Sir, sir.

TRUEMAN: Did you speak, young man, to me?

DERMOT: Yes, faith, sir, and if you be the great new captain that's going to beat the English out of Canada, why, I want to list in your honor's company; for faith, I hate the English and love fighting with anybody but women.

TRUMAN: Are you married, friend?

DERMOT: No, please your honor. Hetty would not have me, because I couldn't maintain her; so when I told her that, she fairly drove me out of the house and swore I was the cares of the world, and no man. So please your honor, I must list to show her I am a man.

TRUEMAN: Ha, ha! Well, my friend, there's the sergeant's tent. He will engage you.

DERMOT: Thank your honor. (*Exits.*)

ACT THREE

Scene One

The village. Enter HARLEY *and* FAIRFIELD.

HARLEY: I tell you, neighbor Fairfield, this war is an excellent thing. 'Tis the only expedient we could resort to, to prove that we are not the poor, mean, pusillanimous nation Europe thinks us.

FAIRFIELD: Well, neighbor, I shall thank you to enumerate some of its advantages.

HARLEY: First, our manufactories will improve; that will call our natural productions into use. Next, the customary luxuries will fall into disuse; that will introduce simplicity of heart and manners. Necessity, the mother of invention, will call up natural ingenuity, and American genius expand. Fourthly, it will clear the country of a number of useless members of society, and leave us, like a long fit of sickness, thoroughly purified.

FAIRFIELD: Ha! Ha! Ha! Well, for the sake of the last useful, I forgive the other absurd advantages; and since I can't help it, and my son and destined son-in-law is engaged in it, why, I will try to think it a wise expedient. But here comes my wife.

Enter MRS. FAIRFIELD.

MRS. FAIRFIELD: So, so, here's a pretty kettle of fish. What's to be done now with the farm? William gone to be a great officer and Dermot a soldier; what shall we do now for plowing and harrowing? All the money must go for day laborers. This comes of the war. I wish I was Congress; I would always be at peace!

FAIRFIELD: Well, my dear, we will run you for President when we want an old woman in the chair.

MRS. FAIRFIELD: Who do you call an old woman, Mr. Fairfield? Not me, I hope. I an't fifty yet, and no woman is to be called old till she is sixty.

HARLEY: Ha! Ha! Ha!

MRS. FAIRFIELD: Aye, you may laugh, neighbor Harley; but when I die for age, you must quake for fear.

HARLEY: Oh, don't be angry, Hannah. Well, how do you like the war? We shall have no more foreign importations; all must be our own country's productions and manufactures.

MRS. FAIRFIELD: Yes, I mean to make my girls spin their own muslin gowns next year; and William's room shall be taken to raise silkworms in, that I may manufacture my own silk. (*Enter* MARIA.) What is Anna doing?

MARIA: Knitting stockings and working lace.

MRS. FAIRFIELD: That's right; nothing like keeping girls at work. (*Exit* MR. *and* MRS. FAIRFIELD.)

Enter CHARLES.

CHARLES: Glorious news, my dear father! The British fleet on Lake Erie is defeated. We remain masters of that noble body of water, and are now going to make a grand attack on York.

HARLEY: Well, my boy, do your duty, and success to the right side.

CHARLES: Oh, we do not fear success. With spirits elated by the brave Perry's brilliant achievement, and led by our gallant commander, victory must be ours. Canada once secured, again will the American flag fly uncontrolled by foreign pride, and free trade bless our flourishing and happy land. But I must to Fairfield. I long to bid Maria farewell.

HARLEY: The girls design to visit camp tomorrow.

CHARLES: I know it. Will you accompany me?

HARLEY: No. Anna expects me, and in defiance of all her heroism, she droops under the pain of parting with you and William. So adieu. (*Exit different ways.*)

Scene Two

FAIRFIELD's *garden.* SOPHIA *and* MARIA *at work.*

SOPHIA: Heigho, my heart is heavy. I feel as if some evil was impending.

MARIA: And for me, sorrow is become so habitual that I scarcely know what pleasure is, and happiness I have never experienced. My mother desires to keep everyone employed; and my love of reading is so constant a source of sorrow to me, that since Charles's life has been endangered by the present war, mine has been a burden too heavy almost to bear. What a dependent state is woman's. I wish I was a man.

SOPHIA: That you might share Charles's danger? Ha! Ha! Poor Maria, its heart is fled, and now she pines like a wood robin in a cage. Can you not raise one sweet song to call the wanderer back? (*Begins to sing "The Wood Robin."*) "Stay, enchanter of the grove"—

Enter CHARLES.

CHARLES: Your voices guided me to your charming retreat. But what has thus exhilarated your spirits, Sophy? You seem more animated than usual.

SOPHIA: A mere exertion of spirits to enliven my sister, which, as it has proved unsuccessful, I leave you to do. So, adieu. (*Exits.*)

CHARLES: Enliven! I fear the news I have to impart will depress that too timid spirit.

MARIA: No, Charles, any new horror will arouse my dormant courage. Hitherto, I have existed in suspense, which has suspended my powers of action. Reason had nothing to awaken her, and I have lived a victim to my feelings. Perhaps, should real sufferings be my fate, I should support them with fortitude.

CHARLES: Your understanding, my Maria, enslaves my soul, while you charm my every sense. Yes, should I fall, Maria will mourn my early doom.

MARIA: Fall, Charles, said you? But proceed; suspense is misery.

CHARLES: Then know that in a few days the whole army is ordered to cross the lake. We must follow victory while she consents to lead us.

MARIA: Alas! Yet heaven may in mercy spare those I love.

CHARLES: Our plans are secret; therefore, no certain intelligence can be sent to you! But do not my love, give despondency such power. (MARIA *leans against a tree in the side scene.*) Is this the fortitude you boasted? (*Takes her in his arms. She leans on his bosom.*) Indeed, Maria, you unman me.

MARIA: Deny me not, Charles, the poor relief that tears can yield; but for them, my heart would break. (*They embrace.*)

Scene Three

HARLEY's *parlor. Enter* ANNA *and* SOPHIA *with a furled flag.*

ANNA: 'Tis finished, thank heaven and our industry.

SOPHIA: Tomorrow our fathers will accompany us to the camp. But Anna, you must present it. You have more courage than any of the girls in the village, so the task devolves on you.

ANNA: Well, so be it. I must dress a la mode de Amazon. Let me see. . . yes, yes, my green riding habit will be the very thing, with a green velvet hat and three white feathers. I really think I shall make a few conquests—nay, without doubt, half the generals, majors, colonels, and captains in the army will bend to my all-conquering eye.

SOPHIA: Well, success attend you; and as you aim at nothing below a captain, you will permit, I hope, your humble hand-maids to exert their powers of attraction on the lieutenants, ensigns, sergeants, and corporals.

ANNA; Oh, by all means, achieve as many conquests in that grade as you please. Nay, I don't know whether I may not toss two or three generals and colonels off to you and Maria, as you are my particular friends.

SOPHIA: (*Curtseying*). Thank you, my dear. That will indeed be generous.

Enter HARLEY.

HARLEY: Well, my girls, let me pass my judgment on your patriotic efforts. (*Takes the flag and examines it.*) Beautiful, indeed. Both the design and the execution is admirable. But who is to present it to the commanding officer?

SOPHIA: Anna.

HARLEY: But she must have five supporters.

ANNA: I am glad of that.

SOPHIA: May they look at the generals, etcetera?

ANNA: Just peep through their fans. Well, Father, as you have been our only confidant, we leave the sole arrangement as to time and place to you. We must now arrange our dresses. So adieu. (ANNA *and* SOPHIA *exit with flag.*)

HARLEY: (*Looks after them*). Charming girls. Oh, can anything equal the sensation of delight a father experiences when he sees his children attain maturity with every sentiment of honor and integrity glowing in their hearts and influencing their actions! 'Tis a happiness as perfect as the world can afford. (*Exits.*)

Scene Four

A wood. Enter HETTY *and* DERMOT.

HETTY: But, dear Dermot, how can you talk of being killed, when you know so well I won't live after you?

DERMOT: Not live after I am kilt? Why, what the devil will make you die?

HETTY: Oh, dear, I don't know, but I am sure that I shall. So, don't go and fight.

DERMOT: Not go, Miss Hetty? What do you take me for—a puppy and a poltroon? Han't I got the bounty, and an't I to get land, that I can have a farm of my own in a few years? And now, when I have got every thing but honor, like a cheating devil as you are, you won't let me have any of that, because you can't have part. No, no, Hetty my dear, when I just get into the thick of the battle, I will be as wide awake as a hawk.

HETTY: Well, then, you will go?

DERMOT: Faith, will I.

HETTY: Then leave me your will and power, that I may get the land; for you will never come back alive. But I suppose your ghost will be crossing the lake every night at twelve o'clock to visit me, oh, ho, ho, ho! (*Cries.*)

DERMOT: Pho, nonsense. My own sweet self will cross the lake to visit you, so don't be after crying there like a fool; but come along to Captain Harley, till you get the will. (*Takes her arm. They exit.*)

ACT FOUR

Scene One

The camp in the woods, the tents ornamented with green boughs, the standards of different regiments displayed. Soldiers busy, sergeants and corporals directing. Enter WILLIAM *and* FREELOVE.

FREELOVE: Then this sister of Harley's is handsome, you say.

WILLIAM: Divinely beautiful. But beauty is her least attraction. She is sensible, spirited, rich, and highly accomplished.

FREELOVE: Oh, I am half gone in love already. And will you, my dear fellow, just introduce me, that's all? My superior endowments will do the rest. (*Strutting, pulling up his neck-cloth, brushing his hair, and looking consequential.*) All the ladies admire handsome Bobby Freelove. Did you never hear the song a dear, sweet, charming, divine creature made on me? Oh, how she did love me.

WILLIAM: Never. Will you favor me with a sight of it?

FREELOVE: Oh, I will sing it for you. Poor thing, how much in love she was; but I could not return it, could not love her, so her parents got her married.

WILLIAM: Then she did not wear the willow. But the song: let us have some proofs of her tenderness.

FREELOVE: (*Pompously*). By all means, sir. You must know bootees were just come in fashion; and, as I looked remarkably well in them, they are the burden. But hem. . . (*Clears his throat.*) Hem, hem! (*Sings.*)

> Of all the gay beaux,
>   That sport their smart clothes,
> There's none that my fancy can please,
>   With their *Spencers*[9] or *crops*,
>   Or wooly *foretops*,[10]
> Like *Bob*, with his *tippy bootees*.[11]

> *Inexpressibles* tight
>   Some fancies delight,
> With bunches of tape at their knees;
>   Yet all must confess,
>   Though snug is the dress,
> It yields to *Bob's tippy bootees*.

> The *blue pantaloons*,
>   As they march in platoons,
> Each lady's attention quick seize;
>   But I let them pass by,
>   And turn round my eye,

---

[9]A spencer was a short jacket.
[10]A foretop was a hair style featuring a forelock.
[11]Short boots with high heels.

For *Bob* with his *tippy bootees*.

    View little Jack Spratt,
    With his head from cravat
Peeping out like a mouse from a cheese;
    With shoes on his toes
    And a handful of bows,
Then look at *Bob's tippy bootees*.

    Then there's Sir Thomas Tap
    With coat and cape,
Like blankets of wild Cherokees;
    Whether quiet or moving,
    He looks like a sloven,
Near *Bob* with his *tippy bootees*.

    With such a dear lad,
    I ne'er could be sad,
Should we wander o'er the mountains or seas;
    And happen what might,
    I'd still find delight,
In my *Bob* with his *tippy bootees*.

WILLIAM: Bravo! Encore! I never heard so convincing proof of a lady's fondness before. But 'tis time to dress. At four o'clock, they are to be here, and now it is near three.

FREELOVE: You will introduce me, then?

WILLIAM: Certainly. Depend on me. (*Exits.*)

FREELOVE: Then my fortune's made. Let me see. . . yes, I will settle here and build a city on the borders of the lake. The city of Erie, founded by Robert Freelove, Esquire, an officer in the United States' Army. Yes, that will do. Oh, I am a great man! My mother always said I would make my own fortune. So welcome, thou fickle dame, to my arms. Oh, Bob, what a damned fine fellow thou art! (*Exits.*)

Enter TRUEMAN, CHARLES, WILLIAM, FREELOVE, *and a number of* OFFICERS *of all ranks.*

TRUEMAN: Major Fairfield, as the lady who is to present the standard has been your companion since infancy, it is presumed she will feel less diffidence in presenting it to you, than a stranger; and soldiers ever respect female delicacy. You are therefore appointed to the high honors of receiving from her fair hands the standard presented by the young ladies of Erie.

WILLIAM: (*Bows*). Thanks, for the lady and myself, are due to our noble commander.

(*Music heard. Shouts and clamors of applause from without. The OFFICERS range themselves on the stage, WILLIAM at front, CHARLES at the side they are to enter. Music. Enter MRS. FAIRFIELD and a few old LADIES. Then ANNA, dressed in a green riding habit, velvet hat the same color with three white feathers, enters, followed by SOPHIA, MARIA, and three OTHERS dressed like Anna. CHARLES receives them, and they march round the stage. The officers salute them. ANNA carries the standard in her hand as she approaches WILLIAM. He advances to meet her, bowing. She holds the flag and unfurls it, presenting it to the audience first, then to the officers. The motto on it: "On your generosity, honor, and courage we depend for protection." OFFICERS half draw their swords, then return them. ANNA and the GIRLS advance to the middle of the front of the stage, and ANNA speaks apparently to the OFFICERS.*)

ANNA: Gentlemen, receive from the hands of the ladies of Erie a simple remembrance of the esteem in which they hold the officers of the army quartered in their neighborhood. This flag— (*Presents it to WILLIAM.*) the work of their hands—is all they have to offer to their country. May it return triumphant, and may the God of battle shield you from every ill. One request they have to make, yet to Americans it may seem superfluous: when urged by a desire of conquest, oh, for their sakes, forget not the soft dictates of humanity. (*She curtsies, and CHARLES hands her to her father. WILLIAM carries the standard up the stage, plants it among the rest. OFFICERS gather round the GIRLS, bowing. Drum beats; they run to their places. TRUEMAN advances.*)

TRUEMAN: Ladies, receive from me the united thanks of the gentlemen of the army, and rest assured that every wish of the ladies of Erie shall be fulfilled. This evening, the last we have to devote to peaceful amusement, we hope you will pass in our society. Alas, perhaps it may be the last we may ever spend together. Let it then be devoted to hilarity. (*GIRLS look at OLD PEOPLE, who bow and curtsey assent.*)

CHARLES: Come, then. The ballroom waits for its enliveners. (*Takes MARIA's hand. TRUEMAN selects SOPHIA. WILLIAM leads ANNA. Other OFFICERS lead off the rest. Then the OLD PEOPLE follow. Curtain drops.*)

Scene Two

The village. Enter HARLEY and FAIRFIELD.

HARLEY: Why neighbor, we must trust to Providence. A few days more will certainly bring us some intelligence.

FAIRFIELD: Ten days of suspense is horror, and aggravated by rumors so various— It is this distracts us. Then, my wife and the girls are so dejected that home is misery.

HARLEY: And abroad is worse; for every eye I meet demands of me the fate of either husband, son, brother, or lover. Then the desolate appearance of every place—fences broke down, gardens not half attended to, fields lying fallow, every necessary of life double price, women dejected, children neglected. If this is war, then God send peace.

(*Drum beats from the lake. Cry, "A flag! Glorious news!" They exit.*)

Scene Three

The banks of Lake Erie. Enter HARLEY, FAIRFIELD, EDWARD, *and* VILLAGERS, OLD MEN, WOMEN, *and* CHILDREN. *(A canoe makes fast.* OFFICER *lands and gives* HARLEY *letters.* FAIRFIELD *advances, but receives none. Exit* OFFICER.)

FAIRFIELD: None for me! Unfortunate father, hast thou then lost the prop of thy declining years? Oh, my poor boy, my son, my son! (*Leans on* EDWARD'*s arm.*)

HARLEY: (*Reading, does not observe* FAIRFIELD, *who continues lamenting*). Huzzah, huzzah! Glory to America! Glorious news! The enemy is ours, Procter defeated, York taken, Charles unhurt, and victory declared for America! Huzzah, the Eagle flies triumphant!

FAIRFIELD: (*In a voice of grief*). But where is William?

HARLEY: (*Reads*). Major Fairfield is now in pursuit of the flying enemy and is, like myself, unhurt.

FAIRFIELD: (*Gradually rouses, then jumps for joy*). Oh, heaven, I thank you! Edward, hasten to your mother with the joyful news.

HARLEY: And we to tell it through the village. Oh, I will have bonfires, feasts, rejoicings, balls, and tea parties for a month! Your girls will do no work for a month, and when they return safe, we will have the dogs married.

Enter ANNA, MARIA, SOPHIA, *and* MRS. FAIRFIELD.

ANNA: Who married, Papa?

HARLEY: William Fairfield.

MRS. FAIRFIELD: What, my son married, and broke his promise to my god-daughter? Oh, the graceless young man! I will disown him, and I will never see his wife—no, no, not if she could spin two dozen a day and never took a book in her hand. (FAIRFIELD *and* HARLEY *laugh.* ANNA *appears very uneasy, but very spiritedly hums a tune.*)

SOPHIA: I do not believe one word of it.

MARIA: Nor I.

ANNA: If he is, why, farewell be. (*Sings.*)

"The loss of one is gain of two,
And choice of twenty more."

I suppose his wife is young and beautiful.

MRS. FAIRFIELD: I tell you, it is no such thing; and John Harley, you are not a friend to my family to raise such a report on my son. (*Shakes her head at* HARLEY.)

HARLEY: Whew, what have I said of your son?

MRS. FAIRFIELD: Why, that he was married.

HARLEY: I deny the charge.

MRS. FAIRFIELD: Girls, I appeal to you.

ANNA: I thought so.

HARLEY: Your thoughts and my words are not always alike.

MRS. FAIRFIELD: Well, good Mr. Wiseacre, what did you say?

HARLEY: William Fairfield, no more. Your own imagination supplied the rest.

SOPHIA: But dear godfather, what news of my brother?

HARLEY: Why, he is gone in pursuit of the British general, and when the campaign is over he shall be married.

MARIA; Heaven, I thank you. (*Puts the letter in her bosom.*)

ANNA: And what of Charles? (HARLEY *gives her his letter.*)

MRS. FAIRFIELD: I knew it could not be so; but what has become of Dermot? If anything happens to him, Hetty will be good for nothing.

HARLEY: He is well, and is made a corporal.

MRS. FAIRFIELD: So, good news! Come, girls, make haste home to work; the wheels must not stand idle now. But I must go and feed my silkworms. Come, girls.

HARLEY: No, no, this is to be a holiday. No work, all play; therefore, old girl, let the young ones go with me. (*Exits with* GIRLS.)

MRS. FAIRFIELD: No work today? Oh dear! 'Tis a sad victory to me. I shall be ruined. Now, I daresay that old fool has some frolic going forward. I will go and see. (*Exits.*)

Scene Four

Moonlight beside the lake. Music heard at a distance. Enter ANNA *and* SOPHIA.

ANNA: What a charming night! How serenely Cynthia rises to our view. Would I could mount aloft on eagles' wings, and ease my fears at once by ascertaining William's fate.

SOPHIA: Why, where would you go?

ANNA: I know not; yet my soul seems as if it could burst its bonds and fly to my soldier's arms. (*Sees the canoe.*) In this, Sophy, we might cross the lake and in a few hours ascertain his fate.

SOPHIA: Mad girl, do not think of such a scheme. Come, let us hasten home. We are not safe here. (*Sound of paddles heard.* ANNA *lingers.* SOPHIA *urges her to go. Indian yell given. A party of* INDIANS *rush on the stage and seize them. They scream, but are carried off.*)

Enter hastily, Captain BELFORD *and Major* CLIFFORD.

BELFORD: What mean those shrieks, Clifford? This way they went, and seemed as if going towards our canoe. (*Screams die away.*)

CLIFFORD: They grow more faint. Methought it was a female voice.

BELFORD: So did I. Let us follow the sound; this way. Though in an enemy's country, let us not forget it is a soldier's duty to protect the fair. (*They exit hastily the way the girls went.*)

Enter EDWARD, HARLEY, *and* FAIRFIELD.

FAIRFIELD: Where can they be?

EDWARD: It was highly imprudent for them to walk away alone.

HARLEY: Search every part of the wood. (*Exit* EDWARD *and* FAIRFIELD.)

HARLEY: Oh! I am half distracted. (*Sees the canoe, jumps into it, and puts off the way the girls were taken.*)

Enter EDWARD *and* FAIRFIELD.

EDWARD: They are gone past recovery.

FAIRFIELD: Where is Harley?

EDWARD: Perhaps at home. This way; further search is vain till daylight. (*They exit.*)

Scene Five

Another part of the lake, more wild. Three canoes moored. Enter
INDIANS, *dragging* ANNA *and* SOPHIA. *(They tie them to trees, then*
get ready their canoes. ANNA *screams.* INDIAN *levels his tomahawk.*
Enter BELFORD *and* CLIFFORD. ANNA *shrieks.* INDIAN *throws the*
tomahawk. BELFORD, *as it passes, strikes it down.* INDIAN *angry.*
CLIFFORD *advances and unties them.* BELFORD *receives* SOPHIA,
fainting. A canoe makes the shore. HARLEY *lands and hallos. The*
INDIANS, *frightened, jump into two canoes and make off.* HARLEY *runs*
to ANNA, *who falls on his shoulder.)*

> HARLEY: My dear daughter.
> ANNA: Oh, my father. *(Faints.)*

ACT FIVE

Scene One

FAIRFIELD's *house. Enter* MRS. FAIRFIELD, MR. FAIRFIELD,
EDWARD *and* MARIA.

> MRS. FAIRFIELD: Ah, this comes of idleness! Had they been at work,
> this could not have happened.
> MARIA: My sister, oh, my dear, dear sister, oh! *(Wrings her hands.)*
> EDWARD: Nothing can be done till morning.
> FAIRFIELD: I shall run distracted. I am sure I heard the Indian yell
> and then a scream. Oh, my child, my darling child!
> MRS. FAIRFIELD: Oh, my poor, dear Sophia. She was always so mild,
> so cheerful, and so industrious. Oh, this comes of war, victories, and
> idleness! Oh, my child! *(Cries.) (Shout without: "Huzzah! Huzzah!")*

Enter HARLEY, ANNA, SOPHIA, BELFORD, *and* CLIFFORD, SOPHIA
leaning on BELFORD's *arm. (*FAIRFIELD *jumps to catch her and embraces*
her, then gives her to MRS. FAIRFIELD. EDWARD *and* MARIA *all hang*
on her, then run to ANNA *and embrace her.)*

Scene Two

The lake. Enter DERMOT *as from it.*

DERMOT: I wonder if it is twelve o'clock yet. Hetty will think it my ghost, for sartin. Well, here goes to try if she can outlive me. (*Goes off.*)

HETTY: (*Calls*). Dermot, Dermot! I am sure that is his old signal. (*Looks out. DERMOT groans. She sees him and calls.*) Dermot, for God's sake, speak if it be you.

DERMOT: (*Speaks in a hollow tone*). Oh, my dear Hetty, and sure I am but the ghost of your poor Dermot, come to put you in mind of your promise not to outlive him. So make haste down and take your lodgings, as I am doing just now, in the lake. Come quick. (*HETTY, frightened, faints and falls on the floor in the room. The fall is heard. DERMOT listens, but hears no sound, gets alarmed.*) Faith, and I believe I have kilt her in good earnest. (*Calls.*) Hetty! Why, Hetty! No answer. Oh faith, poor dear girl, you were true to your promise not to outlive me. And what a damned villain I am to murder you just for a trick. But faith, I must be off, or daylight will overtake me by the way. Oh, goodbye, my poor, dear, dead girl. I suppose your ghost will be after following me over the country and never cease crying, "Dermot, you kilt me." (*Exits.*)

Scene Three

The camp. Time: sunrise. The drum beats the reveille. Enter WILLIAM and CHARLES.

WILLIAM: This day I will solicit leave of absence. I long to see my parents, and here we are doing nothing.

CHARLES: We can certainly get a parole[12] for a few days. I am dying to see my Maria, and perhaps when all hearts are rejoicing, we may have a double wedding.

WILLIAM: Oh, here comes that fop!

Enter FREELOVE.

FREELOVE: This damned early rising I don't like much. Ha, my dear fellow, how goes it? Plenty of laurels? Honor and fame the soldier's mead.

WILLIAM: You, Mr. Freelove, bear yours with great ease.

FREELOVE: Yes, free and easy, that's my motto. (*Sings.*)

> For let the world jog as it will,
> I will be free and easy still.

---

[12]Furlough.

CHARLES: But Freelove, where was you in the engagement?

FREELOVE: Oh, I was roaring, dying with the toothache! Had I have been well, I should have fought like a lion; but I thought I should have died with agony. My limbs shook with pain. This is the cold I caught some time ago.

WILLIAM and CHARLES: Ha, ha, ha.

FREELOVE: Nay, 'tis no joke to be tortured with pain and prevented from sharing the honors of the day.

WILLIAM: Well, be more careful in future to put on your nightcap. But how beats your heart for the lovely Anna Harley?

FREELOVE: Oh, I am dying for another sight of her heavenly charms.

WILLIAM: What impression did you make, at the ball, on her?

FREELOVE: Oh, she smiled so charmingly that I think she was smitten. But I have had no time to improve my victory. And then, this damned toothache has kept me from gaining one poor wreath of laurel to lay at her feet.

CHARLES: I am going, William, to headquarters. Shall I present our united requests for a few days absence?

WILLIAM: I will accompany you. (*Exit* CHARLES *and* WILLIAM.)

Enter DERMOT.

DERMOT: Oh, Ensign, is your toothache got better? Faith, and you owe it to me that your head does not ache this day. If I had not have stood in your place the day of the battle, you would have been tried for cowardice: "But, by my soul, your honor," says I, "the poor fellow howls so loud with pain that no man could stand near him, so just let me hould the colors."

FREELOVE: Thank you, Dermot. I will do as much for you another time, (*Exit* FREELOVE.)

DERMOT: Well, now, I wonder where they will bury poor Hetty. Oh, Dermot, but it was a wicked joke to kill the poor, dear girl that loved you. But hark, I must away. (*Drum beats. Exits.*)

Scene Four

HARLEY's *house.   A parlor with a breakfast table set out.   Enter* HARLEY.

HARLEY: The events of last night have so deranged my ideas, that I almost forget the laws of hospitality to my guests. Oh, here they come.

Enter CLIFFORD *and* BELFORD. *(They salute* HARLEY.)

HARLEY: Good morning, my friends. (*Shakes hands with them.*) To thank you for your noble conduct last night is impossible, but you have bound me to you by the adamantine ties of gratitude.

CLIFFORD: You overrate the merits of the action. We did but fulfill our duty.

BELFORD: Could we have seen those angels suffer, we had been worse than savages.

HARLEY: Well, gratitude is best expressed by action. Tell me your situation. Your uniform bespeaks your country.

CLIFFORD: We were defeated at Yorktown; and, conducted by those Indians who last night forsook us, we were seeking a place of safety.

HARLEY: Such you have found. Remain here as long as you please, and when you depart I will secure you a safe conveyance to Montreal.

CLIFFORD: Duty requires that our departure should be immediate; our services are requisite.

HARLEY: Yet does not nature assert her rights and demand a few days of rest? They will invigorate your minds and bodies.

BELFORD: I am really so exhausted that I cannot proceed for a short time, and as we have no appointed rendezvous—

CLIFFORD: Why, for a day or two we will tarry here.

HARLEY: Thanks for this confidence and courtesy.

Enter ANNA *Harley.*

HARLEY: (*Introduces her*). My daughter. (GENTLEMEN *bow to her.*)

ANNA: (*Curtseying*). To you I owe more than life: my father's peace. And trust me, you will find an American girl feels more than she professes. But breakfast waits. (*Rings the bell. Enter* SERVANT *with coffee.*)

BELFORD: How does the nation in general like the present war?

HARLEY: We are a united people. Our rulers are chosen by the majority, and the minority submit of course.

CLIFFORD: Such have ever been the sentiments of every republic, till increase of wealth introduced luxuries, banished simplicity, and undermined true patriotism. While Rome was poor in wealth, her citizens were rich in integrity; but no sooner was its wealth become boundless than she fell.

BELFORD: America is in one particular an exception from all the republics history record.

ANNA: What is that?

BELFORD: She is grateful to her departed heroes.

HARLEY: You are correct, sir; for the name of Washington still causes our hearts to glow with rapture and an enthusiastic desire to emulate his virtues.

BELFORD: Ha, what angelic form passed the window but now? (*Knocking heard.*)

Enter SOPHIA, MARIA *and* FAIRFIELD, *the girls dressed in white dimity coatdresses, straw hats, and blue ribbons.* (ALL *rise.* ANNA *introduces them.*)

ANNA: This, gentlemen, was my companion in last night's adventure. (*Points to* SOPHIA. BELFORD *gazes at her with evident admiration. She blushes, looks confused, yet steals side glances at him.* ANNA *watches them.*)

FAIRFIELD: Gentlemen, to thank you is impossible, but be assured, 'tis here I feel what I owe you— (*Lays his hand on his breast.*)

SOPHIA: Would I could thank you as I ought, but language is too weak to express what I feel.

CLIFFORD: Then, my dear girl, say no more upon the subject. I have a wife and daughter; heaven knows how soon they may want protection. Come, the morning is so pleasant, methinks I should like to take a survey of your village. What say you to a walk?

HARLEY: Agreed. (BELFORD *offers* SOPHIA *his hand, which she accepts. All exit.*)

Scene Five

The lake. Enter BELFORD *and* SOPHIA.

BELFORD: I shall ever, charming Miss Fairfield, consider last night the most fortunate moment of my life.

SOPHIA: Is it then so delightful a circumstance to rescue two distressed damsels?

BELFORD: To a philanthropic heart, 'tis always pleasing to be serviceable; but to render that service to so much beauty, sense, and intelligence, united with such softness of manners, is ecstasy. And oh, if—as you assure me your heart is yet at your disposal—I may ever hope, no matter at how distant a period, to become master of that gentle heart, what years of happiness may I promise myself. (*Kneels.*)   Speak, angelic excellence.

SOPHIA: (*Confused*). Our short acquaintance, difference of country, time, circumstances, all conspire to—to—

BELFORD: To what, my angel? Proceed.

SOPHIA: I cannot.

BELFORD: What means this agony? Does my passion offend you?

SOPHIA: Oh no, no—but—

BELFORD: Blessings on you for that propitious "no." 'Tis the first time, I believe, a lover ever heard the word with pleasure.

SOPHIA: I have a brother in the American army; you are our enemy. How then can I expect to unite contraries? (*Alarm.*) Hark, what means that noise?

Enter hastily, FREELOVE, DASH, *and his party.*

FREELOVE: Seize the Tory rascal.

BELFORD: Rascal? (*Takes hold him.* FREELOVE *hallos.* DASH *and* SOLDIERS *interfere.* BELFORD *is made a prisoner. Exit* SOPHIA, *hastily.*)

FREELOVE: To the guard-house with him. The other will soon be taken, and (*Exit* DASH *and* SOLDIERS *with* BELFORD.) now see who shall dare to doubt my courage or patriotism. Oh, I shall have a wreath yet to lay at Miss Harley's feet. Laurel wreaths for Yankee soldiers. (*Exits singing.*)

Scene Six

Another part of the lake. Enter CLIFFORD, HARLEY, *and* EDWARD.

HARLEY: Haste, haste. Lose not one moment. In this canoe Edward will conduct you to a place of safety, and should the fate of war ever throw any of our countrymen on your mercy, remember Harley and Fairfield on Lake Erie. (*Puts a purse into* CLIFFORD's *hand, shakes it, hurries him into the canoe, which puts off.* HARLEY *motions till they are out of sight.*) Fear not for Captain Belford. As a prisoner of war, he will be well treated. My house shall be his home, and Sophia Fairfield his jailer.

(Noise of paddles heard. A canoe makes for the shore, moors. CHARLES, WILLIAM *and* TRUEMAN *land. They embrace* HARLEY—CHARLES *first.)*

HARLEY: Welcome, my dear boys. Thrice welcome to your father's arms. Oh, I am so happy, I don't know what to do with myself. (*Sings and dances.*) Yes, hey for the wedding. What think you, Captain? None but the brave deserve the fair.

TRUEMAN: And brave they are.

Enter MR. *and* MRS. FAIRFIELD, SOPHIA, MARIA, ANNA *and* HETTY. *(*MRS. FAIRFIELD *kisses* WILLIAM. MR. FAIRFIELD *shakes* *his hand. His* SISTERS *hang round him.* ALL *seem delighted. He breaks from them, goes to* ANNA. CHARLES *seizes* MARIA's *hand.)*

CHARLES: It is from this fair hand (*Takes* MARIA's *hand.*) I claim my reward.

WILLIAM: And I from this. (*Takes* ANNA's *hand.*) What say you, Captain? Ain't they lawful prisoners of war?

TRUEMAN: Yes, and for life.

HARLEY: Come, come, girls. 'Tis you that must reward your heroes. What say you, neighbor, to our double weddings this night?

FAIRFIELD: With all my heart. The sooner the better.

MRS. FAIRFIELD: No, no, not till all the flax is spun.

HARLEY: Damn the flax and the wheels too.

MRS. FAIRFIELD: Oh, Lord, my work will suffer, that is certain. I am glad Dermot is dead. Hetty can't get married.

Enter DERMOT.

DERMOT: Oh, the devil's mother fly away with me, if I an't just as much alive as you are, ould lady, so here goes Hetty, (*Takes her hand.* HETTY *laughs.* HARLEY *talks to* TRUEMAN *apart.* FAIRFIELD, CHARLES, *and* WILLIAM *join them.*)

TRUEMAN: Certainly, no request of yours shall be refused; but as a prisoner of war, he must have a parole. Till then, I take your word for his forthcoming. (*Exit* HARLEY.)

HETTY: Then Dermot, you an't dead.

DERMOT: Oh the devil a bit, but you dreamt all that about the ghost.

Re-enter HARLEY *and* BELFORD.

HARLEY: This, gentlemen, is the man to whom, under God, we owe the preservation of our dear girls. (WILLIAM *and* CHARLES *eagerly shake hands with him.* TRUEMAN *bows to him.* SOPHIA *and* BELFORD *exchange looks of affection.* ANNA *makes* FAIRFIELD *observe them, who nods assent.*)

WILLIAM and CHARLES: Our gratitude will end but with our lives.

ANNA: If I am not deceived, Captain Belford won't be satisfied with your gratitude. (*Archly.*) Do you think he will Sophy? (SOPHIA *looks confused.*)

HARLEY: Ha, ha, ha! Bravo! Come, Sophy, a triple wedding.

FAIRFIELD: Speak, my child.

BELFORD: Angelic Sophia, on you depends my fate. Give me but that fair hand, and I shall bless the day that made me a prisoner in America.

SOPHIA: As my father pleases.

MRS. FAIRFIELD: Oh dear, oh dear. All the wheels in the house will stand still.

MRS. FAIRFIELD: Take her, sir. (*Gives* SOPHIA's *hand to* BELFORD.) She only can reward your generosity.

HARLEY: Bravo! None but the brave deserve the fair.

TRUEMAN: And 'tis to the American fair the heroes of their country look for reward.

Now war has ceased, and smiling peace again
Permits the ships to plow the azure main.
Our warlike youths returned, to love you,
To claim and to receive the hero's due,
To taste sweet peace and soft domestic ease;
No anxious care but their loved wives to please.

ANNA: Well has each fair of this our western clime
Preserved their hearts for that wished happy time.
Looked not for beauty, prized but genuine worth:
Courage, integrity, and noble truth.
Frowned on the fop, bade libertines away,
But smiled on merit in the face of day.
Faction with all her hideous train doth fly,
And Columbia's fame resounds to yonder sky.

(*Curtain falls.*)

ALTORF

A Tragedy

Frances Wright[1]

1819

First Represented in the Theatre of New York, Feb. 19, 1819.
Originally published by M. Carey & Son, 126 Chestnut Street,
Philadelphia, 1819.

---

[1]Also known as Fanny Wright. Later Frances Wright D'Arusmont.

Preface

I cannot offer this tragedy, with my name affixed to it, to the people of America, without saying a few words that may, in some degree, express my sense of the generous manner in which it has been already received by the inhabitants of this city. Whatever may be its success hereafter, I shall never forget that as the work of a nameless author, it was accepted by the Theatre of New-York, and received with applause by an American audience. In affixing my name to this tragedy, perhaps I am a second time putting to the proof the generosity of the American public. A stranger—a foreigner—a young and unknown woman, my name can draw no attention to the title-page, and give no weight to the work itself. Yet I do not so wrong the people of this country as to apprehend that it will influence them unfavourably. Should it occur to them, while perusing Altorf, that they are perusing the work of a foreigner, it will perhaps also occur to them that that foreigner has sought their country uninvited, from a sincere admiration of their government, a heart-felt love of its freedom, and generous pride and sympathy in its rising greatness.

I know not if my wishes influence my judgment, but I cannot help believing that this country will one day revive the sinking honour of the drama. It is I believe generally felt and acknowledged, by the public of Great Britain as of America, that the dignity of English Tragedy has now degenerated into pantomime; and that rapid movements, stage tricks and fine scenery have filled the place of poetry, character, and passion. The construction as well as the management of the London Theatres perhaps present insurmountable obstacles to any who might there ambition to correct the fashion of the stage. No such difficulties exist here. But this is not all: America is the land of liberty. Here is the country where Truth may lift her voice without fear;—where the words of Freedom may not only be read in the closet, but heard from the stage. England pretends to an unshackled press: but there is not a stage in England from which the dramatist might breathe the sentiments of enlightened patriotism and republican liberty. In America alone might such a stage be formed; a stage that should be, like that of Greece, a school of virtue;—where all that is noble in sentiment, generous and heroic in action should speak to the hearts of a free people, and inspire each rising generation with all the better and noble feelings of human nature.

I am far from supposing myself equal to the forming of such a theatre as my imagination has conceived, but if I might only hope by my example to encourage other and more gifted minds to employ their powers in this work, and thus to effect and complete what I could only imagine, I shall feel that I have not wholly laboured in vain, and merit perhaps to leave my name in remembrance with the people of this great country; which in its infancy, has brought the art of government to perfection, and is destined, I would fondly hope, in its maturer age, to foster and advance every other art, and be at once the land of liberty and of genius.

New York, March 30, 1819.

It may perhaps be as well to advise the Reader that, both as to persons and plot, the Tragedy of Altorf is altogether fictitious. It may be the more necessary to advise him of this, as from the allusions to historical events, and the story being as it were interwoven with a national revolution, he might incline to search the Swiss annals for the name and life of my Hero, neither of which he will find there.

The story of the insurrection of the Swiss Cantons in the fourteenth century; the violent and wanton tyranny exercised by Austria and her Deputies over that intrepid race of mountaineers, and the spirit and heroic firmness with which they rose against that tyranny, and again and again engaged with and overcame the formidable armies by which it thought to terrify and force them into submission—all this is too well known for any abstract of these events to be necessary as a preface to the victory of Morgarten. The opening of the drama supposes that victory achieved, and the Swiss bands, encamped on Mount Sattel, watching the motions of a second division of the Austrian army, that threatened to advance into their vallies.

It only remains for me to apologize for an error, which perhaps the generality of readers might pass over without detection, or at least without comment. I have more than once throughout the piece styled the house of Austria *Imperial*. Perhaps the epithet might admit of defence, not only on the ground that two of that house had already filled the imperial throne, but that even at the time of Leopold's invasion of Switzerland the struggle between the Austrian and Bavarian candidates continued indecided: Frederic no less than Lewis claiming the title of King of the Romans and Emperor elect.

I must confess, however, the propriety of its application to Duke Leopold, a younger brother of Frederic, to be more than doubtful, and, admitting the inaccuracy, I shall only rest its excuse on its unimportance.

New York, Feb. 17, 1819.

Prologue to Altorf
By W. T. Wolfe-Tone

No royal pageantry this night displayed
Crowds your Columbian stage with vain parade,
The pomp of courts, the empty cares of kings
No kindred feeling to your bosom brings.
A nobler inspiration wakes the lyre,
'Tis liberty's unconquerable fire;
That liberty for which our fathers bled
When Washington their free battalions led.
Like them, Helvetia's sons, a hardy race,
Toiled at the plough, or laboured in the chace:
Obscure, but blest, until a tyrant's hand
Stretched its unhallowed grasp over their rugged land.
With generous indignation fired, they sprung,
And the rude horn along their vallies rung;
And, at the call, each peasant mountaineer
Rush'd down his hills, and shook his rustic spear.
The haughty foe, whose chivalry with pride
Rolled up the vale war's undulating tide,
He stood—firm as his native Alpine rock
Each peasant stood the charger's whirling shock,
And calling on Helvetia's sacred name,
Rushed fearless on to victory and fame;
Whilst from each mountain-echo swell'd the cry
Of justice, vengeance, Switz and *liberty*.

    And shall the tale of liberty be told
To ears unwilling and to bosoms cold?
Could self-accusing despots bear the sight
Of Austria humbled in Morgarten's fight?
Oh, no—Columbia, to thy sons belongs
The muse of yet unprostituted songs;
That never yet with mercenary fire,
Strung for a Monarch's ear the adulating lyre.
Freedom, that roused the poet's kindling art,
Will touch the springs of each Columbian heart,
And will associate with a magic spell
The name of WASHINGTON with that of TELL.

Persons of the Drama

Eberard de Altorf, Captain of the Independent Swiss Army
Erlach, the old Baron de Altorf, father to Eberard.
De Rheinthal, a young Swiss soldier.
Werner, Count de Rossberg.
Eustace, attendant of Rossberg.

Giovanna, sister of de Rheinthal and wife of Altorf.
Rosina de Rossberg, daughter of the Count.

Soldiers, Attendants, &c. {Peasants, Soldiers, Servants, Guards}[2]

Scene: Switzerland.

ACT I

Before a wood; cottage appearing through the trees. Enter ROSSBERG, *disguised in poor attire, and a Swiss* PEASANT.

PEASANT: There, friend! In center of that little wood
His cottage lies embosomed. *See where the thatch,
Thick clothed in vines, sends up among the trees
Its curling smoke! And, through the parted boughs,
The lattice, laced with woodbine and the rose,
Looks smiling out.*[3]
ROSSBERG: Thanks, friend. But, ere we part,
Know ye if Eberard, old Altorf's son,
Be yet returned?
PEASANT: How! Ask you of the war?
Surely you are a stranger in our vales
If that you know not of Morgarten's fight

---

[2]Material in brackets was added in the acting edition. This edition, which bears the penciled notation, "Wm. B. Wood," lists the following actors for the major roles: Mr. Wallack as Eberard, Mr. Pritchard as Erlach, Mr. Simpson as de Rheinthal, Mr. Graham as Werner, Mr. Moreland as Eustace, Miss Johnson as Giovanna, and Mrs. Barnes as Rosina.
[3]Passages enclosed in asterisks are omitted in the acting edition.

And young de Altorf, who led on our bands
To victory and freedom.
    ROSSBERG: Stranger I am;
Yet not from land so distant but I know
The tale of your achievements: *how the pride
Of Austria is quelled—her noble chiefs,
Her marshalled legions scattered on the field,
Food for the birds of heaven. How the song
Of proud emancipation rends your Alps,
And every peasant child, as on their sides
Watching his flock or wandering herd he sits,
Teaches the traveler and mountain echoes
His country's freedom, and de Altorf's praise.*
All this I know, but have yet farther heard
That on Mount Sattel still the watch is held
By Altorf and his troops. This seemeth strange,
Or rather useless, might a stranger judge,
Seeing the work of liberty's achieved,
And not a man of Austria's vast array
Remains unto their swords.
    PEASANT: 'Tis this we doubt.
Rumors prevail that other hosts advance,
Not less in number, discipline, and conduct
Than those Morgarten saw. But of these things
The aged Erlach will inform you amply.
    ROSSBERG: Good morrow, then; and thanks, friend, for your
guidance. (*Exit* PEASANT.)
Cautious as brave! By heaven, these rebel churls
Shall cope with peers and princes in the art
Of noble war! Austria, who would have thought
That thy imperial head should yield its laurels
To shepherd mountaineers? *But tremble, Switz.
There is a weapon stronger than the sword,
Whose subtle edge can strike into the marrow,
Sap the foundations of the grandest empires,
Disjoint their strength, and heap them all in ruins.*
Eustace! Come forward, Eustace! (*Calling off the scene.*)

Enter EUSTACE.

    ROSSBERG: We are right,
Behold the roof that tenants Altorf's lord.

Times are sore changed, Eustace—times and manners.
This aged baron, I remember, Eustace,
When Germany, nor France herself could boast
A peer more proud, a knight more chivalrous.
Yet see him now despoiled of states and title,
The aged Nestor of our rebel shepherds;
While his young son, a courtly cavalier,
Acts their Achilles. Fie on't!
Hark'ye, Eustace!
While I accost the sire, seek you the son.
Or one or other I will win, or perish.
    EUSTACE: How look you to succeed?
    ROSSBERG: By art or bribe.
Albeit my kinsman wear these stoic virtues,
None know what cause of secret discontent
May be the parent of them. Blighted hopes,
Ambition disappointed, or sick envy,
Hath made more sages than philosophy,
Saints than religion, patriots than virtue.
    EUSTACE: It may be so! But have you weighed, my lord,
The danger you encounter? Is there one,
'Mid all the leaders of the Austrian Army,
More hateful to the insurgents than Count Werner?
Alone, unarmed, to pass into their camp,
My lord, 'twere madness! No disguise will serve you.
Your face, your form, your voice are all familiar
To thousands of the rebels.
    ROSSBERG: I risk not this.
Pass you into the camp; seek out young Altorf.
Be not too hasty to declare yourself,
But watch him. Watch him silently and closely.
Observe his temper; ask of it from others.
I know that he was proud and hasty somewhat;
And I should deem that in his present station
Of captain to a band of mountaineers,
His pride would meet some rubs. Take your pipe.
'Twill gain you easy passport 'mong the rebels;
And, I remember me, De Altorf loved
To list the wild notes of our mountain airs
When my fair daughter played them. Try your skill;
Observe if you can move him. I esteem
He hath not yet forgot his trothed love,

But yields it only to a father's will.
Examine into this. If the sire fail me,
I'll tamper with the son—work on his pride,
Waken his jealousy, stir up disputes,
Or else relume his now-forgotten passion
For his betrothed Rosina. Now depart.
Meet me again within that hollow valley
Beneath the rebel camp.
  EUSTACE: What hour were best?
  ROSSBERG: The earliest we can.
Before three hours be past I shall be there,
And linger 'mong the rocks until you join me.
A whistle be the signal. Now, farewell. (*Exit* EUSTACE.)
Voices! Perchance 'tis Erlach. I'll withdraw
And list awhile unseen. (*Withdraws among the trees.*)

Enter ERLACH *from the cottage, and an old* SERVANT. (ROSSBERG *concealed.*)

  ERLACH: Not yet arrived? How points the sun, good Hubert?
  SERVANT: Direct from noon.
  ERLACH: Then hie thee, quick,
And choose the freshest fruits the garden bears,
And spread the table 'neath the oaken tree.
I look for them each moment. (*Exit* SERVANT.)
How gaily shines the sun! *Methinks all nature
Knows our tale of freedom. The little birds
Do warble in the boughs with blither note;
The wild goat on the mountain sports more briskly;
The mountain's self doth lift his head more proud,
And, in his joy, doth seem to kiss the heavens,
Too gay to wear a cloud. The very air
Comes to my senses with more balmy breath,
And fans my cheek more sweetly.* Oh, my fond heart!
Thy aged pulses beat as quick with pleasure
As ever bridegroom's on the nuptial day.
My gracious maker, thou hast blessed me fully!
Old Erlach now hath not a prayer to utter;
He can but only praise thee, bless, and die.
(ROSSBERG *comes forward and stands considering him in deep silence.*)
Stranger! Whence comest thou?
What would ye, friend? Why read you thus my face?

ROSSBERG: (*Considering him as before*).
The priest, the moralist, and dreaming poet
Henceforth we may accredit. Who shall teach
Aught strange or novel of the thoughts of men
That might be now disputed?
ERLACH: Who may this be?
Stranger, where tend thy words?
ROSSBERG: To this they tend;
That if men hear, for marketplace reports,
Of crested monarchs who put off their state
And sell their purple for a beggar's rags,
Their palace for a stable, and their realm
For leave to pace the highway, cap in hand,
Craving an alms for love of charity,
They need not cry "God's mercy." They who see
My noble kinsman changed to what I see him
Might hold such tales for just intelligence.
ERLACH: That voice chimes in familiar to my ear.
That eye—that brow—I've seen such heretofore.
Count Werner, as I live!
ROSSBERG: I marvel not
I read amazement in the face of Erlach.
That Rossberg's lord should, through a land of rebels,
Pace in this mean disguise to seek a foe
Is doubtless something strange.
ERLACH: Your pardon, Count?
Who calls this land rebellious speaks not here.
Ere that I ask the motive of your journey,
Resolve to name with honor this free country,
Or part in peace unquestioned.
ROSSBERG: Free, call ye it? Licentious, rather say.
Is it for peasant churls and mountain shepherds
To frame out laws and mock the word of kings?
ERLACH: Hist, lord of Rossberg! Leave injurious words.
Speak quickly to thine errand.
ROSSBERG: You know this signet? (*Showing a ring.*)
ERLACH: Austria's: proceed.
ROSSBERG: Thus saith Imperial Leopold to Altorf:
Albeit the measure of his crimes be full,
That in the eye of nations and of men
He stands arraigned and forfeit to the law;
Yet doth he hold to him his gracious pardon,

Secure to him his lands, his wealth and station.
Nay, more—so he return to his allegiance,
Count of the Empire I have power to hail him.
     ERLACH: Look at these locks, my lord! The snows of age
Have bleached them o'er and o'er. Art not ashamed
To bear such message to so old a man?
Go! Tell him that sent thee, not his empire
Could buy the voice of Altorf from his country.
*Go to! I know the drift. I know you deem
My voice hath weight among this artless people.
And you are right: it hath, I'm proud to say it.
Tush! You have chosen ill. You should have sought
Some hot-brained boy, fresh from his mother's apron,
To catch your bait.* Wealth, rank, and station, Count:
All these I had and freely parted with.
My wealth! I've poured it forth to arm my country.
My rank! I've learned to know it but a name,
And thrown it to the winds. My station—that!
Behold, I've fled for aye the throne of kings,
And found it as the pedestal of freedom!
     ROSSBERG: This might be thought enough; yet I'll speak further.
     ERLACH: No further, Count, if that your drift be treason.
     ROSSBERG: Treason? In Erlach's mouth that word sounds nobly—
Erlach, who's broken oath and loyalty,
And rung rebellion's clamor through the land.
     ERLACH: *Speak not of these things, Count; they are beyond thee.
I tell thee, Rossberg, thou canst not understand
The cause of freedom, nor the patriot's motives.
Why, did I show thee all I think and feel—
All that I've done and would do in this cause,
Thou'dst call me moonstruck and beside my reason.*
Rebellion? Treason? Thou'rt the rebel, Rossberg!
*Thou, who prefer'st the interest of one man,
And that a base and mean and sordid interest,
Unto the weal of thousands. Thou, who stoop'st
A servile knee unto a thirsty tyrant,
Whose hands are dropping with thy country's gore,
And his vile coffers filled with plunder of its poor.
Oh, Rossberg! Rossberg!* Talk no more of this.
Thou'lt break my aged frame with indignation;

It ill becomes so old a man as me[4]
To swell with anger.
    ROSSBERG: Lay it then aside,
And let me claim an answer calmly from thee.
Who hath more cause for wrath—or you or I?
You, who have broke your faith and solemn pledge—
I speak not now of any public matter—
Or I, who took that pledge, and found it rotten?
    ERLACH: I know to what you point: my son's alliance.
Before this country's wrongs cried up to heaven,
Before a Tell defied a Geisler's fury,
*Before a Furst, a Smuffacher, and Melchthal
Held up in Ruttle's field their conjoined hands
And called their God to look down from his throne
And register their oath in his great record,*
Erlach was Rossberg's kinsman and his friend;
And if he is not still, let him see to it
Who is not found where justice, honor call him.
Had Rossberg sided with his injured country,
Our children's loves had not been crossed thus rudely.
    ROSSBERG: Had Erlach not espoused a rebel cause—
    ERLACH: A truce to this! Count Werner sure must feel
That he and I have now no thoughts in common;
And, being so, certain he could not wish
To join his child and mine at heaven's altar.
    ROSSBERG: There you say true. The untainted blood of Rossberg
Certain shall never mix with that of rebels.
But say, hath Erlach with the peasant's garb
Put on the peasant's mind? What, all the fame,
The grandeur, honor, potency forgot
Of this long line of fathers? Forbid it, heaven!
My friend, think better of it. Trust my words:
These churls, for whom you sacrifice your all
Will, when you most attend a good requital,
Turn foul upon you with the canker tooth
Of mean ingratitude. It is their nature.
To look among the base-born and the poor
For virtues of the noble were, as if
We should demand from mules the courser's mettle,

---

[4]The acting edition substitutes "I."

Or lion's magnanimity from foxes.
    ERLACH: *Methinks, when you and I were younger somewhat,
In Mantua's learned halls, that we did read
The golden annals of the men of Greece;
When we did say, that spite of all their errors,
Their pride, their clamor, and their thanklessness,
We rather would have fought, have bled, have died
Upon the hallowed field of Marathon,
Than sat an Alexander on Darius' throne.
So felt we then; so feel I now,* Count Werner.
While that my son and I take up this quarrel,
He aiding with his sword, I with my counsel,
We ask, we wish, we merit none requital
But that sweet payment of approving conscience,
Of which, nor thankless world, nor frowning heaven,
Nor slanderous tongues, nor dungeons, chains, and tortures,
Nor death made vile by scoffings, cord, and gibbets,[5]
The patriot's single heart shall e'er bereave.
    ROSSBERG: You do refuse, then, Austria's proffered bounties?
    ERLACH: I wed in life or death the cause of freedom.
    ROSSBERG: You are fixed on breaking up our children's loves,
Breaking our ancient friendship and our contract?
    ERLACH: So fate and duty have compelled, my lord;
For know, a bar which only death can break
Stands 'twixt my child and thine. My son is married.
    ROSSBERG: How?
    ERLACH: I've said the truth. 'Twas a hard struggle, Count,
For my poor boy: but to a father's prayers
At length he yielded. I knew his love—
How great, how nourished from his boyhood up—
For your bewitching daughter, and I feared
His love should prove a tamperer with his honor,
Should stand betwixt him and his struggling country;
And in this fear—
    ROSSBERG: Oh, no explainings! I doubt not Altorf's heir
Hath found a wealthier and a nobler mate
Than my half-portioned child. But know, false kinsman,
Though Rossberg's lands and titles pass by law

---

[5]Refers to the humiliating form of death employed against criminals, in which the
condemned was led to the gallows with a rope around his neck.

Unto thy son as to the next male heir,
Yet there is wealth and wide estates, too, Baron,
My daughter can inherit!
    ERLACH: Hear me, Count!
Your wealth I never sought. 'Twas not for this
I wished to join our children. And your title,
With the fair lands annexed to it: by heaven,
I covet neither! I claim neither, Rossberg;
I, nor my son. *Doubt not my honesty;
Nor deem I make parade of costly virtues.
This wealth and rank, authority and station
Have* {You} now so little lure to tempt my envy
That yielding them can scarce lay claim to merit,
And barely asks your thanks.
    ROSSBERG: My thanks! Not mine.
Rossberg hath yet too much of human frailty,
Of honor, pride, and chivalrous ambition,
To render praise to monkish apathy,
Or swell the hosannahs of a base-born rabble
To self-deposing lords.
    ERLACH: Nay, scoff not, kinsman!
Albeit opinion make us public foes,
Let us in private wear the heart of friends.
Wilt please you take refreshment ere we part?
    ROSSBERG: I thank you, Baron; here my mission ends.
    ERLACH: Speed quickly, then; for I expect each moment
Some soldiers from the camp, and were you found,
My voice might barely serve to shield your life. (*Exit* ROSSBERG.)
    ERLACH: (*Alone*). Why, what a riddle is the soul of man!
How grand and how contemptible! *Now shining
In such full majesty of godlike virtue—
In thought so high, in feeling so devoted,
In scheme so vast, in action so sublime—
It seems, upon earth's theatre, not less
Than the creating spirit, when it moved
O'er the blank face of chaos, bringing light
And life and joy and loveliness to being.
And then again—and, oh my God, how frequent—
So petty in its aims, base in its feelings,
Gross in its pleasures, sordid in its service,
'Twould be as one with the unreasoning brutes,
Wer't not more rank and loathsome.* Oh, my country!

Remain but simple, frugal, and content.
Hold high in honor still the plough and distaff.[6]
Still think the shepherd's crook more worthy honor
Than idle scepters of more idle kings!
Then shall your hearts be pure, your conscience proud,
Your store be plenty, and your hearth set round
With smiling children and with grateful guests;
Then shall the blessing of your God be with you,
The love, the envy, and the praise of men!

GIOVANNA: (*Entering*). Heaven grant your prayer, my venerable father!

ERLACH: Ah, my daughter! How fares it in the camp?

GIOVANNA: Well! Well. All well—in health—

ERLACH: *In health?
Is't not in all things else?

GIOVANNA: Why doubts our father?

ERLACH: Nay, I doubt nothing, child; only thy phrase
"All well in health," seemed as 'twere left to say
In something all were not well. 'Tis not so?
Why then, all's well; and if with you, with me—
For I now only feel or joy or pain
Through thee, my son, and country.* But where's the rest?
You do not come alone?

GIOVANNA: An accident—some duties, I should say,
Detain your son.

ERLACH: Your brother: he too engaged?

GIOVANNA: He is.

ERLACH: No sound of Austria's approach?

GIOVANNA: None.

ERLACH: Or thought of march to meet them?

GIOVANNA: No.

ERLACH: Some plans to frame or orders to give forth?

GIOVANNA: I heard of none.

ERLACH: Well, well! Perhaps a trifle.

GIOVANNA: A trifle? No; no trifle.

ERLACH: True, for public duties never can be trifling:
'Twas justly said.

GIOVANNA: I meant it not so deep.
Father, you are grave.

---

[6]Spool-like device for winding wool or flax, to spin into yarn.

ERLACH: And you are silent, daughter.

GIOVANNA: *Said I not all was well?*
Unfix your eyes, and smooth your brow, my father,
You look upon me with such searching gaze
As though you waited news of death or life,
And dared not ask, because you feared the worst.

ERLACH: Quick to thy tale! What is the matter? Speak!

GIOVANNA: Now, by my troth, I dare not give it breath,
Lest you should swell my words beyond their meaning,
And pluck disquiet from a childish matter.
It is no more—believe it. Yet such as 'tis,
I wish your counsel and entreat your aid.

ERLACH: Alas, my child, and do you come to me?
Hath Switz no abler man than aged Erlach?
Yet speak; for whatsoever my age can do,
Thou know'st it will.

GIOVANNA: Thy age it is I look to.
*Who like the old and wise can stem the storm
Of bickering passion in the young and thoughtless?
Doth not the counsel of the grey-haired sage
Fall upon angry ears as silken oil
On the troubled ocean?*   Yes, my honored father,
Let but thy voice be heard in yonder tents,
And love and concord shall again be with us!

ERLACH: What, is our camp divided? Holy heaven!
Is Switz undone, betrayed, and all so soon?

GIOVANNA: Nay, God forbid! It is not thus, my father.
'Tis but a little strife, a soldier's quarrel
Betwixt my brother and thy noble son.

ERLACH: My son? What, Eberard? And with thy brother?

GIOVANNA: I mourn to say it.

ERLACH: Quickly, how fell it out?

GIOVANNA: You know—you may have heard, how 'tis agreed
That in four days, if the war hold so long,
My brother, in reward for some late service,
Should take our Eberard's place, and glean the honor
Of driving the invaders from our Alps.
Now, in the council it is judged expedient
Our little camp should tarry on Mount Sattel
Till, lulled into security, the foe
Should tempt again a passage through our valleys;

When, rushing from our rocky fastnesses,[7]
We 'whelm them in destruction quick and certain.
    ERLACH: Where lies the mischief in a plan so wise?
    GIOVANNA: Do you not see that, if the foe delay
Some few days more, your son's command expires,
As he complains, in useless, shameful idlesse;[8]
And when the day of danger comes, he quits
His foremost post, as if afraid to hold it.
Thus, jealous of his honor, and beside
Fond of heroic exploit, he in council
Spoke for more daring action, blamed all delay
As cowardly, unworthy of our nation,
Unworthy of the cause—and, most of all,
Unworthy of those men who wear their scars
Yet green from field of victory.
Thus having spoke,
My brother hasty rose; and, it might be,
From eager wish of honor in command,
Loud pleaded for delay. His voice was heard;
My husband was o'er-ruled. And is it strange
If here was sown the seed of youthful quarrel?
    ERLACH: Oh, fie upon't! Oh, fie! What, is my son
A paltry wrangler for command and station?
I'll to him straight. Run for my staff, dear child!
God's blessing on thee for this timely warning.
I'll forward slowly. Follow with my staff.
    GIOVANNA: I will, I will. But oh, be gentle with them.
Speak not in anger, I conjure you, father.
Kind words alone may heal the strife of friends;
For friends they were, and friends again they shall be.
    ERLACH: Oh, it has cut my heart! Mad, foolish boy!
(*Exit* GIOVANNA *into the cottage.*)

---

[7]Fortifications.
[8]Idleness.

ACT II

Among the Alps, before Altorf's tent. Enter ALTORF *from the tent, with a* SOLDIER.

ALTORF: At noon, at noon. I said before, at noon.
In God's name, tease no more!   (*Exit* SOLDIER.)
What is this life?
Some call't a dream, and some a gossip's story,
And some the tricksome acting of a player,
Forgotten soon as ended. *Psha! An'[9] 'twere such,
Should we find in't so many bleeding rubs?
Should we build up so many fairy hopes;
Grasp at such heights of happiness and greatness;
And plan and feel and act so many things;
And sigh such sighs, and fret so in the core,
For losses, crosses, wants, and disappointments?*
This life, to angels looking out from heaven,
May be an idle dream or passing breath;
But to us men, who have to struggle through it,
It is a time most anxious and most earnest.
Ho, there!   (*Calling off the scene to a* SOLDIER.)
Are our scouts returned?
SOLDIER: (*Enters*). No, Captain.
ALTORF: Went young de Rheinthal forward yester night?

Enter DE RHEINTHAL.

DE RHEINTHAL: No. Yet at your commands, my noble brother.
ALTORF: (*Waving off the* SOLDIER). Indeed!
It is an honor I not quite expected.
DE RHEINTHAL: No, nor quite wished for. Is't not so, my captain?
ALTORF: De Rheinthal! Though you bearded me in council,
And for good order's sake I let it pass,
I'd have you know my temper's not the coolest.
It might be roused, and I were sorry for't.
While that our country stands in risk, 'twere sin
To draw our swords for other cause than hers.
Smooth, then, your brow, and straight your curled lip.

---

[9]If.

I tell you I am hot. Forbear to urge me!
　　DE RHEINTHAL: Hot! I object not. Hot as you will, good Captain.
But is't a matter this, to set the match to't?
All have the right of speech, as of opinion;
Nor do I see, because you think it good
To fight today, I may not like tomorrow.
Nor was I single to advise delay;
The ablest, wisest veterans of our camp
Were on my side.
　　ALTORF: Well, did I object
To bow before their wisdoms, or to yours?
Old age is ever prudent, cautious, cold;
And you, de Rheinthal, doubtless have your reasons—
Doubtless *good* reasons. I object in nothing.
*True, I no more conceive how men should sit
Five days, nor one day, yawning on these hills,
Than catch yon sun upon their tilted spears—*
But this let pass. I only have to say
That not the *purport* of your speech displeased me,
Only the *manner* of it—*accent, air*;
And this I do request for both our sakes,
For peace, good order—if you will, good manners—
That you will leave or change. It is not once,
Nor twice, you have seen it good to tempt me thus.
　　DE RHEINTHAL: Why, in heaven's name, which is to blame? Is't I?
Did I not seek to win you for my friend,
Admiring both your talents and your valor?
And when our parents made the marriage up
'Twixt thee and my dear sister, did I not
Receive you with a brother's open arms—
Try all I could to win your trust and love?
Then, if you only met my love halfway,
Was it my fault? If, when I joked and laughed,
You looked the graver, was the fault with me?
If, when—
　　ALTORF: Truce to your *if*'s. I'll take all blame unargued.
I know my face is grave, my temper gloomy.
'Tis my misfortune; but the man who mocks it
Might never be the brother of my bosom.
You say that I but meet your love halfway;
I told you why I did not—why I could not.
You were the laughing spring, I the cold winter.

You loved the dance, the song, the eye of woman;
I—none of these. Even in arms we differed:
You loved the life, the brilliancy, the pride,
The death, the spirit of the soldier's fortune;
I only sought, setting our cause aside,
The danger and the drowning noise of battle.

DE RHEINTHAL: You do me wrong. I never mocked your ways;
I've thought them strange, as who on earth would not?
In studying you, I find all things reversed.
Why, there's a bridal: i' the world before
I took it for a festival; from you
I've learned to mark it for a day of penance.

ALTORF: Tush!

DE RHEINTHAL: Nay, do you know, de Altorf, you have taught me
That beauty, grace, youth, wit, and loveliness
Are things to shun in women. When I wed,
It shall be some old dame whose wrinkled cheeks
Retain no flush of youth, no blush of love;
Whose eye—no fire; whose voice—no tenderness;
Whose heart—no hopes, no warmth, no kindliness.
I would not, by my soul, crush the fair bud
Of trusting, open-hearted, kindled beauty!
No, not for Austria's throne! What say you, brother?
Should you not marvel if there were a man
Whose face a lovely woman could not brighten?

ALTORF: Again, if such there be, 'tis his misfortune.
I rather pity him than blame him for't.

DE RHEINTHAL: So do not I.

ALTORF: And there's another cause
Why I can only meet your love halfway.
You see we do agree in nothing, brother.

DE RHEINTHAL: I know not how you call your temper hot;
You answer very coolly to my speech.

ALTORF: Yes; for though rude, its cause does not offend me.
You are the brother of a woman such
As Europe scarce might match. That you should love her,
And loving her, should of her peace be jealous,
Is right and natural. That you should blame
The man who seemed too careless of her peace,
Cold to her beauties, blind to her perfections,
Is natural also; yet you are mistaken.
I am not blind nor careless, only cold.

DE RHEINTHAL: Cold! Then you own you do not love my sister?
ALTORF: I have not said so: nor am I bound, I think,
To answer every question you may ask.
DE RHEINTHAL: Whate'er your temper is, I feel mine's hot;
And, if you will not fight, I must not quarrel.
One thing before I go: you marvel, doubtless,
To see me here.
ALTORF: I marvel nothing, sir.
I should have known before I gave my orders,
They would not be obeyed unless they pleased you.
They have not pleased you, and are not obeyed.

Enter GIOVANNA.

GIOVANNA: Both frowning. Fie! Rheinthal, is this your promise?
ALTORF: Fear not, Giovanna; we are both quite cool.
DE RHEINTHAL: 'Tis false! For one at least, I am not cool.
GIOVANNA: Then do not speak. Come, I've a word for you.
This way a moment. (*Exits with* DE RHEINTHAL *into the tent.*)
ALTORF: Would God[10] I had not yielded. Wherefore did I?
To be a patriot, needs it be a husband?
Tush! We'll not think on't. Oh, I'm sick at heart!
Shield us, my father! Sir, how came you here?
ERLACH: (*Entering*). Am I not welcome, son?
ALTORF: Not welcome! Father,
What have I done to merit such a word? (*Pulls off his hat and, stooping on his knee, seizes his father's hand.*)
The hand withdrawn too?
ERLACH: Art thou worthy of it?
ALTORF: How! Worthy?
ERLACH: Aye, son. It is a feeble hand, and old,
Shrunk up from service of the sword and spear;
And yet its thin and shriveled palm is worth
The grasp of noble men. I would not give it,
Old as it is and useless to the touch,
Of him I did not honor.
ALTORF: Ha!
ERLACH: I like the sign:
That start of wonder and that flush of pride

---

[10]The acting edition substitutes "to Heaven" for "God."

Give me my son again. I've wronged thee, Eberard.
ALTORF: Wronged me, indeed, and cut me to the core.
What, soiled and blank in honor? Oh, my father!
ERLACH: Old age, my boy, is often fond and foolish.
Canst thou believe it? In my dreams I saw
The captain of our armies—him whom Switz
Hath chosen for her guard and sentinel—
I saw him in our camp—yea, in our council—
Strike the first spark of discord and dissension!
I saw him fix his eye and selfish heart
Upon the bubble of the world's report—
Ready to barter for the breath of fools,
Faith, freedom, and his country.
    *ALTORF: You've heard it wrong— You've heard it but in part.
ERLACH: That I should hear't at all! Oh, senseless boy!
With lighter heart I'd look upon thy corpse
Than hear this thing of thee.
    ALTORF: Nay, but you wrong me.
No selfish wish, no motive mean or vile
My soul hath known. I swear't, by heaven! By—
    ERLACH: Hold!
Ere thou swear'st, search well into thy heart.
Search—search it clean. Whisper this question to't:
When I gave up the trappings of my state,
Gave up my wealth and my heart's dearest ties,
My first and trothed love—when all I gave
Freely and frankly at my country's call—
Did I then feel I had but done my duty
Right—and no more than right—or did I think
That I had done a thing much to admire,
Felt my heart proud, and said within myself,
My country is my debtor; and when she gave
The keeping of her honor to my hands,
Chose me her captain, setting me above
My elders both in wisdom and in years,
Did I receive the preference as my due,
And think, forsooth, when heaven had blessed the efforts
Of my brave countrymen with victory,
That unto me, the chief, the praise was due,
Great thanks and honors? Whisper thus, my son,
Unto thy heart, and, if it answer well,
Then proudly turn and tell me I have wronged thee.

ALTORF: I may not stand before so pure a judge.
Perhaps, my father, I have something erred;
Perhaps, when dashing in the tide of battle,
I've thought upon myself and felt that death
Would, while it gave my name to future ages,
Release me from a life rough and uneasy.
A thirst for honor I will not deny;
I feel it, and I prize it. Do you blame me?
A sick and aching heart too, I confess.
This may be weakness; is it sin, my father?
ERLACH: I do not chide. I love your thirst for honor.
There's no great soul without it. For your sorrows?
No, no, my boy! I do not chide you here;
Yet if you loved your country as you ought—
But, no, I will not say't! You know your duty.
Now hath my son no errors unconfessed?*
ALTORF: You've heard, I see, th' amount of my offenses,
And heard more than the truth. Am I to blame
Because some like me not? Men's tastes are free.
Must we push through the thronged road of life
And cry "well met" to every fool we jostle?
The short of my offense is: I offend
The brother of my wife. I speak too little,
Am grave at times, or on his sister's beauties
Look with too cold an eye. And when I answer,
My face is as God made it; that my tongue
Speaks when it finds occasion: for my eyes,
If they be blind, the loss is to myself;
That I am past the days of tutorship,
And do not wish a spy upon my steps,
He chafes and throws the gauntlet. I refuse it.
He nurtures up disdain within his breast,
And pours it forth even in public council.
Why, who could take these things with a still pulse?
I am not saint, nor yet philosopher;
Nor do pretend such power o'er myself
As not to feel and not to show my feelings.
ERLACH: And do you dare command some thousand men,
Who are not yet the master of yourself?
Vain, foolish boy! Boy? Thou art not a boy.
Why, on thy head thou bear'st nigh thirty years.
Shame, shame on thee! Go, and throw off that plume.

Throw off your sword, and get you hence to school.
There learn again what 'tis you owe to virtue,
What to yourself, what to your fellow men,
What unto God, and, more than all, your country.
    ALTORF: Enough! Enough! Behold me on my knee.
    ERLACH: Your heart, your stubborn heart! Bow that, my son.
    ALTORF: It is; it is. Command me; I obey.
I'm proud, weak, foolish; I confess it all.
    ERLACH: Oh, mend it all! My son, I'm weak and old.
My feet are on the lowest step of life,
And tremble e'en on that. Thou soon wilt lose me;
Then, if thy stormy passions do awake,
What voice shall lay them? Oh, bethink thee well!
My sand is so near run, this may, my son—
This *may* be the last lesson I shall give thee.
    ALTORF: (*Striking his breast*).
'Tis graven here. Fear not, my honored parent!
Whene'er my proud heart swells, I'll con it o'er.
And be—and be all you could wish, my father. (*Throwing himself at*
ERLACH's *feet.*) Your blessing!
    ERLACH: (*Placing both hands on his head*). There! There!
I cannot speak it, son.

Enter DE RHEINTHAL, GIOVANNA *from the tent.*

    DE RHEINTHAL: Well, well! I'm schooled; I'm schooled!
What have we here?
    ALTORF: (*Rising and holding out his hand* to DE RHEINTHAL).
My friend and brother!
Will you forget the past?
    DE RHEINTHAL: With all my soul.
    ERLACH: Why, that's well said, and comes from a warm heart.
    DE RHEINTHAL: Most worthy sir, I bless you for your present!
Before I had a brother, now a friend.
But (*Turning to* ALTORF.) I hope there's no constraint. I would not owe
My captain's love all to a father's prayers;
No, though that father were the honored Erlach.
    ALTORF: Freely I gave my hand, nor am I wont
To give my hand and to withhold my heart.
    DE RHEINTHAL: The word's enough. And from this hour be
banished
All strife, all coldness, all reserve, all gloom.

ALTORF: Nay, softly, sir! We all are as God[11] made us:
Some gay and spiritous, some staid and heavy,
Some with hearts flowing o'er and faces beaming
With joyous life and love that asks receiving,
Some in less fair and happy fashion cast,
Sunless and chilly, who when most they would,
Cannot draw back the curtain from their souls
And bid men look within. Nay, frown not, sir; (*To* ERLACH.)
Nor arch your brows, de Rheinthal. To be friends
And to *keep* friends, we both must yield a little.
I do not ask that you should change your temper;
Ask it not then of me. Your hand again!
    DE RHEINTHAL: There! (*Giving it coldly.*)
    ALTORF: You are not hurt?
    DE RHEINTHAL: I know not how it is;
You always chill the kindness of my heart.
    ALTORF: Do I? I am sorry for it, *Rheinthal.*
You are a noble, generous young soldier,
And worthy of a kindlier friend than Altorf.
But come, we'll say no more. Wilt please ye in?
We had forgot our father's weary limbs.
(*Aside to* GIOVANNA.) A word, a moment!
(*To* ERLACH *and* DE RHEINTHAL.) We will join you straight. (*Exit*
ERLACH *and* DE RHEINTHAL *into the tent.*)
    ALTORF: Giovanna! Can you pardon me, Giovanna?
    GIOVANNA: Pardon you!
    ALTORF: Aye, noble woman! Thou hast much to pardon.
Oh, had I known thy worth before I wedded,
No—never, never would I so have wronged thee!
    GIOVANNA: Thou hast not wronged me. Be content! Thou hast not.
    ALTORF: Yea, but I have. Oh, it hath weighed upon me—
Weighed on my heart like lead! 'Tis now too late:
To tell thee now what, had I told before
Had saved us both a cup of agony,[12]
Might now seem insult when the cup is drank.
And yet—and yet, I must appear to thee
So very cold, so gloomy, so unkind;
And thou hast such a claim to confidence

---

[11]The acting edition substitutes "Heav'n" for "God.".
[12]The acting edition substitutes "bitterness" for "agony."

That I could almost—
    GIOVANNA: Spare yourself! I know it.
    ALTORF: Know it?
    GIOVANNA: Yes; the father was more generous than the son.
    ALTORF: I merit that. But why conceal this from me?
    GIOVANNA: I would not seem to know what you wished secret.
Sometimes, indeed, I've thought to touch upon't,
But feared to pain you when I wished to ease.
Oft when I've seen you shrink at my approach,
And try to smile and say some idle thing,
I've longed to bid you pour out your vexed soul
Into a sister's bosom. Oh, my Eberard!
I ask not love—I do not wish your love;
I only ask your confidence and friendship.
Do not refuse me these! Unload your heart.
I know it's nigh to burst. Here, turn to me!
Tell me you will forget I am your wife,
And make me as your sister.
    ALTORF: Generous woman!
Come to my heart! My friend, my sister, come!
    GIOVANNA: My Altorf, talk no more of wrongs or pardons!
I am repaid thrice o'er. Yet, I could chide thee,
For that thou did'st not sooner know my nature,
And trust in it for sympathy and ruth.
    ALTORF: And thou dost pity me who never saw her;
Who never heard her speak, nor had her love?
*But, pardon me! Your sufferance, I pray you!
It shall be cured. Yes—yes, it shall be cured.
    GIOVANNA: And thus the cure shall work: I will sit by thee,
And thou shalt count me all her beauties o'er.
Teach me her look, her smile, her air, her motion,
Her voice, her accent, all her little ways,
And what she said, and all she thought or did;
And thou shalt teach me them until I fancy
That I have seen, and known, and loved her too.
And we will hold our converse then in common;
In common think, in common feel, and weep.
And thus by slow degrees your anguished spirit
Shall find relief; and patient, gentle sadness
Steal in the place of agony and ravings.
    ALTORF: Great God, how could'st thou give me such a woman,
And not a second heart to shrine her in!*

Oh, my Giovanna! With a friend like thee,
And with a country bleeding under wrongs,
I were a wretch if of myself I thought.
No! 'Tis on her I think—on her who sits
Alone and comfortless in Rossberg's towers,
And takes no sleep by night, no food by day,
But wastes and sickens in her early prime,
Breaking her heart on Altorf's broken faith.
    GIOVANNA: Oh, had I known it sooner—had I known
You loved so deeply, so eternally,
Never should'st thou have sworn away thy freedom.
Our fathers might have prayed—prayed on their knees,
I never would have yielded. Shall I confess,
And wilt thou not despise me? When I heard
My destined husband was the brave de Altorf,
My conscious heart heat high. Yes! I had seen thee—
Seen thee returning from the wars of Savoy,
And said, as on thy noble form I gazed,
If e'er I loved it should be such a man.
*It was an idle thought, and might have vanished,
But busy fame, spreading abroad thy praises,
Fixed it and shaped it in my youthful fancy,
Till all my dreams by night, or idle day,
Were on the man I saw ride by from Savoy.*
    ALTORF: What, did you come to me a lover, then?
    GIOVANNA: Fear not. 'Tis past.
    ALTORF: Past? You loved me, and 'tis past?
*Oh, what a tale is here! And have I foundered
Another peace, another virgin heart?
You loved me, and 'tis past.* But I deserve it.
Yet wherefore follow me? Why share my fortunes?
Why bear with the unkindness of a man
You loved and love no more?
    GIOVANNA; Did I say that?
You sure mistook my words. I follow you,
Not with a weak and sickly woman's dotage.
Hearts are not won by importunity,
Nor, if they were, would one so gained
Suffice to do me pleasure. No! I have followed you
For that I saw your stricken soul required
The tendance of a friend, and for I thought
You had no friend on earth so true as I.

I do not say that I now love you, Eberard,
As when you led me blushing to God's[13] altar,
*And took my maiden troth. No, that is gone.
The burning flame of love, if left uncherished,
Must wane its fervor.* Yet, I *have* a love
That I do think beyond the love of woman—
One that will wear out my poor husband's days,
Or last me to my grave.
    ALTORF: Thou generous woman!
Oh, teach me how to merit such a heart!
Come with me to my father; at his feet
Let me breathe out again my marriage vows. (*Exit into tent.*)

ACT III

A wild place among the mountains. The Swiss camp visible upon the tops of the rocks in the distance. Enter ROSSBERG, *disguised as before. He gives a loud whistle, which is answered by* EUSTACE, *who suddenly appears among the precipices and descends them rapidly towards* ROSSBERG.

    ROSSBERG: His ready answer flatters my best hopes.
Eustace, what fare?
    EUSTACE: My pipe hath served me well.
All gathered round me, boys and bearded men,
And silver-headed ancients.
    ROSSBERG: But de Altorf?
    EUSTACE: *I've that to speak.* I saw him but this moment.
Watching my time, I stole from out the crowd,
And seating me alone beside his tent,
I took my pipe and played a gentle air
That I had sometime heard your daughter play
When Altorf came a wooer to your castle;
*When he would sit—I saw it more than once—
With breath restrained and cheek all flushed with rapture,
And eyes that rained down tears.* That air I played;
And, to my thought, scarce had I breathed a prelude,
When forth unto my side he troubled came.

---

[13]The acting edition substitutes "the" for "God's."

His cheek was pale, his look most strangely wildered,[14]
His eyes suffused with tears; and when I ceased,
Such store of pitying sighs he poured me forth,
As if I'd sent a death-knell o'er his heart.
    ROSSBERG: He spoke to you?
    EUSTACE: No; but cast his gaze up to the sky,
As if he thought the harmonist was there.
And still he sighed, and ever and anon,
Pressed on his heart his hands.
    ROSSBERG: He loves her still.
    EUSTACE: A bootless love, then. Know you he is married?
    ROSSBERG: More hope in that. Love grows with obstacles.
Let Hymen weave him chains against his liking,
He'll seek the mistress but to fly the wife.
    EUSTACE: But how would you propose—
    ROSSBERG: List! I'll explain.
I've interest with Austria and Rome.
Seduce him from this cause, divorce is easy.
And, though the father be so iced in virtue,
The son's young blood may show some sin to work on.
Wealth, honors, love! Eustace, I'll have him yet!
    EUSTACE: But is it worth the risk?
    ROSSBERG: 'Tis worth all risk:
This Altorf is my kinsman and my heir.
    EUSTACE: Austria will null the claim.
    ROSSBERG: Suppose he cannot.
Suppose the rebels prosper? We have learned
The chance is possible. And shall I bear
To let the titles and the power of Rossberg
Pass from my line into a line of rebels?
*For what though Erlach nor his son should claim them,
Will not their heirs? Nor need we wait for this.
Have not these peasants conquered at Morgarten?
Soon may we see the lands of Austria's friends
O'errun and ravaged by these lawless robbers.*
No! We must win their chief, divide their councils.
If we can sow dissension in that camp,
The day is ours.
    EUSTACE: But have ye hope of this?

---

[14]Bewildered; confused.

ROSSBERG: Nay, here I look to thee. Caught you no sound
Of jealousies, intrigues, or stirring envies?
No quarrel current? Caught you none of this?
    EUSTACE: Something there was. Altorf and young de Rheinthal—
    ROSSBERG: What! His wife's brother?
    EUSTACE: Yes. And it is whispered
They sort not well in temper—nay, of late,
That they have differed often. Yet the breach,
Whate'er it be, I judge nor wide nor deadly.
I saw them stand together, heard them commune—
Coldly, indeed, yet with much mastered ease
And careless courtesy.
    ROSSBERG: I like the news.
Take you this paper. 'Tis addressed to Altorf;
Meant for the father, but 'twill serve the son.
It is from Austria's duke, and bears within it
Offers of high perferment. Watch your time,
And throw it where de Rheinthal's hand may find it.
    *EUSTACE: Where shall I meet you?
    ROSSBERG: Here.*
Hush! Someone comes. Hie quickly to the camp.
Ere midnight I'll expect you. (*They exit separately.*)

A young PILGRIM *enters and seats himself at the foot of a rock. Enter* ALTORF.

    ALTORF: Oh, solitude! Sweet solitude! How is't
That men do fly thee? Why, methinks to habit
A little cell upon some mountainside,
Where the wild trees should give my simple food,
The rill—my drink, the scented turf—my bed,
The winds my visitants, the heaven my study,
And the poor, timid beasts by kindness tamed
To frisk as my companions: wer't not sweet?
What idle wishes doth our fancy frame!
All that we have we ever hold in scorning;
All we have not we robe with hues of heaven.
*The royal hero, decked in Philip's crown
Could envy the poor cynic in his tub.
Is there a fool so dull, or sage so wise
That hath not seen a rainbow in his mind,
And run to catch the image?*

And who art thou that with a pitying face
Sit'st reading the dull earth?
    PILGRIM: One reft of all
Save the dull book he reads.
    ALTORF: Alas, my boy!
So very young, and yet so very friendless.
    PILGRIM: While young in years we may be old in sorrows.
The tender sapling oft by heaven is set
Alone to brave the ravings of the storm,
In lieu of the tough oak.
    ALTORF: But we'll transplant it.
Yes, yes, my boy, lift up thy drooping head.
Thou shalt have shelter from my stronger branches.
Wilt have me for thy friend, thine elder brother?
    PILGRIM: (*Rising and looking up in* ALTORF's *face*).
My master, is't not? To that martial plume
And lordly carriage I should bow the knee;
My lord, I'll be thy servant.
    *ALTORF: Up! Up! Thou dost offend me. Stripling, thy look,
Thy pale and pensive cheeks, thy deep-sunk voice,
Thy face so still, thine air so melancholy
Have won for thee a passage to my heart.
    PILGRIM: Is my cheek pale? But late 'twas fresh and blushing.
Is my face still? But late it played with smiles.
Is my voice sunk? But late it caroled gay
As the young lark when wooing in the spring.
Thanks to thee, noble stranger! But the cell
Of gloomy penitence and cold religion
Were fitter shrine for such a cheerless guest
Than the gay heart of proud and crested warrior.
    ALTORF: Than the gay heart! Nay, youth! There may be hearts
Beneath the dingy garb of fasting friar
That throb more gay than some beneath the corselet.[15]
An' all the outward livery of the man
Should fit the temper of the hidden spirit,
Perchance these knightly trappings were exchanged
For thy poor russet—yea, this doughty sword
For such another pilgrim staff as thine.*
    PILGRIM: Nay, then, I'll follow you, most gracious sir!

---

[15]Piece of armor.

And yet—and yet—should I not fear to do it?

ALTORF: My trade of arms—is't that?

PILGRIM: Oh, no, sir: no.

The tent to me were welcome as the hall,
The chilly skies as kind a canopy
As silken hangings! 'Tis not that, sir—but—

ALTORF: But what, my boy? Speak out thy fear. But what?

PILGRIM: Yourself, sir.

ALTORF: Myself?

PILGRIM: Aye, sir, yourself; I have no other fear.

Kindly you speak—yes, very kindly, sir;
But so did others, and they used me hardly.
I had a master, sir, who loved me well—
Who said, at least, he loved me—and, in truth,
His deeds were such I could not doubt his words.
I loved him, sir, and served him faithfully—
So faithfully as never servant served.
His favor was my pride, his will my law,
*His lips my oracle, his smile my sun,
His eyes my mirror, and his face the book
In which I studied all things.* Was't not hard?
Just when he saw my soul was at his feet,
That I did look on him as 'twere my God,[16]
He turned me broken-hearted to the world
Without so much as one poor "God be with you."
I crave your pardon, sir! My tale seems idle;
My sorrows, too, perchance.
They who ne'er felt the sting of mocked affection—
Felt in youth too, for 'tis keener then—
Can little understand the venom of it.

ALTORF: What say'st thou then to those who give that sting?
No, boy! Come not to me; thou fear'st me justly.
Aye, know, all kind and gracious as I spake thee,
I—I myself have stung a faithful heart
That loved me—oh, *my God*—as I love her.

PILGRIM: Altorf! *My Eberard!* (ROSINA *throws off her hat and stretches out her arms to* ALTORF.)

ALTORF: That face![17] Great heaven!

---

[16]The acting edition substitutes "Heaven."

[17]This scene follows the sequence of the acting edition. In the original edition. Altorf first recognizes Rosina's voice, and then she reveals her face.

My Rosa! My beloved! Speak! Speak again!
ROSINA: I cannot speak. Oh, God! The joy's too much.
Thou art faithful! Thou art faithful!
ALTORF: Did'st then doubt?
ROSINA: Oh, yes, I did. Forgive me, love! Forgive me.
Canst thou believe it? I came now to chide thee.
And yet—not that—I did not mean to chide;
I only came to steal one other look
And crave the boon to die upon thy bosom.
*ALTORF: To die upon my bosom! Aye, my love!
'T hath been a cruel, treacherous one to thee;
And yet not false—I swear it is not false.
ROSINA: Thou need'st not swear. I see—I feel thy truth.
Thine eyes speak all thy soul. Oh, Eberard!
To find thee true is worth to have thought thee false.*
ALTORF: To die upon my bosom. No, my Rosa!
'Tis I should die, and if I live, I live
Only to right my country. Loved of my soul,
Oh, aid me in this task! Do not unman me!
Thou canst—thou hast— But oh, forbear, my love!
Leave me! Forget me, for thy peace—for mine!
ROSINA: Leave thee? Forget thee? *For my peace? For thine?
What, were it peace to thee should I forget thee?*
Thou art then changed!
ALTORF: No, no; I am not changed.
Tied as I am—sold as I am to honor—
My heart, my soul, my all is thine, Rosina!
*ROSINA: What ask I more, then? Why, my Altorf's love
Is all I seek on earth or ask of heaven.
Wrong not our love, to say it mocks at honor.
I know but little of these public quarrels,
But love like ours hath every thing in common.
Are we not wedded? What though earthly priest
Ne'er joined our hands, have not our hearts been joined?
What though no altar sanctified our vows,
Hath then our love no seal? Aye, that it hath!
Our vows are registered by angels, Altorf!
The heavens have been our sanctifying altar,
And God himself the priest who made us one.
Yes! I am thine, and thou art mine—all mine*
Thy fate, thy fortune, country, country's wrongs!
ALTORF: (*Aside*). All-pitying heaven, she knows not of my marriage.

*ROSINA: What says my Altorf? Eberard, what's on thee?

ALTORF: Nothing, my love. 'Tis joy, my love; that's all.
Thou art pale, Rosina. Art not wearied, love?

ROSINA: I've journeyed far afoot; yet I'm not wearied.
Before I found thee, when I thought thee false,
I was too sick in mind to ail in body;
And now I've found thee—now I've found thee true—
I am too blessed to have an ail in either.
Why dost thou look so on me?

ALTORF: Look on thee?
Is it forbidden e'en to look on thee?

ROSINA: Forbidden? How? What mean you?

ALTORF: (*Falling on his knees*). Oh, do not curse me! Do not curse
me, Rosa!
I swear it thee—I swear it thee by heaven!
I swear it by thyself—thy precious self—
I love but thee! I ne'er have loved but thee!
I never will love woman but Rosina.

ROSINA: What means thy frenzy? I don't doubt thy love,
I know thou ne'er wilt love but thy Rosina.
Who should'st thou love but her?

ALTORF: Oh! None, none, none.

ROSINA: My Eberard!

ALTORF: My Rosa!*

ROSINA: Is all well with thee?
Thou look'st— 'Tis not like joy.

ALTORF: Thou lovely flower!
And is it Altorf's hand shall mar thy beauty?
Go! Fly me!

ROSINA: Fly thee?

ALTORF: Aye, quickly! Quickly!
Know it is sin to love thy Altorf, girl!
Know that his arms can only work thee shame.
Know that— Oh, fly! I pray it of thee, fly!

ROSINA: All holy heaven, what horrid secret hast thou!
Tell me! I'll know it. Tell me!

ALTORF: I cannot tell thee.

ROSINA: Thou must; thou shalt.

ALTORF: Could no one tell it thee, but only I?
I'm married—
Oh, my beloved! My Rosa! Hear me, angel!
My heart is thine. My faith has never swerved.

A father's prayers—my country—duty—oh!
Call me not false! Look not so motionless!
    *ROSINA: Married?
    ALTORF: I swear to thee I'm thine. If 'twill appease thee,
Know I am wretched, maddened, broken-hearted.
    ROSINA: Married! Married! To whom? When? Where?
Married?
    ALTORF: Oh, ring not o'er that word! Would'st break my heart?
    ROSINA: Dost talk to me of breaking hearts? Oh, Altorf!
Thou'st cleaved mine asunder. Married! Ye heavens!
Where is the faith of man? Where are the oaths
Thou swor'st me, traitor? Where the sighs, the tears,
The burning kisses we have mixed together?
Married! 'Tis false! Thou had'st no faith to give.
Mine was thy faith; mine were thy loves; mine all.
Mine, said I? Mine? Fond fool, that I should think it!
    ALTORF: Think it; believe it still. I'm thine—all thine!*
A rigid father, and a bleeding country—
    ROSINA: Did'st owe thy father all, and Rosa nothing?
I have a father, too; yet see me here.
Thy country? Thine were mine; its wrongs my wrongs.
Did'st thou not know all this? Oh, little love!
Oh, little trust in such a love as mine!
    ALTORF: Oh, do not pierce my heart with thy reproaches!
If thou did'st ever love me, spare me, Rosa!
I merit thou should'st hate me; hate me then;
But do not tell me that thou hat'st me, love!
    ROSINA: Hate thee! *Who said I hated thee?* Oh, that I did!
Oh, that I could! Oh, that I e'er had hope
My love would slacken! Hate thee, traitor? No!
Hear! Hear, and tremble at Rosina's sin!
She loves the married Altorf! She will love
Nothing but married Altorf. *See thy work!
See, triumph in, the mind that thou hast ruined!
Oh, God, forgive my ravings! Eberard!
Forgive me, my best loved, my first—my last!
Forgive me! I don't chide thee—don't upbraid thee.*
I'll go, my love; I'll go. My blessings on thee!
May peace, may joy, may every good be thine!
    ALTORF: Go? Go? Where would'st thou go?
    ROSINA: Oh, stay me not! I have not too much strength.
Enough! Enough! One last embrace!

(*A bugle sounds from the camp.*) Hark, hark!

*ALTORF: Thou shalt not go. I've thousand things to tell thee,
Thousand to ask.

ROSINA: Our minds are too distracted.
What use of words? We cannot understand them.

ALTORF: Yes, there is use; there shall be use.
A moment!*

ROSINA: The bugle sounds again!
See! Someone descends the rock.

ALTORF: Go, then; *but come again.

ROSINA: Again! When? Where?

ALTORF: You would not travel back this night to Rossberg?

ROSINA: I know not where I travel: I know nothing.*

ALTORF: Meet me but once—once more! Dost fear me, Rosa?

ROSINA: No, Eberard—but—

ALTORF: *No but.* Say you will come.
I can't part with thee thus.

ROSINA: The time, the place?

ALTORF: Before the midnight watch. *Curse the intruder.*
Here, before midnight. Wilt thou, Rosa? Say it.

ROSINA: The soldier will observe us. Speak no partings.
Till night, then; till the night.

ALTORF: You will not fail?

ROSINA: I will not. (*Exits.*)

Enter DE RHEINTHAL.

ALTORF: Oh, God![18] This has unmanned me.

DE RHEINTHAL: A visitor from Holy Land? (*Looking off the scene.*)
A pilgrim, is't not?
Gentle and young he seemed for such a trade.
Captain! (*Aside.*) I cannot understand this man.
Captain!

ALTORF: Oh, de Rheinthal!

DE RHEINTHAL: A strange report runs current in the camp.
'Tis said the Lord of Rossberg—

ALTORF: Rossberg! What of Rossberg?

DE RHEINTHAL: Nay, only that he lingers in disguise

---

[18]The acting edition reads, "This! This has unmanned me," rather than "Oh, God! This has unmanned me."

Among these valleys.

ALTORF: In disguise? Count Rossberg?

DE RHEINTHAL: Yes, Count Rossberg.

ALTORF: He will have traced his daughter. Evil chance!

DE RHEINTHAL: Why muse you so on't? Does the matter touch you?

ALTORF: Touch me, sir? No.

DE RHEINTHAL: Still must you find offense?

ALTORF: I crave your charity. I'm somewhat ill.

DE RHEINTHAL: In troth you have the hue on't. You look fevered.

ALTORF: Nothing. I thank you, nothing—a poor weakness;
I have had it from a boy. Seek you the camp? (*Exits, crossing* GIOVANNA.)

Enter GIOVANNA.

GIOVANNA: Why, how is this? He flies me as a scorpion.
Brother, what means it?

DE RHEINTHAL: That you should follow him,
That you should soothe and woo him for a smile.
Have you as yet to learn your husband's temper?
Follow him, soothe him. He is sick, good sister.

GIOVANNA: Sick!

DE RHEINTHAL: Aye, of a deadly sickness. Haste you! Fly!
He needs a nurse, perchance; perchance a slave;
If so, he needs his wife.

GIOVANNA: Oh, my rash brother!
And still unkind as rash.

DE RHEINTHAL: By heaven, Giovanna,
An' thou wilt brook his scorn, I will not for thee!
I am a soldier, sister! A young soldier,
And one not practiced to pass by affronts,
Or stoop my own before another's pride.
So I shall tell your husband.

GIOVANNA: Hold, de Rheinthal!
Who made thee umpire 'twixt me and my husband?
If that I am not offended for myself,
Why art thou for me? 'Tis my pride, not thine,
That should be touched by his neglect or scorning.
And when it is so, I shall know myself
How best to right me.

DE RHEINTHAL: And when it is so, say'st thou?

An' it be not so now, thou hast, by heaven,
A spirit tamer than a Turkish slave.
> GIOVANNA: Let me so pass with thee; I am content.
But only, as thou lov'st thy country's good,
As thou dost feel the merit of her cause,
Forbear dissension. And if the plea will move thee,
As thou dost love thy sister's peace, forbear it.
> DE RHEINTHAL: Why still connect our country and her cause
With Altorf's humor? Let him chafe or leave us!
I wis[19] we lack not soldiers brave as he,
Nor chiefs as skillful. And, if fame speak true,
He serves us with a mind not wholly willing.
This very spy that lingers round our camp,
Count Werner, is, 'tis said, his friend and kinsman.
'Twas something strange too, when but now I named him,
The blood forsook his cheeks.
> GIOVANNA: What mean you, brother?
You would not, surely—nay, you dare not throw
Suspicious word upon de Altorf's honor?
> DE RHEINTHAL: No, no. I mean not that! 'Twas said in temper.
I mean not that. No man can doubt his honor.
But for his haughtiness and wayward temper:
I'll humor them no more. I, too, am proud,
As proud as he; nor care I though he find it. (*Exits.*)
> GIOVANNA: (*Alone*). Count Werner in these vales? And in disguise?
I like not this. The blood forsook his cheeks!
Oh, fie! I scorn myself for such a fear.
My life upon his honor! Yet, I'll see him.
Count Werner is the father of his love,
His kinsman too, and friend. Yes, I must see him. (*Exits.*)

ACT IV

Among the mountains as before. ALTORF *is discovered lying on the earth.*

ALTORF: The sun hath sunk. The heaven's bright glories fade,
And grizzly eve comes onward with her dews
To dim fair nature's face. Yet thou, oh earth,

---

[19]Deem.

Shalt soon wipe off the stain—soon clear away
The offending vapors and, exulting, hail
The golden lord's return in strength recruited!
Oh, were it so with man! *Had he but hope,
When sorrow drew her curtain o'er his mind
And scared the gladsome tenants of his heart,
That the fair season of his bygone days
Would yet return, and the bright wings of joy
Play in his sight again! Yet some we see*
To whom this is. Nay, some we see, blessed souls,
*Of such a lucky, easy temper made,
Or good or ill, with all vicissitude
Comes equal kindly. We are varied creatures,
As different in our power to suffer ill
As is the weight of the ills we are called to suffer.*
Some, an' they weep today, can smile tomorrow—
Nay, like the infant, whilst the teardrop trembles
Upon the quivering eyelid, laugh to see
The frolic of a fly. The fools are sages.
(*Enter* GIOVANNA. *She advances softly towards him and stands observing him in silence.*)
My wife!
Why com'st thou like an evil spirit on me?
    GIOVANNA: It had been kinder said, a watching angel.
    ALTORF: Perchance it had, but when was Altorf kind?
That mood is past—is dead in me, Giovanna;
And I conjure thee, as thou lov'st the peace
Of thy fair youth, to seek my face no more.
    GIOVANNA: Thou might'st have known ere this Giovanna's peace
Was one with thine. I would not seem to boast;
Yet, as I have an urgent prayer to put,
I will recount my claims—not on thy love,
But on thy gratitude and thy respect.
Be patient, Eberard, and answer me.
Say, have I not in summer of my youth,
When that the heart is warm and temper smiling,
Resigned myself unto a husband's service
Who never gave me for my pains a smile?
    *ALTORF: All true. All true. No more, Giovanna!
    GIOVANNA: Nay, there is more, and thou shalt hear it yet.
Have I not slept upon thy soldier's couch;
Have I not fed upon thy soldier's food;

Have I not kept thy soldier's fasts and vigils;
Have I not footed all thy soldier's travels;
Nay, have I not my tender bosom steeled
In soldier's mail, and shared thy risks of battle?*
    ALTORF: Thou hast; thou hast.
    GIOVANNA: And when I did all this,
Did'st thou perceive I thought it much to do it?
*Did I by look, by sigh, by little word,
By speaking face of trouble or fatigue
E'er give thee chiding or leave room to doubt
My thoughts looked backward to my father's home?
    ALTORF: Thou never did'st. And tell me now, Giovanna,
And 'tis in kindness said—in pity too,
That the fair blossom of thy tender spring
Should be so coldly nipped—say, canst thou bear
To throw thy sweets upon a wintry cloud?
To let thy beauties wither in the arms
Of a dull senseless specter—a man's shadow,
A blasted wretch whose fire is all burnt out,
And cannot throw one spark back to thy blaze?
    GIOVANNA: That is for me to find, not you to ask.
Have I complained I found thy service cold,
Been urgent in my love, or claimed from thee
What thou wert slack to grant? Thou know'st I have not.
Thou know'st my love has been as pure as fervent,
Distant though tender, silent though awake—
Yea, that it hath been such as proves it, Altorf,
Of high, of countless price.*
    ALTORF: And thinks my wife,
By pressing thus her heavy claims upon me,
To win a heart that I have not to give?
    GIOVANNA: Hast thou so soon forgot this morning's converse?
I do not ask thy love; but this I ask,
By all the debt of gratitude thou ow'st me,
To guard thy honor! Start, but hear me, Altorf!
Look to thy honor! As thou art a man,
As thou art a soldier, as thou art a patriot,
As thou art a husband—guard thy honor!
    ALTORF: (*Aside*). A husband! Knows she of Rosina's coming?
    GIOVANNA: My fears are true? You've seen him? Tell me!
You've seen Count Werner.
    ALTORF: No, by this hand!

GIOVANNA: Nor mean to do it?

ALTORF: No! Heaven save me from it!

GIOVANNA: Amen. I ask no more.

ALTORF: But wherefore asked you this? How should I see him?

GIOVANNA: If it be true he sojourns in disguise
Among these hills, 'tis doubtless for a purpose.
And, though I'd swear to thy integrity,
Some enemies, if such thou hast, or else
Some busy babbler, might to thy discredit
Connect this spy with Altorf. 'Tis well known
Your former friendship for the Count of Rossberg;
Nay more, the tale of your unhappy love—
You understand me. Take it not unkindly
If I remind you, not what honor asks,
But thy peculiar station and position.

ALTORF: I do believe thou art the noblest woman
That ever walked God's earth. Still is't for me,
And never for herself, Giovanna feels.

GIOVANNA: She finds her pleasure in't. There needs no praise.

ALTORF: Aye, but there does, if thou did'st know, good spirit!
Yet, no; thou ne'er shalt blush for me. Thy image
Shall stand betwixt me and the tempting demons.
I shall come spotless from this trial; trust me!

GIOVANNA: What trial speak'st thou of, if not with Rossberg?

ALTORF: Of none—of none but with myself, good wife.
(*Aside.*) She must not tarry here. Should Rosa come!
I'll win her to the camp, and so return.
(*To* GIOVANNA.) Shall we not hence? The dews are falling thick. (*Exit.*)

Enter ROSSBERG *and* EUSTACE.

EUSTACE: They have the scent. We may not tarry longer.

ROSSBERG: *Only this night. I know the mountain passes,
And well can slip pursuit. I understand
Young Altorf hath the practice oft o'nights
To wander past the precincts of the camp.
Could I but cross him! Or,* could'st thou deliver
A letter from me?

EUSTACE: It were not possible.
I doubt suspicion rests on me already,
And now the papers found by young de Rheinthal
Will instant seem to point me for their bearer.

ROSSBERG: What of the papers? Are they rightly stowed?

EUSTACE: I saw myself de Rheinthal gather them.

ROSSBERG: That's good. Where did he find them?

EUSTACE: At the very entrance of his captain's tent.

ROSSBERG: It may work much—but hist! A stranger comes.
Stand backward to that cavern. (*They conceal themselves.*)

Enter ROSINA.

ROSINA: *I am the first, who should not be at all.
And why not be?* I come to seek the man
Who rules my destiny, who hath my faith,
My thoughts, my love, my soul, my all in keeping;
And do I wrong to seek the face of such?
I know not; *but this world hath strange opinions,
And very wondrous creeds of right and wrong.
If with our little lips we speak an oath
That men do register, albeit the heart
Cries out aloud and damns the sounding falsehood,
'Tis still a saintly seal, and passeth current
In earth and heaven. But when two pure hearts
Seek testimony at the ear of God,
And have the record of their true affections,
Here is no saintly bond, no gordion knot[20]
But what the sword of law may cleave asunder.*
Poor, trusting, simple Rosa! *Oh, ye young hearts,
Who come confiding on this slippery world,
That I could teach you but my piteous tale
And save you from my very cruel heartache!*
Would I had never come! *And do I wish it?
I wis I do not. No, I'll see him yet!
See him once more—gaze once, but once again
Upon that worshipped face— *Ha! Is that he
Upon yon hilltop, marked against the sky?
Forbid it, heaven! A woman! Then, his wife.
He stoops—he kisses her—he waves his hand!
Oh, traitor! Traitor! Traitor! I will away.
I'll fly— I have not strength. Oh, I have heard on't—

---

[20]A legendary knot tied by King Gordius of Phrygia, which could only be untied by extraordinary force.

Heard of jealousy: its sting, its venomed tooth—
I've heard on't oft. I never thought to feel it.

Enter ALTORF.

    ALTORF: Rosa! My Rosa! Do I find thee, love?
Is it thyself, and dost not turn to me?
'Tis Altorf, Rosa! Eberard—thy lover—
Art ill, my love?
    ROSINA: No, no! Not very ill;
Only some little way towards madness, or—
Leave me, thou double traitor!
    ALTORF: Nay, art thou angry? Dearest, do not chide me!
This last—last meeting—
    ROSINA: Aye, last. Go, go!
Thy wife is there and waits to know I'm gone.
Well, tell her—tell her. I will not trouble her.
I meant—I do believe—I meant to curse thee,
But do not fear: thou see'st my poor heart's weakness.
    *ALTORF: My love.
    ROSINA: Nay! Do not act it more. It is not needed.
I give thee joy—upon my soul I do!
I'm very glad that thou dost love thy wife,
And she loves thee; for that I'm sure she must,
An' she have eyes and ears and half a heart!
May she be happy as. . .I soon shall be,
An' priests teach truth of heaven—
    ALTORF: Rosa!
    ROSINA: Unhand me, Altorf! Do not mock me, pray—
I do not merit this of thee; thou know'st it.
The world will say I do. I heed not it.
But thou—thou canst not charge it for a crime
That I have loved thee even to forsaking;
And, throwing men's opinions at my back,
Have followed thee o'er mountains such as these.
    ALTORF: I do implore thee, by my peace and reason,
Forsake this style! If I have ever loved,
If I do love—if e'er I love hereafter—
Other of womankind save thee, Rosina,
May'st thou thyself at this foul, lying heart
Aim with a poisoned dagger!
    ROSINA: Do my ears err?

Or did my eyes? Ere thou proceedest further,
Tell me, —I am so very fond a fool,
I will believe thy words before my sight—
Did I on yonder hilltop see thee hold
A woman's hand that was not thy Rosina's?
Did I on yonder hilltop see thee print
A kiss on woman's cheek that was not hers?
    ALTORF: I see the error. Angel of my life,
No kiss of love it was I printed there!
    ROSINA: I do not understand. With me, a kiss
Speaks always love. Witness: I would as lieve[21]
Upon this mouth, this cheek—nay on this hand—
Take touch of other lip than Eberard's;
I would as lieve, I say, before the shrine
Of some false, heathenish saint or deity
Do impious homage, as permit this thing.
I see I am a fool. The breath of man
Woos like the wanton winds from every flower
The scented nectar. Eberard can lip
Each cheek that's fair, and, doubtless, many cheeks
That tears ne'er washed and pining never wasted
Are fairer now than these.*
    ALTORF: Prythee, don't break my heart,
If thou dost love me! Oh, *Rosa,* when thou wert
All blooming, blushing in youth, life, and health—
*Thy lips the coral and thy cheeks the rose,
Thine eyes the diamond and thy brow the heaven—*
Thou wert not half so fair—so passing fair—
In my fond sight, as now that hapless love
And pining agony have dimmed thy lustre.
Thy wasted cheek, my love, speaks volumes to me.
For me—it is for me it wears that hue,
That woeful livery of faithful love.
    ROSINA: Thou know'st I shall believe whate'er thou say'st;
So tell me one thing more, and I'll look on thee.
Though married, yet as free, though lost, yet mine—
Tell me, oh, tell me quick—that thou dost hate her.
    ALTORF: Who? Hate who?
    ROSINA: Why she—she—oh, God, she whom men call thy wife!

---

[21]Willingly.

ALTORF: I love her not: witness, you listening heavens!
ROSINA: But hate her; swear it.
ALTORF: I were a fiend to do it—
My heart is yours. Oh, Rosa, on my knees,
I never loved but one, nor never will,
Though fate could curse me with an endless life—
And endless youth to boot—I swear thee this!
Yet do not ask of me to hate the woman
Who hath for me, with more than angel's goodness,
Ta'en all the scorn of unrequited love
And paid me back with such a suffering patience,
Such tender sympathy of all my woes,
Such generous pity of the hapless Rosa,
That—that—I were a very devil could I hate her.
    ROSA: And is she such? Why, then, *I'll* pity *her*.
To have thy company and not thy love;
To call thee husband, and yet find no fondness?
*No! I'm no longer jealous. I would rather
Three zones should lie betwixt us—nay, the grave—
Than sleep upon thy bosom, and be loved
One poor iota less! Swear it me, then,
That when we part to meet on earth no more,
That when my voice shall meet no more thine ear,
Mine eye—thine eye, my throbbing heart—thy heart,
When death shall clutch my wretched soul away,
And when poor Rosa's name shall be rubbed out
From every human memory beside
That *thou* wilt think on her—that *thou* wilt love her
As truly, wholly, fervently as now.
    ALTORF: My love! My angel, cease!
    ROSINA: Nay, swear it.
    ALTORF: Do Rosa this by me, as I by her.*
    ROSINA: Oh, pardon *me! I doubt I much distress you,
My Eberard.*   And can it be heaven's will
That two such hearts as ours, so knit together,
Should be for aye divided?
    ALTORF: I think no.
    ROSINA: Who hath a claim on thee, if 'tis not I?
Or who is bound to me, if 'tis not thou?
    ALTORF: By heaven! There's none, Rosa; there's none but I
Dare call thee his. Oh! Let me hold thee, angel!
Say that thou wilt not go—thou wilt not leave me;

Or if thou dost, I'll after thee to—

Enter ROSSBERG *from the cavern.*

ROSSBERG: Hold!
ROSINA: Ha!
ALTORF: Who art thou, cursed intruder?
ROSINA: Support me, heaven! It is—it is my father.
ROSSBERG: Well may you both stand blank![22] Daughter, is't thus—
Is't thus thou dar'st insult thy father's name,
His rank, his honor, blood, and dignity?
ALTORF: Spare—spare reproaches! God of heaven, she dies!
ROSSBERG: *Die?* Let her die. Leave her, I say, vile traitor!
Thou base seducer, dost not fear a father?
ALTORF: My Rosa, speak! It is thine Altorf, love.
Patience a moment, Count! Art better, angel?
ROSSBERG: Look to thy sword, I say.
ROSINA: Oh! Mercy, mercy! (*Faintly throwing herself between them.*)
Father, point here the steel! I only am guilty,
If guilty either be. *Oh, sheath it, father!
Altorf, thou dar'st not draw.
ALTORF: No; fear it not.
Rossberg, a moment's audience.
ROSSBERG: Audience, traitor!
Is't not enough to see my daughter's shame,
But must I hear it?
ALTORF: You wrong me, sir.
ROSSBERG: Wrong you! Hast thou not broken faith
To me and to my child? Hast thou not wedded,
In very face of the signed bond with us,
The daughter of another? And, false villain,
Dost thou not stand—stand here a married man,
Pouring thy wiles in that poor virgin's ear?
ROSINA: Father! Altorf, be patient.
ALTORF: I will; I am. Rossberg, no tongue save thine—
But thou art privileged. Thou hast much cause,
Much seeming cause.
ROSSBERG: Seeming!
ROSINA: *Nay, father, list!

---

[22]The acting edition substitutes "be surprised" for "both stand blank."

List to the only guilty! Here alone,*
Unwooed, unwished for, did thy daughter come.
*She is the only vile, the only tempter.
    ROSSBERG: Then more vile he, that could so change my child.
Once who so pure, so modest as Rosina?
Who more a father's pride, or a world's envy?
Thou wretch! And hast a heart to see that flower,
So lately blushing sweetly on her stem,
Rifled and soiled, cast forth to common scorn,
The jest and byword of each passenger.
    ROSINA: Regard him not, Altorf; regard him not.
'Tis not as he hath said. None know my flight;*
None know that I have sought thee here unwooed.
And when I die, the world will never know
I die for love of thee.
    ALTORF: Oh, spare me, Rosa! Spare me, both of ye!
One with her kindness, one with his upbraidings,
Goes nigh to shake my reason. Tell me, Rossberg—
Tell me how I may work you satisfaction.
    ROSSBERG: Too late, too late. Saith she her flight none know:
How am I here then, an' it be not known?
What cause could I have in this mean disguise
To seek your armed camp, wer't not to find
My fallen child and to revenge her ruin?
Draw, I say.
    ALTORF: I will not.
    ROSSBERG: Back, child! Rosa, retire!
    *ALTORF: Rossberg, but hear me speak.
    ROSSBERG: What canst thou have to speak that's worth the listing?
Draw, I say!*
    ROSINA: All gracious heaven! Ye meet but through my heart.
Oh, father! Altorf! Lover! Father! Lover!
Will not such words as these arrest your fury?
    ALTORF: My Rosa, fear not me! I will not draw.
    ROSSBERG: Back, child, and let us parley! Altorf, one way—
One only way may'st thou arrest my vengeance.
    ALTORF: Speak it; command my life.
    ROSSBERG: Daughter, retire!
That which I ask of thee, thy honor asks;
That which I ask of thee, thy passions ask;
That which I ask of thee may save her ruin.
    ALTORF: Speak it: the way—the way!

ROSSBERG: To wed her.

ALTORF: To wed her?

Why, know'st thou not I'm wedded to another?

*ROSSBERG: To one thou lov'st?

ALTORF: It needs not answer that.

ROSSBERG: Or who loves thee?

ALTORF: Who doth most kindly by me.

But whom, God knows, I make most truly wretched.*

ROSSBERG: Rome shall annul the marriage.

ALTORF: Ha!

ROSSBERG: What say'st thou?

ALTORF: Impossible, impossible.

Don't tempt me, Rossberg. As thou art a man,

As thou art a soldier, name it not again.

All else but this.

ROSSBERG: What else is there, sir?

ALTORF: Nay, nought but misery.

ROSSBERG: And infamy,

At least for her thou dost profess to love.

And wherefore hesitate? For what? For whom?

A wife thou lov'st not, who were happier,

From thy confession, with another man.

ALTORF: True, true. Yet, Rossberg, I dare not do it—

Not yet, at least. When that my country's free;

When that— Enough; I dare not listen to the thought.

Take not advantage of my weakness, Rossberg.

Thou art a man of honor, though my foe;

Respect mine then. I do so love your daughter

That passion might impel me on to madness;

To worse—dishonor.

Enter EUSTACE.

EUSTACE: Fly! Fly, ye are surprised!

ALTORF: By whom? How? Where?

EUSTACE: From the Swiss camp.

ROSSBERG: Goodnight, then, to my life.

ALTORF: Fly, and I'll save pursuit. (*Draws his sword.*)

Enter DE RHEINTHAL, *followed by three* SOLDIERS.

DE RHEINTHAL: Seize him! 'Tis Rossberg.

*ROSSBERG: (*Draws.*) Rossberg sells his life.

DE RHEINTHAL:* What, Altorf? Almighty heavens! Altorf.

ALTORF: Altorf. And know he risks his life for these.

DE RHEINTHAL: Traitor! Thank God, thou'rt ta'en.
Throw down thy sword and yield thee.

ALTORF: This to me?

*DE RHEINTHAL: To thee. Soldiers, seize them all.

ALTORF: Seize none.

DE RHEINTHAL: Traitor, dost thou command? Throw down thy
sword!

ALTORF:* I had forgot appearance made against me.
Forbear awhile. Soldiers, stand back!
Hear me, de Rheinthal! *Put thy sword aside.*

DE RHEINTHAL: By heaven, and dost thou mean to fool us still?
Know, traitor, that I hold the damning proofs
Both of thy league with Rossberg and with Austria.
I have the letters.

ALTORF: Letters? I know of none.

DE RHEINTHAL: Indeed!
Nor know that man, perchance. Oh, fie upon't!
By heaven! I did distrust my very eyes.
I could have sworn the letters were a cheat.

ALTORF: Thou'rt mad, I say, or else a knave. What letters?

DE RHEINTHAL: No idle parley. Yield thee for a traitor.

ALTORF: Hold, de Rheinthal!
Speak but the word again. *Beware of swords.*

DE RHEINTHAL: And dost thou then deny? Thou hardened villain!
Soldiers, your duty.

ALTORF: Hah! Try then our strength.
Rossberg, canst dare the odds?   (*They fight. ALTORF disables* DE
RHEINTHAL, *while* ROSSBERG *and* EUSTACE *engage the* SOLDIERS.)

DE RHEINTHAL: *My sword arm's gone.*
Ho, *for more* succor,[23] ho! (ALTORF *turns also on the soldiers, who are
driven off.*)

ALTORF: Quick! Up the vale. Rosa, my love, with me.
Rossberg, I'll see ye safe beyond our confines.
De Rheinthal, ere the morning I return,
And meet, and answer to this charge in council.   (*Exit* ALTORF,
ROSSBERG, ROSINA, EUSTACE.)

---

[23]Help; reinforcements.

DE RHEINTHAL: Curse on his skillful fencing! He hath 'scaped;
And yet I'm glad on't. Traitor as he is,
To see him die a traitor's death had touched me.
GIOVANNA: (*Arriving*). What is the uproar? Rheinthal, gracious
heavens!
Bleeding and fainting!
DE RHEINTHAL: A flesh wound; nothing more.
Lend me your scarf. (*She binds his arm.*)
GIOVANNA: How came you by it?
DE RHEINTHAL: Fighting with a traitor.
GIOVANNA: Rossberg?
DE RHEINTHAL: Altorf.
GIOVANNA: Altorf? Fie on thee! What, upon the proof
Of these forged papers? Forged I'll swear they are.
DE RHEINTHAL: Swear not, good sister. Very honest papers.
Yonder your courteous husband flies with Rossberg.
GIOVANNA: With Rossberg?
DE RHEINTHAL: True.
GIOVANNA: Immortal heavens!
I'll after him. Perchance there yet is time.
Tell none that I have followed.
DE RHEINTHAL: A word—
One word, I pray. 'Tis chance that you may meet—
Enough. He is not worth—not e'en your pity.
GIOVANNA: Speak out your thought. What is there chance I meet?
DE RHEINTHAL: A woman.
GIOVANNA: Ha! How know ye this?
DE RHEINTHAL: A tender youth he had in company,
Whom in his arms half dead he bore away.
The pilgrim's garb but ill concealed the woman.
GIOVANNA: Rosa de Rossberg. Then he's lost indeed.
You're faint, my brother. Lean upon my arm.
DE RHEINTHAL: Hark to our soldiers' shouts! They have the scent.
GIOVANNA: Which way did they speed?
DE RHEINTHAL: Right up that valley.
GIOVANNA: Oh, God! Why did I leave him? (*They exit.*)

ACT V

The hall of an ancient castle. ROSSBERG *and* EUSTACE.

EUSTACE: My lord, he will not stay.
ROSSBERG: He must and shall.
Hath he consented only to repent?
Yet this we should have looked for. As a soldier,
I can respect his doubts and his compunctions.
De Altorf is a man so pure in honor
That but the thought of taking taint upon it
Will wound him in the quick. And, for I know this,
I do the more rejoice to win his friendship—
To win him from a cause unworthy of him
And lead him back to his first-sworn allegiance.
We have him now secure. His promise past,
His flight, my proffered friendship, Rosa's love,
And, stronger yet, his pride and temper chafed
By Rheinthal's passion and the camp's suspicion—
All this must fix him ours. But tell us, Eustace,
Came there not tidings from the Austrian's army?
EUSTACE: None that I hear, my lord.
ROSSBERG: 'Tis strange, methinks.
I cannot judge them distant; yet, an' they be,
Our castle's in some danger. Send forth scouts,
And let them keep good watch upon the tower. (*Exit* EUSTACE.)
ROSSBERG: This silence of the Austrian alarms me.
Can he be panic-struck, and so retreating?
I know not what to think. But first to Altorf. (*Enter* ALTORF.)
Ah, to my wish!
ALTORF: Count, I must hence.
ROSSBERG: You shall not hence, brave kinsman.
You risk your life.
ALTORF: No more, good sir; no more!
I care not what I risk. I will return.
ROSSBERG: By heaven, thou shalt not. We will lock our gates.
List but one moment to the words of reason.
You've enemies; your prowess hath stirred envy.
De Rheinthal hates you. I have means of knowledge,
By spies and others, of most devilish plots
Contrived against you.
ALTORF: I'll defeat them, then;

Meet my foes face to face.
    ROSSBERG: Impossible.
You're hunted as an outlaw. Heard we not
In every vale, from every nook we passed,
Curses and execrations muttered on you?
Your head is priced. *What an' you meet their scouts?*
The first will hang you on the nearest tree,
Or shoot you to the heart.* Or if you reach—
In safety reach your camp—what then?
What have you but your word—your single word
'Gainst circumstance more strong than that of thousands?
    ALTORF: My honor, sir? My honor? Answer that.
    ROSSBERG: 'Tis pledged to me.
'Tis pledged to me and to my daughter, kinsman.
Have you not passed your word?
    ALTORF: Nay, spare me, *Count.*
Recount not o'er my villainy and weakness.
You cannot mean to hold me to a promise
Passed in the mad and thoughtless heat of passion?
Chafed by de Rheinthal's taunts, pressed by pursuit,
The cry of traitor thundering in my ears;
Hunted with execrations, and your daughter—
Your lovely daughter—fainting in my arms,
Joining her feeble cries to your entreaties—
*Oh God! What could I do but yield myself
To you, to her, to any one that led me?*
    ROSSBERG: Nay, calmly, Altorf! Calmly! Weigh the matter.
Return: you but return to death or insult.
And why return? To clear yourself? You cannot.
Be then advised. Stay where you are. *I ask not
That you should turn your sword against these peasants,
But leave their cause. If 'tis decreed in fate
That it should prosper, 'twill without your aidance.
And wherein lies the crime? How are you guilty?
You have betrayed no trust. You have not sold
Your comrades, nor yourself. All men are free
To choose the way of life or mode of action
Best fitted to their interests or desires.
And, tell me, kinsman, were there no dishonor
In leaving me and thy too fond Rosina?
A love like hers might claim some sacrifice;
So might her father's friendship. And—what is it?*

We only ask you to accept a shelter
From the pursuit of some ungrateful peasants,
For whom you've freely poured your wealth and blood,
And who, in turn, will not bestow so much
As thanks and confidence. What say you, kinsman?
　　ALTORF: My speech and reason, too, have left me, Rossberg.
I see that I am lost. Return or stay,
I ne'er can be again the man I was.
Well! Let it pass. The die is cast. I'm reckless.
I've passed my word to thee, and I will keep it.
Switz, freedom, virtue, honor: fare ye well!
　　ROSSBERG: Come! Look not thus upon it. Trust me, Altorf.
There may be honor—aye, and freedom too,
In other camp than that of Switz rude peasants.
Rouse ye. Compose your thoughts! Confide in me.
Trust to my wiser age for wiser judgment,
And to my honor for its care of thine. (*Exits.*)
　　ALTORF: I am a shipwrecked man. Where'er I turn
Disgrace, dishonor stare me in the face.
I'm lost beyond redemption. *Cursed fool!
I've erred. I've sinned. Nor yet well know I how.
And were it all to do and act again,
Likely I should in all do much the same.
Oh! Wherefore came I here? What madness drove me?
Oh, my cursed love, cursed marriage, and cursed fortune!* (*Throws himself
into a chair.*)
That I could think! That I could see one way,
One gap for exit! Oh! My head is dizzied.
I'm stupefied, besotted; my brain's foundered.
Now would I bless the man could prove me mad.
And sure I am. A phantom? (*Rising.*)
(*Enter* ROSINA.) Is't Rosina?
*Then as I saw her in our wooing days,
In garb of virgin white.* Beloved, why here?
Why not at rest?
　　ROSINA: At rest? Oh, why not thou?
Altorf, why thus cast down? Here all are friends.
Here may'st thou rest in peace from thy pursuers.
　　ALTORF: Pursuers, love? And who is't that pursue?
My countrymen—my fellow-soldiers—brothers.
Oh Rosa! Thou hast laid thy honor, sweet,
At feet of him thou lov'st, and on it he

Must wreck his own.

ROSINA: What speak'st thou of?

ALTORF: My honor, love, the jewel I have lost.
My spotless name, my bright integrity,
My good report on earth.

ROSINA: High heaven forbid!
No! *Thou shalt clear thee,* Altorf. I will clear thee—
*I—I, the fool who lost thee.

ALTORF: Thou, my love?

ROSINA: Aye, I will tell—cry it aloud in Switz,
How I, alone, disguised, unwished for, came,
And drew thee to thy ruin. Ruin! No!
It is not ruin—'tis not ruin, Altorf!
Oh, God of heaven, don't tell me I've undone thee.

ALTORF: Rosa! My generous Rosa! And wilt do,
Wilt sacrifice so much for thy true love,
And shalt not be repaid? Hear me, my sweet!
Sooner than thou shalt cry aloud in Switz,
That thou unwooed, unwished for, sought thy lover,
I'll have me written traitor and adulterer
On every city sign and highway tree.
Think'st thou me such a poor, cold, heartless coward
To make thy honor scapegoat of my own?
To have it said I robbed thee of thy heart,
And, having soiled thy fame and culled thy sweets,
Then threw thee like a used flower away?
No, no! I am not so vile, nor yet so cold.
Honor is gone, so let us hold by love.
As Egypt's queen took Roman Antony,
Who gave the world to die within her arms,
So thou, my love, take me.

ROSINA: Too much! Too much!
Thou generous man! And shall I 'vantage take
Of thy devoted, blinded, headstrong passion?
Oh, no! I dare not.

ALTORF: Thou would'st as much for me.

ROSINA: As much?* What is there that I would not?
Ah! Well thou know'st it—know'st that on this head
I would the flouting world's opprobrium take:
Proud man's disdain, unfeeling woman's scorn—
All shame, oppression, want, death, infamy—
So that I had the proud, the glorious boast

That all was ta'en for sake of him I loved.

ALTORF: And shall he less? Angel, I yield me thine.
Whate'er betide, it shall betide us both.
Lost, ruined, perjured, at your feet I throw me,
Perjured in all but in my faith to thee!

Enter ERLACH.

ROSINA: Rise, Altorf! Rise! A stranger! How he gazes!

ALTORF: Who gazes? Where? Ye powers of darkness, shield me!
Sire! Father! Do I see? Is't truth?

ROSINA: Great heaven!

ALTORF: Speak to me! Look not so! For mercy, speak!
Father! How came you here? With whom? For what?

ERLACH: To see with these old eyes thy damning sin.
To hear with these old ears thy damning guilt.
To speak with these old lips thy father's cursing.

ALTORF: Await—in mercy!

ERLACH: Touch not my garment, wretch!
Up from thy knees, and sing the hallelujah!
A father's dying groans shall swell thy revels,
A father's dying curse—

ALTORF: Hold!

ROSINA: Heap thy curses here.
On me—on me, offended father, deal
Thine anger and revenge! Thy son is guiltless.

ALTORF: Angel, forbear! Rise, love! He heeds thee not.

ROSINA: But he shall heed. He shall not curse thee, Altorf.
Oh, list me, reverend sire! List her thou once
Did'st love and bless and call thy chosen daughter.

ERLACH: I've seen it, God of heaven! Almighty ruler,
Thou who dost 'venge the cause of outraged nations,
Thou who dost hearken when the upright call,
And, at the patriot's cry, with thunder smit'st
The tyrant's head, and scar'st the traitor's heart,
Hear now the cry of Erlach!

ALTORF: Hold! Thou shalt not speak it.
I am thy son. Old man, I am thy son!

ERLACH: *My* son? Thou liest. Thy mother played me false.
A son of mine a traitor and a villain?
A son of mine so base a wretch as thou art?
A son of mine sell honor and his country,

Its cause—its righteous cause—for one weak woman?
Look here, thou poor, despised, fallen coward!
Thou worse than coward, look at these grey hairs!
And, as thou'st brought them to the grave with shame,
So may thy God and mine revisit thee
With all his choicest plagues. May he requite
Thy father's anguish. As he asked of old
The fratricide for blood of murdered Abel,
So may he ask of thee my broken heart;
And, in the revels of thy wanton chambers,
Cry aloud in thy appalled ear
My solemn—dying—curse! (*Falls backwards.*)
    ALTORF: Horror! Despair!
Father! Father! Speak! Father! Rouse thee! Speak!
    ROSINA: Help! Help! *Rouse thee, old man!* Altorf, be calm!
He faints; he does but faint.
    ALTORF: 'Tis death; 'tis death.
Oh, ope thine eyes! Father, ope once thine eyes!
I'll be a murderer, a parricide—
Be anything so thou revoke thy curse!
Revoke thy curse! Live to revoke thy curse!
Depart not thus! I am thy son—thy boy!
Give me one look—one dying look of pardon!
    ROSINA: *Oh God!* What can I do? Help! Succor! Help!
    ALTORF: Too late; too late. The holy spark is gone.
Cold—cold and still! I am a wretch, indeed.
Leave it to me. Call not for help! No noise!
Here, father! Here I'll find revenge for thee! (*Is about to fall on his sword.*)
    ROSINA: What, at thy life? (*Dashes aside the weapon.*)
    ALTORF: Avaunt! Leave me!
    ROSINA: To die? No, no. Altorf! Eberard! Help! Help! (*Struggling with him.*)
    ALTORF: Would'st have me kill thee, fool?
    ROSINA: Yes; and I'd bless thee for't. Here! Here! But spare thyself.
Oh, curse me, strike me, if thou wilt, but hear me!

Enter ROSSBERG.

    ROSSBERG: Who calls? Rosina? Altorf? What's the matter?
    ROSINA: Help, father! Help! The sword! Prevent him! Help!
    ROSSBERG: How, at your life? Almighty heaven, what mean you?
    ALTORF: There! Take it. And now leave me.

No need of swords. Father, thy curse hath killed me! (*Rushes into an inner chamber, and bolts the door.*)[24]
    ROSSBERG: What means this, child? That body, too—who is't?
    ROSINA: His father, sir; his father.
    ROSSBERG: Whose? Not Altorf's?
    ROSINA: Aye.
    ROSSBERG: Dead?
What, ho! Help here! Dead? Most heavy chance!
Bear in this body. (*Speaking to two* SERVANTS *who enter.*)
Seek out some skillful leech.[25]
I fear 'tis all too late; but bear him in. (*The* SERVANTS *bear off the body.*)
*How did it chance? Rosa! What make you there?
    ROSINA: (*Listening at the door*). Close locked? Oh, open! Let me in!
Help, father!
Help! Help! Break down the door!
    ROSSBERG: Leave him awhile. Passion will spend itself.
And hearken, child! You are the hope I rest on.*
Let not young Altorf hence. I have my reasons.
He parts not hence until he is thy husband.
    ROSINA: My husband? Never, never. *Hear it, heaven!
'Tis I—'tis I who broke his father's heart.
'Tis I who shall break his. Altorf, oh, hear me!
    ROSSBERG: Peace, child! I have his sword.
    ROSINA: His sword? Oh, God!
He hath a dagger in his heart, my father,
Whose wound—whose poisoned wound—no hand shall heal.
Oh! Oh! The noble being I have ruined!
    ROSSBERG: Hush! Patiently, my child! Confide in me.
This burst of grief shall pass. Deal with him gently.
I should not much regret old Altorf's death
'An it had chanced in any place but this.*
The father gone, the son is fixed our friend.
Austria now gains his sword, we his alliance.
Himself, his lands, his title—all are ours.
    ROSINA: (*Starting up from the door and rushing forward*).
What hear I? Holy heaven, is this the cause?
Is this the cause why thou hast wooed him here?

---

[24]The acting edition omits this action and all other actions pertaining to it. While the substituted action is not specified, it appears, from the way the text is cut, that at this point Altorf loses consciousness and remains so during subsequent lines.
    [25]Physician.

Have I been made the tool in such foul dealings?
*Oh God, my brain! My brain! Speak! Tell me, quick!
Thy words—thy look—have conjured up a thought,
A fear will drive me mad.
  ROSSBERG: What would'st thou, child?
Hast not thy Altorf here?
  ROSINA: Oh, that I had not!*
Yes, I see it. The daughter's love hath been
The helping hand to the sire's avarice,
The ladder to his aims and worst ambition.
  ROSSBERG: *This to thy father?* Peace, thou raving fool!
Art mad? An idiot?
*(Going to the door.) Altorf! Strange, he hears not!
Altorf! What, ho!*

Enter EUSTACE.

  EUSTACE; My lord! My lord!
  ROSSBERG: What bear'st thou? Quick!
  EUSTACE: The armies have engaged; Austria's defeated.
The whole rank's slaughtered; scarce a man escaped
To tell their fate.
  ROSSBERG: What say'st thou?
  EUSTACE: The truth.
  *ROSSBERG: Lies; all lies.
  EUSTACE: Truth, as I breathe, my lord.*
Nay, more, we hear the distant shout of foes.
  ROSSBERG: Friends, fool! Friends!
  EUSTACE: Look forth yourself, my lord.
  ROSSBERG: *Saints! 'an thou speak the truth, would thou wert
hanged!*
Run quick! Alarm the vassals! Man the walls! (*Exit* ROSSBERG *and*
EUSTACE.)
  *ROSINA: (Alone, listening always at the door).
I can hear nothing. Altorf! Altorf! Answer!
For mercy—oh, for mercy, speak one word!
Hark! Was't a sound? A groan? All still again.
Altorf! Love, madness, give me strength!
(With a dreadful effort, she breaks down the door, and falls senseless.)
  ALTORF: What! Are the bars of hell broke down upon us?
What is the clang? Are we all in a dream?
  ROSINA: (Feebly rising). I see thee. 'Tis enough.*

ALTORF:[26] *My love! My life!* Why, sure thou should'st be Rosa.
Speak to me, love. Canst tell me where I am?
Why on the earth, my sweet?
    *ROSINA: Oh, too kind lover,
Dost thou not hate me yet? What look you on?*
    ALTORF: I pray thee pass thy hand across my eyes;
I sure have dreamt or dream.
    ROSINA: Oh! Eberard.
    ALTORF: You had best leave me, love. I think 'twere best.
    ROSINA: Leave you? All, all but that. I cannot—dare not.
    ALTORF: Oh! What a murky gulf is this I gaze in:
No light, no hope. Oh Rosa! Thou'st undone me.
    ROSINA: I have! I have. That I should live to know it.
But stop! A little while—all shall be well.
But if thou lov'st me— Love me? That thou canst not.
But if thou ever did'st, oh, look not thus!
    ALTORF: I hear it yet. Oh, was it well, my father,
To add thy curse unto the curse of God[27]?
Sure I was born beneath some blasting comet.
How hath it come to pass? What have I done
That I should be the buffet thus of fate,
And mark for heaven's thunder?
    ROSINA: Hark! I will tell thee.
*Thy fair branches, love, did meet and twine
Into a poisoning, blasting upas[28] tree.
Fair did it seem, and thou did'st cling and cling,
Closer and closer, till the death-draught wrought;
And, one by one, thy boughs and leaves did droop,
And all thy sap and beauty passed from thee.
But, lo, the axe we'll lay unto the root.
Thy killing mate shall fall; then, green and fair,
Scented and vigorous, thy boughs shall lift
And proudly touch the heaven.* Dost hear me, love?
Fly from these walls; trust not my treacherous father.
Back to thy camp, thy troops, thy country, Altorf.
And I the while—I'll seek thy father's ghost,
And he shall hear and know 'twas I that sinned.
Then shall he blot his curse from th' angel's record,

---

[26]It is at this point, in the acting edition, that Altorf apparently revives.
[27]The acting edition substitutes "heaven."
[28]A tree of the mulberry family, which has poisonous bark.

And, from the opening heaven, speak out thy pardon—
A word, a whisper in thine ear. (*She leans suddenly over him, plucks his dagger from its sheath, and stabs herself.*)
    *ALTORF: Ha!
    ROSINA: Contend not!* It is done. *Well done, my Altorf.*
Now thou art free. *The blasting upas dies.
Look not so frenzied! Hear me! All is well.*
Return unto thy country—to thy virtue.
*Altorf, dost hear me?
    ALTORF: Did I need this lesson?
Well done, and bravely. Quick, my love; this way.
I had forgot the steel. But there is time. (*Struggles with her for the dagger.*)
    ROSINA: No; as thou lov'st me, Altorf, by our love—
Our love that made this wound and makes it sweet,
Touch not thy life, Altorf! Oh, God! (*Falls back in his arms, flings away the dagger, and grasps him in the convulsions of death.*)
Swear it!
Touch not thy life! Live to redeem thy honor!
    ALTORF: Past, past, my love! My angel!
    ROSINA: So! I am blest.
Too blest—* Altorf, thy sire's revenged! Thou'rt free,
And I—I die. Oh, let my death atone!
My love, my life! I die upon this bosom. (*Dies.*)
    ALTORF: Where is the steel? Let be! I need it not.
The blow hath struck. Death knocks upon my heart.
My faded lily! My too faithful Rosa!
(*A loud noise of arms without.*)
*Lie on this rising breast. So—let me gaze!
The fiends let loose their hellish hurly round me;
Yet will I gaze awhile before they clutch me.
Lovely—too lovely flower! They say death's horrid:
Thou might'st enamor gods of it, my love.
See, how he gently streaks with ivory fingers
The lovely cheeks—there, softly seals the lips,
Yet keeps their smile, that breathes love's music still!
Yea, that discourses more sweet eloquence
Than the best words of life. (*The noise of arms increases without.*)
How sweet thy sleep!
The din awakes not thee. How calm the brow!
How placidly repose those closed lids,
Their fringes lie upon the velvet cheek
Like streaks of night upon a moonbeam cloud.*

GIOVANNA *rushes in, rolled in a soldier's mantle.*

GIOVANNA: Where shall I turn? Where find him? Ha!
Is't thou? Fly, fly! The castle's yielded.
ALTORF: Who comes to break upon my dying dream?
Giovanna!
GIOVANNA: Dead! Who's she thou hold'st? Thy Rosa?
*ALTORF: Said I not true she had an angel's air?
In death, if thus, what was she when I wooed her?
GIOVANNA:* Oh, stir thee! Fly! I hear our soldiers enter.
The castle has surrendered; Rossberg's prisoner.
ALTORF: Thanks, thanks. I know not what thou say'st, but thanks.
Giovanna, thou hast been to me a generous friend.
Protect my name. Tell all thou canst t' excuse me.
Say that I have more hapless been than sinning,
More weak than wicked. I can't tell thee all.
Death comes, but comes too slow. This dagger'll serve. (*Snatches dagger and falls on it.*)
*GIOVANNA: No way but this? Was there no way but this?
ALTORF: None; none.* (*Shouts off the scene, "Victory! Victory!"*)
Ha! Victory! Whose is the cry?
GIOVANNA: Freedom's.
ALTORF: Enough. (*The back scene opens, and* DE RHEINTHAL *rushes in at the head of the Swiss* SOLDIERS.)
GIOVANNA: Cease! Cease those shouts! Turn here your eyes, my brother,
In sadness, not in triumph.
DE RHEINTHAL: What heap is that,
Bleeding and dying? Am I then too late?
Live, Altorf, live! Rossberg hath cleared thy fame.
Wounded, expiring, he reveals the arts
By which he wooed thee here.
*ALTORF: Rossberg is prisoner? Lead him hither, then,
And let his closing eyes behold this death scene.
I ask no greater vengeance.*
GIOVANNA: Eberard!
ALTORF: Kind friend!
Thou hast been very kind. God bless thee, wife!
Send thee a better—happier—mate. . .than. . .Altorf. (*Dies.*)
GIOVANNA: Art gone? Both gone? Poor maid, I envy thee.
In life thou wert beloved, in death united;
And ye shall have one grave, poor, hapless lovers!

And one sad, only mourner there to weep you. (DE RHEINTHAL *and the* SOLDIERS *gather mournfully round the dead. The curtain falls.*)

THE END

Epilogue

By H. T. Farmer.
Spoken by Mrs. Barnes in the character of Rosina.

Waked by the grateful tribute of applause,
I burst my bonds and spurned death's icy laws.
Methinks e'en now I see Elysium beam—
But soft, ye fair, and I'll repeat my dream.
Old Shakespeare led me to ambrosial bowers,
And Dryden crowned me with a wreath of flowers,
While Otway wept, for that sad pilgrim knew
The bliss of genius and her curses too.
How soon, alas, that fleeting bliss expires!
She dreams of roses, but she sleeps on briars;
Convenes in robes a magic court of air,
Then wakes, and finds her wildered bosom bare!
Nay, more; though lorn and weary and distressed,
Suspense, that vampire, banquets on her breast,
While sleepless Envy, with her shuddering brood,
Relentless dips a dagger in her blood.

Ye who award to sterling worth its due,
And love the floweret that your garden grew,
With heart, with impulse, and with fostering hand,
Greet this sweet scion of your native land.
The lovely dew-queen, in succeeding years,
Shall bathe its future buds in sparkling tears,
Unnumbered leaves its cherished blossoms shed
To deck the Patriot's grave and virgin's bed.

Author's Epilogue (from manuscript)

With cypress crowned, with brow of solemn gloom,
The Muse stands thoughtful over Altorf's tomb.
Hushed is her lyre, its shattered chords unstrung.
Cold is her hand, and powerless now her tongue.
Yet, soft! She stirs, she lifts her marble brow;
She moves her lips, in accents soft and low.
She breathes the moral from her tale of woe.
"Ye sons and daughters of this blessed land,
Where Freedom holds her rod, and Peace her wand,
Turn not with careless ear this night away
From the feigned story of my tragic lay.
From upright Erlach catch the Patriot's fire;
And shun from Altorf's tale, Love's fierce desire:
Thus to the youth. And let the maiden learn
A solemn lesson from Rosina's urn.
See all the woes that come in passion's train,
Nor yield her ear unto this syren strain.
To all: in what is good, example find;
Warning from errors. Thus to all mankind.
But children of Columbia must aye
Follow the upright; the base, the abject flee;
For where should virtue dwell, if not among the free.

ERNEST MALTRAVERS

Louisa Medina

Originally published by John Dicks, 313, Strand, London.
Dicks' Standard Plays, Number 379.

Characters

John Walters
Armstrong
Dick Darvil
Alice Darvil
Lumley Ferris
Ernest Maltravers
Sir William Maltravers
Lady Florence Saxingham
Zerrigueo
Lord Saxingham
Octavia de Montaigne
Colonel Montaigne
Castrucci
Officers, servants, gondoliers, peasants, brigands, and pilgrims

ACT I

Scene One

Dark wood. Storm. Cries of "Follow! Follow!" Enter WALTERS *and* ARMSTRONG. ARMSTRONG *has a dark lantern.*

WALTERS: Douse the glim. Skulk, man, skulk—hush! Are they gone?
ARMSTRONG: (*Closing the lantern*). Yes, they have taken the cross path to the factory, where Dick Darvil threw the sledgehammer. We have escaped the bulkies[1] this time, John Walters.
WALTERS: Yes, we may thank our heels for the safety of our necks, this time, my covey.[2] I wonder if we will ever be so fortunate again. But where the devil can Dick Darvil be?
ARMSTRONG: He can't be far off. But I say, John Walters, did you ever see anyone like Dick Darvil in all your life? He hates the rich as

---

[1]Police.
[2]Fellow.

though he had been wronged by them more deeply than ever man was wronged before. It is easily seen that Richard Darvil was not always what he is now.

Enter DARVIL.

DARVIL: You're right, worthy associates and most honorable comrades. I was not always the friend and fellow of beaten hounds, who feel the lash, yet lack the heart to show their fangs. Brave men ye are. Could ye but fight one half as well as ye run, he'd be a hero who drove you from your purpose. Why, ye fled from your own shadows that, had not fright rendered you scant of breath, I should have scarce overtaken you. Oh, he may boast himself a man that excels the bettermost of you—especially in running.

WALTERS: Why, the odds were too much against us, and how were you to escape else? Had we made any resistance, to a dead certainty they'd planked you. How did you escape?

DARVIL: How! Which way did poverty ever escape power by violence? How! Had I not the sledgehammer in my hands, and in my heart the will to use it? How escape! Even as I would from a baying cur that flew upon my throat—dash him down and spring upon his body. Since I am to be hunted like a beast of prey, it will go hard but I dip my fangs in blood.

WALTERS: Humph! Murder is a big word, Darvil, and one would be likely to scrag[3] for it. We have worked together, we have stolen together these several years, but to take the actual life of a man—is—

DARVIL: Better than to lose ours by starvation! Every man's hand is against us. Why not ours against every man? Perdition! Had you ever known the wild delight of having your clutch upon a rich man's throat—to hear the lordly accents whine for mercy, to see him quail and shake beneath the power of the poor man he oppressed—you'd give your life—aye, twenty lives— for such another triumph.

WALTERS: Hush! That sort of gab will string us up to dance on nothing one of these days. No, no, Darvil, a better way might be found to touch the ready—in your own little Alice there at home.

DARVIL: What of the girl?

WALTERS: Why, she's mighty beautysome, and there's many a rich cove[4] would fork down handsomely to have the kissing of her.

---

[3]Hang.
[4]Fellow.

DARVIL: Wretch! Would you have me sell my flesh and blood? Make a market of my daughter's shame? Hark ye, sirrah, there be ties that have made a civilish bond between us—and I endure the brutish nature of the thing I use—but breathe you no more words against that girl, as you would hope to live!

ARMSTRONG: Oh, damn your sentiment, Dick. You're on your high horse tonight, so goodbye. Here, John, take the lantern. I'll see you again in the morning. (*Exits.*)

WALTERS: Well, now, I meant no harm. We are safe now. Let's go home.

DARVIL: Home—aye, to starve! Home to a cold hearth and a penniless purse, and with an ungratified hate. Foiled and beaten, we must sneak back like hungry wolves to our lair.

ERNEST: (*Without*). Hallo! Hallo!

WALTERS: Hush, may I be scragged if the bulkies aren't after us. I heard voices, and as soon as Oliver[5] peeps out, we are lost chickens.

DARVIL: Not without a deadly struggle first. He'll be a bold man who leads the chase when the boar's at bay. (*Looks out.* ERNEST *hallos.*) No, no, 'tis but a single man. What can bring a man to this lonely common at this time of night? Back, back, I say, and watch him! (*They retire. Storm increases.*)

Enter ERNEST.

ERNEST: Hallo! Hallo! No sign of human form or habitation on this lonely waste! No guide but those distant watch-fires that glimmer with a preternatural glare amidst the darkness! How am I to make my way to the village? I think the wandering spirit of the Will o' the Wisp[6] must have led me here so late. Shall I never forget that I am no longer a student of Gottingen, counting those coquettish stars, but Ernest Maltravers, heir to the oldest and wealthiest family in Cumberland, and just returning to my paternal home. What the devil is to become of me tonight in all this pitiless pelting? Hallo!

DARVIL: (*Advancing*). Who calls?

ERNEST: Ha! Thank heaven, I have a companion in my wanderings! Save you, friend, can you direct or guide me to the nearest shelter? I have lost my path in this wild common.

DARVIL: The village is far off—full five miles distant.

---

[5]The moon.
[6]A moving light seen over marshes at night.

ERNEST: So far, and I am fearfully tired. Will you accompany me?

DARVIL: It is very late. (WALTERS *advances with lantern.*)

ERNEST: (*Draws out watch*). Stoop your lantern—yes, half past eleven. (DARVIL *and* WALTERS *exchange signals.*) But it matters not complaining. If you will accompany me, friend, I will pay your trouble handsomely. (*Takes out purse.*)

DARVIL: No offense, sir, you're a grandee,[7] but if you would condescend to rest beneath my humble roof, it stands hard by, and I will go with you at daybreak to the village.

ERNEST: Offense, indeed, to a man ready to drop, and beaten to numbness by the storm! Lead on, friend. Any shelter will be welcome, however poor, so it be honest.

DARVIL: Of its honesty, sir, you shall be better convinced before we depart.

ERNEST: On, then—but stay. I dropped my valise but now from sheer fatigue. With the prospect of present shelter, I can endure to recover it. Wait one moment. (*Exits.*)

DARVIL: Hell fights for us: the watch, the money. Follow us to the house, but keep quiet until I summon you.

WALTERS: Why not rob him here with less ado?

DARVIL: No, it is not safe. He is young and strong, and will make a desperate resistance. The body, too, would soon be found, and so near our dwelling, cause suspicion.

WALTERS: The body! Why, you won't murder him!

DARVIL: Wretch! Did you not bid but *now* a father sell his child for gold? For gold, pollute the pure and vital stream that flows from his own veins! For gold, hurl down the only holy thing that remains to plead for him above! Yet, you would have me tremble now, as if a stranger's blood was dearer than my own! Go to! Hide yourself in the shed behind the house. There shall be no *murder*, as you call it.

WALTERS: That's right, Dick, it ben't safe—hush, he's here.

Re-enter ERNEST *with valise.*

DARVIL: Now, sir, if you please, I'll show you to a place of rest. (*As* ERNEST *passes out,* DARVIL *leans back and whispers to* WALTERS.) Bring the sledgehammer with you. (*Music. They exit,* WALTERS *carrying the hammer which* DARVIL *had left on.*)

---

[7]Nobleman.

Scene Two

Interior of DARVIL'*s cottage, everything presenting the appearance of wretched poverty. Before a few embers,* ALICE *is discovered kneeling and blowing them into a flame. A door, right, and a staircase, the door fastened by a rough bar of wood through two staples. Furious storm.*

ALICE: (*Rises*). It is almost midnight, and yet no sign of Father. What a dreadful night. How the rain plashes from the leafless branches of those weird-like trees, and the blue lightning streams over the wild common, as if the earth were all on fire! In such a night, I have heard that terrible murders have been done, and pale specters arisen from their graves to fright the living into madness. (*Thunder and lightning.*) It is a dreadful thing to be thus lonely: no eye, no ear, no help within miles, save ONE—that which is above. On such a night, too, it is said the evil one has power to tempt poor wretches to sell their souls for gold. Heaven preserve us! (*The door is shaken, and* LUMLEY FERRERS *calls softly, "Alice! Alice!"*) Ha! Have my thoughts conjured a spirit? Yes, the human spirit of evil! He, the tempter to infamy! But he shall not enter. I am cold and hungry, poor and ignorant, but I am honest and will keep so. (FERRERS *calls again, "Alice! Alice!"*) What shall I do? Would that my father were here. Stern as he is, he is still my father; though rough be the stem, the root is nature's planting. (FERRERS *dashes open the window and looks in.*)

FERRERS: Alice Darvil!

ALICE: Ha! You here again?

FERRERS: Undo the door and let me speak with you. The rain is pouring.

ALICE: I shall not. Pray, be gone. I have no dealings with you. You shall not enter here. (FERRERS *leaps in at the window.*)

FERRERS: There go two words to that, my pretty one. All this dignity is very becoming, but very much out of place. I am a man of fortune and birth, in love with you. You are the daughter of the most notorious thief, vagabond, poacher that—

ALICE: Silence, sir! Whatever may be my father's failings, his daughter's ear is not the one to listen to their detail!

FERRERS: Then I'll speak of yourself. Here you live in a wretched hovel without even the necessaries of life—you, whose budding youth and excelling beauty might well become a coronet.

ALICE: Truly, sir, I am often cold, thinly clad, and hungry. Where's the remedy?

FERRERS: In my love, my sweet little cowslip of the common. Trust yourself to me, and I will wreathe that perfect brow with pearl and fold those graceful limbs in silk. Thou shalt sleep on down, eat off gold, and have no care save to vary pleasure.

ALICE: And when that pleasure surfeits, to be turned forth to suffer bitterer poverty without that best of antidotes—an honest heart! Oh, sir, sir! Poor and ignorant as I am, I can confound your rhetoric. You talk of *love*! *I* know that love exalts, not debases, its object. You despise the peasant Alice too much to call her *wife*; she scorns you too much to be your wanton!

FERRERS: (*Aside*). Humph! A very pretty sermon. I look damned silly here. (*To her.*) All this is very fine, Alice, but in two words take my reply. I love you; you are necessary to me. If you do not listen to reason, you shall be mine by force. (*Approaches her.*)

ALICE: Attempt no violence here. I am not alone.

FERRERS: The devil you're not. Why, who protects you?

ALICE: (*Takes up gun*). Myself and this. You called my father "poacher." A poacher needs a gun, and his child knows how to use it.

FERRERS: (*Aside*). What a virago! (*To her.*) Well, Alice, I see you have a spice of the devil in you, and that will fit you the better for me. Farewell, this time. The next time I come for you, it will not be alone. (*Exits, leaving door open.*)

ALICE: What have I done thus to be singled out for insult? Should he return—and oh, horror to think on, should he win my father to his purpose! Hark, he comes. Oh, heaven, there are two steps! My father ushers the seducer to his child! (*Sinks in a chair.*)

Enter DARVIL *and* ERNEST.

DARVIL: How's this? What means the door unfastened? Alice, girl—daughter, see you not the gentleman?

ALICE: (*Sinks at her father's feet and hides her face in her hands*). Father, Father, force me not to look upon him. Am I not your child?

DARVIL: Are you besotted, girl? Fool, I ever knew, but now you must be either mad or drunk. Up, up, I say!

ERNEST: Do not be so rough, friend. (*Raises* ALICE.) Look up, my pretty maid, and tell me if my presence here be painful to you. If so, I'll brave the storm, and quit this shelter instantly. Nay, do not tremble so. No one shall harm you.

ALICE: (*Looks up in confusion*). A thousand pardons. I thought— I feared— Excuse me, sir, I will come again instantly. (*Exits.*)

DARVIL: The girl's gone mad, I think. Why, Alice, bring what we have for supper. (*Calling.*) Are you known in these parts, sir?

ERNEST: Oh, no, not now. I have been abroad for years and am just returning home.

DARVIL: Probably they expect you?

ERNEST: No, not for these six months. But why do you ask? Are you a resident here?

DARVIL: I am.

ERNEST: And work in the factories, I suppose?

DARVIL: My employments are various. But here's your supper. (*Enter* ALICE *with supper.*) It is but little we have, sir, but you'll fare better tomorrow.

ERNEST: Nay, a worn traveler is not fastidious. This supper, and this chair for a bed, are luxuries compared with a night passed on the common.

DARVIL: No doubt you will sleep sound tonight.

ERNEST: (*To* ALICE). Prettiest of lasses, after having frightened you so much on my entrance, I must hear from those sweet lips that I am welcome, ere I can eat with pleasure. (*As he kisses her hand,* DARVIL *locks door and takes away the key.* ALICE *sees him and is going to speak to* ERNEST, *when* DARVIL *comes between them.*)

DARVIL: Eat, sir, eat. Alice is country bred and understands no fine words. I will fetch more fuel, and then leave you to sleep. (*Exits with gun. Music.* ERNEST *sits at table.* ALICE *examines the door, looks for the gun, and finding that* DARVIL *has taken it, softly approaches* ERNEST.)

ERNEST: Sweetheart, these coarse crusts would be well digested by one sweet kiss of those coral lips.

ALICE: Hush! Have you much money about you?

ERNEST: (*Advancing*). Oh, the mercenary baggage! Does she sell her kisses so high? Why, my dear?

ALICE: Give it to Father, or it may cost you your life!

ERNEST: Ha! What mean you?

ALICE: I hardly know, yet I fear for you. Escape when we are gone. Rain, wind, and darkness are better to brook than the envy with which poverty views wealth. Hist! He is here.

Enter DARVIL *with faggots.* (*Music.* DARVIL *comes between* ALICE *and* EARNEST *and throws off* ALICE *with fury.*)

DARVIL: Forward wench, begone! And you, Mr. Gentleman, take notice that my daughter is no safe manor to poach on. Come, mistress.

ALICE: I follow you. (*Music. As* DARVIL *makes up fire,* ALICE, *in pantomime, tells* ERNEST *not to sleep—to fly.*) Goodnight, sir. You'll not let the fire out, if you please! Goodnight. *Pray remember!*

ERNEST: I shall not forget. (ALICE *and* DARVIL *go off, upstairs.* DARVIL *takes the bar of the door with him.*) Forget! If I die tonight or live till age chill my blood, I shall never forget you, lovely, generous girl! Fool that I am, shall I never learn prudence? Well, here I have at least the kitchen poker, and, at the worst, it is but man to man. He will not find an easy prey. Thus I await him. (*Takes up poker and stands in attitude of defense.*)

Scene Three

The shed behind the cottage. Dark. Enter DARVIL *with lantern and hatchet.*

DARVIL: Why should I hesitate? It is but a blow, and one that insures me wealth for months to come. Am I to blame, that must either starve or murder? Is not self-preservation the first law of nature? Shall I rot by inches and see my fair girl pining to the grave, to save a stranger's life? One, too, of those accursed *gentlemen*, who think, because they roll in gold, they may insult the poor and pollute their children with impunity. (*A low whistle heard.*) Ah! Walters is here; then his fate is fixed. Come in, fool. Why do you linger? His purse and watch are worth two hundred guineas!

ALICE: (*Who has entered*). And how does that concern you, Father?

DARVIL: Death! Alice here! I thought 'twas Walters I spoke to.

ALICE: And what would bring John Walters here at this time of night? What work is on hand?

DARVIL: Fool! What's that to you? But, since you must know, we intend tonight—

ALICE: To commit a murder.

DARVIL: Ha!

ALICE: Father, what means this hatchet? Why are you here? What bloody work needs the aid of Walters? Father, you would murder the stranger for his gold, but you shall not!

DARVIL: Fool that you are, think you I would risk my neck? Should I not lose my life?

ALICE: Aye, and deserve to lose a thousand! Father, he who lifts his hand against a sleeping guest is guilty of a crime that has no name save that of horror. He who violates the sanctity of faith, and breaks through nature's holiest rites, deserves to be thrust forth from man and herd alone with beasts. You would do this, but you shall not!

DARVIL: I shall not? Who will prevent me?

ALICE: I will prevent you. You shall strike through my heart, ere you harm a hair of that noble stranger's head. Father, I have said it! (*Exits.*)

DARVIL: Curse on the snivelling wench. Ho! Walters!

Enter WALTERS, *staggering.*

WALTERS: Heigh, ho! Dick Darvil, is that you or the devil!

DARVIL: Silence, beast! Death and hell, have you been soaking when most you need your senses clear? Be silent and be sober, brute, or I will begin this night's work of blood by dashing out your brains!

WALTERS: How you talk, Dick. By the hokey,[8] man, there's no knowing what to make of you. Sometimes when I hear your big words and see you hold your head so high, I think you were not always Darvil.

DARVIL: You're right. I was not always the wretch I have become. Listen to me, and then wonder if you can that I hunt the proud ones of the earth with a hatred unto death. I was born a younger brother, to a race possessed of fortune, rank, and power. But because I could not bow and fawn and cringe in slavish acquiescence to my father's will, he cast me from his heart and gave my eldest brother that love which was once my soul's inheritance. God, how I once loved that brother! Even now, when I recall his noble features, courteous accent, and winning smiles, which made all hearts his own, I feel my heart grow womanish. Let me remember how he wronged my love, and turn my tears to blood. I loved; the object was rich in beauty and in worth, but poor and lowly born. I married her, for I hadn't learned the cruel cunning of the great to trample all beneath me, And for that I could not be a villain, my father called me a disgrace and cast me from his heart and doors.

WALTERS: Cursed rough, to be sure.

DARVIL: We wandered forth as outcasts and beggars for years. My young and lovely wife was made to suffer the bitterest gnawings of poverty and hunger. I saw her drooping unto death before my eyes. I snared a hare to give her food, was seized, manacled, and dragged before the great man whose game laws I had broken. That great man was my brother.

WALTERS: Oh, hookey!

DARVIL: My proud father had gone down to the tomb of his ancestors. My brother was the sole lord of house and lands, and--as I then thought—offered to share them with me. Fool that I was—dolt, idiot—I believed his smooth professions and gave him from my heart the deepest, warmest gratitude. To my wife he seemed the kindest, gentlest—the most damned of villains! She became, for the first time, a mother. Alice was born, the loveliest thing the earth e'er shone upon, but hell rose in my heart; for I thought the infant smiled too like my brother. Then I saw the cause of all his cursed care. Maddened with my wrongs, I struck the monster to the earth—and rushing, bathed in her seducer's blood, before my faithless wife, cursed her in the bitterness of soul. I saw her fall senseless to

---

[8]Nonsense.

the earth. I could not—no, I could not take her life—but I seized the unconscious infant and rushed away to be a hunted criminal and a branded felon. She died, they said, withered like a broken lily. So—so, I struggled to forgive her in my heart and cherish little Alice for her sake; but I have revenged her fall upon the proud oppressors of the land, and am deeply sworn to lay her cursed betrayer as low as his perfidy hurled down his hapless victim. (*Walks away, agitated.*) No more of this. Remember the business for which we are met. The time has come.

WALTERS: You're a desperate man, Darvil. It's true I've been lushing a little, but I am not so boozy as not to remember the work on hand. So don't begin flashy, but tell me what's to be done with the body of the swell cove when we have finished him!

DARVIL: Yonder deep pond shall answer for it. Forward. Now, remember to strike one blow, and a sure one. (*Exit. Music.*)

Scene Four

Interior of DARVIL's *cottage.* ERNEST *discovered.*

ERNEST: This, then, is the end of all my wanderings: to be murdered within a few miles of the home I've not seen since boyhood. Can it be so? Courage! Courage, Ernest Maltravers, and you will balk the villain yet! Let me but once get out upon the common, and I will trust my life to my speed, but first I'll prevent their return for awhile. (*Goes to door.*) By heavens! The staples are empty; the bar is gone. Their plan is deeply laid. Nothing remains for me but flight. (*Goes to door.*) Locked and the key gone! Then am I lost, indeed. Since I must die like a rat in a cage, at least I'll die biting. Ha—voices! I hear the steps of two—'tis fearful odds. Oh, God! My father! (*Music. Sinks in a chair.* ALICE *enters from staircase, comes behind him.*)

ALICE: Arise, arise, for shame! Are you a man! And do you despair when resolution alone can save you! Away—you are free—I have saved you!

ERNEST: Generous maiden! Thanks for your kind endeavors, but I cannot fly. The door is locked.

ALICE: (*Produces key*). Behold the key. I watched him where he laid it. I waited until he left the house. I besought your life in vain. I told him he should not harm you, and he shall not. (*Unlocks door.*)

ERNEST: How shall I thank you?

ALICE: Hush, they are in the shed. Yet, stranger, remember he is my father, and do not betray him, for my sake.

ERNEST: Thy virtues, lovely Alice, might atone the crimes of devils; yet do I fear to leave you. Rather than expose you to danger, I will stay and brave it with you.

ALICE: Oh, no, no, they will murder you! Oh, for the love of heaven, begone! Will you stay and let me see you slaughtered before my eyes? Fly! Each moment is laden with your life—away! Away!

ERNEST: Farewell awhile. We will meet again, sweet Alice, and then I'll say how much I love you. (*Presses her to his breast and exits. She stands looking out and calls after him.*)

ALICE: To the left—to the left! Keep to the left hand of the river. He springs away with the fleet step of youth and liberty. His form is lost in darkness. He is saved! I have saved him! Hark, they come! Not yet—he is not yet far distant. (*Goes to the door of the staircase and passes her arm through the staples.*) The bolt is gone, but noble stranger, Alice guards you!

DARVIL: (*Without, pushing door*). Stand from the door!

ALICE: You cannot enter here!

DARVIL: Open the door, or I will burst it open!

ALICE: You cannot, it is firmly barred.

DARVIL: Liar! The bolt is gone.

ALICE: Aye, but into the staples I've thrust my arm, and he who enters first must break it.

WALTERS: (*Leaps in at the window*). You forget the window, my covess. (*Music. Chord. He drags her from door. DARVIL enters with hatchet.*)

DARVIL: Here's to the heart of your paramour! Ha! Where is the stranger?

ALICE: Gone! Safe! I told you, you should not harm him.

DARVIL: Eternal curses seize you for it. Speak! Which way went he? Out, Walters and pursue. (*Exit WALTERS.*) He is a stranger to the common. Which path went he? Speak, wretch, as you value your life!

ALICE: Do not kill me, Father! I am your child!

DARVIL: 'Tis false! If you were mine, you would not league against me! Death! You have roused a thought of hell within me! Speak, or I'll strike you dead! Which path went he?

ALICE: The path to liberty and home!

DARVIL: Die, then, accursed child of guilt and shame! Perish in your treachery! (ALICE *presses her hand over her face. DARVIL heaves up the hatchet, when ERNEST and FERRERS rush in, accompanied by SERVANTS. A desperate struggle ensues. DARVIL is secured. ERNEST supports ALICE. ARMSTRONG enters, with others.*)

ERNEST: Alice! Alice, my brave and beautiful Alice! Look up. You are safe. Heaven be praised, we came in time to save you. (*To FERRERS.*) Oh, sir! Surely it was the interposition of heaven that sent you across the common tonight to save this angel from a fate so shocking!

FERRERS: 'Twas opportune, indeed. (*Aside.*) If it was heaven sent me, I was coming on an errand for the devil! Hark'ee good fellow. (*Beckons to* ARMSTRONG.) Our plan of carrying off the girl tonight has failed. Say nothing of it, and you shall be paid the same.

ARMSTRONG: All right, sir. Good evening to you, Mr. Darvil. (*Aside to* DARVIL.) You have escaped the gallows long enough, but we've got you now. Gammon, Dick. Fifty dollars reward for the notorious smuggler, poacher, and house-breaker. Bind him, lads. That rope becomes him as if the hemp was grown for him! (*Retires.*)

ALICE: (*Kneels to* ERNEST). Spare him. Spare my father, even as I saved you. Have mercy upon him. If they take him hence, a shameful death awaits him!

ERNEST: You plead in vain, sweet Alice. His life is forfeit to his country's laws, and he must pay the penalty. Take him away to prison!

ALICE: Then take me with him. If my father goes to prison, his daughter will go too.

ERNEST: Virtuous girl, you have conquered. On condition that he leaves the country this hour, I will pay these men the ransom and let him free. (*To* DARVIL.) Do you accept the terms?

DARVIL: I do. Alice, come near to me. For sixteen years I have reared and cherished you, in want, in disgrace—in danger. My first thought has been of you. In death, my last words would have been your name. In you has lived the last gentle feeling of my wronged and hating heart. In you has dwelt the last human tie of my corroded nature. This night you have sold me for a kiss from a stranger's lips, and now we part for ever. Come closer to me. My manacled hands would fain touch your beauteous head once more!

ERNEST: Unbind his hands! (*They free his hands; he draws* ALICE *gradually closer.* ERNEST *approaches.*)

DARVIL: Thanks. This done, I shall depart in peace. Alice, receive the last token of a father's vengeance. (*He rapidly draws a knife, and with a loud shout, aims it at her heart. Music.* ERNEST *catches his arm from behind, and he is again secured.*)

DARVIL: Curses blast you! Disease prey upon your beauty, and sorrow drink your blood! May the sharp pangs of scorn cut to your soul! May the deep curse of withering hate corrode your heart! False serpent! Unnatural fiend! May you live to be forsaken—trampled upon—spit upon! May you drink to the dregs the wormwood of a father's curse! (ALICE *falls.*)

Tableau. Curtain.

ACT II

Scene One

A parlor in Maltravers' Hall. Enter SIR WILLIAM MALTRAVERS *and* FERRERS.

SIR WILLIAM: You are a very sensible young man, Mr. Lumley Ferrers—a very extraordinary young man, as I may say—and I only wish it had been my luck to have had such a son and heir instead of my headstrong, brain-sick, romantic Ernest.

FERRERS: Oh, sir, you do me too much honor. But you must remember that my friend Ernest is yet very young, and— (*Hesitates.*) Perhaps he has not fallen into the very best hands.

SIR WILLIAM: Oh, sir, there you touch the very life, the very marrow, as I may say, of my apprehensions. What else can account for his long absence from home and his perverse indifference to the beautiful heiress, Lady Florence, whom I have chosen for his bride! Here he is away mystifying at Gottingen for five years. He comes home one night when no one expects him, in a thunderclap, looking like a ghost, and with a long rigmarole story about being waylaid and murdered by the way.

FERRERS: (*Smiling*). Not quite murdered, sir. (*Aside.*) Though I wish to heaven he had been.

SIR WILLIAM: Well, I introduce you to him; he has made your acquaintance before. He praises your courage, vows he owes his life to your opportune arrival, and, when curiosity is at the highest, declares he has bound you in honor to be silent. Is not this aggravating and, as I may say, devilish conduct?

FERRERS: Why, it is rather annoying, I must confess, but that promise must plead my only excuse for not satisfying your very reasonable curiosity.

SIR WILLIAM: Ah, Lumley, my dear fellow, be a good boy, and give me a hint. Not tell, you know—oh, no—but just drop a hint of the affair.

FERRERS: Oh, sir—my honor!

SIR WILLIAM: But I will put it in an honorable point of view. You told me that you owe money. I have a few loose hundreds much at your service. You can pay your debts, and that is honorable conduct.

FERRERS: I confess, sir, your arguments are most conclusive. Well, suppose—only suppose, you know—

SIR WILLIAM: Aye, yes, suppose—or, as I may say, imagine.

FERRERS: That Ernest had become entangled—only entangled—

SIR WILLIAM: To be sure—only entangled—or, as I may say, taken in with—

FERRERS: Yes; taken in with—with—a woman.

SIR WILLIAM: The devil! Oh, the vicious—or, as I may say, the shameless young dog! Keep a girl! Abominable!

FERRERS: (*Aside*). Here's a precious old rogue! By all accounts, half a dozen didn't serve him. (*Aloud.*) Oh, fie, my dear sir, for shame! I didn't insinuate such a thing at all. Ernest is too virtuous. No, if he is indeed connected with this female, depend upon it she is his wife.

SIR WILLIAM: His wife! What? By all the blood of the Maltravers! You stagger—as I may say—astound me! His wife! What? He dare to marry a nobody knows who? And he the heir to all the Maltravers! I'd rather he kept a seraglio! I'll turn him out of doors! Let him marry Lady Florence, or look to it.

FERRERS: Pray, sir, remember he is your son.

SIR WILLIAM: Son me no son, sir. Go to him, Ferrers. Talk to him. Tell him what I say. For I swear to you, if he has done this, I'll never see him more—I will not, by all the blood of the Maltravers! And I'll marry Lady Florence myself. (*Exits.*)

FERRERS: So the first stone of the building is well laid. Ernest has married Alice Darvil, and, if I mistake not, begins to be rather sorry for his romantic Quixotism. This fury of his father's will finish his disgust for his cottage bride, and the pretty Alice will be very much at Lumley Ferrers' service. Lady Florence, too, if I do not flatter myself, casts softer glances at the obsequious Lumley than on the indifferent Ernest, and her large fortune is quite desirable. Ha! Here she comes.

Enter LADY FLORENCE, *singing.*

LADY FLORENCE:

> And it's oh, dear, what will become of me,
> Oh, dear, what shall I do?
> There's nobody coming to marry me—
> Nobody coming to woo.

What, Lumley Ferrers, the gallant and gay, imitating the cold philosophy of Ernest Maltravers and giving himself up to pensive, holy contemplations in the lonesome cells? Pray, what may be the subject of so unusual a reverie?

FERRERS: (*Bows*). As the subject now presents itself, any attempt to describe the picture would be useless.

LADY FLORENCE: (*Looks cautiously around*). The original! Might a body see it?

FERRERS: By glancing in yonder mirror, you will.

LADY FLORENCE: Excellent! What, then, you mused on me! Well, now I know the text, may I not hear the commentations?

FERRERS: Certainly. The first division was beauty, the second grace, the third virtue, and the whole wound up with love.

LADY FLORENCE: Then the subject was vastly ill-argued. The preface should have been fortune, your first chapter treated of filial obedience, your second of neglect, and indeed you might have summed up with pity. (*Turns aside, agitated.*)

FERRERS: (*Kneels and takes her hand*). Pity! Pity you—the loveliest, the most beloved of all living creatures! Can pity be connected with you? Yes, it can! I pity myself that I have ever seen—have ever loved you!

LADY FLORENCE: Oh, pray rise, Mr. Ferrers. You know I must not listen to this language. I came here, indeed, by my father's will to be courted, but not by you, unless Mr. Ernest Maltravers has delegated the disagreeable office to you as his proxy. My friendship, however, is yours, and were I blessed with a free choice, it might—

FERRERS: Ripen into love. Thanks! Thanks!

LADY FLORENCE: I can't tell, but I will sing you a song about it. (*She acts as she sings.*)

Song:
"Temple to Friendship"—Moore's Melodies.

A temple to friendship, said Laura, enchanted,
I'll build in the garden. The thought is divine.
Her temple was built, and she now only wanted
An image of friendship to place on the shrine.

She flew to a sculptor, who set down before her
A friendship, the fairest his art could invent;
But so cold and so dull that the youthful adorer
Saw plainly this was not the idol she meant.

"Oh, never," she cried, "could I think of enshrining
An image whose looks are so joyless and dim.
But you, little god, upon roses reclining:
We'll make, if you please, sir, a friendship of him."

So the bargain was struck. With the little god laden,
She joyfully flew to a shrine in the grove.
"Farewell," said the sculptor. "You're not the first maiden
Who came but for friendship and took away love."

Enter ERNEST, *reading.*

LADY FLORENCE: (*Crosses to* ERNEST). A fair good morning to you, most serious, solemn, and sagacious cousin. May we in all humility inquire of your wisdom what it is you study so profoundly?

ERNEST: (*Bows stiffly*). It is a German work, madam: Zimmerman on the pleasures of solitude.

LADY FLORENCE: Indeed! Doubtless you are his admiring disciple. Mr, Ferrers, I know not how you may receive the hint, but my woman's wit interprets it into an intimation that Mr. Ernest Maltravers wishes to be alone. Zimmerman revered—good morning. (*Curtsies and exits.*)

ERNEST: Ferrers, give me your advice. My situation is replete with difficulties. I am acting like a brute to a lovely, amiable woman, and she pesters me with entreaties to acknowledge her as my wife.

FERRERS: Doubtless—doubtless she is in haste to claim her new honors, Ernest. I am sorry to give you cold comfort. Some officious, prying busybody has given your father a hint of this. He's enraged beyond bounds. He questioned me and bade me tell you if that were true, you were no more son of his.

ERNEST: Gracious heavens! He is likely to keep his word. My grandfather, as I am told, disinherited my uncle Richard for marrying against his will and choice. Her birth and connections are not only poor, but shameful. What shall I do?

FERRERS: There is only one way to escape ruin. Your father may forgive your not marrying Lady Florence, but never your union with Alice Darvil. That he has heard of her it is plain. Alice must be content to call herself your mistress.

ERNEST: By heaven, Lumley, you are mad! Never would I consent to such a scheme. You do not know Alice if you believe she would. I tell you, there is more pride of virtue in that low-born girl than in twenty women of rank and fortune.

FERRERS: Humph! Ernest, do you believe me to be your friend, and can bear to hear the truth?

ERNEST: Can you doubt it? You are my only adviser.

FERRERS: Then hear me with calmness and with patience. The character of Alice Darvil was not unsuspected when you married her. (ERNEST *starts angrily.*) Nay, if you flame out, I have done. Ernest, worlds could not have forced me to reveal this, did you not by the obstinacy of this very girl stand upon the brink of ruin. Ernest Maltravers, you have often asked me how I came so opportunely that night upon the common. Now I answer you: I was going to Alice Darvil.

ERNEST: (*Seizing him wildly*). Wretch! And yet you stood by and saw me married to a wanton!

FERRERS: By heavens, you would not hear me! I did but notice to you that her father called her vile, and you were ready to strike me dead! You would not eat, drink, sleep, or scarcely breathe, till you were married to her.

ERNEST: Fool! Dolt! Idiot that I was! The dupe of a lascivious wanton! But I will break the marriage—

FERRERS: Be calm, and you may. The clergyman is dead, and I, your friend, am the only witness. Yet be advised: I insist on her passing to your father as your mistress; so shall you see if love to you make any motive to her deception. Farewell, and pray be patient.

ERNEST: Yes, as a criminal on the rack! To seem so purely, so proudly virtuous! Damned, designing, deceitful woman! (*Exits.*)

Scene Two

A garden with trelissed arbor, in which a small table is set with wine and fruit. In the back a neat little cottage is seen through trees. Pen, ink, and paper on table. Garden chair center. Two garden chairs left. Door key on chair. Time: sunset. ALICE discovered reading.

ALICE: (*Reads aloud*). "I did not take my leave of him, but had most pretty things to say. Ere I could tell him how I would think of him at certain hours, or to have made him swear at morn and noon to encounter me with visions, or ere I could give him that parting kiss which I had set between two charming words, lo! he was gone."[9] Oh, beautiful, charming, natural Shakespeare! How every page of yours speaks to our heart of hearts. There the fond wife pours out her soul's devotion; here sorrow blinds our sight with weeping for its woe; and here anger, hatred, fear, all live and breathe and have their being! Valued page, ever valued friend, who taught me first to love thee! (*Lays down the book and looks out.*) Beloved Ernest! How tedious is the time when thou art away! Sink quickly, sun, and bring the welcome night which brings my Ernest here! (*Enter* ERNEST, *muffled in large rough coat.* ALICE *springs to his embrace.*) My life! My love!

ERNEST: I am tired and heated. This cursed coat I'm forced to wear for a disguise drags heavily enough about my neck, without the burden of your arms besides.

ALICE: (*Takes the coat*). Dearest! Are you not well? Come, give it to

---

[9]From Shakespeare's *Cymbeline*, Act I, scene 3.

me. There, now. Sit down, dear Ernest, while I mix your favorite wine with water I brought myself fresh from our little fountain. (*She busily arranges table. He sits gloomily and opens book.*) Oh, you see I am not idle in your absence. I have been studying your favorite Shakespeare.

ERNEST: Indeed! There are many true sayings there. Alice, what think you of this? (*Opens book.*) "Oh, curse of marriage, that we can call these delicate creatures ours, and not their appetites."[10]

ALICE: Thank heaven, my husband will never call his marriage a curse.

ERNEST: Be not too sure of that.

ALICE: Ernest, something has displeased you. Do you not wish me, love, to stay? 'Twas you first taught me to understand and love you. To you I owe all I have and all I know.

ERNEST: And you are grateful, doubtless?

ALICE: Oh, if to love with woman's truest, fondest, best devotion—if to think of you by day and dream of you by night—if to behold in you my benefactor, friend, instructor, lover—if to scarce hold my life mine own unless 'tis dear to you: if this is gratitude, then is poor Alice grateful. (*Brings down chair.*)

ERNEST: (*Aside*). Can this be art that wears the loveliest face of truth? Could Ferrers be mistaken? No. Was he not himself that night to meet her? (*Aloud.*) Words, Alice, are air. Actions are the heart's index. My evil face forces me to test your gratitude and love.

ALICE: (*Springing up*). Oh, joy! Joy! Joy, past all expression. Can the poor, the lowly Alice do aught to serve her Ernest?

ERNEST: Sit and listen to me. (*Both sit.*) You cannot have forgotten, Alice, when we married, I told you that I braved my father's anger, the loss of my inheritance, and—far more than wealth—my rank and standing amongst my fellow men.

ALICE: Forgotten? Ernest?

ERNEST: This danger has come to pass. My father has discovered your retreat, and knows you live here under my protection.

ALICE: Will that move his anger?

ERNEST: Will it? Are you mad, girl? Will it incense the proudest man in England—the head of a family so high in their own standing that they have refused a peerage? Will it incense such a man to know that the heir of his house and blood is married to Alice Darvil, a common felon's daughter, to be connected with whom, even in the sixtieth degree, would tarnish all the honors of a king?

ALICE: (*Sinks gradually to his feet*). Alas! My father's crimes are not

---

[10]From *Othello*, Act III, scene 3.

mine!

ERNEST: From the inevitable ruin that awaits me, you alone can save me. My father will see, will question you. Then my hopes, my honor, my all is in your hands.

ALICE: Speak! Speak! How can I avert his wrath?

ERNEST: By denying yourself to be my wife. A father will easier pardon a son's immorality than disgrace. Say what you will, so you say not the truth! This may redeem me!

ALICE: (*Rising*). And brand me with the name of wanton! No, sir. If your honor sleeps, mine remains awake. I will not so wrong myself and you as to stamp infamy upon your wife. If, while rich in honesty and fame, I am unworthy to share your name, how shall I dare assume it when blighted with the withering mildew of my shame? No, Ernest, my life is yours, if you demand it. My honor is my own.

ERNEST: (*Takes chairs up*). You would do well, madam, to drop the veil of art you have worn so long, now that your end is gained. But learn: your dupe—your crazy fool—your blinded lover is no more. I know you, Alice Darvil, for what you are. I rue the hour I ever saw your face. I hate your falsehood and cast you from my breast for ever. (*Going.*)

ALICE: (*Screams and catches his arm*). Stay! I conjure you to stay! Ernest, by all our hours of love—by all the passionate vows you've spoken—by all my easy faith and fond devotion, stay! I conjure you, stay! (*He struggles to go.*) Nay, then, by all the solemn rites with which God's minister has bound us, I do command you, stay!

ERNEST: (*Stops, surprised*). Speak, then. I listen.

ALICE: Ernest Maltravers, I have heard your proposal. Do you now hearken to mine. Take me by the hand and lead me to your father. Say, in a moment of infatuation, allured by fancied beauty and wrought on by my own generous nature, I made this poor but virtuous girl my wife! I now repent my folly and cast her from me. Say but this, Ernest. Give me back the spotless truth I brought you, and then forsake me, if you will. Your stern father will forgive, and Alice—poor, broken-hearted Alice—will retire to die!

ERNEST: Ha! Ha! Excellent. Give me your hand! I will lead you to my father's. I will say, look on the fairest face that e'er foul vice disgraced, and wonder not that I became its dupe! Deceiver! Plague spot! Vile, licentious woman! Release me. I hate you! Your reign is ended! Thus do I cast you off to the infamy you merit. (*Releases her, dashes her off, and exits. ALICE falls, fainting.*)

Enter FERRERS, raises her.

FERRIS: Ha! So low already! Now, by heavens, as I gaze upon this face, so lovely in its death-like beauty, my heart smites my treachery. Alice! Alice! Dear Alice! Look up and live.

ALICE: (*Recovering*). Gone! Is he gone? Is Ernest gone? (*Stage gradually to half dark.*)

FERRIS: Ernest is gone! But here behold a tenderer, truer, fonder one than Ernest, who never will cause your heart the pangs his treachery has given.

ALICE: (*Rising haughtily*). Is my disgrace so public, then, that every fool must offer me the insult of his pity?

FERRIS: So haughty, Alice! Have you not yet learned to confess your master? Then know, 'tis I have worked for you this woe; I, that set your credulous spouse against you; I, that have stirred his stern, old father's anger. Provoke me, Alice, and I will ruin you with father and with son. Consent, and I will raise you far above them both.

ALICE: (*Aside*). What shall I say or do? Direct me, *Thou*, that art the orphan's friend.

FERRIS: (*Aside*). She hesitates. (*Aloud.*) Hear me, fairest Alice. I, who loved you first, alone am constant to you. Give yourself to me—to rank—to riches.

ALICE: Alas, sir, I am young and weak. I have been ill-treated and may scarcely trust the vows of men. Will you insure me this in writing?

FERRIS: (*Going to table*). Willingly. (*Aside.*) She's mine. All—all alike: wavering, inconstant woman. (*Aloud.*) Willingly. (*Writes at table.*) And now, loveliest, when may I reap the boon my constancy deserves?

ALICE: Be here tomorrow at this hour. Be sure you come unsuspected and unseen, and *you shall have what you so well deserve.*

FERRIS: Enough. Till that blest hour, dearest, farewell. (*Exits.*)

ALICE: (*Seizes the paper*). Yes! Gained. 'Tis gained! In his own snare the wicked one is taken! Ernest! Ernest! Why did I censure you? Treachery alone had galled your noble nature! This will convince you, and here you will come tomorrow to hear, unseen, the villain's falsehood from himself. But how shall I meet my Ernest? To seek admittance to the castle were to be refused. Ha! His coat here; perhaps his coat may contain the key? That key by which, on many a happy night, he's left his castle door to come to Alice's arms—that happy key he used to call his passport to his heaven. (*Takes up coat and gets key.*) Thanks to kind heaven, 'tis here! 'Tis almost dark by this. I'll enter, unperceived, and hide myself until I see my husband. Then, then—oh, then—once again will happiness await me! Eternal Power, that art the friend to innocence, I thank thee. (*Music. Sinks on her knees.*)

Scene Three

Part of a forest adjoining Maltravers Hall. A large black cross is marked on an oak. Moonrise. Stage dark. Music (cautious). Enter DARVIL, *wrapped in disguise, and carrying large mask.*

DARVIL: At last, after long years of toil and danger, do I revisit the spot where first I drew my breath. Ye ancient towers, ye lordly oaks coeval with my race, over whom the house of proud Maltravers long has reigned: ye hasten to your fate. And the proudest and most detested of thy name, William Maltravers: tremble! He on whom you laid the curse—the curse which sleepeth not—he to whom you gave poverty, hate; he whose forsworn wife, whose recreant daughter now rise up in judgment against you; he—he is near, and with no friendly purpose. Tonight my debt of revenge will be paid. (*Examines around, and reads paper.*) This is the very spot, the center of the wood, within a bird's flight from the hall, beneath a large oak, marked with a cross of black. This is the spot. Now, to call my comrades. (*Exits. Music, soft.*)

Enter ALICE *cautiously, cloaked.*

ALICE: How fearfully I tremble! The knotted thickness of the wood excludes the light and baffles my skill to trace the path. Surely the hall cannot be far distant, and yet I dare not take the open wood, lest that dark villain spy me. Why should I fear? Do I not go on nature's holiest errand? Woman's faith reclaiming recreant love! Ha! I see lights! Who at this time frequent the woods? Poachers or thieves, I fear, who may molest my path. I will retire and watch them. (*Music.* ALICE *retires.*)

Enter DARVIL, WALTERS, *and* ARMSTRONG, *cloaked and masked. (One bears a torch, which is planted upright on the stage. As they confer,* ALICE *is seen at intervals listening.)*

DARVIL: Are all here? Are all here?
OMNES: All, all. We are.
DARVIL: Ye all know what our purpose is tonight. Which, among us, has not suffered imprisonment, stripes, poverty, and wrong from the proud gentleman, the active magistrate, William Maltravers?
ALICE: (*Aside*). Ha!
OMNES: All—all hate him.
DARVIL: Ye know, besides, that in Maltravers Hall, there is accumulated plate and gold enough to make us rich for life. By sure report,

I learn his son, the boy Ernest, is every night from home, and the servants we can easily overpower.

WALTERS: But this Ernest—he is the poor man's friend. What if he cross our path?

DARVIL: Strike him dead. (ALICE *evinces great emotion.*) No man, nor boy, nor devil, stays my hand tonight. One thing alone I bargain for between ye. I leave the spoil, but no hand but mine must combat with the Maltravers.

WALTERS: How shall we force our way?

DARVIL: (*Produces large scroll*). See, here, this is a plan of the house. I have had cause to know it well. At this door we must force entrance. This staircase leads to the room I seek, this gallery to the treasures you would have. (*As they bend over the paper,* ALICE *approaches from behind, and also examines attentively.*)

WALTERS: Which is the room of Ernest?

DARVIL: This, bloodhound. Be it your task to bathe the floor in blood. None of the race must live!

(*Music, chord, hurry.* ALICE *utters a faint scream. They all start and see her. She strikes down the torch. Stage in darkness.* DARVIL *flies.* ALICE *drops her cloak, dodges, and exits. The rest exit tumultuously.*)

Scene Four

Chamber of SIR WILLIAM MALTRAVERS. *Furniture, antique and rich. A toilet[11] on which lies a pair of pistols. Small table with gold goblets and pitchers, lights, books, etc. Two practicable doors. Stage dark.* SIR WILLIAM *discovered at table.*

SIR WILLIAM: What strange creatures we are of time and circumstances. Here am I depressed, or, as I may say, downcast with what I know not, just at the time I have most reason to be mirthful. My wayward son, Ernest, has been tonight attentive, or, as I may say, particular in his *devoirs* to Lady Florence; and my good friend, Ferrers, assures me that he will prove in all things comfortable. Yet neither the lively dance nor joyous song could amuse me for an instant, and I retired alone to wonder at my melancholy. Ah, me! 'Tis this night seventeen years ago that poor Richard's wife, in this very room, gave birth to poor little Alice, the child of misery and guilt. (*Door opens slowly, and* DARVIL *appears.*) Wronged, unhappy brother, perhaps he wanders far, far from his paternal home!

---

[11]Dressing table.

Would I could again behold him!

DARVIL: (*Confronts him*). Your wish is granted: behold him here!

SIR WILLIAM: Eternal heaven! Can I believe my senses? Do I, indeed, look upon my brother Richard?

DARVIL: William Maltravers, you do! You see again that brother whom your acts first made a common outcast to poverty and scorn.

SIR WILLIAM: By heaven, you wrong me! I had no share in your undoing.

DARVIL: 'Tis false! Yes, you see again that brother whose easy faith believed your false regard—who trusted to you all that the earth contained for him, holy or dear—whose confidence you broke—whose wife dishonored and whose hate provoked. Aye, William Maltravers, he is here, and with no friendly purpose.

SIR WILLIAM: Richard, I swear, your wife for me was as pure as an angel!

DARVIL: Liar! You made her as foul as devils! Take heed! Add not perjury to the black catalogue of all your other crimes, for you must quickly answer them.

SIR WILLIAM: Powers of mercy! What do your words portend? What fearful object do you seek?

DARVIL: Your life, seducer—liar—slanderer! Die by the roused vengeance of a brother's arm. (*Seizes* SIR WILLIAM, *drags him up to chair upstage of table, lifts a knife, which* SIR WILLIAM *catches, and struggling, falls and throws open his arms.*)

SIR WILLIAM: Strike, then! But by all your hopes of eternal life, hear me ere you strike. (DARVIL, *agitated, releases his hold.*) In the last hours of life, your injured wife addressed a letter to you. You will find it yonder, locked in my private casket. Disbelieve, if you dare, the awful adjurations of the dead. Read that, and then strike home. The breast is bare.

DARVIL: Wretch, would you escape me?

SIR WILLIAM: My powers are gone. (*Sinks into a chair.*)

DARVIL: (*Goes to door*). What, ho! Walters, this way. Keep guard here. If he makes sound or stir, strike him dead. The casket! The casket! (*Music, cautious. Exit* DARVIL.)

Enter WALTERS. (*He comes down, sees* SIR WILLIAM, *and exits through door.*)

Enter ALICE, *from door opposite, slowly, very pale, her hair loose, and her white dress spotted with blood.*

ALICE: All still—all quiet. Heaven be praised, I am not too late. The wound I have received is slight, yet fear and faintness quite overcame me, and as I sank exhausted in the wood, oh, how I trembled, lest I might be too late. I passed the hall, and heard the merry dance, but dared not be seen this wild and ghastly figure. The private door has led me here, unnoticed. Now to communicate my fearful tidings. This, then, is Ernest's father. Sleeps he? I must awaken him. How like to Ernest—the same majestic brow and smiling lips—and though the frosting snow has mixed with the bright brown of Ernest's hair, how like it shades his temples! Sir William, awake. Hear me! Ha! Someone comes. What will they think of me!

Enter WALTERS, *masked, carrying a small casket.* (ALICE *retires.*)

WALTERS: (*Softly*). Dick! Dick, I say! Now, on my conscience, ain't he a pretty fellow to lead us here, in peril of our necks, and then to fly off on some precious whim of his own! I've got something, however. It's wonderful heavy. I wonder if it's full of gold. Ah, here's cups and goblets too. (*Approaches table. He rattles goblets, which wakes* SIR WILLIAM, *who then sees the casket.*)

SIR WILLIAM: Wretch! Ruffian! Put down that casket! You shall have my life sooner!

WALTERS: That we'll soon see. (*Music. Draws a knife.* ALICE *seizes one pistol from the toilet and rushes between them.*)

ALICE: Villain! Forbear.

WALTERS: What, is the house alarmed? Stand back, girl. Your defenseless arm is useless.

ALICE: 'Tis false! I'm armed! Man! Man! I would not shed a human creature's blood, but touch that revered head with a hand of ill, and the same moment you rush into eternity. (*Music.* WALTERS *strives to unclasp the hand of* SIR WILLIAM *from the casket, then stabs him. When he falls,* ALICE *fires.* WALTERS *falls back, wounded.*)

WALTERS: Curses on you! That shot has done for me! One blow for vengeance! (*He staggers, holding up the knife, to* ALICE, *who has seized the bell and rings violently. He falls short of her, then staggers off.*)

Enter DARVIL, *masked.*

DARVIL: Hoary villain! Thou hast deceived me. (*Distant murmur.*) Ha, the cry is up! Death and hell! What do I see, the victim slain? And Alice Darvil *here*—in this house! Then is the falsehood clear! Eternal curses seize you, fiend! Come thou with me. (*Bell rings. Shouts. Music. Hurry.* DARVIL *seizes* ALICE, *and his mask falls off. She exclaims,* "My father!" *and struggles violently. Shouts.* FERRERS *stumbles on.* SERVANTS *drag in the*

other ROBBERS. OTHER GUESTS *and* PEOPLE *crowd in. Stage light.*)
    FERRERS: Good heavens! What have we here? (LADY FLORENCE
kneels by the body of SIR WILLIAM. SERVANTS *secure DARVIL, who
offers no resistance.* ALICE *stands motionless, still holding the pistol.*) Sir
William slain, and robbers in the hall! How could they enter here?

Enter SERVANT, *speaking.*

    SERVANT: The private wicket door is open, sir, and the pass-key of
Mr. Ernest is in it.

Enter ERNEST, *speaking.*

    ERNEST: Here! What do I see? Merciful heaven! My father? Oh, my
father! (*Kneels by the body.*)

Enter two SERVANTS, *with* ALICE's *cloak.*

    SERVANT: The police have traced the robbers to their hiding place,
and on the spot found this cloak.
    ERNEST: (*Starting up*). The cloak of Alice! (*Sees* ALICE.) Merciful
heaven! What may this horror mean?
    DARVIL: Ha! Ha! Ha! Can you not read the riddle? Why, then, for
old acquaintance sake, I'll solve it for you. That girl led us from the forest
by with her pass-key. We entered at the wicket gate. By her hand your
father bleeds. See you not the pistol in her hand, the blood upon her dress?
    FERRERS: It is the robber, Darvil, and his daughter. (ALICE *starts
from her trance with a scream, and drops the pistol.*)
    ALICE: No! No! No! What frightful sounds are these? My brain is
whirling. My eyes are dim with blood. Ernest! Ernest, my husband, speak
to me!
    DARVIL: Your husband! Nay, that is glorious! Ernest Maltravers your
husband? The measure of your crimes is full. Look upon me, all. (*Throws
off his hat and cloak.*) What! See you no lineaments of your proud race?
(*To* ERNEST.) Has seventeen years so altered me that none call me by my
name? Why, then, I'll name myself. Richard Maltravers stands before you!
The convicted robber—the branded murderer, Richard Maltravers! Yes,
Ernest, your father was my brother, and my direst foe. Fearfully has the
retribution for his treachery fallen. (*Speaks low and hoarse.*) He wronged
my faith, seduced my wife, and—Ernest Maltravers, hear you me? *Alice is
your sister.* (*Chord. Dreadful horror shown.*) Ha! Ha! Ha! Alice
Maltravers, is my curse fulfilled? Wretch! You have slain your father and

married with your brother! (ALICE *falls senseless.* ERNEST *catches pistol from toilet and puts it to his breast.* FERRERS *holds his arm. Music.*)

ACT III

Scene One

Beautiful view of the Lake of Como. On one side, an Italian villa with practicable balcony. Time: morning to early sunset. Music. Soft serenade heard gradually approaching, with the voices of the singers. As it increases, a gondola floats on, in which are are party of GONDOLIERS *and Italian* PEASANTS, *some with guitars.*

Serenade

Softly, oh softly, rest on your oar,
And wet not a billow that sighs to the shore;
For sacred the spot where the starry waves meet,
And the breath of the orange and citron is sweet.
       Softly, oh softly.
(*They row a little between the verses, keeping time with their oars.*)

Then awake thee, sweet lady, and list to our song.
Like love are thy steps on the souls of the strong,
As the moon to the earth—as the soul to the clay—
As love to the heart is thy smile to our lay.
(*They spring on shore. The window of the villa opens, and* LADY FLORENCE *comes out on the balcony.*)

ZERRIGUEO: Blessings on that sweet face! Although it be a foreign one, 'tis lovely! I'm sure the whole country round have reasons to bless the generous English family. See, she comes, led by her noble father!

Enter LORD SAXINGHAM, *leading on* LADY FLORENCE. (*All greet her.*)

LADY FLORENCE: Thanks. Thanks to all! Pray, good friends, pass within and partake of the refreshments your early gallantry so richly merits.
LORD SAXINGHAM: You are all very welcome.
LADY FLORENCE: (*Looking after*). How happy they all seem! So happy! Heigho!
LORD SAXINGHAM: What means that sigh, my daughter? Need the wealthy and accomplished Lady Florence Saxingham sigh, to speak of

happiness?

LADY FLORENCE: Wealth, my dear father, is a poor caterer for the heart. And as to accomplishments, the arts of music, drawing, and dancing would have been just as serviceable to Robinson Crusoe on his desert island as to me here.

LORD SAXINGHAM: It is true, we have retired, but at whose wish has it been done? Your intended husband shuns the very name of stranger.

LADY FLORENCE: My intended husband! Oh, my dear father, can you call a melancholy recluse—one whose whole heart and feelings are buried in dreadful memories—my husband! How can we tell that his wretched, ill-fated wife is dead for a certainty?

LORD SAXINGHAM: No more of that. You well know that it was surely ascertained that the unfortunate Alice Maltravers died in the madhouse to which she was conveyed. Florence Saxingham, hear me! To you I have ever been a fond, foolish, indulgent father, but from your very childhood my heart has been set upon this union. Had Sir Ernest, after he recovered from the dreadful illness which followed that fearful night—had he declined this alliance—I must have been content to give it up; but amidst all his misery, he still clings to you only. Take notice, therefore, if you be my daughter, you will be his wife. If not, you are a stranger to my blood, my heart and house. He is here. Leave us. (*Enter* ERNEST.) You are welcome, Sir Ernest. Your name was on our lips.

ERNEST: Can lips so sweet syllable a sound so mournful?

LADY FLORENCE: (*Crosses*). Ah, sir! Lips are like harp-strings: they must be obedient to the player's touch; but if too often touched, and forced to utter ungracious discords, they will break. (ERNEST *leads her to the steps. She exits.*)

LORD SAXINGHAM: Ernest Maltravers, matters too long have remained in this uncertain state between my daughter and yourself. Her feelings are affected by it, and it becomes my duty as her father to demand when your union is to be solemnized.

ERNEST: (*Starts*). Our union—mine!

LORD SAXINGHAM: Do you make the sound so strange, sir? Yes, your union. For years has my girl been affianced to you. 'Tis time she became your wife.

ERNEST: Wife! Ill-omened name! Never may another bear it.

LORD SAXINGHAM: How, sir—never?

ERNEST: Your pardon, Lord Saxingham, and by your tender feelings as a father, I conjure you to answer me: is this the wish of Lady Florence?

LORD SAXINGHAM: Undoubtedly. Few of even common feelings can quietly submit to be slighted, much less the Lady Florence.

ERNEST: I thank you, my lord, and will meet your wishes. That I have delayed to speak upon the subject has been for your daughter's sake, not mine. The blossoming clematis twined round the blasted oak may for a time conceal its rottenness, but inevitably must share in its decay. I would have wished a happier fate for one so young and fair, but since the victim courts the sacrifice, the priest may not withhold the knife. (*Exits.*)

LORD SAXINGHAM: I sincerely believe they are both mad together; but were they fit for Bedlam, married they must and shall be. (*Exits.*)

Scene Two

Part of the garden. Trees. Enter LADY FLORENCE.

LADY FLORENCE: Oh, woman, woman! Man's choicest blessing and his slave! The sport of feeling and the puppet of fortune—how hard a lot is thine! Like the modest violet, panting for the shade, thou livest to pour thy odors on the lowly valley; yet when transplanted to the hotbeds of pride, the hand that tore thee from thy native home rejects and scorns thee! Well, I never felt more in a humor to moralize in all my life. I am condemned without judge or jury. Let me see: yon beautiful sycamore will do for the Council of Ten. So, "Oh, yes! Come into court, Florence Saxingham, Lady of Touwood Lee, and answer to the charge of love!" Mercy, what a crime! "Guilty or not guilty of love for Ernest Maltravers?" Oh, not guilty, my lords and gentlemen—not guilty! "Answer to a second charge: guilty or not guilty of love for Lumley Ferrers?" Oh, guilty! Very guilty, my lords, but recommended to mercy. (*Enter* ERNEST, *behind.*) For pray consider, what can a poor woman do but fall in love with goodness, courage, and kindness? So in love I am, and pray, my lord, forgive Florence Saxingham; she'll never do so any more. (*She curtsies to the trees and finishes pantomime, turns and sees* ERNEST.) Ha! Ernest here!

ERNEST: So sweet and soft a fault may well move stocks and trees to commit the same with the offender.

LADY FLORENCE: Bless me! How you frightened me!

ERNEST: Nay, then, I will in my own person be the executioner of the judge's sentence, and stamp with the seal of her offense the lips of my sweetest, fairest Alice. (*He has passed his arm around her, but as he pronounces the last word, both start. He walks aside, much agitated.*) Lady Florence, I have been rightly punished for assuming a tone foreign alike to my heart and circumstances. Forgive me, lady. Thy worth and beauty deserve the fondest love, but the tree blasted by lightning lives not again. If a green leaf spring from its withering stem, it but gilds the inward canker. I never can love woman more! If you can accept from me the reverence of a friend—the affection of a brother—they are yours; but, lady, I can love no more!

LADY FLORENCE: Thank you, sir, for this sincere confession, and I will repay it by one as honest. My heart is given to another.

ERNEST: And that other is—

LADY FLORENCE: The poor but noble Lumley Ferrers.

ERNEST: I do not know a worthier. Fear not, dear Florence. Trust the management of this to me, and I will not wrong your confidence. Ferrers must be summoned here.

LADY FLORENCE: That is done already. 'Tis some time since I wrote, and expect him hourly.

ERNEST: You have done well. But as the passes all around are infested by mountain robbers, I will set out to meet him. Lost to happiness myself, I still retain the pleasure of beholding it in others. Trust all to me. (*They exit.*)

Scene Three

Mountainous defile.[12]   A rude path descending to the stage.   Groups of BRIGANDS *of the Abbruzzi discovered, keeping watch.   At center, beneath a large tree,* OCTAVIA DE MONTAIGNE *lies in a trance, her father, the* COLONEL *standing over her in deep emotion.   Other* BRIGANDS *lying about.   Entrance to a cave.   Stage half dark.   Time: before sunset.   All rise from their positions as* DARVIL *comes down the pass and takes center stage.*

COLONEL: (*Goes up to him*).   You, then, are the leader of these robbers—chief of this lawless horde?

DARVIL: I am the captain of men whom there is little need to describe, since their actions speak more for them than their words.

COLONEL: To you, then, I speak. Will you not release my child and allow me to remain in your hands as a hostage for the payment of our mutual ransom?

DARVIL: Impossible! Our laws, indeed, are of our own framing, but more binding than those of kings. If at the return of our messenger, your friends send not the stipulated ransom, your life is not worth half an hour's purchase!

COLONEL: My life I think not of. I am a soldier, and have faced death so oft that his form has lost its terror; but my child—my young, my innocent daughter, who now lies insensible before her father's eyes—what will become of her?

---

[12]Narrow mountain pass.

DARVIL: She falls by ballot to the band.

COLONEL: Monster! Have you no children?

DARVIL: None! And more, I hate the name of father and delight to break the bonds of parentage. But we war not with the life of women. There are lusty fellows here who will prefer her to the enviable rank of a bold brigand's bride.

COLONEL: Detested wretch! Rather than that, let her encounter death, and from a father's hand! (*Rushes toward her with dagger uplifted, taken from his breast, as* ALICE *appears on the pass above, wild and fantastically dressed.*)

ALICE: Hold, madman! The bride of the mountain thunder, who sports with the lightning's flash and holds communion with the mighty dead speaks! Pray for me. I have saved your band from blood.

(*At the moment* ALICE *appears,* DARVIL *turns downstage, and* ARMSTRONG *comes down to* COLONEL MONTAIGNE.)

ARMSTRONG: Stand not appalled! Her speech is wild, but her purpose harmless. 'Tis Alice, the mountain wanderer.

DARVIL: Armstrong, how comes it that yon crazy wench roams thus at large? Why is she not confined?

ARMSTRONG: You might as well bind the will-o'-the-wisp, or confine the mountain thunder. Bolts and bars cannot hold her, and if chained, she would soon droop and die.

DARVIL: (*Gloomily*). The better for us both!

Enter ALICE *from below.*

ALICE: No, Richard Darvil, not for you; for when the clay is cold, the spirit wanders to demand a fearful retribution. I have seen their ghastly shapes in the still moonlight—an old man weltering in blood, who calls for vengeance on Richard Darvil!

DARVIL: (*Raising his gun*). Wretch! Call me that name again, and I will dash your mad brains to my feet!

ALICE: (*Calmly*). No, Richard Darvil, you will not and you *dare* not! *Hate* your victim you may, but in your own despite you *fear* her too. You won't kill me, Richard Darvil! (*He turns angrily upstage, and* COLONEL MONTAIGNE *comes down.*)

COLONEL: Poor maiden. Even desolate and woebegone as thou art now, may my poor child become!

ALICE: (*Violently*). Your child! Your daughter! And did you bring her here to this piteous pass? Does she love you? Would she have died for you? And did you brand her with a nameless horror? Chain down her limbs in darkness and in straw until she became a howling maniac? Drag her from the quiet grave to misery, madness, and despair? Ha, ha, ha! (*Rushes up and drags* DARVIL *down.*) Rejoice! Rejoice! Excellent, worthy Richard Darvil! You have met your compeer in guilt—ha, ha! What rejoicing there must be in hell over such a peerless pair!

DARVIL: Fiend! Wretch! Madwoman! Unloose thy hold, or by death and hell, I swear—

ALICE: (*Solemnly*). Hush—hush! He hears you. (*He turns away.*) Come, come. I'll take this maiden to my care.

ARMSTRONG: 'Tis well until our messenger returns. Let her remain with Alice. You, sir, must go with me.

COLONEL: (*Raises up* OCTAVIA). Never! What, trust my child to this poor, mad creature?

ALICE: Silence, man! Madness is a mighty mystery—a wild and wondrous destiny—but it comes from *Him*! And woe unto that man who mocks at the infliction of heaven! Come, come, lean on me. Softly, softly. (*Exits with* OCTAVIA. COLONEL MONTAIGNE *is led off.* BRIGANDS *exit.*)

DARVIL: (*Seems lost in thought*). Am I grown chicken-hearted, or have years brought me a second dotage? At the words of that ill-fated girl, my blood chills, my pulses pause, and all my frame shivers with horror! "God sees and hears you, Richard Darvil!" If that be true, what—what am I?

Enter ARMSTRONG.

ARMSTRONG: A traveler, accompanied by a single guide, ascends the mountain pass, taking the road directly to the lakes.

DARVIL: (*Hastily*). Let him pass free!

ARMSTRONG: How, captain—free? That is not bandit law.

DARVIL: Well, disarm and bring him here, but see you harm him not. I have begun to weary at the thoughts of blood. Has our messenger yet returned from Milan?

ARMSTRONG: No; and by our rules, if he comes not at sunset, the prisoner must die! (*Exits.*)

DARVIL: Speed be his course. I have spilled too much blood already. Yet was not my nature cruel. How does at times my heart. . .my early home. . .my aged father, and my noble, generous brother—ha! Do I name his name! Whose crimes have made me what I am! Yet I thank heaven he died not by my hand. (*Music. Seats himself on a bank.*)

Enter ARMSTRONG *with* FERRERS, *led by two* BANDITS, *who retire.*

DARVIL: So, Sir Stranger, methinks you are bold to venture into these mountain gorges unattended. Know ye not we are monarchs of this soil and suffer no intruders to pass without a toll, except, indeed, the pilgrims of the shrine, and they take out their debts in the absolutions?

FERRERS: The errand I came called by sets fear at naught.

DARVIL: What is your name and quality? (ALICE *listens at cave.*)

FERRERS: My name is Somers, my profession the painter's art, humble by birth and almost bankrupt in fortune. My imprisonment can avail you nothing. Be generous, and set me free! (ALICE *comes down center, behind.*)

DARVIL: Are these statements true?

FERRERS: Both true as heaven!

ALICE: (*Comes between*). Both false as hell! Liar and slave! Thou hast another name written in the chronicles of blood. a name savoring of treachery and guilt—the name of Lumley Ferrers!

DARVIL: Now, by heaven, it is true! What ho, there, Armstrong! (*Exits, hastily.*)

FERRERS: Discovered! Confusion! Away, mad fool! 'Tis false!

ALICE: Ha! Ha! The mad forget not. They can see the serpent in the heart and hear the bones of the dead rattle with horrid life! Know you me? (*Throws back her hair and looks at him.*)

FERRERS: Is it possible? Do I dream? Do mine eyes deceive me? Do the dead live? Can this be Alice Darvil?

ALICE: (*Mournfully*). Aye! That was my name when I was innocent and happy! Now it is misery! Alice Darvil! Oh, with that wound comes memories of the past—the happy, gone by past. They press upon my brain; they crowd upon my heart; they whisper of another name bound up in memory with it.

FERRERS: He lives. Ernest Maltravers lives!

ALICE: (*Gives a wild shriek*). Ah! That's a name no one has dared to mention for ages—ages past! What fiend of hell art thou who breathes it to the air! Dost thou not see the solid rocks around us shake at the unnatural horror? Ernest, my life, my husband! Hear me! See—see! He rides the clouds! He holds the thunder! Blood is in his path, and might upon his arm! I come to thee! I come! I come! (*Rushes madly off.*)

FERRERS: Merciful heaven! And in this frightful havoc I have had a share! Is this the once beautiful—the gentle Alice? May heaven forgive us all the wrong we wrought!

Enter DARVIL, *holding the ebony casket, seen in Act II.*

DARVIL: Lumley Ferrers, as you do hope for heaven and fear a hell, answer me how you came by this casket!

FERRERS: Strange man! Who are you that ask me?

DARVIL: (*Dashing off his hat*). Richard Maltravers! He whom you last saw on that fearful night of blood—who fled from justice and have here since made my trade of blood and rapine. This casket was that night the object of my search. How came it in your hands?

FERRERS: After that night, I was left by Ernest sole guardian and agent of his affairs. The family mansion has been closely shut, and the room in which the murdered died never since opened. Before I quitted England I entered it. This casket caught my eye, and knowing it to be the secret depository of the Maltravers, I brought it with me.

DARVIL: But why to Italy? Why here? Juggle not with me!

FERRERS: Because even now I was upon my road to Ernest, and bringing the casket to him.

DARVIL: Ah! Then Ernest Maltravers lives?

FERRERS: He lives upon the Lake of Como.

DARVIL: It is so, then. It is the same unopened casket in which he said the *letter* laid. I stand like one who topples on the precipice's verge! I tremble— (*Sees* FERRERS *and resumes his haughty manner instantly.*) For you, sir, you are free. Depart unharmed. Instantly tell your friend what you have seen, and add, besides, that if—that if—fool that I am, the accents will choke me—all be as I hope, happiness may still be his. (*Enter* ARMSTRONG.) Conduct this stranger safe through the defile. His ransom's paid. (*Exit* FERRERS *and* ARMSTRONG.)

DARVIL: (*Looks eagerly around*). Now I am alone. Now I shall know that truth, the doubt of which has poisoned all my life! If I should have wronged her—the palsy of fear is on my heart and hands. I am cold in my very veins! (*Music.*) I cannot break the seal! (*Music. He takes up the casket, starts, trembles, opens casket, and takes out letter, which he reads in agitation.*) "To my husband, from the point of death." Her husband! 'Twas me she meant—yes, I was her husband. Was I not her murderer too! "Richard Maltravers, my first, last, and only love, I am dying! In a few hours—minutes, perhaps—I shall face the God that made me. By this awful name, I now swear—" (*Pauses and shades his eyes in deep emotion.*) My eyes swim. My brain burns. The faint and feeble lines seem traced in molten fire. From every word looks out the accusing spirit of the lost writer. Ha, let me read on—let me end this terrible suspense. "I swear to you my faith has been unbroken as my love, and the poor babe who, tonight without a mother, is your child, the living pledge of your wedded wife." (*Drops letter and falls on his knees.*) I thank thee, merciful heaven! I thank thee mine eyes are dim! For twenty years I have not wept, yet now my tears are flowing. Lost spirit of my injured wife, cannot the immortal blest forgive! Oh, from thy blissful home bend down and teach me to redeem the past! (*Music. Enter* ALICE, *and timidly approaches him. He springs up in deep emotion.*) My child! My child! My wronged—my hapless child! These outstretched arms—these choking tears implore thee to forgive thy father. (*She rushes into his arms.*)

ALICE: Father—Father, your eyes are wet; your voice is troubled. The fountain of my heart is stirred to hear you call me child!

DARVIL: My injured child, forgive me if you can!

ALICE: Oh! We have all many sins to be forgiven. He forgives us all. Come, my father, where the softened moonlight falls like the pitying smile of heaven. There we'll go and kneel together, and when this poor, distracted brain wanders from its devotion, you will gently chide it back. And I—oh, I will wash your head and hands in tears, and heaven will pity both! Come, come.

DARVIL: I dare not! (*Music, low and sacred, is heard, and the voices of pilgrims descending the pass, chanting the "Vesper Hymn."*)

Ave Maria! Thou who ne'er
Did'st from a sinner part—
Ave Maria! Hear, oh hear,
And smile upon his heart.
Ave Maria!

(*As the* PILGRIMS *descend slowly,* ALICE *draws* DARVIL *back to them.*)

ALICE: Hark! Heaven invites you! (*He hesitates, yields tremblingly, approaches the* PILGRIM *who carries the cross, kneels slowly, kisses it, and falls prostrate, with* ALICE *kneeling by.*)

Scene Four

Part of the ravine, wild and dreary. Enter LORD SAXINGHAM *and* ERNEST, *leading* LADY FLORENCE.

ERNEST: Courage—courage, dear Lady Florence. Our guides are diligently searching through the woods, and will find ere long the path. What, can your high spirits fail?

LADY FLORENCE: No, but my legs do, sadly; and after all should we miss the object of our journey—

ERNEST: Do not fear, we will not; but rest you on yonder bank, and I will explain all to your father. (LADY FLORENCE *rests on bank.*)

LORD SAXINGHAM: What was that Florence said about the object of our journey? Did you not tell me the object was to make my girl a bride?

ERNEST: I did so, my lord, and trust still to redeem my word by giving her to Lumley Ferrers.

LORD SAXINGHAM: Lumley Ferrers!   Now, by heaven, this is insolence.

ERNEST: Good my lord, give me your patience, and I hope to convince you in this matter your interest sides with your consent.

LORD SAXINGHAM: How so?

ERNEST: Your father and mine settled upon your life one thousand pounds a year in case this union should take place. Now, I refuse the lady's hand. I bear a widower's heart, which never can love more; and thus is the contract made between us void.

LORD SAXINGHAM: If thus you choose to violate your word, undoubtedly it is; but this can never wring from me my consent to marry Lumley Ferrers.

ERNEST: Once more, be patient. And in consideration of my refusal, I will from my own estate settle an equal sum upon you, which your dutiful child, when once the wife of Ferrers, will double out of hers.

LORD SAXINGHAM: Oh! Oh! This is a different story. Come hither, Florence. You have my blessing and consent to be happy your own way. (*Exits.*)

LADY FLORENCE: All hail the age of gold! But softly—who comes here? My eyes reflect the image in my heart, or do I in good truth behold—

Enter FERRERS.

FERRERS: Your friend and lover—Lumley Ferrers!

ERNEST: Welcome, my friend! Sure, heaven smiles propitious on our desires, sir. We have journeyed far to meet you, and now demand your congratulations to the bride.

FERRERS: (*Much moved*). Lady Florence is married then?

ERNEST: No, but shortly will be, to—

LADY FLORENCE: To Lumley Ferrers, if he will accept of her. Fie, fie, Sir Ernest; this is not cordial greeting to your friend. But my virtue is sincerity. So take my hand, as you have ever had my heart. (*Offers her hand. He kneels and kisses it.*)

FERRERS: To win and wear this coveted gift has been the object of my life; yet, now with grief and deep remorse, I own myself unworthy to profane its touch. Hear me, sweet lady—and you, too, my companion, my confiding and abused friend—hear the confession wrung by conscience from unwilling lips. Led on by jealousy and hate, I invented foulest falsehood against the most unhappy Alice. Nay, turn not away until you hear me swear that she was pure as stainless innocence. Had it not been for me, she would not that night have taken refuge in your father's house, where double treachery laid in wait to ruin her.

ERNEST: No more—no more. You have turned back a fearful page of guilt. Long since have I believed the wretched girl was, like myself, the prey of fate, not sin. Enough. You are forgiven, but never more name this dread subject to me. (*Exits.*)

FERRERS: And my judge—what is her sentence?

LADY FLORENCE: Oh! If I myself were faultless, I should be inexorable to another; but being full of errors, I cannot grieve because my lover is not peerless. Receive my pardon. Once more accept my hand. See you refuse it not again, lest it be not offered more.

FERRERS: I will guard it as my heart of hearts! Come, let us on, and as we go I will relate to you a wondrous tale. You should best know how to reunite two hearts too long divorced by cruel fortune. (*They exit.*)

Scene Five

The mountainous defile. Night closing in. (Music.) Enter, from various entrances, ARMSTRONG, CASTRUCCI, *and* BRIGANDS.

ARMSTRONG: Hist! Hist! Are we all assembled?

CASTRUCCI: All!

ARMSTRONG: Well, friends and fellow-thieves, I have certain knowledge that a small party of English folks will pass by here within the nighttime, and what's more, they are old acquaintances of the captain's and mine. They will be slimly attended and are as rich as kings; but if the captain hears their names, he will not suffer us to touch them.

CASTRUCCI: Why, that's nothing less than sheer robbery to the band. Oh, honor among thieves, say I.

ARMSTRONG: So to cut a long story short, to depose and murder the captain, to elect me in his stead, and lay our hands on all the English gold this very night. What say you all?

CASTRUCCI: Why, as to fingering the gold, it's likely we're all agreed about that; but about the deposing and murdering the captain, that is another story. Now I propose that we make him a fair offer to act with us, and if he won't act handsomely, why, his blood be on his own head.

ALL: Bravo! Bravo! Right!

ARMSTRONG: I'm agreed, and here he comes. Now, Castrucci, do you pop the question. (ALL *retire up to hut.*)

CASTRUCCI: Not I. I haven't half the gab that you have. Besides, a word and a blow, and sometimes both together, is our noble captain's general way of arguing.

Enter DARVIL.

ARMSTRONG: Good evening, Señor. You've come in time. We have just heard of excellent booty to be had tonight.

DARVIL: Not by me. I will kill and rob no more.

ARMSTRONG: (*Aside*). There, didn't I tell you so? Why, captain, you wouldn't betray us, sure.

DARVIL: Betray! Only a heart as base as thine could harbor such a thought. But I'm sick of rapine and of blood. As I found you, so I leave you. My course of life is far away from yours. (ALL *murmur.*) How, now, ye mountain tigers, what growl ye for? Is there one among your band who dare accuse this hand of treachery, this heart of cowardice? Have I not glutted you with gold and made your names the terror of the land? What danger have I shunned or what reward demanded? And dare you mutter, paltry jackals, because the lion, who for awhile has hunted with your troop, retires again to his solitary lair?

ARMSTRONG: Fine words, captain, but if we be jackals we are not jackasses.

ALL: No! No! No!

ARMSTRONG: So, in a word, be one of us or nothing! We do not wish your blood, but you must lead the attack tonight.

DARVIL: And if I do not, you will murder me.

ARMSTRONG: Self-defense demands it. Say I well, comrades?

ALL: Huzzah for Armstrong.

DARVIL: Well, ye shall prevail tonight, at least. I will be one among ye, and as the first proof of your returning to your duty, retire all to your concealment.

ALL: Huzza for our noble captain. (*They exit.*)

DARVIL: Bloodhounds! I will be one among ye, but it shall be to save and not destroy. Once let me use my lawless power for noble ends, then lay it down for ever. (*Goes to cave.*) Within, there—come forth!

COLONEL: (*Comes out.*) Is then my hour arrived? I am ready. Heaven protect my child!

DARVIL: Aye, thy hour is come, but not to die! Prisoner, would'st thou have liberty? Father, would'st thou preserve thy child? Soldier, would'st thou do thy duty to thy king? The way and hour is come. Tonight a party of armed sbirri[13] will cross the upper path. Haste you to meet and lead them here.

COLONEL: You forget, sir, that if I do it, it must be to make you my prisoner.

DARVIL: (*Proudly*). Sir, you cannot make a prisoner of one who yields

---

[13]Police.

himself. But away. Stay not to parley, for life hangs on your speed. I myself will guide you on your way up to the pass.

COLONEL: And my daughter—dare I leave her to your honor? (DARVIL *buries his face in his hands.*)

DARVIL: I have deserved your doubt. Man, man, you wring a heart already breaking! I tell you, sir, could immortality be purchased by one drop of your daughter's blood, they should kill me before they shed it! Away! Away! (*They exit up the pass.*)

Enter ERNEST, *much agitated, and* FERRERS. (*Music.*)

FERRERS: Once more do I entreat you to return. This spot appears to me to be near the place where I this morning was, but confused by the thousand hills and thickening gloom, I cannot well distinguish it. See, the moon is shining brightly and will betray us to any lurking spies. Let me entreat you to turn back.

ERNEST: You urge in vain. The tale you told has set my blood on fire. Lost as she is to me for ever, I will once more behold my poor, ill-fated Alice—will speak of peace and comfort to her distracted brain—will take her from this savage horde and lodge her in some holy sisterhood, then take a sad farewell, and in some foreign battle throw away my worthless life.

FERRERS: Heaven comfort you in this terrible affliction.

ERNEST: It does. The deepest sting of anguish was to think my Alice guilty. Now, terrible as has been our unconscious sin, I dare look forward to a union. There. (*Points upward. Music.* FERRERS *bends his head respectfully.* ERNEST *motions to go. They go off.*)

Enter ARMSTRONG.

ARMSTRONG: So, Richard Darvil triumphs again. One word of his rends what I for months have labored to effect. By heaven and hell! I will have signal vengeance on him and all who bear the name. Ah! Who's here? Answer or die! (*Enter* FERRERS.) A stranger! In our lair—by heavens, the very one whom I this morning captured. Ho! What ho, there! Brigands awake! Treason and treachery. What, ho! The captain has sold us to the soldiers! (*Music.* CASTRUCCI *and* BRIGANDS *rush in.* ARMSTRONG *speaks through the music.*) Down with the spy! (BRIGANDS *on at every entrance.* ARMSTRONG *and* CASTRUCCI *fall on* FERRERS. *Enter* DARVIL *from cave. They are fighting close by. He strikes up their swords.*)

DARVIL: What, two men on one? And he armed with only a sword? Shame on ye. Put up, if ye be men. And you, sir—(*Turning to* FERRERS.)

Ha! Is it possible, Lumley Ferrers? Do I again behold you here?

ARMSTRONG: You do—for the last time. (*Draws a pistol and fires at* DARVIL, *who staggers and falls. At the same moment* ERNEST *rushes in, and is attacked by* BRIGANDS. FERRERS *is wounded, staggers, and falls dead.* ERNEST *is overpowering* CASTRUCCI, *when* ARMSTRONG *rushes to him.*)

ARMSTRONG: Die! Die! Ernest Maltravers, your life is a forfeit.

ERNEST: Ah, villain! Robber! Murderer! Well do I remember you. My father's blood is on your sword.

ARMSTRONG: And yours now mixes with it. (ERNEST, *overpowered, falls on one knee.* ARMSTRONG *raises in the act to strike him, when a wild scream is heard, and* ALICE *rushes down between them and catches* ARMSTRONG's *uplifted arm.*)

ALICE: Hold! Hold! Or strike through my heart. It is the shield of his! (*Music. All the* BRIGANDS *rush to present their carbines, but immediately lower them, and fall on their knees, as* COLONEL MONTAIGNE *appears with* SOLDIERS, *who secure* ARMSTRONG.)

ERNEST: Eternal heavens! What do my eyes behold? (ALICE *regards him fixedly in a wild and wondering manner. Then, with a scream, she falls to the ground.* ERNEST *regards her with horror.*)

DARVIL: Ernest Maltravers, approach. Sole remaining scion of my father's house, listen to the last words of Richard Maltravers! Fear not to take yon fainting form within your arms. I, whose curse brought death and woe, now speak of peace and blessing. Take her—take her. She is pure as heaven's own stainless angels. The grasp of death is even now upon my heart here—'tis here. (*Draws letter from his breast, gives it to* ERNEST.) The messenger of peace and joy, Ernest—my brother's. Canst thou forgive me? (ERNEST *glances rapidly at the letter.*)

ERNEST: Merciful heaven! Let not my senses reel. Speak, Richard Maltravers—speak. Oh, God! He sinks! One word—one sign. Alice is—is—

DARVIL: (*In a clear voice*). Your wife, and my much injured daughter. (*He falls.* ERNEST *clasps* ALICE.) And now, spirit of my lost and injured wife, accept this expiation. Bless—bless— (*Music.* DARVIL *raises himself faintly, makes a sign of blessing, falls and dies.*)

ERNEST: Alice, my own wife. My own dear Alice. (*Music.* ALICE *listens, at first carelessly, but gradually begins to mark the tune, then places her hand upon her brow and rises gently.*)

ALICE: Sure I have slept a heavy sleep. The last chimes of the village bells are ringing. My father's late. No, my husband. Did I dream that I was married? Alas! I tremble. Ernest—Ernest—Ernest, I am very cold. Prithee, take me to thy heart, and bid mine beat no more. (*Music. She begins to look around in a startled way, and at length sees* ERNEST.) Dear Ernest, on that fearful night of your good father's murder, I had sought the hall to prove to you that I was guiltless of the sins with which you charged me. I was bringing you this paper. Read. (*Hands letter.*)

ERNEST: (*Reads*). "Dear Alice, I love you to distraction. It was this love that caused me to arouse the jealousy of your credulous husband and incite the anger of his father. You are now mine. Provoke my wrath, and you are ruined. Grant my wishes, and I will raise you to rank, wealth, and happiness. Lumley Ferrers." Villain! Justly has heaven punished him for his crimes! But how shall I ever atone for the deep wrongs that you have suffered?

ALICE: My own, my own—once more, thou art my own. (*Group forms around for the picture. Soft music as curtain falls.*)

THE FOREST PRINCESS
OR, TWO CENTURIES AGO

An Historical Play in Three Parts

Charlotte Mary Sanford Barnes[1]

1844

First performed in Liverpool, England, 1844. American premiere: Arch
Street Theatre, Philadelphia, April 16, 1848.
Originally published in *Plays, Prose and Poetry*. Philadelphia, 1848.

---

[1]Later Charlotte Barnes Conner.

INTRODUCTION

The lack of intelligible chronicles has left the early history of the red men imperfect; the prejudice and injustice of their dispossessors have too often falsified or obscured their traditions; and the various dialects and rapid disappearance of many tribes render perishable the historic songs some rude Homer may have chanted. The life of Pocahontas is an exception to this rule: the great charm of all connected with her is its certainty and truth. All the particulars of her biography are confirmed by relatively distant and unimpeachable testimony, recorded by writers who, (so far from adding to narrative a single charm,) by their uncouth style and barren enumeration of events denude them of all beauty save their intrinsic worth. While the mere fact that some of the most worthy families in our land are the living descendants of Pocahontas, gives an almost prosaic reality to her existence.

Considered in her individual career, Pocahontas stands forth from first to last the animated type of mercy and peace, unselfishness and truth. Her benevolence, (of which the limits of this play can record but a small part,) is neither a momentary impulse nor a cold system of utility: it is a warm, all-pervading and abiding principle. Her life was pure, active, and affectionate: her "beautiful, godly, and Christian death" was a theme of praise to all beholders.

Considered in relation to the events which resulted from her instrumentality on earth, her character assumes still greater importance. The various historians and colonists concur in the assertion that but for the benefactions of Pocahontas, Virginia would have been lost to England. The Dutch and the Spaniards were then aiming at a settlement, and would have established themselves there during the delay which must have inevitably occurred, had the British colonists starved to death or abandoned the spot,—a result which Pocahontas alone prevented. How far the aspect of civilization, of national character and government, of literature and science, in America, would have been affected, had other lands given customs, laws, and language to so extensive and central a portion of our continent, is a question well worthy of consideration, and in justice to Pocahontas, should ever be associated with her name.

The great difficulty in the construction of a drama from this subject,—its unconquerable defect, rhetorically speaking, lies in the division of the interest. Were it a romance, it were easy to heighten the attraction tenfold by representing love as the result of Pocahontas' compassion and Smith's gratitude, and thus perfecting the unity of the plot. But this tale is no fiction; and though precedents illustrious in literature exist where the acts of historical personages have been misrepresented to embellish romance, the justice of such a course may be questioned, especially when, as in the present case, it would detract from the pure disinterestedness of a woman's fame. However rude may be the shrine on which Vesta's fire is kindled—however dim its blaze may seem, viewed through the misty atmosphere of centuries,—even the laws of classic fable forbid us to employ the torch of Hymen, or Cupid's "purple light" to replenish the celestial flame.

To the official courtesy and kindness of our minister, the Hon. Edward Everett, and to the facilities afforded by that admirable institution, the Library of the British Museum, I am indebted for the historical details of this play. It would appear only an affectation of pedantry to name the works, (at least twenty in number,) which were consulted previous to the writing of this ephemeral production.

The incidents of this play are historical in their most minute detail, but the unities of the stage required the condensation of events into days instead of months and rendered several anachronisms necessary. The reader of history will at once perceive them.

Persons of the Drama[2]

EUROPEANS:
Charles, Prince of Wales, aged 17
Sir Thomas Dale, Governor of Virginia
Captain John Smith, "Sometime Governor of Virginia, and Vice- Admiral
    of New England"
Master John Ratliffe, President of the Council
Master John Rolfe, a gentleman
Master Robert Hunt, Preacher
William Volday, a Switzer
Anas Todkill
Adam Francis
Master Newton
Page
Drawer
Colonists, Mechanics, Soldiers, &c.
Queen Anne, Consort of James the First
Mistress Alice
Maud

NORTH AMERICANS:
Powhatan, King of the Twelve Tribes of *Powhatan*[3]
Opachisco
Mosco
Americans of the tribes of the Paspaheghes, Monacans, &c.
Pocahontas, the *Forest Princess*, named also Matoka, daughter of Powhatan,
    and afterwards baptized under the name of Rebecca[4]

---

[2]Author's note: All the names in the play, without exception, are historical.

[3]Author's note: The correct pronunciation of *Powhatan* by the Indians themselves
lays the emphasis on the last syllable.

[4]Author's note: Pocahontas was the *title*; Matoka, or Matoax, the *name*. The Indians
kept the latter a secret, lest the whites should avail themselves of it to practice sorcery
upon the forest princess.

FIRST PERIOD, 1607

ACT I

Scene One

The banks of the Powhatan River in Wingandacoa, the land of Powhatan, named Virginia by Sir Walter Raleigh, in compliment to Queen Elizabeth. On one side is the entrance to the fort, on the other a clump of trees crowning a small acclivity. Rude dwellings are seen near the fort and in the distance. The British flag flies from the fort. All the colonists are discovered in various groups, some of the mechanics still retaining their tools. MOSCO is discovered seated on the ground, listening attentively. ROLFE, SMITH, RATLIFFE, HUNT, FRANCIS, TODKILL and VOLDAY advance. The rest assemble around them with respectful attention.

RATLIFFE: Now, my brave friends and comrades, rest we here;
For well is leisure earned by zealous toil.
There stand complete the first abodes by hands
Of British artisans upreared, upon
The Paspaheghes' land—the settlement
Of fair Virginia. And by full consent
Of this good council, we shall call the fort
And dwellings Jamestown, honoring the king
By whose commission we explore these lands.
    ALL: Long live King James!
    RATLIFFE: Your counsel, friends, I seek.
Right worthy Captain Smith, as thou hast learned
The languages of many native tribes,
And all their customs and geography,
To thee I first address myself.
    SMITH: The same
Fair praise is merited by Master Rolfe,
Who, all unused to labor, still hath toiled
Without reward, hard as paid artisan,
And from the savage brought to Britain young,
Learned e'en as much as I.
    ROLFE: You wrong me there.
You are my elder and my better, too—
A soldier prudent, brave and tried—while I,
Wild for adventure, only hope to see
The Indian countries noble Raleigh named,

And with my sword to carve my way to fame
And fortune, if I can.
    SMITH: What more wouldst have?
Who would at home drag out an aimless life,
When honorable, bold ambition calls
To lead through forests vast the arts and faith
Of polished, civilized life; like pioneers,
To hew a road to glory's farther goal,
And write on her imperishable page
The opening chapter of a nation's story?
    HUNT: Thy words like fire warm each heart that hears.
    RATLIFFE: Now to our plans.
(*Pointing to Mosco.*) This friendly Indian says
Yon noble stream and lands of vast extent
Are ruled o'er by Virginia's mighty king,
Great Powhatan, who lives in savage state
At Orapaks, about four leagues from this.
We must with him a treaty make, that may
Secure supplies of corn and other food
When we've exhausted all our vessel's store.
A deputation to this king must go.
    HUNT: Might I advise, but two should bear the news.
A number of strange faces would convey
Semblance of hostile purpose.
    RATLIFFE: Well you speak;
And Captain Smith first named. The other— (*Reflecting.*) Stay—
    SMITH: Most worthy president, I'll go alone.
Each arm and head are needed to preserve
The safety of the colony.
    ROLFE: Let *me*
Thy danger share.
    SMITH: (*Apart to him*). Thou art more needed here.
Besides, if thou wouldst serve me, stay. A few
There are who love me not, and might instill
Wrong thoughts among the council. Doctor Hunt
And you may serve me *here.*
    ROLFE: So be it, then.
    SMITH: With your good leave I will go forth at once.
    RATLIFFE: Are you accoutred for the task?
    SMITH: I am. (*Looking at his pistols.*)
A little harmless powder strikes with awe
The savage tribes. This (*Pointing to his sword.*) proves my trusty friend

Should danger threaten; and an axe to cut
My way through pathless, tangled brakes.
(ROLFE *goes into the fort.*) The sun
Will be my guide to Orapaks; his beams
In setting gild its rude abodes—so tells
The Indian here. (ROLFE *returns with an axe and gives it to* SMITH.)
Thanks, friend, I will not lag
Upon the road. The wild grapes and the stream
Will feast me in my absence. Fare ye well,
Most worthy council and my trusty friends. (RATLIFFE *and* VOLDAY
bow. HUNT *and* ROLFE *advance to say farewell.*)
    HUNT: Heaven speed thee on thy errand.
    SMITH: Reverend sir,
Amen. (*Exits.*)
    RATLIFFE: Now let us in, and feast this wild
But friendly man, and after send him home
Well pleased, laden with glittering gifts, to bear
A good report of us among his tribe. (*They are conducting* MOSCO *to the fort as the scene closes.*)

Scene Two

The adjacent forest. Enter VOLDAY.

    VOLDAY: 'Tis ever thus—in Britain, on the seas,
And now in forests—still this Captain Smith
Is foremost in our council and our wars.
No other name can gain a eulogy.

Enter ROLFE, *equipped for the chase.*

    ROLFE: See, the sun shines bright on Smith's adventure.
    VOLDAY: On Smith! Is there no other brave, bold man,
That he must be the burthen[5] of each song?
    ROLFE: For shame! Thou lik'st him not, because, of all
The lawless spirits here (and they are many),
Thou art the hardest to control. Why, man!
We are among an untaught race, whom we
Would make our friends.

---

[5]Central theme.

VOLDAY: What then?

ROLFE: What then?
Why thus: thou did'st endeavor to defraud
The Indians who first came to sell us venison.
Thou wouldst have robbed, not bartered. Captain Smith
Made thee pay what with us values little,
But is a treasure to the forest-bred.
For this, I grieve to see, thou ow'st him grudge.

VOLDAY: What right has he to lord it o'er the rest?

ROLFE: The right of rank bestowed for service tried;
The right of valor and integrity;
Prudence, experience, generosity;
Endurance and the pride of conscious worth:
These give him right to rule o'er me, and thee.

VOLDAY: A man's opinions are as free as air,
And I have mine.

ROLFE: But if they tend to ill,
Discard them, pray. We are a little band
Amidst an unknown country, and should be
United. Come, meet Smith on his return
With friendship. I will try my sporting skill
Till sunset. Fare you well. (*Exits.*)

VOLDAY: Young scatter-brain!
Your boyish dreams of honor and desert
Will ever keep your purse filled scantily.
You aided Smith in public to disgrace
My name. I *will* bear friendship—in my *looks*,
And wait the hour to crush ye both. (*Noise without.*) But hark!
(TODKILL *rushes on, much frightened.*) How now? What ails thee? Speak!

TODKILL: Speak! I've hardly breath, I've run so fast.

VOLDAY: Run! Wherefore? Why
Dost tremble so? Are foes at hand?

TODKILL: I'll tell you, only wait. (*Recovering himself.*) Master Ratliffe
sent me into the forest for Master Rolfe, when two great, glaring eyes
looked out upon me from the thicket. Then I heard an angry growl. It
was a wolf, or a bear, or one of those more hideous beasts you wise heads
call a panther.

VOLDAY: Of course,
You shot him dead.

TODKILL: Oh, no! I ran away.

VOLDAY: Coward!

TODKILL: No, no! I don't deserve that name. I've no objection to fair fight with *men*, but wild beasts are my particular aversion.

VOLDAY: Weak fool! To let
The brute escape, surrounded as we are
By dangers.

TODKILL: If you are so anxious, seek him out yourself; and if he makes a meal of you, I don't think many will shed tears.

VOLDAY: Cease your senseless gossip!

TODKILL: Senseless! Umph! If it was a *bear*, he'll have a fellow-feeling and make friends with you.

VOLDAY: Psha! (*Exits angrily.*)

TODKILL: (*Laughs*). Ha, ha! I think that I was even with him there. I wonder where young Master Rolfe is gone. (FRANCIS *enters.*) Ha! Francis!

FRANCIS: So, Todkill, no more work, at least today.
It is to be a holiday.

TODKILL: Not before we want it. Such a life! Cutting down trees, chopping up trees, sawing, digging! Whew! My arms ache at the recollection.

FRANCIS: Yes, the work is hard.

TODKILL: Hard! Aye, I believe it is! And at night, before we can go comfortably to sleep, we must light fires to keep off—ugh! The wild beasts.

FRANCIS: Yes, fires large enough to roast—

TODKILL: Roast! Don't talk of roasting! Shall I ever see a joint of meat served up in a Christian way again, or go to sleep without the singing of those vile mosquitoes in my ears?

FRANCIS: And then we cannot have a jovial bout, forsooth, because the wine is doled out daily to us!

TODKILL: These savages—poor, ignorant, unhappy creatures— have no wine, anything, except tobacco. That's my only comfort here—to smoke a pipe; for then I think of pretty Mistress Alice whom I left in England, and how comfortable I should be seated at home with her by a nice *coal* fire, a cup of mulled wine and a pipe by my side. That's comfort, Francis.

FRANCIS: Comfort, yes! Hark'ye, you're a merry fellow, and if you will give your word to keep a secret—

TODKILL: Close as the grave. What is it?

FRANCIS: When poor Captain Smith gave out the wine yesterday, I stole a flagon, and here it is. (*Producing it.*) But mind, in confidence. I'll share it with you before we go back to the fort.

TODKILL: Ah, Francis, you're a worthy soul. Here's the health of comely Mistress Alice. (*Drinks.*)

FRANCIS: Mistress Alice! (*Drinks.*)

TODKILL: Bless her pretty face. I think I see it now. (*Drinks again, then gives the flask to* FRANCIS.)

FRANCIS: Here's success to the new colony. (*Drinks.*)

TODKILL: Ah! This forest life is very dreary.

FRANCIS: Well, you can return in the next ship.

TODKILL: No, I must stay with Master Rolfe, heaven bless him! I've known him since we were both little boys. He always stood up for me when I was in trouble; and in our merry game—Lord, how he used to thump me! Bless him! I wouldn't leave him for the world.

FRANCIS: Well, then, think of fame and money.

TODKILL: Yes, money's very well; but as for fame, that's charming enough for Master Rolfe, who wants to live in story. I'd rather live in England and die undistinguished. Oh, Mistress Alice! (*Takes the flask and drinks.*)

FRANCIS: Console yourself with the adventures you can relate on your return. (*They are going.*)

TODKILL: Ah, yes! How Alice will stare with astonishment! I'll tell her all I've seen, and more too. Travelers, you know, are not bound to tell the truth. If they were, their books wouldn't be half so entertaining. (*Exit* TODKILL *and* FRANCIS, *laughing.*)

Scene Three

POWHATAN's *wigwam at Orapaks. A rude throne on one side, on the other a pile of huge stones.* POWHATAN *enters from without.*

POWHATAN: The sun has set, yet Pocahontas
Returns not with the forest's blooming spoil.
Why does she linger? Hark! It is her step. (POCAHONTAS *enters the wigwam, bearing a basket of wild fruit.*)
My child is welcome.

POCAHONTAS: Pocahontas brings
A dainty for her father's evening meal.
Her task was shortened by surprising news.
A weary wanderer from that peaceful tribe,
The Paspaheghes, met her on the road.
He says the pale-faced men, whose homes are where
The sun doth rise, are come unto our shores
Once more, in their white-winged canoes.

POWHATAN: The God
Of ill rain curses—

POCAHONTAS: (*Beseechingly*). No!

POWHATAN: They come to seize

The red man's lands—to slay—

POCAHONTAS: Though some were false,
My father will judge all harshly. Think!
Even amongst our own and other tribes
There oft are wicked and deceitful men.
So may it be with these. Remember, too,
'Mongst those who landed here, and since went home
O'er the big waters, years ere I was born,
I've heard my father praise—aye, more than one!
Many for bravery stood eminent.

POWHATAN: Thy voice breathes kindness ever. Pocahontas
Is her father's dearest child.

POCAHONTAS: And fondly
She loves him. Were he the meanest of the tribe,
She'd share with joy his base, inglorious lot;
But as he is a mighty chief and brave,
She loves his glory dear as she loves him,
And ever will entreat him not to cloud
His fame by judgment harsh or cruelty.

Enter OPACHISCO *with the axe used by Smith in Scene One, followed by two* INDIANS.

OPACHISCO: Mighty chief, we have surprised a stranger
Wandering near this wigwam! Not of our race
Is he, though speaks he our tongue. We would
Have seized and brought him hither, when aside
He cast this tomahawk he held— (*Pointing to the English axe.*) and raised
A short, black wand. A flash gleamed in the air.
The spirit he invoked, 'mid smoke denounced
Our rashness, and we fled, but soon returned
When he, great wizard, beckoned and besought
To see the mighty Powhatan.

POWHATAN: Ye fools!
It was no spirit, but a tool of war
The pale-face fights with, as you arrows use.
He is no wizard. Go, conduct him here. (*Exit* OPACHISCO *and the other* INDIANS.)
See, even as Pocahontas said, 'tis one of those.
(SMITH *is conducted in by* OPACHISCO *and other* INDIANS.)
He comes. What brings the pale-face here?

SMITH: I am called Captain Smith. With other friends

Just landed from a long and stormy voyage,
I came to seek Virginia's mighty king.
    POWHATAN: Where are the white man's countrymen?
    SMITH: Upon
The banks of thy broad river, Powhatan.
They wait my coming with assurance fair
Of amity from thee. A bond of peace,
With presents rich, I offer; and besides,
Bright beads and hatchets, tools of every kind,
Arrow heads, glass, wrought iron, copper too,
Your corn and venison taking in exchange.
    POWHATAN: Powhatan will no treaty make, no peace.
The pale-faced brethren come to spy, to seize
His lands, to make his tribes their slaves, to bow
Him down with tribute.
    SMITH: Chief, you wrong me much,
And wrong still more your father, England's king.
Ambition, avarice may be the curse
Of some who sought your friendship to betray.
My word is sacred as my bond. In deeds,
As well as speech, I proffer amity.
    POWHATAN: (*Surprised*). Do *young* men speak in the pale-face's councils?
Where are their white-haired sages? Powhatan
Suspects them all; and even now, perhaps
Their treacherous band in ambush lurking near
May spring upon us. One, at least, shall be
Secure. (*He gives a signal, and the* INDIANS *advance stealthily behind* SMITH *and prepare to seize him, directed by* OPACHISCO.)
    POCAHONTAS: (*Springing forward*). What means my father?
    POWHATAN: Seize the stranger! (*Before* SMITH *has time to draw his sword, the* INDIANS *spring upon him and pinion his arms. After a struggle,* SMITH *is overcome and held down by the savages.*)
    POWHATAN: He shall die, appeasing the Great Spirit
Who then may drive all rash intruders hence!
So, bind him hard. (OPACHISCO *does so.*)
    SMITH: Yet hear me, savage chief!
    POWHATAN: Plead not! 'Tis vain.
    SMITH: Plead! 'Tis for thyself
I'd speak. Beware the vengeance of my king.
Plead, never! Death I fear not. I will meet
Its stroke with firmness, as a soldier should.

My peace, I trust, is made above. My life,
Risked for my country oft, is England's still.
POWHATAN: Prepare the instruments of death. (SMITH *is led to the*
pile of stones and assisted to lie down with his head upon the stones. The
INDIANS *bring their clubs.*)
POCAHONTAS: No! No!
Will not my father spare him?
POWHATAN: Get thee hence.
Our chiefs admit not women's counsels.
POCAHONTAS: True.
Poor Pocahontas is a woman, but
She's child of a great warrior and king—
Of Powhatan—and, as she shares his blood,
So may she share his counsels.
(*Beseechingly.*) Let her stay!
POWHATAN: Thou art the dearest daughter of the king.
Provoke him not to wrath. Begone.
POCAHONTAS: The voice
Of mercy louder speaks than Powhatan.
POWHATAN: Thy father hates these strangers. Mark me well.
They came in numbers ere thyself wast born.
Their deeds, their history, their conduct *then*,
To our tribes will *ever* be the same.
The time will come they'll spread o'er all the land.
Foul tyranny and rapine they'll return
For friendly welcome and sweet mercy shown,
Defrauding or exterminating still
Our ancient race, until the red man's name
Will live but in the memory of the past,
Or in some exile powerless, who sells
For a few ears of corn his father's land,
Lord of that soil where then he'll beg a grave.
POCAHONTAS: And *should* our race thus pass from earth away,
The shame will not be theirs, but their oppressors',
Who then, amidst the chronicles they keep,
This act of mercy by a forest king
Full surely must record. Oh, spare him, father!
POWHATAN: Is Powhatan a woman, to be moved
By tears? The stranger dies. (*Turns from her.*) Now, warriors,
Obey your king. When I raise my arm,
Dash out his brains! (*The* INDIANS *brandish their clubs.*)
POCAHONTAS: (*Rushing to her father*). No! No! In mercy stay!

Perhaps he has a child in that far land—
A babe just straying from its mother's arms—
Both watching for his coming, praying to
The good Great Spirit to protect him still!

POWHATAN: (*Incensed*). Let women snatch from wolves the prey their fangs
Have torn, but thwart not Powhatan. Begone!

POCAHONTAS: Think, were my father captive far o'er seas,
Thus doomed to die alone—no hand to save—
His daughter helpless here in agony—
For her sake, spare him!

POWHATAN: (*With terrible anger*). Dare not speak again!
He dies! Away! (*Goes up to his throne and raises his arm. At the same moment,* POCAHONTAS *rushes to* SMITH *and clasps his head in her arms, laying her own head upon his, as the* INDIANS *are in the act of striking the blow.*)

POCAHONTAS: (*Exclaims*). Then slay him thus!

POWHATAN: Hold!   Hold!   (*The* INDIANS *pause.*)   (*To* POCAHONTAS, *with surprise and admiration.*)   Thou art a worthy daughter of thy race—
A warrior's spirit in a woman's form.
Thou wilt not doubt the word of Powhatan.
'Tis pledged. (POCAHONTAS *relinquishes her grasp of* SMITH *and comes forward.*)
(*To the* INDIANS.) Release the pale-face! (*They raise and unbind him.*) He is free!
(POCAHONTAS *falls at the feet of* POWHATAN, *who stands upon his throne repelling* SMITH's *expressions of gratitude. The* INDIANS *group around in wonder, and* OPACHISCO *points to the entrance, directing* SMITH's *departure, as the curtain falls.*)

SECOND PERIOD, 1609

ACT II

Scene One

Jamestown. The same scene as the first of the play. The COLONISTS *discovered in various groups, some reclining on the ground leaning against the trunk of a tree, some leaning on their guns, and all more or less feeble and haggard from the effects of famine.* RATLIFFE, ROLFE, VOLDAY,

TODKILL, *and* FRANCIS *are most prominent in the group.*

ROLFE: Look cheerly, friends; we'll not despair as yet.
Each hour brings hope of near arrival from
The shore of dear, old England. Come, bear up!
VOLDAY: *Bear up!* With famine's squalid frown upon
Each face? I say, away with this control.
We're in extremity; then let us try
Each for himself—the strongest win the day.
Break open the stores, and let us make
One jovial meal, at least.
ROLFE: A selfish counsel;
For there are many sick within the fort.
VOLDAY: Let the sick die or heal, whiche'er they please.
I say, break open all the stores.
ROLFE: For shame!
RATLIFFE: The ship is fit for sea. Why not set sail
(Those who are able), to the nearest port,
With what provisions yet we have?
ROLFE: And leave
The rest to perish by starvation here—
Give up all prospects of the colony—
Desert the post our country gave in charge?
No! Let us act like men! *I* will not stir
While there's a dog alive within the fort
To make a meal of.

SMITH *enters from the fort.*

RATLIFFE: With what strength we have,
Let's arm, and rush upon the savages,
And seize whate'er we want. (*Night begins to close in the scene.*)
SMITH: (*Coming forward*). A villain's thought!
Besides, the tribes to us are score to one.
'Tis madness, Ratliffe.
VOLDAY: (*To* RATLIFFE, FRANCIS, *and others*).
Come, then, friends. We will
Provide for our own safety. Oh!
ROLFE: (*Drawing his sword*). By heaven,
He dies that stirs! (*They pause.*)
Friends, comrades, ye will not,
Selfish and reckless, crush the little hope

Of what a few days' fortitude may bring,
And leave so many sick inchmeal to die!
Like brothers, let us stand together!
    VOLDAY: No!
Make way! (*Advancing with* RATLIFFE, FRANCIS, *and the rest.*)
(SMITH *whispers to* ROLFE, *who goes off hastily.*)
    SMITH: Then hear me, by St. George! If ye
Will thus desert your comrades, as ye pass—
For pass ye must—within the cannon's range,
With sakre-falcon[6] and with musket shot
I'll fire upon your pinnace,[7] and I'll sink
Ye all![8] (VOLDAY *levels a pistol at* SMITH.)
Aye, fire! Young Rolfe will execute
My plan! Desert us if ye dare! (*Distant shout.*)

HUNT *enters.*

    HUNT: Joy! Joy!
From Lady Pocahontas come her brave
Young brother and six Indians more, with stores
Of food. (*A loud shout from all except* VOLDAY.)
ROLFE *enters.*
    ROLFE: Aye! Shout! And thank the Indian maid
Who watches o'er our safety. I bring news
Of more good fortune. From the tallest tree
Beyond the fort, you may afar descry,
In gallant trim, a ship that steers this way.
    SMITH: Indeed! Good news crowds in. On to the fort!
A hearty meal to each, and then prepare
To welcome all our countrymen.
    RATLIFFE: (*To* SMITH). Come, friend,
Give me your hand. I own I've been to blame.
    SMITH: That cancels all. (*Grasps his hand.* HUNT, ROLFE,
RATLIFFE *and* SMITH *confer together.* FRANCIS *approaches timidly.*
SMITH *beckons, and in actions, expostulates with and forgives him.*)
    VOLDAY: (*Apart*). Were not these fools so tame,
So swayed by Smith and Rolfe, I know that some

---

    [6]Small cannon.

    [7]The small boat used to reach the ship.

    [8]Author's note: These are the words recorded as having been uttered by Smith on that occasion.

Would back me in the strife. So let it be.
The secret messages I've sent unto
The savage king have prospered, and he knows
The fitting time for ambush and surprise.
These *patient* victims then will fall, and I,
Rewarded, honored by the savages,
In time in lawless luxury may live,
And reign amid these forests. (*Meanwhile,* ROLFE *and his friends have been accosting the* COLONISTS *and aiding the feeble to rise and approach the fort.*)

    ROLFE: (*To* SMITH). I'll remain.
For while my hungry comrades feed on what
This Indian Ceres has bestowed, 'tis fit
The outskirts of the forest here should not
Be left unwatched.

    SMITH: Thy caution is well-timed.
Farewell awhile. (*To the* COLONISTS.) Now follow to the fort. (*Exit* SMITH *to the fort, followed by the rest, tumultuously.* VOLDAY *goes off slowly.* ROLFE *takes up his gun, which was resting against a tree.*)

    ROLFE: (*Alone*). That I could see her! Such a gentle maid
Were pleasanter acquaintance in these wilds
Than yon rough comrades. I am half in love,
Already, with this forest maid, and could
I see her—hark! A step is rustling through the brake.
Is't man or brute? I'll climb this knoll and watch. (*He ascends and looks off.*)
It is the panther's stealthy tread. I hear,
But cannot see him. (*Looks through the branches of the tree.*)
Stay! Beneath the shade
Of yon old tree, an Indian girl reclines.
I'll nearer steal. (*Advances nearer and starts with horror.*)
Is she the panther's aim?
Yes! There I see him. Look! He's crouching low,
Unseen by her, on her recumbent form
To spring. Now— (*Leveling his gun.*) Heaven nerve my arm!
(*Fires and looks off.*) Well shot!
The brute is down, the maid unhurt.
(*With surprise.*) No shriek!
Yet, 'tis a woman, and she comes this way. (POCAHONTAS *descends.*)

    POCAHONTAS: A gun! The weapon of the pale-faces. (*Sees him.*)
Thou art the stranger whom the forest maid
Must thank. Within yon shady nook, where she

A moment sat to rest her wearied feet,
In death a panther lies. One instant more,
Without thy aid, the death would have been hers,
Not his. How shall the forest maiden thank
The stranger?
    ROLFE: Nay, no thanks, sweet maid. Enough
To have preserved thee. Mention it no more.
    POCAHONTAS: Had I been slain, my warning had been lost.
Time wears. The wanderer must not delay.
Young brave, take thou this string of beaded shells.
Despise it not; for show this token when
Thy fair locks tremble in the red man's hand,
His tomahawk will fall unstained to earth. (ROLFE *kneels to receive it.*)
Whate'er thy peril, send the forest maid
That little chain, her tribe will free thee straight.
    ROLFE: No sainted relic e'er was treasured more
Than this shall be for sake of her who gave it.
But may I ask the gentle donor's name?
    POCAHONTAS: Matoka is my name. Virginia's tribes
Know me as Pocahontas.
    ROLFE: Princess! What,
Our guardian angel? She who saved the life
Of Smith?
    POCAHONTAS: Thou know'st him?
    ROLFE: He's my dearest friend.
    POCAHONTAS: Indeed! Too long I've tarried. I must speak
With Captain Smith alone, and quickly too.
My life is periled by my stay.

VOLDAY *enters from the fort, and retires observing them.*

    ROLFE: Your life!
For him you risk it?
    POCAHONTAS: Not for *him*, young brave.
For peace and mercy's sake alone. But when,
In bonds expecting death I saw him stand,
Compassion made us kin at once, and now
Dear as a father is thy friend to me.
    ROLFE: Sweet maiden, would that *I* might share such love!
    POCAHONTAS: More like my own brave brother is thy youth,
And Pocahontas as a brother trusts thee.
The time draws on. Oh, haste!

ROLFE: This way, dear lady. (*Leads her into the fort.*)

VOLDAY: (*Advancing*). How's this? An Indian girl conferring with Young Rolfe! Are then my plans revealed? Their words I scarce could catch. I'll follow to the fort. If aught I see betoken I'm betrayed, I'll quick to Powhatan for refuge. Yes, And spur the savage to attack at once. (*Exits into the fort.*)

Scene Two

The interior of the fort. ROLFE *leads in* POCAHONTAS.

ROLFE: Princess, rest here. I'll seek out Smith. Meanwhile, A reverend friend shall guard thee from intrusion: For see, he comes this way.

Enter HUNT, *much agitated.*

HUNT: Oh, woeful news! Brave Smith is wounded unto death.

ROLFE: Oh, heaven!

HUNT: Still first in toil, he launched his skiff to meet His friends in boats fast pulling from the ship That now, with England's flag displayed, hath cast Her anchor in the stream. A bag of powder That near him lay, by some mischance caught fire, Exploded, and the captain wounded lies In cruel suffering.

ROLFE: Where is he?

HUNT: They Have borne him to the ship, where surgeon's care Is busy round him.

POCAHONTAS: Then to *ye* must I Reveal my errand, or 'twill be too late. First, tell me where my noble brother is, For I am Pocahontas. (*To* HUNT.)

HUNT: Generous maid, Thy brother and attendants, long ere this, Are safe at Orapaks. Their mission o'er, They left us instantly.

POCAHONTAS: Then they are safe. A villain lurks among the pale-faces

Who hath betrayed ye all to Powhatan.
With presents a few red men soon will come,
And while ye feast, your weapons they will steal,
And giving signal to the ambushed tribes,
Will massacre ye all.
    ROLFE: What fiend can thus
Have sold us?
    POCAHONTAS: Strangers, hearken unto me.
Your faith, 'tis said, e'en more than ours, commands
That ye should speak the truth. By all ye hold
(*Taking a hand of each.*) Most sacred and most terrible, I claim
Your word to act as Pocahontas wills.
In peace and pity, slaughter to prevent,
I give this warning. But, whate'er betide,
Ye must attempt no strife. In mercy act;
Nor slay, nor *harm* the tribes of Powhatan.
Ye promise this?
    HUNT: (*Solemnly*). For Pocahontas' sake,
The council shall their honor pledge to this.
    ROLFE: (*With equal solemnity*). As we do ours.
    POCAHONTAS: Send one you can trust
To Powhatan, and tell him you've received
From o'er the waters, in that great canoe,
Food, warriors, and arms. But name not *me*!
Oh, haste! (*A salute is heard from the cannon of the fort.*)
    ROLFE: The governor has landed. Worthy sir,
Go seek our countrymen. Let all be done
In strict obedience to this maiden's will.
    HUNT: (*To* POCAHONTAS). May heaven ever bless thee for this act!
(*Exit* HUNT.)
    POCAHONTAS: Farewell, young brave. Ere dawn I must again
Within my father's wigwam be.
    ROLFE: Return,
Without repose, that distance through the woods
On foot?
    POCAHONTAS: The forest maids can travel far
Untired.
    ROLFE: Thou wilt miss the way.
    POCAHONTAS: We see
Unfailing landmarks in the trees and stars;
Nor e'er forget a path we once have trod.
    ROLFE: But darkness will surround thee.

POCAHONTAS: The Good Spirit
Will see and guard me, then. Farewell. (*Another salute is fired.*)

HUNT *enters, showing in* SIR THOMAS DALE, *preceded by* RATLIFFE, VOLDAY, FRANCIS, *and followed by the other* COLONISTS *and a* GUARD *of honor.*)

HUNT: (*Pointing to* POCAHONTAS).
This is the princess who hath twice preserved
This colony from famine and from death. (*Day is seen to break through the windows of the fort.*)
DALE: Her plans we've followed, and her message now
We send to Powhatan. (*To* VOLDAY.) No moment waste,
But swiftly seek the king and strongly paint
Our reinforcing strength.
VOLDAY: (*Obsequiously*). Doubt not my zeal
Or aptness for the task. (*Apart.*) Fate seems to aid
And hasten my revenge. (*Bows and exits.*)
DALE: Princess, no arm shall 'gainst your tribes be raised.
You're welcome here.
POCAHONTAS: The red king's child will seek her father now;
Yet would she learn if Smith still lives.
DALE: He does.
And prays to bid thee, Master Rolfe, farewell. (RATLIFFE *goes up to* DALE *and talks with him, pointing to* POCAHONTAS, ROLFE, *and* HUNT.)
ROLFE: First let me tend thee, Princess, on thy path.
POCAHONTAS: No, no. Farewell!
And when thou seest my father,
The stranger he will love who saved his child.
ROLFE: Thy bidding I obey. But soon, I trust,
We'll meet again.
DALE: (*Advancing*). And thou, good Doctor Hunt,
Go, soothe Smith's dying pillow with thy prayers.
HUNT: An old man's blessing be with thee, sweet maid. (*Exit* ROLFE *and* HUNT.)
DALE: (*To* RATLIFFE). My friend, your counsel is most excellent.
POCAHONTAS: Strangers, farewell. (*Going.* RATLIFFE *intercepts her.*)
RATLIFFE: (*Rudely*). You pass not here, young girl.
POCAHONTAS: (*With dignity*).
I am a warrior's daughter, and am called

Virginia's princess. Stranger, stand aside.

Dale: All courtesy we'll show thee, lady, but
Thy father's peace and friendship we would gain
By this one act. (*He gives a signal, and each entrance is guarded.*)

POCAHONTAS: The child of Powhatan
Ye will not keep a prisoner?

DALE: But until
Her father signs a peace. (POCAHONTAS *starts, but instantly recollects
herself.*) You deem this strange?
Policy demands this step.

POCAHONTAS: No policy
Doth Pocahontas know, save justice. She
Hath succored ye, for she believed ye friends.
But if your arms should e'er be leveled 'gainst
Her race, mark well: her country's foes are hers!

RATLIFFE: Why should we trust her tale? We have no proof
The peril she announced was really near.

POCAHONTAS: Powhatan's daughter is no mockingbird.
Her voice sings but one strain, and that is truth.

DALE: Fear not.

POCAHONTAS: I am a warrior's child, and know
No fear.

RATLIFFE: And yet thine eye is moist. Thy hand,
Though clenched, doth tremble.

POCAHONTAS: The red woman's soul
Is strong, although her frame be weak.

DALE: A chair! (FRANCIS *brings down a chair.*)
Here rest thee, lady, while the plans I tell
Of England's king, thy father, in whose name
I speak.

POCAHONTAS: (*Waving back* FRANCIS).
"The sun's my father, and the earth
My mother: on *her* bosom I'll repose,
When I have need of rest."[9] If I *must* stay
Within your wigwam, solitude, at least,
A maiden and a princess may command.

DALE: Lady, thy haughty wish shall be obeyed.
(*To* RATLIFFE *and* FRANCIS.) Conduct her in. (*The doors of an inner*

---

[9]Author's note: speeches enclosed in quotation marks are taken from "recorded
examples of Indian eloquence."

room are thrown open.)

RATLIFFE: Hope no escape. The fort
Is closely guarded. (POCAHONTAS *looks at him with suppressed contempt and turns to* FRANCIS.)

POCAHONTAS: I will follow *thee.*

DALE: Thou hast a bold heart, lady.

POCAHONTAS: Though alone,
I'm not defenseless. The Great Spirit's eye
Sleeps never, and His ear is never closed.
(*Apart.*) Father and brother, ye shall find me true.
From these I'll hide my grief; but once alone,
I'll quench my fire in tears. (*Going.*)

DALE: (*To* RATLIFFE). Now to send news
To Powhatan touching the chance we've seized
To thwart his treachery. (*At that word,* POCAHONTAS *turns around hastily.*)

POCAHONTAS: In a daughter's ear,
Who dare to breathe that word against her sire?
To free his country from invader's tread,
He tries the arts his rugged life has taught.
Ye blame the red man, yet adopt his wiles.
Why do ye practice treachery, deceit,
Trampling on hospitable gratitude
By thus constraining me? Oh, shame! The stream
Of patriot love flows in *my father's* heart,
Though shadowed so by dark, enlacing woods,
The sun of mercy cannot always pierce
Their thick unwholesome gloom. No such excuse
Is *yours*; for from the current of your souls
The tomahawk of ages has hewn down
All that impeded the pure light of heaven! (*She is going in, while* DALE *and his party stand in mute surprise. The doors are opened upon her.* DALE *and his friends exit.*)

Scene Three

The forest near Jamestown. In the distance, the waters of the swamp are seen through the woods. Clumps of trees in the foreground at the foot of a declivity. Daylight. Enter HUNT *and* ROLFE.

ROLFE: Cruel mischance!

HUNT: Unfortunate, that ere we reached the bank,

The boat was on her way.

ROLFE: Ah! Much I fear
Some ill is plotting, and the message given
A deep-laid scheme.

HUNT: Here's Francis.

FRANCIS *enters hastily.*

FRANCIS: In the fort
You both are wanted. The young princess is
Detained a hostage till her father comes
To sign a peace.

ROLFE: Oh, shame and treachery!

FRANCIS: You, Doctor Hunt, she'd speak with. Lose no time. (*Exits.*)

ROLFE: Base policy! I'll go remonstrate with—

HUNT: (*Detaining him*).
Stay! Even my grey hairs would fail to gain
For me a hearing. How much less couldst thou!
Let old experience check thy youthful wrath.
Calm thee, my son. Come on. (*They are going.*)

VOLDAY *enters and intercepts them.*

VOLDAY: Stay yet awhile.
You pass not here, good youth.

ROLFE: Who'll stay me?

VOLDAY: (*Drawing his sword*). I!
Resist not. I have those at hand whose darts
Ne'er miss their aim.

ROLFE: *Thou* art the traitor, then! (HUNT *is restraining him.*)
Hold me not, worthy sir. Forbearance now
Were cowardice. (*Draws his sword.*)

VOLDAY: (*Sarcastically*). Chivalrous youth! Stand back.
The odds are desperate. (*He gives a signal, and a number of* INDIANS,
armed, start forth from behind the trees and mounds.) Behold!

ROLFE: Villain!
Detain me not. (*He endeavors to pass* VOLDAY, *who rushes upon him. They
fight.* HUNT *has drawn his sword, but has been almost instantly seized by two*
SAVAGES. VOLDAY *is about to slay* ROLFE, *when* POWHATAN
appears, followed by OPACHISCO *and other* SAVAGES.)

POWHATAN: Desist! Shed not the blood
Of thine own people. Powhatan demands

His scalp-lock. (*Approaches* ROLFE *with his tomahawk to execute his intention, when he sees the chain around Rolfe's neck.*)
Pale-face, whence that token? Speak!
No English hand hath wrought it.
  ROLFE: By thy child,
If thou art Powhatan, 'twas given.
  POWHATAN: Rise.
Thou and thy friend pass free.
(*The* INDIANS *release* HUNT.) That token is
A pledge of faith, which by a red man ne'er
Was broken or forgot. (VOLDAY *advances threateningly.*)
Molest them not,
On peril of thy life.
  ROLFE: Thanks, savage chief!
  POWHATAN: Return not to the fort, for there I plan
Destruction.
  HUNT: Know you not your hopes are foiled?
Each outlet guarded, food and arms supplied,
By troops in ships now landed?
  POWHATAN: (*Wonderstruck*). What?
  HUNT: (*Pointing to* VOLDAY).
I heard Sir Thomas Dale that villain charge
To bear this news to thee.
  ROLFE: He speaks the truth.
  VOLDAY: (*Sullenly*). He does. I own it.
  POWHATAN: Double traitor! Yes,
False to thy countrymen, and false to me.
  VOLDAY: I sought revenge—as thou dost, Powhatan.
  POWHATAN: The red man wars with strangers, enemies;
But thou wouldst slay thy brothers. Such excuse
Blackens still more thy deed. (VOLDAY *is about to speak.*)
Silence! They most
Who profit by a traitor's arts, despise,
E'en while they use him.
(*To* ROLFE.) Stranger, speak! My child
Has left her father's house. Where did she give
That pledge?
  ROLFE: Last night within the fort, where now
She is detained a hostage.
  POWHATAN: There? *My child?*
And but for thee might Powhatan ere this
Have given signal for the darts to slay

His daughter! (*To* VOLDAY.) Monster! Did'st thou seek to wade
Through Pocahontas' blood to vengeance?
(*To the* INDIANS.) Braves,
Away with him to death! (VOLDAY *darts through the trees.*)
Pursue him! Though
Your speed o'ertake him not, your arrows will. (*A party of* INDIANS
headed by OPACHISCO *rush in pursuit of* VOLDAY, *shouting the war
whoop.*)

RATLIFFE *enters with a white flag.*

RATLIFFE: Virginia's king, of thy child's freedom now
I come to treat.
POWHATAN: Inform the white man's chief:
How great soe'er the ransom, Powhatan
Will pay it, and here offers all the arms
In traffic bought, and seven pale-faced men
Captured near Orapaks, and prisoners now,
With corn five hundred measures, for his child!
RATLIFFE: I'll bear your message, chief. But say, are these
Your prisoners too? (*Points to* ROLFE *and* HUNT.)
POWHATAN: No, they are free. Depart,
Young brave. Seek and protect my child.
ROLFE: While life
Remains. Till in thy arms again she rests,
I'll guard her with a brother's jealous care. (*Exit* ROLFE *and* HUNT.)
RATLIFFE: With speed, great chief, I will return and bring
The governor's reply.
POWHATAN: Here Powhatan
Will wait for thee. (*Exit* RATLIFFE.)

OPACHISCO *enters, followed by the* INDIANS.

OPACHISCO: Great king, we fast pursued
The stranger! Thick our arrows round him flew.
In the dark waters of the swamp he plunged;
Nor could we trace him more.
POWHATAN: There let him drown,
Or starve, if he have reached the bank. 'Tis well. (OPACHISCO *retires up
the stage.*)
POWHATAN: (*Reflecting*). More ships, arms, food—more men! 'Tis
vain to strive.

Like swollen streams they gain upon the land,
And one day will possess it. Yes, I hear
My father's prophesying spirit speak
In the low moanings of the forest trees:
He bids me end a struggle useless now.
The red man's portion is. . . decay! Your voice,
Brave father, whispers! Powhatan obeys. (*Retires and leans against a tree,
surrounded by the* INDIANS, *some reposing, others listening for the envoy's
returning footsteps.*)

Scene Four

The interior of the fort.

Sir Thomas DALE *enters, attended by* ROLFE, HUNT, FRANCIS,
TODKILL, *and all the* COLONISTS, *meeting* RATLIFFE, *who enters
with white flag.*

DALE: Returned so soon?
ROLFE: I gave the king your answer,
That lasting peace alone could free his child.
He answered not. With hundreds in his train,
He followed, and now stands without the fort.
He asks a pledge that if he enters here,
He may depart unharmed.
DALE: Go, Master Rolfe,
And in our monarch's name a promise give
Of safety, and with deference due, conduct
Him here. (ROLFE *exits with* RATLIFFE *and a* GUARD *of honor.*)
(*To his* ATTENDANTS) From yon recess, bring forth the deeds
And gifts prepared to please this forest king. (*They bring forth a large table
on which are pens, ink and paper; a large deed closely written on parchment
and sealed with the royal arms of England; a scepter; a crown upon a cushion;
and a regal robe.*) 'Tis well.
(*A flourish of trumpets.*) Behold, the savage chieftain comes.

Enter ROLFE, RATLIFFE, *and the* GUARD, *escorting* POWHATAN,
OPACHISCO, *and other* INDIANS.

DALE: Virginia's king, we give thee greeting from
Thy father, England's monarch.
POWHATAN: The red man

Has come to seek his child.

DALE: She's safe and well.
She'll come anon. Our royal master sends
Across the seas by me his greeting.

POWHATAN: (*Looking around*). Where
Is he called Captain Smith?

DALE: An accident
Detains him in our ship; no surgeon's aid,
Though it may mitigate, can cure his wounds,
Unless he should return to England's shores.

POWHATAN: Then Powhatan is sorry. Smith is brave.
The red man honors a brave enemy.

DALE: A friend, I trust, as we all soon shall be.
We come in peace to settle in this land.

POWHATAN: And why? Across the waters, are there not
Broad plains where *you* may dwell? The Great Spirit
To his *red* children gave *these* hunting grounds.
There is not room for us and you. Ye will
Extinguish our council fires, destroy
Our stony chronicles, and trample down
The mounds 'neath which our sage's bodies rest.
The red men love their fathers' graves.

DALE: Nor will
Our nation reverence them less. We hope
In amity to dwell. Our monarch doth
Confirm thee in thy titles and thy state—
King of Virginia and its many tribes,
In proof whereof these robes, this scepter, and
This crown— (FRANCIS *and an* ATTENDANT *advance with the robe and scepter.* ROLFE *approaches with the crown.*)
Symbols of rank with English kings—
He sends to thee, and representing him,
I'll place it on thy brow. (ALL *present except* Sir Thomas DALE, *take off their hats.* DALE *takes the crown in his hands and approaches* POWHATAN.) Kneel, Powhatan!

POWHATAN: Forbear! Powhatan never bends his knee,
But standing, prays to Him Who, of all creatures,
Made *man*, alone, erect.[10] The crown doth give

---

[10]Author's note: Powhatan's refusal to kneel is minutely dwelt upon by the historians; but as no motive is assigned, I have given that which seemed most probable.

No rank to him who was a king before.
I take these gifts as proof of friendship from
The white man's chief. (*Takes the crown and gives it to* OPACHISCO. *The other gifts are placed in the hands of the* INDIANS.) Such wealth as Powhatan
Can give in gold or pearls or silver, and
Whatever else the red man's skill can make,
Bear to your king, my brother, back from me.[11]
Where is my child? (*Suspiciously.*)
    DALE: We'll send for her anon.
    POWHATAN: Let her come *now*. Virginia's chief will make
No treaty till he sees his child.
    DALE: Conduct
The princess hither, worthy Master Rolfe. (*Exit* ROLFE.)
The treaty now, great chief. (*Offers it.*)
    POWHATAN: (*Still resolved*). Powhatan waits
To see his daughter.
    DALE: Look, she comes!

ROLFE *leads* POCAHONTAS *from the inner room. She runs to her father.*

    POWHATAN: (*Together*). My child!
    POCAHONTAS: (*Together*). My father!
    POWHATAN: Yes, 'tis she unharmed, quite safe!
    POCAHONTAS: Does Pocahontas see her father once
Again! Alone, imprisoned, terror filled
Her heart. But all is well. He's here! Till now,
She never knew how much she loved her own,
Dear father.
    POWHATAN: (*Rapturously*). Powhatan's joy! His treasure!
(*Recollecting himself.*) Stand from me, child. Let not men see a brave
To woman turn. A tear had almost dimmed
The warrior's sight.
    HUNT: Then check it not. My friends
Will not revere thee less. The glistening tear
Of sweet affection in a parent's eye
Is jewel for an angel's diadem.
    POWHATAN: Why came my child among the pale-faces?

---

[11]Author's note: Pearls were found in great profusion in North Carolina and Virginia, and were an important article of barter.

POCAHONTAS: (*With one arm twined round her father, she lays her other hand upon his tomahawk, and looks appealingly in his face*).
To blunt the tomahawk.
(*Points to* HUNT.)   Much kindness has
This good man shown.
(*Turning to* ROLFE.)   This youthful brave, the friend
Of Smith, preserved thy daughter when she lay
Within the panther's spring.
POWHATAN: In deeds, not words,
Her father thanks him.   The young brave shall be
A son to Powhatan. (*Giving his hand.* ROLFE *bows respectfully over it.*)
DALE: Virginia's king,
Now wilt thou make the treaty?
POWHATAN: (*With firm dignity*).   Yes.
DALE: 'Tis here,
By England's monarch signed and sealed.   To you
It shall be given.
POWHATAN: Take this wampum belt,
The pledge of faith.   "Around the council fire
We'll smoke the calumet[12] of friendship, deep
Inter the tomahawk, and o'er it plant
The tree of peace, beneath whose spreading shade
Our children's children fondly shall entwine
Their arms together." (*Gives the belt and takes the treaty.*)
We are brothers now.
DALE, and all the COLONISTS: Long live King James, and long live Powhatan! (*Flourish of trumpets.*)
HUNT: (*Advancing*).   Now hear *me*.   If this peace ye would cement,
There is a way to make it last for aye.
This youthful pair, by providential hap
Together thrown, have read each other's hearts,
And found the same fond characters in each.
Let Powhatan his princess wed unto
Young Master Rolfe, and in that marriage, strife
Will die forever.
ROLFE: It were happiness
Too great for me to hope.
DALE: Without demur,
I speak my sovereign's approbation.   What

---

[12]Ceremonial pipe.

Does Virginia's king reply?
POWHATAN: The pale-face
Is brave and young. He saved my daughter's life.
But he will take my child away, unto
His wigwam o'er the waters.
(POCAHONTAS *clings fondly to* POWHATAN.) Powhatan
Is no weak woman. He's a warrior brave—
But Pocahontas is his dearest child.
He cannot spare her.
ROLFE: 'Tis my wish to build
My home beside Virginia's flowing streams.
POWHATAN: So be it then. The red man's king consents.
The birds, when *fledged*, go forth; they meet their mates,
And ne'er unto the parent nest return—
'Tis nature's law. My child shall speak her thought.
If Pocahontas loves the stranger, well.
If not, she shall not wed him. Powhatan
Will still keep faith with England.
DALE: Then what says
The princess?
ROLFE: (*Advancing to her*). Lady, speak!
POCAHONTAS: The red man's child
Will ne'er desert her father's autumn days.
ROLFE: E'en shouldst thou visit England, brief would be
Our stay. For all my race are not like these:
In iron clad, embrowned by foreign suns,
With voices striving against the billow's roar.
No, there are hundreds skilled in graceful wiles
To win a maiden's heart. Couldst thou with them
Compare my plain address, I fear thou wouldst
Repent thy choice.
POCAHONTAS: Such doubt wrongs Pocahontas.
Whene'er a forest maiden gives her heart,
Around her the Great Spirit casts a spell:
Before her eyes, the husband of her soul,
Even while absent, ever seems to stand,
And from her sight shuts out all other men.
HUNT: That faith is worthy of a holier creed. (*Retires and confers with*
POWHATAN *and* DALE.)
POCAHONTAS: 'Tis Pocahontas who has most to fear.
Unlike the fair-haired maids, she has not learned
Those small, strange characters of wondrous power (*Pointing to the treaty in*

Powhatan's hands.)
That speak without a voice. Thou'lt blush to show
The fair-faced dames an untaught bride.
    ROLFE: Had I
A soul so mean, I should deserve to blush
At my own baseness. I have little lore,
Save what my parents early made me con:
To use plain honesty in speech and act,
To share my purse with those who want it, still
To love my native land and fight for her
When needed, ne'er to yield, or triumph o'er
The fallen, to protect woman whene'er
Oppressed—and love her too. If thou canst prize
Such simple precepts and a faithful heart,
I give them, princess, with my hand. Oh, speak!
    POCAHONTAS: Powhatan's daughter will not hide her thought.
No harm can surely dwell in that which gives
Such happiness and joy. Stranger, thy wife
Will Pocahontas be. (*Timidly laying her hand in his.*)
    ROLFE: My life shall speak
My thanks. (*Kisses her hand.*)
    HUNT: (*Pointing to* POCAHONTAS).
To such a heart the Christian faith
Must penetrate and spread conviction there.
Virginia's king, and you who represent (*To* DALE.)
The majesty of England, go with me.
Within the humble chapel of this fort
Our church's rites shall make these lovers one:
The first of the two nations joined, as yet,
In wedlock's sacred bonds.
    DALE: This deed unites
In peace and love the old world and the new.
    POWHATAN: Young brave, I give thee here my daughter's hand.
Nor shalt thou take her dowerless. The king
Of Powhatan's twelve tribes can send his child
Well portioned to the stranger's wigwam. Thou
Wilt love, protect her when her father's eyes
Are closed, her kindred driven from the earth,
As soon they will be, beneath the crushing strides
Of thy vast nation. And when Powhatan,
Like a true brave, his death song calmly sings,
Amid his greatest feats of war, he'll proudly boast

His richest trophy was his daughter's love. (*Joins their hands.* ROLFE *and* POCAHONTAS *kneel.* POWHATAN *lays his hand upon* POCAHONTAS' *head. The other characters group around them. A flourish of trumpets as the curtain falls.*)

THIRD PERIOD, 1617

ACT III

Scene One

A street in London. On one side a tavern, with the sign "The Arquebus: Anas Todkill, Vintner." Enter VOLDAY, *miserably clad and weak from privation and fasting.*

VOLDAY: Is this to be my doom? Exhausted, faint,
To die of want and poverty? Abroad,
For months, alone I lived amid the woods
In suffering, till an artful tale obtained
My passage in a Spanish ship. Since then,
Each pang of wretchedness I've known! 'Tis strange
A will unscrupulous and stalwart arm
Combined, should lack employment. Curses shrink
That child of fortune, Smith! He ever was
My bane. He hath at last recovered from
His wounds, I hear, and is in London. Oh!
What pangs acute shoot through my heart!
(*Looking off.*) Who comes?

Enter Captain SMITH, *looking around him.*

SMITH: Sure I have missed the street, and yet he said—
(*Seeing* VOLDAY, *accosts him.*) Friend, canst thou guide me to—
VOLDAY: (*Apart*). Great heaven!
SMITH: (*Surprised*). What?
Changed as he is, 'tis sure the Switzer, Volday.
VOLDAY: You know me, Captain?
SMITH: Though four years have passed,
I recognize thy face.
VOLDAY: (*Bitterly*). I'm somewhat changed
From what I was in wild America;

For there I dared to brave thee, noble captain.
    SMITH: Tut, man! Those days are past. I had forgot
Thy mad rebellion. I no malice bear
To living soul, and least of all to old
Companions sunk into misfortune. Go, (*Forcing money into his hand, which*
VOLDAY *takes unwillingly.*)
Supply thy wants. Soldiers should share their purse. (*Retires, looking around him.*)
    VOLDAY: What, more humiliation! But that weak,
Tyrannous nature craves some sustenance,
I'd hurl his alms in anger back. (*Looks off.*) Who's here?
The comely Master Rolfe! What, do I meet
Each of my foes at once? Curses o'ertake
And cling to me, if I forgive them! (*Retires, observing them.*)

SMITH *advances to meet* ROLFE *as he enters.*

    SMITH: Rolfe!
    ROLFE: My honored friend, a thousand welcomes.
    SMITH: I
Have loitered here to meet you, for I missed
My way but now. How doth your gentle wife?
    ROLFE: Well, I would hope; and yet her slender form
Daily more fragile grows. A life of bliss
So radiant cannot last. Much I rejoice
At your return.
    SMITH: I come to speed you on
Your voyage tomorrow to Virginia's shores.
    ROLFE: Come, pledge our welcome meeting here. This house
Affords good wine. Thou know'st the owner well:
An honest vintner—our companion once. (*They go into the tavern.*)
    VOLDAY: (*Advancing*). Returning to Virginia—wealthy—safe!
I yet may mar your projects. (*Exits into tavern.*)

Scene Two

Interior of Arquebus, denoting wealth and comfort. A casement at the back, through which passers-by are seen before they enter at the door. A long settle[13] at the back near the door. A cabinet between the door and window.

---

[13]Wooden bench with a back and armrests.

On one side of the stage is a table with wine cups and flagons, at which four GUESTS *are seated carousing. On the other are a table and two chairs.* TODKILL *and two* DRAWERS *are attending upon the guests.*

TODKILL: (*Bustling about*). You say truly, neighbor Varney; it was desperate cold that night. I remember it well.

SMITH *and* ROLFE *enter.* (TODKILL *bows.*)

SMITH: Ah! Well met,
Master Todkill. (*Offers his hand.*)
TODKILL: (*Taking it with deference*). Captain, your notice honors me.
ROLFE: Well, old friend, how fare you?
TODKILL: Never better, master, never better. I'm more expert at chalking down reckonings than cutting down trees, can draw a cup of wine more easily than a sword, and like loading my "Arquebus" here better than trying to shoot a live stag for my dinner. You take, Master Rolfe?
ROLFE: (*Smiling*). I do.
SMITH: How's this? No hostess yet?
TODKILL: In good time, worthy captain. Mistress Alice waits with all duty upon Lady Rolfe, and only delays our marriage till her departure.
SMITH: Much joy
To you, old friend.
TODKILL: I thank you, Captain.
(*During the previous dialogue,* VOLDAY *has entered. The* DRAWER *expostulates with him. He offers money, and after some hesitation, the man takes the coin, brings* VOLDAY *a large cup of wine, points out the settle.* VOLDAY *sits and drinks, observing* SMITH *and* ROLFE.)
ROLFE: Good Anas, here, a flagon
Of your best wine.
TODKILL: Directly, Master Rolfe. (*He brings a salver with flagon and cups, and places it on the vacant table.* ROLFE *and* SMITH *seat themselves.*)
The king, I say it with all reverence, drinks no better. What else, good gentlemen?
ROLFE: Naught else, my friend. (TODKILL *sees* VOLDAY *and appears to reprove the* DRAWER *for having admitted him, then goes busily among the other* GUESTS, *still noticing* VOLDAY. ROLFE *fills glasses.*)
The king
And royal Charles.
SMITH: No news from Raleigh yet?
ROLFE: A vessel from Guiana brought today
Despatches to the king. Prince Henry's death

Lost Raleigh a firm friend, whom he will need
When he returns, I fear.
  SMITH: Not if he thrives.
Success is always faultless—most of all,
In royal eyes. Here's Raleigh's health.
  ROLFE: With all
My heart. (*They drink.*)
  SMITH: The Lady Pocahontas.
  ROLFE: Thanks. (*They drink again.*)
Shall we ne'er see thee wedded, Captain?
  SMITH: No.
Renown and arms are still my only love.
When wrecked on Gallia's coast, a woman nursed
And succored me. In America,
The Lady Pocahontas twice preserved
My life at peril of her own. None more
Can honor woman than the man who thus
In every clime finds her his guardian angel.
(TODKILL *advances to meet* NEWTON *who enters the tavern.*)
  TODKILL: Welcome, neighbor. You are late.
  NEWTON: Yes, I had great difficulty in making my way through the
streets. Everyone is out of doors listening to the news.
  TODKILL: What news? (*The* GROUP *at the table listens eagerly.*)
  NEWTON: Very bad, Master Todkill. Sir Walter Raleigh's expedition
has failed, his brave son has been killed, and Sir Walter is now on his way
to answer for his conduct to the king.
  ROLFE: (*Rising*). My friend, I pray, explain more fully. Speak!
Hast thou further tidings? (SMITH *rises also.*)
  NEWTON: Nay, master. I know no more than this, which
I gathered from the gossip round me. (*Bows and goes up to table.*
TODKILL *gives him a vacant chair and converses with him and the other*
GUESTS. *The* DRAWER *fills their cups. They drink.*)
  SMITH: Ah, poor Raleigh!
  ROLFE: I dread the worst; for Spain's ambassador,
All potent now with James, will work his fall.
My father honored Raleigh, and his fame
First roused adventure in my boyish heart.
  SMITH: Be cautious in your words. King James, I know,
With eye suspicious looks on *you.*
  ROLFE: The king?
Absurd! What grounds—
  SMITH: (*They take their hats*). Are you not wedded to

Virginia's princess? Heir to crown and lands
Of Powhatan?

ROLFE: (*Smiling*). James has no cause for fear.

SMITH: Yet be more wary in thy praise of Raleigh.

ROLFE: Foolhardy is that man, 'tis true, who thrusts
Unasked opinion in the ears of those
Who wish him ill; but 'tis a coward's heart
That praises not his friend as cordially
In peril as in triumph.

SMITH: Rolfe! Thy hand!
Now farewell for awhile. (*They approach the door together.*)
But at thy house
We meet again at noon. (ROLFE *and* SMITH *exit.* SMITH *is seen to pass the casement.* VOLDAY *is concealed by the open door as* TODKILL *shows them out.* VOLDAY *advances.*)

VOLDAY: Most fortunate. I have overheard enough.
After long fasting, wine hath fevered me.
No matter, if it gives me strength to work
My plot. Now, quick—here, host, more wine.

TODKILL: (*Advancing*). What did you call for?

VOLDAY: More wine!
Pen, ink, and paper. Never stand, man! Here,
I've that will pay the reckoning. (*Gives money.*)

TODKILL: You shall have it, although your money and your dress
don't suit each other, friend.

VOLDAY: Make haste! (*The* DRAWER *brings wine.* TODKILL *brings writing implements from the cabinet.* VOLDAY *sits at the table Rolfe has quitted, and drinks frequently.*)

TODKILL: I'm coming, friend. There's a scrivener lives next door.
Shall I send for him?

VOLDAY: A scrivener? No. (*Writes during* TODKILL'*s speech.*)

TODKILL: No offense, I hope; but one don't look for such
accomplishments in your condition. (*Looking at him.*) You are a ready
scribe, and write as fair a hand as the young master who just now left us.
(VOLDAY *looks up.*) Well, you need not stare. You know him, surely; for
you watched him narrowly enough.

VOLDAY: (*Apart*). The meddling fool! Did he
Observe me? (*Finishes and folds the letter. Pours out the last drop from the flagon.*)

TODKILL: Shall I send the letter?

VOLDAY: No! (*Rises and sinks back.*)

TODKILL: What's the matter?

VOLDAY: Nothing. (*Drains the cup.*)
Give me more wine.
TODKILL: My conscience won't let me. You look wild enough already. A hearty meal you shall have, and welcome—at my expense, too—but no more wine.
VOLDAY: (*Seizing him*). Thou babbler! Give me wine!
(*Releases him from exhaustion.*)
TODKILL: (*Terrified*). Stay! Stay! I'm a peaceable man. I'll get it you. (*Going slowly.*) I'll wager my new jerkin against his rags, it is that rascal Volday.
VOLDAY: The fool speaks truth.
The fire is in my pulse and in my brain.
Now, let me read this o'er.
(*Reads half aloud.*) "Raleigh's friend—
Rolfe—seeks Virginia's crown—conspires against
The throne—Raleigh's confederate"—so— (*Continues reading to himself.*)
TODKILL: (*Apart*). That letter bodes no good, I'll swear. I know him, though he don't remember me—the sour-looking rogue. I'll follow him and see where he goes to. And if I can spoil any villainy he's after, I'll do it as sure as my name's Anas Todkill. (*Gives directions to the* DRAWER, *who brings him his hat.*)
VOLDAY; (*Closing the letter*).
'Twill do. This nameless missive to the king
Shall go. Rolfe's ruin will involve his friend.
Together must they fall. My brain's on fire!
My limbs scarce bear me onward, and my heart
Irregularly leaps as hard as if
'Twould burst its bonds. Let me but be revenged!
No matter *then* what dunghill is my grave.[14] (*Totters out and is seen to pass the window, followed cautiously by* TODKILL.)

Scene Three

An apartment in Master ROLFE*'s house in London.* MAUD *enters, showing in* HUNT *and* SMITH.

MAUD: So please you, wait. I'll seek my mistress, sirs. (*Exit* MAUD.)
HUNT: (*To* SMITH).

---

[14]Author's note: Volday's fate is summed up in history in these words: "he perished miserably."

Poor, fading flower, each day more near her end,
Each day more fit for heaven! (MAUD *enters*.)
    MAUD: My lady's here. (*Exit* MAUD *and enter* POCAHONTAS.)
    POCAHONTAS: My aged friend and monitor!
    HUNT: How fares
My gentle lady?
    POCAHONTAS: E'en more feeble still
Than yesterday.
    HUNT: And yet you look not so.
    POCAHONTAS: So says my husband, and delusive hope
Still cherishes.
    HUNT: Thy dear friend Smith now waits
To greet thee. Look. (SMITH *advances*.)
    SMITH: Well met, dear lady! (*She looks at him in silence, then turns
from him and hides her face.*) What!
Does my presence grieve thee?
    POCAHONTAS: (*Recovering herself, gives him her hand*). No, I joy
To see thee, but a host of memories speak
Of home and father, in thy well-known voice.
'Tis o'er. My husband will rejoice to see—
    SMITH: We left
Each other, lady, not an hour since.
He tells me that tomorrow you return.
You like not of Britain then?
    POCAHONTAS: Not like it! Yes!
For beautiful is England, with her groves,
Her castles, palaces, and abbeys old.
Like fairy homes her vales and streams appear.
Each landscape glows with history and wears
The sober perfectness of ripened age.
No classic lore adorns my native land;
But rich, redundant nature reigns alone.
Great rivers, giant lakes in silence sleep,
And rushing torrents by their solemn voice
Call man to praise his Maker. Insects steal
The summer's lightning there, and tiny birds
Bring rainbow beauty from the spirit land.
There autumn forests on their leaves reflect
The gorgeous colors of the setting sun,
Whose throne, scarce vacant, night usurps, nor waits
Strange twilight's mournful smile. My father's grave
Will be ere long 'mid those familiar haunts.

It is my home! It is my native land!

Enter TODKILL *hastily, not seeing* POCAHONTAS.

TODKILL: Oh, Captain! Such dreadful news! Master Rolfe has just
been arrested in the street yonder! I saw a crowd and asked what was the
matter. The constables told me they'd an order from the Secretary of State
to take him prisoner to the Tower, on a charge of treason.
POCAHONTAS: The Tower! Treason? Did my husband speak?
TODKILL: (*Confused on seeing* POCAHONTAS). No, madam. That
is, he had no time; but he beckoned to me, and said one
word—"Pocahontas," and threw this to me. (*Takes out the chain given by*
Pocahontas to Rolfe.) I made no answer, for I couldn't speak; but I looked,
as much as to say, "I understand." And then the dust flew in my eyes, I
suppose; for I couldn't see any more. (*Gives her the chain.*)
SMITH: Arrested! On what grounds?
TODKILL: Conspiracy with Sir Walter Raleigh to establish an
independent kingdom in Virginia. That was all I could learn amidst the
confusion.
POCAHONTAS: (*Gazing on the chain*). This chain he's worn
Since first I gave it him. It calls me now
To save him. Counsel me what first to do. (*Placing the chain around her*
neck, and pressing it to her lips.)
SMITH: Go, seek the king, while I trace out the source
Whence flows this accusation, or they soon
May plot thy peril too.
POCAHONTAS: Mine! (*With sudden thought.*) Ah, my child!
(*To Doctor* HUNT.) Good friend, to thee I give my boy. Depart,
For my sake, to Sir Lewis Stukely; he
Loves well my husband, and will guard my child.
At court he's in high favor. Wilt thou go?
HUNT: I will, dear lady, and will send to thee
News of his safety.
POCAHONTAS: Thanks. Wilt thou, good friend,
(*To* TODKILL.) Bid Alice deck him for his journey? Go! (TODKILL *goes*
off.)
I dare not clasp him to my heart once more.
'Twould shake my purpose; for I feel, I know,
I never shall behold my boy again!
My blessed child! My only one!
HUNT: Yet hope!
The clouds will break. The sun will shine again,

For Providence is with thee.

POCAHONTAS: Best of friends!
Bear to my boy my blessing and farewell.
Now go! (*Exit* HUNT. TODKILL *returns.*) 'Tis done!

SMITH: Rebecca! Sure thy frame
Will ill support this trial.

POCAHONTAS: Heaven implants
In woman strength for all her duties. Now
The mother's task is o'er; the wife alone
Remains. I go to seek the king. Again
At Gravesend I will see thee—or in prison. (*Exit* POCAHONTAS.)

TODKILL: (*Advancing to meet* SMITH). I tell you, Captain, I see
through the whole. Anas Todkill is no fool, I promise you. I traced
Volday to the palace, which is, you know, hard by my house. Volday
spoke to a lackey, who spurned him; then he offered money, and the man
listened. I saw Volday give the coin and the letter. I saw the lackey present
the letter to a nobleman who was dismounting from his horse. He read the
paper, muttered, "It is as I suspected," and beckoned to one of the king's
messengers who was standing near. They went into the palace together. I
dared not approach any nearer. But in a few minutes, out came the
messenger and several constables. As luck would have it, neighbor Newton
passed me, and I bade him follow Volday, while I ran hither to warn Master
Rolfe: when, as I came, I found the constables here before. Who would
believe so much mischief could be done in a quarter of an hour?

SMITH: To Volday lead me first, and on my way
I'll take two trusty friends in company
As witnesses. How shall we thank thy zeal?

TODKILL: Don't name it. It pleases me more to serve Master Rolfe
than if the king and the whole court had sat down to supper in the best
room of the Arquebus.

SMITH: I do believe it, worthy friend. Lead on. (*Exit* SMITH *and*
TODKILL.)

Scene Four

Garden of the Palace at Whitehall.   Enter CHARLES *and* ANNE *in
conversation.*

CHARLES: Madam, I doubt these cruel whispers against
The friends of Raleigh will involve them all
In his approaching ruin.

ANNE: Much I fear

'Tis true.

CHARLES: Oh, could my influence protect
The innocent, I'd use it freely! (*Enter* PAGE.) Well?

PAGE: May it please your royal highness, Lady Rolfe
Most earnestly entreats an audience.

CHARLES: (*Surprised*). What?
Lady Rebecca? Go, conduct her here. (*Exit* PAGE.)

ANNE: It is the first sad pleader in the cause
Of which thou spok'st but now, my son. But see,
The mourner comes.

PAGE *shows in* POCAHONTAS.

POCAHONTAS: Most gracious, gentle Queen,
And you, kind Prince, oh, grant a wife's sad prayer!
Your royal father will not hear my suit.
To you I come for mercy.

CHARLES: Lady, speak,
But calm your grief! What would you ask?

POCAHONTAS: My life!
For in my husband's life is mine involved.
Oh, deign to sue unto the king for him.
His safety—nay, his life's unjustly periled,
For he hath done no wrong.

CHARLES: Be of good cheer.
Although thy husband is arrested, yet
'Tis on suspicion only.

POCAHONTAS: A strong foe!
'Tis like that reptile of our wilds, whose sting
Is fatal and whose rattle shrill, the knell
Of him who hears. But 'tis *more* merciless;
Suspicion gives no warning ere it stings.

ANNE: (*Advancing to her*). Hope for the best, dear lady.

POCAHONTAS: Hope alone
Cannot obtain the boon I seek. Oh, then,
Kind lady, hearken to my prayer! Mercy,
The brightest gem in royal crowns, will gild
Thy brow with greater lustre than the hues
Of loveliness and splendor. Plead for me.

ANNE: My husband's will I scarcely hope to change;
Yet his displeasure would I risk for thee.
I'll seek him, but I dare not promise aught.

My heart's best wish, dear stranger, goes with thee
Unto my husband's throne. (*Exit* ANNE.)
    CHARLES: Rebecca, yet
Droop not. A trial will exonerate
Thy husband.
    POCAHONTAS: Not if Raleigh be condemned.
Sweet Prince, since death hath claimed thy brother dear,
Thou wilt be king. Then think (for who can read
The future): clouds may dim thy reign, and woes
Arise, such as crowned heads but rarely know.
Should troubles swarm, and death close up thy path,
The thought that thou hast e'er the wretched soothed,
Redressed a wrong, protected virtue—cheered,
Sustained the weak—will more avail thee *then*
Than all the thousands who thy crowning hail
With, "Long live Charles the First!"
    CHARLES: Cease, lady, cease!
Thy words prophetic seem, and touch my soul.
Should woes like these assail my dying hour,
Thy pleading voice will echo in my ear,
And bid my conscience answer the appeal.
Farewell. Thou hast my royal word. I'll seek
The king. If just entreaty can avail,
Enforced with strongest arguments of truth,
And each appeal that filial love can make,
Thy husband shall be free. Thou faintest!
    POCAHONTAS: (*He supports her*). Yes!
The joy—the hope—my grateful heart o'ercharged!
A wife, a mother, and a *stranger's* thanks
Call blessings on thy head!
    CHARLES: Let me lead thee
First to thy friends, then seek my father. Come,
Look cheerily! This way. We'll save him yet. (*Leads her out.*)

Scene Five

MASTER ROLFE's *house at Gravesend. The back of the stage is nearly all occupied by a large casement, which being opened, discovers a view of the banks of the Thames at Gravesend, with the "George" lying at anchor. Sunset. Near the windows a large antique chair with cushions. Enter* TODKILL.

TODKILL: I begin to find out what a clever fellow I am. Opportunity is everything. I took the captain and his friends to that villain's den, and then came down here to meet Captain Smith on his return. Odso, I should like to thrash Volday myself!

Enter ALICE.

ALICE: Ah, Master Anas!

TODKILL: What, Mistress Alice, is that you?

ALICE: What were you thinking of when I came in, clenching your fists and looking so valiant?

TODKILL: Valiant! I believe I am valiant, Mistress Todkill that is to be.

ALICE: How came you here on such a busy day? Who will take care of the Arquebus?

TODKILL: (*Pompously*). The Arquebus must take care of itself. I have had important business. I've been rescuing the innocent and exposing the guilty.

ALICE: You! Mercy on the man!

TODKILL: At least, I've helped to do it, which is the main thing.

ALICE: What do you mean?

TODKILL: I've been assisting Captain Smith to save Master Rolfe.

ALICE: I rejoice to hear it. No man is better able to save a friend than Captain Smith. Such a brave—

TODKILL: Brave! Truly he is. Why, years ago he was chosen out of a whole army to fight the Turkish champion.

ALICE: Was he indeed?

TODKILL: Yes. Master Rolfe told me. The Captain not only fought *one* but *three*, and killed them all! And ever since, he carries their heads on his shield. I've seen them.

ALICE: (*Shuddering*). Oh! How dreadful!

TODKILL: Foolish woman! Not the heathen Saracens themselves. Don't you understand? The heads are his arms, and he'll hand them down to posterity.[15] He is a brave man, and so is Master Rolfe, and so am I!

ALICE: What, Master Anas! You, brave?

TODKILL: Yes, you should have seen me in America. Nobody would believe how valiant I was there, among the wolves and the bears and the panthers.

---

[15]Author's note: The coat of arms of Captain Smith was confirmed by Garter King at Arms in London: three Turks' heads, on a shield.

ALICE: Heaven's mercy! And had you the courage to fight those terrible creatures?

TODKILL: Courage! Why, Alice, I couldn't tell you how many I killed.

ALICE: What dangers there are abroad!

TODKILL: And at home too, of another sort. Look at this villainy toward Master Rolfe. Alice, have they been here to search?

ALICE: Yes, and placed huge seals on all the doors and presses. They ransacked every drawer and paper they could find, and cross-questioned me—

TODKILL: Indeed? It's well I was not here.

ALICE: Then they went away muttering that their search had been unsatisfactory.

TODKILL: To them, which means very satisfactory to us. They found nothing. Has Lady Rebecca returned from the palace yet?

ALICE: No, not yet, poor lady. I know not what I shall do when she is gone.

TODKILL: (*Pompously*). You will then be Mistress Todkill, hostess of the Arquebus, and will have enough to do in looking after the guests and attending to your husband.

ALICE: (*Looking off*). Hush! Here comes my lady.

TODKILL: Then I'll go down to the river's bank and wait for news from London.

ALICE: Bless thee, thou hast a kind heart, Anas.

TODKILL: To be sure, I have. That's why I'm going away now. I've no consolation to offer the poor lady, and I'll not stay to stare at a sorrow I can't relieve. Goodbye, Alice. (*Exit* TODKILL.)

ALICE: She comes. Alas! How slow she moves!
Sorrow has shattered her enfeebled frame. (*Runs to meet her.*)

POCAHONTAS *is led in by* ALICE *and* MAUD.

POCAHONTAS: No news from Captain Smith? (MAUD *brings down the chair, into which they place her.*)

ALICE: No, madam, none.

POCAHONTAS: Nor of my child?

ALICE: Not yet.

POCAHONTAS: I gasp! More air!
Throw wide the casement! Let me see the sun. (MAUD *throws open the window, while* ALICE *adjusts the cushions and supports the head of* POCAHONTAS.)
Its sinking beams will cheer my dying hour,

And even now in splendor of noonday
It gilds my native land. Hark! 'Tis the tramp
Of horses' feet. Run, girl, and see! (*Exit* MAUD.) My heart,
Hold yet awhile. (MAUD *re-enters with a letter.*) Now speak.
    MAUD: From Doctor Hunt,
This letter, madam. (*Gives it.*)
    POCAHONTAS: (*Opening it eagerly and attempting to read*).
Ah, my sight is failing!
I cannot read it. Alice—(*Gives it to her and sinks back, exhausted.*)
    ALICE: (*Reads*). "Dear lady,
Sir Lewis bids me say, no harm shall reach
Thy boy beneath his roof, where now we rest
In safety."
    POCAHONTAS: (*Having listened eagerly*). Heaven, accept my thanks!
My son,
Thou'lt not forget thy mother's fond caress!
Father and brother: are ye living yet?
There rides the ship that was to bear me home.
My journey *home* will be more quickly made.
I faint with weariness! (*She relapses into a slumber, her attendants watching her.*)

In the performance of this drama, the stage thus illustrates the Vision of Pocahontas:
A strain of invisible music is heard, and thin clouds obscure the view from the casement. The clouds gradually disperse and discover the open sea, across which the "George" is seen to sail. This view fades and gives place to the mouth of the James River with its forest, its rude fort, and wigwams. On the bank stands Powhatan, awaiting his daughter's arrival in the ship, which is seen approaching the shore. Clouds again obscure the scene, and through them a figure of Time passes, beckoning Peace, who follows. The clouds partially disperse, and disclose in the distance the form of Washington. The Genius of Columbia stands near him. Time hovers near, and Peace encircles with her arms the Lion and the Eagle. A mist then conceals the allegorical group, and again dispersing, discovers the view of Gravesend, at sunset, with the "George" at anchor, as it appeared previous to the vision. The music dies away.

    POCAHONTAS: (*Awakes suddenly and exclaims, after gazing round her*).
No, 'tis no dream! (*As if endowed with temporary strength, she starts up, clasping her hands in thankfulness.*)
Souls of the prophet-fathers of my race,
Light from the land of spirits have ye sent

To paint the future on my mental sight.
Like the great river of far western wilds,
Improvement's course, *unebbing*, shall flow on.
From that beloved soil where I drew breath
Shall noble chiefs arise. But one o'er all,
By heaven named to set a nation free,
I hear the universal world declare,
In shouts whose echo centuries prolong,
"The Father of his Country!" O'er the path
Of ages, I behold Time leading Peace.
By ties of love and language bound, I see
The island mother and her giant child
Their arms extend across the narrowing seas,
The grasp of lasting friendship to exchange! (*As the prophetic enthusiasm dies away,* POCAHONTAS *sinks exhausted in the arms of her wondering attendants.*)[16]

SMITH *enters hastily.*

SMITH: Lady, hope on! Led by an humble friend,
I sought the dying Switzer. By revenge
And famine tortured, nature found relief
In madness. Volday's ravings soon revealed
His motives and his slanders. Witnesses
With me to royal Charles have borne the news,
Which long ere this is laid before the king. (POCAHONTAS *falls on her knees.*)
I stayed not to hear more, but hastened on
To bring thee hope. (*The women raise* POCAHONTAS *and place her in the chair.*)
    POCAHONTAS: Oh, take my fervent thanks!
The thanks of one whose name and race will die
Together!
    SMITH: No! Thy country's sons will task
The sculptor's and the limner's art to pay
Hereafter homage to thy memory.

---

[16]Author's note: The belief in prophetic inspiration at the hour of death was, and is, general among the American red men; and although Pocahontas died a Christian, the new faith could not fail to be tinged by the hues of early association. The embodiment of her prophetic vision by allegorical scenes and figures, was a necessity consequent upon the acting of the drama.

In Britain, too, whole ages hence, the tale
Of Pocahontas' noble life and death
Will love and admiration claim from all.
Thy name will live forever!
POCAHONTAS: (*Who has exhibited all the restlessness of approaching dissolution, now exclaims*). Listen! Hark! (*A murmur heard without.*)
ALICE: A murmur in the hall, and rapid steps.
ROLFE: (*Speaks without*). Where is she? Speak!
POCAHONTAS: (*Starting up and tottering forward*).
It is my husband's voice!
ROLFE: (*Rushing in, exclaiming*). My wife! (POCAHONTAS *falls in his arms.*)
POCAHONTAS: He's safe! He's here!
ROLFE: Dearest! See,
Restored to thee! Look up!
SMITH: Acquitted? Free?
ROLFE: My innocence confirmed, Prince Charles himself
Brought me my prompt acquittal from the king.
But say, dearest, why sink you thus? I'm safe. (POCAHONTAS *raises her head and gazes at him.*)
Great heaven! How changed thou art!
POCAHONTAS: Our child will be
Thy stay in after years. My husband! I—
Must leave thee.
ROLFE: Say not so! My wife! My love!
POCAHONTAS: I warned thee of this parting months ago.
Our peaceful lives rob death of half its sting. (*Extends her hand which* SMITH *presses reverentially to his lips. She then flings her arms around* ROLFE, *exclaiming.*) Bless thee! (*Sinking back in the* WOMEN's *arms.*)
ROLFE: (*In anguish falling on his knees*). Live, Pocahontas! Live!
POCAHONTAS: (*With a faint smile of joy*). That name!
My own! The first by which thou knew'st me, love!
'Tis music to my soul. (*Her trembling hands vainly attempt to lift the little chain from her neck. Her* WOMEN *raise it for her, and* POCAHONTAS, *with fading sight and uncertain action, at length casts it around* ROLFE's *neck.*) I lose thee now.
My eyes behold Virginia's grassy turf.
I hear my father. Husband, fare thee well.
We part, but we shall meet—above! (*Her right hand, which has been momentarily pointed upwards, falls, and she dies in the arms of her* WOMEN. ROLFE *still remains upon his knee, clasping her hand and gazing upon her in utter despair.* SMITH *bends over him in silence.*)

Adams. L. B.
  See Swanwick, Catherine.
Addison, Julia de Wolf Gibbs, b. 1866.
  Blighted Buds. A Farce in One Act, 1896. Pub. Boston: W. Baker (Baker's Plays).
Additon, (Mrs. J. H.).
  The Operetta of Carlotta. In Five Acts, 1870. Music by James Wright. Pub. Rockland, ME: 1870.
Alcott, Louisa May, 1832-1888.
  Comic Tragedies (By "Meg" and "Jo"), 1893. With Anna Bronson Alcott Pratt. Pub. Boston: Roberts Brothers. Includes: *Norma, or, The Witch's Curse*; *The Captive of Castile, or the Moorish Maiden's Vow*; *The Greek Slave*; *Ion*; *Bianca, An Operatic Tragedy*; *The Unlov'd Wife, or, Woman's Faith*.
Alden, Ruth.
  The Sniggles Family. A Humorous Entertainment in One Act, 1892. Pub. Philadelphia: Penn Publishing.
  Easy Entertainments for Young People, 1920. Pub. Philadelphia: Penn Publishing.
Aldrich, Mildred, 1853-1928.
  Nance Oldfield, 1894. Adap. of C. Reade. Pub. Boston: W. Baker (Baker's Edition of Plays).
Allen, Lucy Grace, b. 1872.
  Debutantes in the Culinary Art; or, A Frolic in the Cooking Class. Musical Comedietta for Young Ladies, 1899. Music by R. Thiele. Pub. NY: Roxbury; Chicago: Dramatic Publishing.
Amory, Esmerie.
  The Epistolary Flirt, c. 1896. In *Four Exposures* (Chicago: Way and Williams, 1896).
Anon. with indications of female authorship:
  Dramatic Pieces Calculated to Exemplify the Mode of Conduct which Will Render Young Ladies Both Amiable and Happy when their School Education is Completed, 1791. By P.I. Pub. New Haven: A. Morse.
  The Little Country Visitor. A Drama in Two Parts, 1798? Pub. Boston: W. Spotswood.
  The Little Trifler. A Drama in Three Parts, 1798. Pub. Boston: W. Spotswood.
  Americana; or, A New Tale of the Genii, being an Allegorical Mask in Five Acts, 1802. Pub. Baltimore: W. Pechin.

Sheperdess of the Alps. A Play in Four Acts, 1815. By a citizen of New York. Pub. NY: T. Low.

Catharine Brown, the Converted Cherokee. A Missionary Drama Founded on Fact, 1819. By a Lady. Pub. New Haven.

May Day, or, The Celebration of the Return of Spring. Being a Play for the Amusement of Young Girls on the First Day of May, 1819.

Mary of Scotland, or, The Heir of Avenel. A drama in three acts founded on the popular novel of The Abbot (by Scott) and originally performed at the theatre in New York, with universal applause, 1821. Pub. NY: H. Megarey.

Evenings in New England. Intended for Juvenile Amusement and Instruction, 1824. Pub. Boston: Cummings Milliard.

Morning Visitors, or, A Trip to Quebec, 1830?

My Husband's Mirror, 1857(?) Pub. Boston: Spencer (Spencer's Boston Theatre, no. 69).

The Maid of Florence; or, A Woman's Vengeance. A Tragedy, n.d. Charleston.

Armstrong, L. M. C.

Gertrude Mason, M. D.; or, The Lady Doctor. A Farce in One Act for Female Characters Only, 1898. Pub. NY: Dick and Fitzgerald.

Augusta, Clara.

See Jones, Clara Augusta.

Ayer, Harriet Hubbard, 1849-1903.

The Widow. A Comedy in Three Acts, c. 1877. Adap. of *La Veuve* by Meilhac and Halévy. Pub. NY: DeWitt (DeWitt's Acting Plays, no. 213).

Bacon, Delia Salter, 1811-1859.

The Bride of Fort Edward. Founded on an Incident of the Revolution, 1839. Pub. New York: S. Colman.

Baker, Delphine Paris. (Pseud.: Delphine).

Solon; or, The Rebellion of '61. A Domestic and Political Tragedy, 1862. Pub. Chicago, S. Rounds.

Baker, Irene.

A Day in the Vineyard, n.d. With Alexander Drummond. Reprint pub. Kennikat Press, 1972.

Baker, Rachel E.

See Gale, Rachel E. Baker.

Bancroft, Frances Marsh.

See Paul, Anne Marie.

Bannan, Martha Ridgway.

The Fisher Maiden, 1899. "A vaudeville written for the Court at Weimar." Pub. Philadelphia: J. Yorston.

The Lover's Caprice. A Pastoral Play in Verse, 1899. Adap. of Goethe's *Die Fischerlein*. Pub. with above.

Barnes, Charlotte Mary Sanford, 1818-1863.

The Last Days of Pompeii, 1835. Adap. of Bulwer-Lytton. Perf. New Orleans: American Th., May 7, 1835.

La Fitte; or, The Pirate of the Gulf, 1837. Perf. New Orleans: American Th., April 15, 1837.

Octavia Bragaldi; or, The Confession, 1837. Perf. NY: National Th., Nov. 8, 1837. Pub. in *Plays, Prose and Poetry* (Philadelphia, 1848). Pub. in *Plays, Prose and Poetry*.

The Forest Princess; or, Two Centuries Ago, 1844. First perf. in Liverpool. American premiere Philadelphia: Arch Th., April 16, 1848. Pub. In *Plays, Prose and Poetry*, 1848.

Plays, Prose and Poetry, 1848. Pub. Philadelphia: E. H. Butler. Includes: *Octavia Bragaldi*; *The Forest Princess*.

A Night of Expectations, 1848. Adap. of popular French novel. Perf. Philadelphia: Arch Th., April 9, 1850.

The Captive, 1850. Perf. Philadelphia: Arch Th., March 8, 1850.

Charlotte Corday, 1851. Adap. of historical material. Perf. Philadelphia: Arch Th., March 18, 1851.

Barstow, Ellen M.

The Mission of the Fairies, as Exhibited by the First Universalist Sunday School, 1869. Pub. Portland: S. Berry, 1869 and 1871.

Bascom, Ada Lee.

The Bowery Girl, 1896.

The Queen of Spades, 18-?.

Bateman, Sidney Frances Cowell, 1823-1881.

The Mother's Trust; or California in 1849, 1854. Perf. San Francisco: Metropolitan Th., June, 1854.

Self. An Original Comedy, 1856. Perf. St. Louis: People's Th., 1856; Woods Th., Aug. 31, 1857. Pub. NY: S. French (French's Standard Drama, no. 163). Also pub. in *Representative Plays by American Dramatists, From 1765 to the Present Day*, ed. M. Moses, vol. 2 (1925).

The Golden Calf; or Marriage a la Mode. A Comedy in Three Acts, 1857. Perf. St. Louis: Woods Th., Aug. 31, 1857. Pub. Missouri Republican Office, 1857.

Geraldine; or, Love's Victory, 1859. Variant title: *The Master Passion*. Blank verse. Premiered in Philadelphia, then perf. NY: Wallack's Th., Aug. 31. 1859.

Evangeline, 1860. Adap. of Longfellow. Perf. NY: Winter Gardens Th., March 19, 1860.

Rose Gregorio; or, the Corsican Vendetta, 1862. Perf. NY: Winter

Gardens Th., May 12, 1862.

Fanchette; or, The Will o' the Wisp, 1871. Adap. *Die Grille*, German version of George Sand's *La Petite Fadette*. Perf. London: Lyceum Th., 1871.

The Dead Secret, 1877. Adap. of Wilkie Collins. Perf. London: Lyceum Th., 1877. Pub. London: E. Boot.

Bates, Ella Skinner.

The Convention of the Muses. A Classical Play for Parlor and School for Nine Females, 1891. Pub. Boston: W. Baker (Baker's Edition of Plays).

Baum, Rosemary.

That Box of Cigarettes. A Farce in Three Acts, c. 1892. Pub. Boston: W. Baker (Baker's Edition of Plays).

Love in a Lighthouse. A Farce in One Act, c. 1896. Pub. Boston: W. Baker (Baker's Edition of Plays).

The Dolls' Frolic. An Entertainment in One Scene, c. 1898. Pub. Boston: W. Baker. In *Little Plays for Little Players*, c. 1910.

Bell, Lucia Chase.

Bouyant, A Dicken's Charade in Three Scenes, c. 1889. In *A Dream of the Centuries and other Entertainments for Parlor and Hall*, ed. G. Bartlett (Boston: W. Baker, c. 1889).

Belmont, Eleanor Robson, b. 1879.

See Ford, Harriett.

Bergen, Helen Corinne, b. 1868.

When Jack Comes Late. A Comedy-Monologue for a Lady, 1893. Pub. NY: E. Werner.

The Princess Adelaide, 1900. Pub. Washington: Neale.

Bidwell, Jeanne Raymond.

Under Protest. A Comedy in One Act, 1896. Adap. from Spanish. Pub. Boston: W. Baker (Baker's Edition of Plays).

Blanchard, Amy Ella, 1856-1926.

Hearts and Clubs. A Comedy in Three Acts, 1896. Pub. Philadelphia: Penn Publishing, 1913.

Blandin, Isabella Margaret Elizabeth.

From Gonzales to San Jacinto: A Historical Drama of the Texas Revolution, 1897. Pub. Houston: Dealy and Baker.

Booth, Helen.

After Twenty Years, n.d.. In *Dramatic Leaflets. Comprising Original and Selected Plays* (anthology), c. 1877 (Philadelphia: P. Garrett). Also pub. separately: Philadelphia: Penn Publishing, 1903.

At the "Red Lion," n.d. In *Dramatic Leaflets*, as above.

An Electric Episode, n.d. In *Dramatic Leaflets*, as above.

A Fifty Dollar Milliner's Bill, n.d. In *Dramatic Leaflets*, as above.

Bordman, Georgiana N.

   The Kingdom of Mother Goose. A New Fairy Play for Vestry and School Entertainments, c.1877. Pub. Boston: Ditson, c.1905.

   Odd Operas for Eventide, 1893. Pub. Chicago: Dramatic Publishing. Includes: *A Glimpse of the Brownies; Market Day; Queen Flora's Day Dream; The Boating Party; Six Little Grandmas; Jimmy Crow; A House in the Moon.*

Botsford, Margaret, fl. 1812-1828.

   The Reign of Reform; or, Yankee Doodle Court, 1829. Pub. Baltimore, 1830. 2nd ed., 1832.

Bowers, Elizabeth Crocker.

   The Black Agate; or Old Foes with New Faces, 1859. Adap. of Rev. C. Kingsley's *Hypatia*. Perf. Philadelphia: Academy of Music, Sept. 5, 1859. Pub. Phila. (for the author) U.S. Steam-Power Book and Job Printing.

Bradbury, Louise A.

   Game of Dominoes. A Comedy in One Act, 1885. Adap. from the French of Dubry. Pub. Boston: W. Baker.

   Easy Entertainments for Young People, 1920. Pub. Philadelphia: Penn Publishing.

Bradbury, Sophia Louise Appleton.

   The Pirate. A Serio-Comic Opera in Three Acts, 1865. With partly original music and adaps. of Mozart, Rossini, Donizetti, Verdi, and Old English ballads. Pub. Cambridge: (for the author) Welch, Bigelow.

Bradley, Nellie H.

   The First Glass; or, The Power of Woman's Influence, 1868. Pub. in *New Temperance Dialogues* (Rockland, ME: Z. Vose).

   The Young Teetotaler; or, Saved at Last, 1868. In *New Temperance Dialogues*, as above.

   Marry no Man If He Drinks; or, Laura's Plan and How It Succeeded, 1868. In *New Temperance Dialogues*, as above.

   Reclaimed; or, The Danger of Moderate Drinking, 1868. In *New Temperance Dialogues*, as above.

   The Stumbling Block; or, Why A Deacon Gave Up His Wine, 1871. In *New Temperance Dialogues*, same publisher, 1871.

   Wine as Medicine; or, Abbie's Experience, 1873. In *New Temperance Dialogues*, same publisher, 1873.

   A Temperance Picnic with the Old Woman Who Lived in a Shoe, 1888. With music compiled from various sources. Pub. N.Y.: National Temperance Society and Publication House.

   A Collection of Temperance Dialogues, ed. S. T. Hammond (Ottawa: S.T. Hammond, 1869) contains additional plays by Bradley.

Brazzà-Savorgnan, Cora Ann Slocomb di, Contesa, b. 1862.
> *A Literary Farce*, 1896. Pub. Boston: Arena, 1896.

Brewster, Emma E.
> *Aunt Mehetible's Scientific Experiment. A Farce in One Act*, 1880. Pub. Boston: W. Baker (Baker's Edition of Plays), 1901.

> *A Dog that Will Fetch Will Carry. A Farce in Two Scenes for Female Characters Only*, 1880. Pub. Boston: W. Baker (Baker's Edition of Plays).

> *Eliza's Bona-Fide Offer. A Farce in One Act for Female Characters Only*, 1880. Pub. Boston: W. Baker (Baker's Edition of Plays), 1901.

> *How the Colonel Proposed. A Farce in Three Scenes*, c. 1880. Pub. Boston: W. Baker (Baker's Edition of Plays).

> *Parlor Varieties. Plays, Pantomimes, and Charades*, 1880. Pub. Boston: Lee and Shepard, 1880. Contains many of Brewster's plays in their original publication. Part II written with Lizzie B. Scribner, pub. Boston: Lee and Shepard, 1886.

> *Poor Peter. A Farce in One Act*, 1880. Pub. Boston: W. Baker.

> *Zerubbabel's Second Wife. A Farce in One Act*, 1880. Pub. Boston: W. Baker (Baker's Edition of Plays).

> *Cent-Any-All. Centennial Charade in Three Acts*, 1881. In *Parlor Varieties*.

> *Beresford Benevolent Society. A Farce in One Act*, 1885. With Lizzie B. Scribner. Pub. Boston: W. Baker (Baker's Edition of Plays), 1906.

> *The Christmas Box*, c. 1887. Pub. in *Christmas Entertainments for School and Home*, ed. J. Kaye (Boston: W. Baker).

Bridgham. Lillian Clisby.
> *The Marriage of Jack and Jill. A Mother Goose Entertainment in Two Scenes*, 1899. Pub. Boston: W. Baker.

> *The Famous Brown vs. Brown Separate Maintenance Case: A Woman's Suffragette Mock Trial*, 1912. Pub. Boston: W. Baker.

> *A Suffragette Town Meeting: An Entertainment in One Act*, c.1912. Pub. Boston: W. Baker (Baker's Edition of Plays).

> *Margery Makes Good. A Comedy in Three Acts*, c.1915. Pub. Boston: W. Baker (Baker's Edition of Plays).

Brown, Abbie Farwell, 1871-1927.
> *Quits. A Comedy in One Act*, 1896. Pub. Boston: W. Baker (Baker's Edition of Plays).

> *The Green Trunk. A Masque Written for the Fiftieth Birthday of the Saturday Morning Club*, 1921.

> *The Lantern and Other Plays for Children*, 1928. Pub. Boston and NY: Houghton Mifflin.

Browne, Frances Elizabeth.
> *Ruth,* 1871. In her *Ruth: A Sacred Drama and Original Lyrical Poems* (NY: Wynkooop and Hallenbeck).

Bullock, Cynthia, b. 1821.
> *Dialogue, Poet and Musician,* 1847. In her *Washington and Other Poems* (NY: [for the author] Reid and Cunningham).

Burnett, Frances Eliza Hodgson, 1849-1924.
> *That Lass o' Lowrie's,* 1878. Adap. of her novel. With Julian Magnus. Perf. NY: Booth's Th., Nov. 25, 1878.
>
> *Esmeralda. A Comedy Drama in Four Acts,* 1881. Adap. of her novel. With William Gillette. Perf. NY: Madison Square Th., Oct. 26, 1881. Pub. NY: S. French, c. 1881-1909 (French's International Copyrighted Works of the Best Authors, no. 72).
>
> *Young Folks' Ways,* 1881. With William Gillette.
>
> *The Real Little Lord Fauntleroy,* 1888. Adap. of her novel. Perf. NY: Broadway Th. Dec. 11, 1888.
>
> *Little Lord Fauntleroy. A Drama in Three Acts, Founded on the Story of the Same Name,* 1889. Adap. of her novel. Pub. NY: S. French (French's International Copyrighted Edition of the Works of the Best Authors, no. 42).
>
> *Phyllis,* 1889. Adap. of her novel *The Fortunes of Philippa Fairfax.* Perf. London: Globe Th., July 1, 1889.
>
> *Nixie,* 1890. Adap. of her novel *Editha's Burglar.* With S. Townsend (Variant sp.: Townshend). Perf. London: Terry's Th., Apr. 7, 1890.
>
> *The Showman's Daughter,* 1892. With S. Townsend. Perf. London: Royalty Th., Jan. 6, 1892.
>
> *A Lady of Quality,* 1896. Adap. of her novel. With S. Townsend. Perf. NY: Wallack's Th., Nov. 1, 1897.
>
> *The First Gentleman of Europe,* 1897. Adap. of her novel. With Julia Fletcher (Pseud.: George Fleming). Perf. NY: Lyceum Th., 1897.
>
> *A Little Princess,* 1911. (Variant title: *A Little Unfairy Princess.*) Adap. of her novel. Perf. NY: Criterion Th., Jan. 14, 1903.
>
> *A Pretty Sister of José,* 1903. Adap. of her novel *Louisiana.* Perf. NY: Empire Th., Nov. 10, 1903.
>
> *That Man and I,* 1904. Adap. of her novel *The DeWilloughby Claim.* Perf. London: Savoy Th., Jan. 25, 1904.
>
> *The Dawn of Tomorrow,* 1909. Adap. of her novel. Perf. NY: Lyceum Th., Jan. 25, 1909.
>
> *The Little Princess. A Play for Children and Grown-Up Children in Three Acts,* 1911. Adap. of her novel. Pub. NY: S. French. Also in *A Treasury of Plays for Children,* ed. M. Moses (Boston, 1921).
>
> *Racketty Packetty House. A Play in Prologue and Three Acts,* 1926.

Adap. of her novel. Perf. NY: Children's Th., Dec. 23, 1912. Pub.
Boston: Little, Brown.
Burnham, Clara Louise Root, 1854-1927.
    *Santa Claus' Mistake; or, The Bundle of Sticks. A Christmas Cantata for
Children.* c.1885. Music by George F. Root. Pub. Cincinnati: J.
Church.
    Judge Santa Claus; A New Departure. A Christmas Cantata, c.1887.
Libretto. Music by George F. Root. Pub. Cincinnati: J. Church.
    Snow-White and the Seven Dwarfs. A Juvenile Operetta, c.1888.
Libretto. Music by George F. Root. Pub. Cincinnati: J. Church.
    Santa Claus and Company. A Christmas Cantata for Children, c.1889.
Libretto. Music by George F. Root. Pub. Cincinnati.
    Phyllis, the Farmer's Daughter. An Operatic Cantata, 1892. Libretto.
Music by George F. Root. Pub. Cincinnati: J. Church.
    The Right Princess. A Play in Three Acts, 1902. Pub. Boston:
Houghton Mifflin.
Burton, (Mrs. Henry S.)
    *Don Quixote de la Mancha. A Comedy in Five Acts, Taken from
Cervantes' Novel of that Name,* 1876. Pub. San Francisco: J. Carmany.
Buxton, Ida M.
    How She Has her Own Way: An Interlude in One Scene, 18-?. Pub.
Clyde, OH: Ames (Ames' Series of Standard and Minor Drama, no. 50).
    Taking the Census. Original Farce in One Act, 1883. Pub. Clyde,
OH: Ames (Ames' Series of Standard and Minor Drama, no. 137).
    A Sewing Circle of the Period. An Original Farce in One Act, 1884.
Pub. Clyde, OH: Ames (Ames' Series of Standard and Minor Drama,
no. 138).
    Matrimonial Bliss: A Scene from Real Life, 1884. Pub. Clyde, OH:
Ames (Ames' Series of Standard and Minor Drama, no. 139).
    Tit for Tat. An Original Sketch in One Scene, c. 1884. Pub. Clyde,
OH: Ames (Ames' Series of Standard and Minor Drama, no. 142).
    Our Awful Aunt. A Comic Drama in Two Acts, c. 1885. Pub. Clyde,
OH: Ames (Ames' Series of Standard and Minor Drama, no. 146).
    Why They Joined the Rebeccas. An Original Farce in One Act, c. 1885.
Pub. Clyde, OH: Ames (Ames' Series of Standard and Minor Drama,
no. 155).
    On to Victory: A Temperance Cantata in One Scene, 1887. Pub.
Clyde, OH: Ames (Ames' Series of Standard and Minor Drama, no.
215).
    Carnival of Days, 1888. (Variant title: *Festival of Days.*) Pub. Clyde,
OH: Ames (Ames' Series of Standard and Minor Drama, no. 250).
    Cousin John's Album. A Pantomime, 1888. Pub. Clyde, OH: Ames

(Ames' Series of Standard and Minor Drama, no. 260).

Byington, Alice.

> "*Cranford*" *Dames. A Play in Five Scenes for Female Characters*, c. 1900. Adap. of novel *Cranford* by Elizabeth Gaskell. Pub. NY: H. Roorbach.

Campbell, Amelia Pringle.

> *The Great House; or, Varities of American Life*, 1882. Pub. NY: E. Jenkins.

Campbell, Marian D.

> *An Open Secret. A Farce in Two Acts*, 1898. Pub. Boston: W. Baker.
>
> *A Chinese Dummy. A Farce in One Act for Female Characters Only*, c. 1899. Pub. Boston: W. Baker (Baker's Edition of Plays).
>
> *Sunbonnets. A Farce-Comedy in Two Acts*, 1900. Boston: W. Baker (Baker's Edition of Plays).

Cantell, Lilia Mackay.

> *Jephthah's Daughter. A Biblical Dance Drama in Three Scenes*, 18-?. Libretto and music. Typescript promptbook.

Careo, Zella.

> *The Hidden Treasures; or, Martha's Triumph. A Drama in a Prologue and Four Acts*, 1883. Pub. Clyde, OH: Ames (Ames' Series of Standard and Minor Drama, no. 141).

Carr, Mary.

> See Clarke, Mary Carr.

Carter, Alice P.

> *The Fairy Steeplecrow. A Play for Children in One Scene*, c. 1887. Pub. Boston: W. Baker.
>
> *A Sad Mistake. A Musical Comedy in One Act*, 1895. Pub. Boston: W. Baker (Baker's Edition of Plays. Also in *Clever Comedies for Female Characters* (Boston: Baker, 1915).

Case, Laura U.

> *May Court in Greenwood*, c. 1887. In *Dramatic Leaflets. Comprising Original and Selected Plays* [anthology] (Philadelphia: P. Garrett, c. 1887).
>
> *The Veiled Priestess*, c. 1887. In *Dramatic Leaflets*, as above.

Castle, Harriet Davenport, b. 1843.

> *The Courting of Mother Goose. An Entertainment*, n.d. Pub. Chicago: Dramatic Publishing.
>
> *Castle's School Entertainments*, vols. 1-4, 1887-1905. Pub. Chicago: A. Flanagan.

Chaney, Caroline I.
William Henry, 1875. Adap. of "William Henry" books by Abby M.
Diaz. Pub. Boston: J. Osgood, 1875.
Chartres, Annie Vivanti, 1868-1942. (Pseud. Anita V. Chartres.)
The Ruby Ring. Comedy in One Act, 1900. San Antonio: Maverick-
Clarke Litho.
Also wrote at least three plays in Italian.
Clarke, Helen Archibald, 1860-1926.
Baulustion's Euripides, 1915. Perf. Boston: Plymouth Th. Pub. *Poet-
Lore.*
Starrylocks in Butterflyland, n.d. Musical for children.
Hermes at School, n.d. Perf. Boston: Little Powers Theatre.
Clarke, Mary Carr.
The Fair Americans. An Original Comedy in Five Acts, 1815. Pub.
Philadelphia, 1815.
Return from Camp, 1815. Perf. Philadelphia: Chestnut Street Th.,
Jan. 6, 1815. Probably variant title of *The Fair Americans.*
The Benevolent Lawyers; or, Villainy Detected. A Comedy in Five Acts,
1823. Pub. Philadelphia, 1823.
*Sara Maria Cornell; or, The Fall River Murder. A Domestic Drama in
Three Acts*, 1833. Perf. NY: Richmond Hill Th., Aug., 1834. Pub. NY.
Clayton, Estelle.
Favette, the Story of a Waif. A Comedy in Four Acts, 1885. Perf. NY:
Union Square Th., Feb. 6, 1885. Pub. NY.
A Sad Coquette. A Modern Comedy of Error in Four Acts, 1887. Perf.
NY: Union Square Th., Dec. 15, 1887. Pub. NY: Richardson.
*The Viking. Comic Opera in Two Acts. An Original and Romantic
Version of the First Discovery of America by the Ancient Norsemen*, c.
1893. Music by E. I. Darling and E. R. Steiner. Perf. NY: Palmer's Th.,
May 9, 1895. Pub. NY: Springer and Welty.
Clifton, Mary A. Delano.
In the Wrong Box. An Etheopian Farce in One Act, n.d. Pub. Clyde,
OH: Ames (Ames' Series of Standard and Minor Drama, no. 47).
Schnapps. A Farce in One Act, n.d. Pub. Clyde, OH: Ames (Ames'
Series of Standard and Minor Drama, no. 48).
Der two Subprises. A Farce in One Act, n.d. Pub. Clyde, OH: Ames
(Ames' Series of Standard and Minor Drama, no. 49).

Cobb, Josephine H.
The Oxford Affair. A Comedy in Three Acts, 1896. With Jennie E. Paine. Pub. Philadelphia: Penn Publishing, 1911 (Dramatic Library, vol. 1, no. 109).
Cobb, Mary L.
Poetical Dramas for Home and School, 1873. Pub. Boston: Lee and Shepard. Collection of short plays adap. from poems.
Colburn, Carrie W.
His Last Chance; or, The Little Joker. A Comedy in Three Acts, 1895. Pub. Boston: W. Baker (Baker's Edition of Plays).
A Romantic Rogue. A Comedy-Drama in One Act, 1902 (?). Pub. Boston: W. Baker (Baker's Edition of Plays).
Colclough, Emma Shaw, 1847-1940.
An Object Lesson in History. A Historical Exercise for School Exhibitions, 1896. Pub. NY and Chicago: E. Kellogg, 1896.
Coleman, (Mrs. Wilmot Bouton).
Maud Stanley; or, Life Scenes and Life Lessons. An Original Romantic Drama in Five Acts, 1874. Adap. of story by Elvira L. Mills. Ms. promptbook. In NY Pub. Lib.
Colman, Julia, 1828-1909.
The Boys' Panorama of the New Year. A Holiday Concert, 1872. Pub. NY: Nelson and Phillips.
No King in America. A Patriotic Temperance Program in Three Parts, 1888. Pub. NY: National Temperance Society and Publications House.
Our Cider Entertainment. A Concert Exercise With Tableaux Vivants, 189-?. Pub. NY: National Temperance Society and Publications House.
Commelin, Anna Olcott.
Hymettus, 1894. Adap. of her poem "Of Such is the Kingdom." Pub. NY: Fowler and Wells.
Atala, An American Idyl. A Poetic Dramatization of the Work of Chateaubriand, with Original Poems, 1902. Pub. NY: E. Dutton.
Conner, Charlotte Barnes.
See Barnes, Charlotte Mary Sanford.
Conway, (Miss), pseud.
Lamora; or, The Indian Wife, 1849. Perf. NY: National Th., Nov. 27, 1849.

Cook, Eliza, 1818-1889.
>   *The Mourners*, c 1856.   Pub. in *Massey's Exhibition Reciter and Drawing Room Entertainments*, nos. 1-2. Pub. NY: S. French.

Corwin, Jane Hudson, 1809-1881.
>   *A Dialogue Between Mr. Native and Mrs. Foreigner, on Literary Subjects*, 1858. Pub. in her *The Harp of Home* (Cincinnati: Moore, Wilstach, Keys).

Corwine, Mary R.
>   *A Woman's Blindness*, c.1874. In *Beadle's Dime Dialogues*, no. 14 (1874).

Côté, Marie.
>   *The Witch of Bramble Hollow. A Drama in Four Acts*, 1899. Pub. NY: W. Young.

Cox, Eleanor Rogers, 1867-1931.
>   *A Duel at Dawn. A One-Act Tragedy*, 1894. Pub. NY: P. Kenedy (Kenedy's New Series of Plays).
>   *A Millionaire's Trials. A Comedy*, 1894. Bound with above.

Coyle, Susan Edmond.
>   See Paul, Anne Marie.

Crane, Eleanor Maud.
>   *The Lost New Year. A Play in Two Scenes for Children*, c. 1897. Pub. NY: Dick and Fitzgerald.
>   *Just for Fun. An Up-to-Date Society Comedy in Three Acts*, 1899. Pub. NY: Dick and Fitzgerald.
>   *A Regular Flirt. An Up-to-Date Society Comedy in Three Acts*, 18-?. Pub. NY: Dick and Fitzgerald, c.1903.
>   *Men, Maids, and Matchmakers. An Up-To-Date Comedy in Three Acts*, c.1901. Pub. NY: Dick and Fitzgerald.
>   *A Pair of Idiots. A Comedy in Two Acts*, 1902. Pub. NY: Dick and Fitzgerald.
>   *Ye Village Skewl of Long Ago. An Entertainment*, c. 1904. Pub. NY: Dick and Fitzgerald.
>   *When a Man's Single. A Rural Society Comedy in Three Acts*, c.1905. Pub. NY: Fitzgerald Publishing.
>   *The Bachelor Maids Reunion. An Entertainment in One Scene*, c.1906. Pub. NY: Dick and Fitzgerald.
>   *In the Ferry House. Character Sketches in One Act and One Scene*, c.1906. Pub. NY: Dick and Fitzgerald.
>   *Next Door. A Comedy of Today*, 1906. Pub. NY: Fitzgerald Publishing.
>   *A Little Savage. A Military Comedy in Three Acts*, 1907. Pub. NY: Dick and Fitzgerald.

The Rainbow Kimona. A Comedy in Two Acts for Girls, c. 1908. Pub. NY: Fitzgerald Publishing.

The Best Man. A Comedy in One Act, c.1910. Pub. NY: S. French (French's International Copyrighted Edition of the Works of the Best Authors).

Billy's Bungalow. A Comedy in Three Acts and One Scene, c.1910. Pub. NY: Dick and Fitzgerald.

Raps. A Vaudeville Sketch, c.1911. Pub. NY: Dick and Fitzgerald.

The Real Thing. An Up-to-Date Comedy, c.1911. Pub. NY: S. French (French's International Copyrighted Edition of the Works of the Best Authors, no. 204).

The Honor of the Class. A School-Room Sketch in One Act and One Scene for Girls, c.1912. Pub. NY: S. French.

Fun in the Farmhouse. An Entertainment Especially Adapted to Church Societies, Dramatic Clubs, Social Evenngs, Etc., 1913. Pub. NY: Dick and Fitzgerald.

Pegg's Predicament. A One-Act Farce for Girls, c.1915. Pub. NY: Dick and Fitzgerald.

Her Victory. Comedy in One Act, 1920. Pub. NY: Dick and Fitzgerald.

His Soul. A Farce in One Act, c.1922. Pub. NY.

Fads and Fancies. A Sketch for Girls, c.1917. Pub. NY: Dick and Fitzgerald.

Ye Quilting Party of Long Ago. An Amusing Entertainment in One Set, 1935. Pub. NY: S. French

Crane, Elizabeth Green.

Berquin. A Drama in Three Acts, 1891. Pub. NY: Scribner's.

The Imperial Republic. A Drama of the Day, 1902. Pub. NY: Grafton Press.

The Necken. A Play in Two Acts, 1913. Pub. NY.

Are You Men? A Drama in Four Acts, 1923. Pub. NY: Minden Press.

Crosby, Fannie J., 1820-1915. (Full name: Van Alstyne, Frances Jane Crosby.)

The Flower Queen; or, The Coronation of the Rose. A Cantata in Two Parts, 1852. Libretto. Music by George F. Root. Pub. NY: Mason Brothers.

Daniel; or, The Captivity and Restoration. A Sacred Cantata, 1853. Libretto, with M. C. Cady. Music by George F. Root and William R. Bradbury. Pub. NY: Mason.

The Pilgrim Fathers, 1854. Libretto, with George F. Root. Music by Root. Pub. NY: Mason.

Conquered by Kindness. A Juvenile Operetta, c.1881. Libretto. Music by Hart P. Danks. Pub. NY: W. Pond.

Glitter and Gold; or. The Conquest of Faith, c.1883. Libretto. Music By Hart P. Danks. Pub. NY: S. Gordon.

St. Nicholas' Visit to the School. A Christmas Cantata, c.1884. Libretto. Music by William H. Doane. Pub. NY: Biglow and Main.

Santa Claus' Home; or. The Christmas Excursion. A Christmas Cantata, c.1886. Libretto. Music by William H. Doane. Pub. NY: Biglow.

Zanie. An Operetta, 1887. Libretto. Music by Hart P. Danks. Pub. Cincinnati: J. Church.

Santa Claus' Prize and Who Got It. A Christmas Cantata, 1888. Music by William H. Doane. Pub. NY: Biglow.

The Wise Men from the East. A Christmas Cantata, c.1893. Libretto. Music by Hart P. Danks. Pub. NY: Biglow and Main.

Summer Roses, n.d. Libretto. Music by Hubert P. Main.

Crumpton, M. Nataline, 1857-1911.

Ceres. A Mythological Play for Parlor and School in Three Acts, c. 1890. Pub. Boston: W. Baker (Baker's Edition of Plays).

Pandora. A Classical Play for Parlor and School in Three Acts, 1890. Pub. Boston: W. Baker (Baker's Edition of Plays).

Theseus. A Play for Parlor and School in Five Acts, 1892. Pub. Bostob: W. Baker (Baker's Edition of Plays), 1902.

Greek Costume Plays for School and Lawn Performance, 1914. With Mary L. Gaddess. Pub. Boston: W. Baker.

Cunningham. H.

The Golden Goose, c. 1890. Adap. from "Gammer Grethel" (German peasant woman whose stories were retold by the Brothers Grimm.) Pub. Boston: W. Baker.

Cunningham, Virginia Juhan, 1834-1874.

The Maid of Florence; or, A Woman's Vengeance. A Pseudo-Historical Tragedy in Five Acts, 1839. Pub. Charleston: S. Miller.

Madelaine, the Belle of Faubourg. A Drama in Three Acts and a Memoir of Mrs. Virginia Cunningham, c. 1848. Pub. Boston: W. Spencer, 1856 (Spencer's Boston Theatre, no. 49). In *Modern Standard Drama*, vols. 32-33 (1848).

Curtis, Ariana Randolph Wormeley ("Mrs. Daniel S. Curtis"), 1833-1922.

The Spirit of Seventy-Six; or, The Coming Woman, A Prophetic Drama, 1868. With Daniel Sargent Curtis. Perf. Selwyn's. Boston, 1868. Pub. in her *The Spirit of Seventy-Six* (Boston: Little, Brown), 1868. In *On to Victory: Propaganda Plays of the Woman Suffrage Movement*, ed. B. Friedl (Boston: Northeastern U. Press, 1987). A burlesque of the suffrage movement.

A Change of Base, 1868, In vol. above.

Doctor Mondschein; or, The Violent Remedy, 1868. In vol. above.

A Practical Demonstration, 1874. In *Beadle's Dime Dialogues*, no. 14 (1874).

The Coming Woman; or, The Spirit of Seventy-Six. A Prophetic Drama, n.d. London: S. French.

Cusack, Mary Frances Clare, 1830-1899. (Also Sister Mary Francis Clare; The Nun of Kenmare.)

Tim Carty's Trial; or, Whistling at Landlords. A Play for the Times, 1886. Pub. NY: S. Mears.

Cushing, Eliza Lanesford Foster, b. 1794.

Esther. A Sacred Drama, 1840. Pub. Boston: J. Dowe.

Dallas, Mary Kyle, 1830-1897.

Our Aunt Robertina. A Comedietta in One Act, 1891. Pub. NY: E. Werner. Repub. Boston: W. Baker (Baker's Edition of Plays), 1902.

Aroused at Last. A Comedy in One Act, 1892. Pub. Chicago: Dramatic Publishing (Sergel's Acting Drama, no. 440).

Dana, Eliza A. Fuller.

Iona. An Indian Tragedy, 1864. Pub. in her *Gathered Leaves* (Cambridge: Private ed. printed by H. Houghton).

D'Arusmont, Frances.

See Wright, Frances.

Davenport, Fanny Lily Gypsy, 1850-1898.

Olivia, Vicar of Wakefield, 1878. Adap. of play by W. G. Wills, based on Goldsmith's *The Vicar of Wakefield*. Pub. NY.

La Tosca, 1888. Adap. of Sardou.

David, Mary Evelyn Moore, 1852-1909.

A Christmas Masque of Saint Roch, 1896. Pub. Chicago: A. McClurg.

A Bunch of Roses. A Romantic Comedy, c. 1899. Pub. NY: E. Werner.

Christmas Boxes, c. 1899. Pub. NY: E. Werner, 1907.

A Dress Rehearsal, 1899. Pub. NY: E. Werner, 1907.

The New System, 1899. Pub. NY: E. Werner, 1907.

Queen Anne Cottages, 1899. Pub. NY: E. Werner, 1907.

Davidson, Belle L.

A Visit from Mother Goose. A Christmas Play for Primary Grades, c. 1896. Pub. NY: E. Kellogg.

Davison, E. Mora, d. 1948.
> *The New Englanders. A Comedy of the Revolution in Three Acts*, 1882.
> NY: Priv. Printing by Collins.

Dawson, J. H.
> *Lights and Shadows of the Great Rebellion; or, The Hospital Nurse of Tennessee. A Grand Military Drama of the Great Rebellion in Four Acts and Five Tableux*, c. 1885. With B. G. Whittemore. Pub. Clyde, OH: Ames (Ames' Series of Standard and Minor Drama, no. 194).

Dean, Julia, 1830-1866.
> *Adrienne the Actress*, 1853. Perf. Charleston: Charleston Th., Dec. 22, 1853. Played lead role herself.
> *The Priestess*, 1854. Boston, 1855.
> *Mary of Mantua*, 1855. Perf. NY: Broadway Th., Dec. 7, 1855.

Debenham, L.
> *Grannie's Picture*, c. 1899. Pub. NY: S. French (Children's Plays, no. 18).

Delanoy, Mary Frances Hanford (Pseud.: Marion Eddy.)
> *The Outcast's Daughter. A Drama in Four Acts*, c. 1899. Pub. Chicago: Dramatic Publishing (Sergel's Acting Drama).

De Lesdernier, Emily Pierpont.
> *Heloise. A Drama of the Passions in Four Acts*, c. 1853. In her *Voices of Life*. Pub. NY: (for the author) Cornish, Lamport.

De Mille, Beatrice M., d. 1923.
> See Ford, Harriet.

Denton, Clara Janetta Fort.
> *Little People's Dialogues. For Children of Ten Years*, 1888. Pub. Philadelphia: National School of Elocution and Oratory.
> *To Meet Mrs. Thompson. A Farce in One Act for Female Characters*, c. 1890. Pub. Boston: W. Baker (Baker's Edition of Plays).
> *When the Lessons Are Over. Dialogues, Exercises and Drills for the Primary Classes*, c. 1891. Pub. Chicago: T. Denison, c. 1891.
> *Surprised. A Comedy in One Act for Eight Female Characters*, 1892. Pub. Philadelphia: Penn Publishing, 1898.
> *All Is Fair in Love. A Drama in Three Scenes*, 1897. Pub. Boston: W. Baker (Baker's Edition of Plays).
> *A Change of Color. A Drama in One Act*, 1897. Pub. Boston: W. Baker (Baker's Edition of Plays).
> *From Tots to Teens. A Book of Original Dialogues for Boys and Girls. Some Merry Times for Young Folks*, c. 1897. Pub. Chicago: T. Denison.
> *The Man Who Went to Europe. A Comedy in One Act*, 1897. Pub. Boston: J. Baker (Baker's Edition of Plays).
> *"W. H." A Farce in One Act*, 1897. Pub. Boston: W. Baker (Baker's

Edition of Plays).

All Sorts of Dialogues. A Collection of Dialogues for Young People, with Additional Stage Directions, 1898. Pub. Chicago: T. Denison, 1898.

All the Holidays. A Collection of Recitations, Dialogues, and Exercises for All School Holidays, 1905. Pub. Chicago: A. Flanagan.

Denton's Best Plays and Dialogues. The Happy Book of Stageland, 1905. Pub. Chicago: A. Flanagan.

Jack Frost's Mistake. One-Act Operetta for Thanksgiving, 1907. Pub. Lebanon, OH: March.

Pat and His Countrymen. A Dialog for Two Boys, 1907. Pub. Lebanon, OH: March.

Bobby's Help, 190-?. (Clara J. Denton Monologues.) Pub. Franklin, OH: Eldridge.

The Birthdays. A Lincoln and Washington Birthday Dialogue, 1910.

Entertainments for All the Year, 1910. Pub. Philadelphia: Penn Publishing.

Mademoiselle's Mistake. A Farce in One Act for Two Girls, 1910. Pub. Franklin, OH: Eldridge.

The Old Ship. A Dialogue for Three Boys, 1910. Pub. NY: J. Fischer.

Sammie's Lesson. A Dialogue for a Boy and a Girl, 1910. Pub. NY.

Seeing Uncle Jack. A Two-Act Comedy for Seven Girls, 1910. Pub. NY: J. Fischer.

The Yellow Law. A One-Act Play for Thanksgiving Day, c. 1910. Pub. NY: J. Fischer.

The White Chief. A Thanksgiving Playlet, c. 1915. Pub. Franklin, OH: Eldridge.

Merry Dialogues for Country Schools, 1924. Pub. Dayton, OH: Paine.

Christmas at Happy Valley. A Two-Act Play, c. 1925. Pub. Dayton, OH: Paine.

Dialogues for Closing Day, 1925. Pub. Dayton, OH: Paine.

Denton's New Program Book: Plays, Dialogues, Recitations, Pageants, 1926. Pub. Chicago: Whitman.

Dot Pooty Gompliment, 19-?. Pub. Franklin, OH: Eldridge.

Getting Track of the Mallories, n.d. Pub. Franklin, OH: Eldridge.

The "Left-Handed" Sleeve, 19-?. Pub. Franklin, OH: Eldridge.

One Little Chicken, n.d. (Clara J. Denton Monologues.) Pub. Franklin, OH: Eldridge.

Seen and Not Heard and *Vi'let's Troubles*, n.d. (Clara J. Denton Monologues.) Pub. Franklin, OH: Eldridge.

Sorry for Billy, n.d. (Clara J. Denton Monologue.) Pub. Franklin, OH: Eldridge.

Uncle Peter and the Widow, n.d. (Clara J. Denton Monologue.) Pub.

Franklin, OH: Eldridge.

    Waiting for Oscar, n.d. (Clara J. Denton Monologue). Pub. Franklin, OH: Eldridge.

Diaz, Abby Morton, 1821-1904.

    Mother Goose's Christmas Party. A Rhymed Drama, 1891. Pub. Chicago: Searle and Garton.

    Also see Chaney, Caroline I.

Dickinson, Anna Elizabeth, 1842-1932.

    Laura; or, Trusts Herself, 1876. Perf. Philadelphia, Dec., 1876.

    Mary Tudor, 1876.

    A Crown of Thorns; or Anne Boleyn, 1877. Perf. NY: Eagle Th., Apr. 2, 1877.

    An American Girl, 1880. Perf. NY: Fifth Avenue Th., Sept. 20, 1880.

Dickinson, Eva Lyle.

    A Thanksgiving Lesson and *A Real Thanksgiving*, c. 1899. With Stanley Schell. Pub. NY: E. Werner (Werner's Magazine, vol. 24), 1899.

Dillaye, Ina.

    Ramona. A Play in Five Acts, c. 1887. Adap. of Helen Hunt Jackson's novel. Pub. Syracuse, NY: F. Dillaye.

Dix, Beulah Marie, 1875-1970.

    Cicely's Cavalier. A Comedy in One Act, 1897. Pub. Boston: W. Baker (Baker's Edition of Plays).

    At the Sign of the Buff Bible, 1898. Perf. NY: Empire Th., Dec. 1, 1898. Pub. 1915.

    Apples of Eden, 1898. Perf. NY: Empire Th., Dec. 2, 1898.

    The Beau's Comedy, 1902. With Carrie A. Harper. Pub. NY: Harper.

    A Rose o' Plymouth Town. A Romantic Comedy in Four Acts, 1902. With Evelyn G. Sutherland. Perf. NY: Manhattan Th., Sept. 29, 1902. Pub. Boston: Fortune Press, 1903.

    The Breed of the Treshams, 1903. With Evelyn G. Sutherland.

    The Road to Yesterday. A Comedy of Fantasy, 1906. With Evelyn G. Sutherland. Perf. NY: Herald Square Th., Dec. 31, 1906. Pub. NY: S. French, 1925.

    Matt of Merrymount, 1907. With Evelyn G. Sutherland.

    Boy O'Carroll, 1907. With Evelyn G. Sutherland.

    The Lilac Room, 1907. With Evelyn G. Sutherland. Perf. NY: Weber's Th., Apr. 3, 1907.

    Young Fernald, 1908. With Evelyn G. Sutherland.

    Allison's Lad: A Drama, 1910. Perf. NY: Lyceum Th., Dec. 23, 1910. In *Representative One-Act Plays by American Authors*, ed. G. Mayorga, 1929. Also in *Fifty One-Act Plays*, ed. C. Martin (London, 1934).

    Alison's Lad and Other Martial Interludes, Being Six One-Act Dramas,

1910. Pub. NY: Holt.

Across the Border. A Play of the Present in One Act and Four Scenes, 1914. Perf. NY: Princess Th., 1914. Promptbook (1916 ed.) has photos. Pub. NY: Holt, 1915.

A Legend of St. Nicholas, 1914. Pub. in *Poet-Lore,* vol. 25, no. 5.

Moloch: A Play about War in a Prologue, Three Acts, and an Epilogue, 1915. Perf. NY: New Amsterdam Th., Sept. 20, 1915. Pub. NY: A. Knopf, 1916.

A Pageant of Peace. Written for the American School Peace League, 1915. Pub. Boston: American School Citizenship League, 1930.

The Captain of the Gate, c.1921. In *The Atlantic Book of Modern Plays* (Boston, 1921).

A Legend of St. Nicholas and Other Plays, 1925. Pub. NY: S. French.

The Girl Comes Home. A Comedy in One Act, 1927. Pub. NY: S. French (French's International Copyrighted Edition of the Works of the Best Authors, no. 625).

The Hundredth Trick. A Romantic Tragedy, c.1929. In *Twelve One-Act Plays for Study and Production* (Boston, 1929).

Ragged Army. A Modern Play in Three Acts, 1934. With Bertram Millhauser. Perf. NY: Selwyn Th., Feb. 26, 1934.

Hugh Gwyeth, n.d.

Donnell, Florence T.

Drackkov. Russian Drama in Five Acts, 1890. Pub. NY: W. Jenkins.

A Revolutionary Marriage. Drama in Five Acts, 1890. Pub. NY: W. Jenkins.

Moneymaking and Matchmaking; or, New York in 1890. Comedy in Five Acts, 1891. Pub. NY: W. Jenkins.

Dorbesson, Fern, d. 1960.

Aldemon's Daughter (Cassilda.) Tragedy in Prose in Four Acts, 1890. Pub. NY: T. Wright.

Doremus, Elizabeth Johnson Ward, 1853-1934.

The Sleeping Beauty, 1878.

A Fair Bohemian, 1888. Perf. NY: Madison Square Th., May 11, 1888.

The Circus Rider, 1893. Perf. NY: Daly's Th., April 27, 1893.

Mrs. Pendleton's Four-in-Hand, 1893. Adap. of story by Gertrude Atherton. Perf. NY: Empire Th., Jan. 16, 1893.

A Full Hand, 1894. Adap. of *Les Petites Godines.* Perf. NY: Madison Square Th., Jan. 23, 1894.

The Fortunes of the King, 1904. With L. Westervelt. Perf. NY: Lyric Th., Dec. 6, 1904.

The Duchess of Devonshire. A Romantic Comedy in Four Acts, 1906.

Perf. Newburgh, NY: Opera House, Oct. 8, 1906.
> *Grif. A Play in One Act*, n.d. With Frank Allen. Adap. of B. L.
Farjeon.
> *Pranks*, n.d.

Downing, Laura Case, 1843-1914.
> *Defending the Flag; or, The Message Boy. Military Drama in Five Acts*,
1894. Pub. Clyde, OH: Ames (Ames' Series of Standard and Minor
Drama, no. 342).

Duer, Caroline King, 1865-1956.
> *Overheard in a Conservatory* and *Dialogue*, c.1896. With Alice Duer
Miller. Pub. in her *Poems* (NY: G. Richmond, 1896).
> See also Ford, Harriett.

Duncan, Florence I.
> *Ye Last Sweet Thing in Corners. Being ye Faithful Drama of ye Artist's
Vendetta*, c. 1880. Pub. Philadelphia, Duncan and Hall.

Dunn, Norah E.
> *Mrs. Plodding's Neices; or, Domestic Accomplishments. A Comedy in
One Act for Young Ladies*, c. 1899. Pub. Chicago: Dramatic Publishing
(Sergel's Acting Drama, no. 453).
> *Miss Tom Boy. A Comedy in One Act*, c. 1899. Pub. Chicago:
Dramatic Publishing (Sergel's Acting Drama, no. 539).

Dyer, Elizabeth.
> *A Tangled Skein, In Three Knots*, 1881. Pub. Providence, RI: J. and
R. Reid.

Edgarton, Sarah Carter, 1819-1848.
> *The Beauty of Piety*, c. 1877. Pub. in *Dramatic Leaflets* (Philadelphia:
P. Garrett, c. 1877).

Edouin, Winnie.
> *A Bunch of Keys; or, the Hotel*, c. 1883. With Charles Hoyt. In
America's Lost Plays, vol. 9 (Princeton, 1940).

Ele, Rona.
> *Woman's Lefts. A Drama in Three Acts*, n.d. Pub. Philadelphia and
Boston: G. Maclean.

Eliot, Annie, 1857-1949. (Full name: Trumbull, Annie Eliot).
> *From Four to Six: A Comedietta*, c.1894. In *Stories of New York* (NY:
1894).
> *Matchmakers. A Comedy in One Act*, c.1884. Pub. Boston: W. Baker
(Baker's Edition of Plays).
> *A Virginia Reel. A Comedietta in Two Parts*, c.1888. Pub. Hartford,
CT.
> *St. Valentine's Day. A Comedy in One Act for Female Characters
Only*, 1892. Pub. Boston: W. Baker (Baker's Edition of Plays).

A Masque of Culture, 1893. Pub. Hartford, CT: Case, Lockwood and Brainard.

The Green-Room Rivals. A Comedietta in One Act, 1894. Pub. Boston: W. Baker (Baker's Edition of Plays).

The Wheel of Progress, 1898. Pub. Hartford, CT: Case, Lockwood and Brainard.

Haman. A Tragedy, 1907. Typescript.

A Christmas Party, n.d. Pub. Hartford, CT: Payne Printing.

Mind Cure; or, When Doctors Agree. A Farce, n.d. Pub. Hartford, CT: Case, Lockwood and Brainard.

Ellet, Elizabeth Fries Lummis, 1818-1877. (Pseud.: Cyril Turner.)

Ephemio of Messina. A Tragedy, 1834. Trans. of S. Pellico. Pub. NY: Monson, Bancroft.

Teresa Contarini. A Tragedy in Five Acts, 1835. Adap. of Niccolini. Perf. NY: Park Th., March, 1835. In her *Poems, Translated and Original* (Philadelphia: Key and Biddle).

Wissmuth and Company; or, The Noble and the Merchant, 1847. Perf. NY: Park Th., Apr. 13, 1847.

The Slave Actress, 1856. Perf. NY: Burton's Th., Dec. 10, 1856.

White Lies. A Drama, c. 1858. Adap. of novel by C. Reade. Perf. NY: Laura Keene's Th., Jan. 30, 1858. Pub. NY: H. Roorbach.

Ellis, Sarah Stickney, fl. 1812-1872.

The Duke of Buckingham, 1809. Perf. NY: Park Th., June 21, 1809.

Marmion; or, The Battle of Flodden Field, 1812. Perf. NY: Olympic Th., Mar. 20, 1812.

Elwyn, Lizzie May.

Millie, the Quadroon; or, out of Bondage. A Drama in Five Acts, c. 1888. Pub. Ames (Ames' Series of Standard and Minor Drama, no. 251).

Dot, the Miner's Daughter; or, One Glass of Wine. A Drama in Four Acts, c. 1888. Pub. Clyde, OH: Ames (Ames' Series of Standard and Minor Drama, no. 254).

Sweetbriar; or, The Flower Girl of New York. A Drama in Six Acts, 1889. Pub. Clyde, OH: Ames (Ames' Series of Standard and Minor Drama, no. 266).

Murder Will Out. A Farce in One Act for Six Female Characters, c. 1890. Pub NY: H. Roorbach.

Switched Off. A Temperance Farce in One Act, 1899. Pub Clyde, OH: Ames (Ames' Series of Standard and Minor Drama, no. 413).

Rachel, the Fire Waif. A Drama in Four Acts, 1900. Pub. Clyde, OH: Ames (Ames' Series of Standard and Minor Drama, no. 420).

Uncle Sam's Cooks. A Farce in One Act, 1904. Pub. Clyde, OH: Ames (Ames' Series of Standard and Minor Drama, no. 446).

A Ruined Life; or, The Curse of Intemperance. A Temperance Drama, 1904. Pub. Clyde, OH: Ames (Ames' Series of Standard and Minor Drama, no. 452).

Enebuske, Sarah Folsom.

A Detective in Petticoats. A Comedy in Three Acts for Female Characters Only, c. 1900. Pub. Boston: W. Baker (Baker's Edition of Plays).

Faugeres, Margaretta V. Bleecker, 1771-1801.

Belisarius, A Tragedy, c.1795. Pub. NY: T. and J. Swords, 1795.

Fessenden, Helen May Trott.

Troublesome Children; or, The Unexpected Voyage of Jack and Pen. A Play for Children, 1892. Adap. of W. Newton. Pub. Pittsfield, MA: J. Maxim.

Fezandié, Margaret.

The Tennis Drill, 1889. In *Harper's Young People*, June 11, 1899. Also pub. Boston: W. Baker (Baker's Edition of Plays), 1891.

The Soap-Bubble Drill. An Entertainment for Girls, 1892. Pub. Boston: W. Baker (Baker's Edition of Plays).

Edith's Dream. An Operetta for Children, 1893. Libretto. With Edgar Morette. Music by Eugene Fezandié. Pub. Chicago: Dramatic Publishing.

Field, Henrietta Dexter.

Collected Works. The Muses Up-To-Date, 1897. With Roswell M. Field. Pub. Chicago: Way and Williams. Includes: *Cinderella. A Fairy Comedy in Three Acts*; *A Lesson from Fairyland. A Tribute to Early Convictions, in Three Acts and an Intermezzo*; *The Modern Cinderella, An Exploded Fairy Tale in Three Brief Acts*; *Trouble in the Garden, A Horticultural Episode in Three Acts, with Living Pictures*; *The Wooing of Penelope, An Incident of Depravity in Three Acts (A Shadow Pantomime)*.

Field, Kate, 1838-1896. Full name: Mary Katherine Field Kemble.

Mad on Purpose. A Comedy in Four Acts, 1868. Trans. of Cosenza. Pub. NY.

Extremes Meet. A Comedietta in One Act, c.1877. Pub. NY: S. French (French's Acting Edition, no. 1652). In *The New York Drama* (NY: 1878).

The Drama of Glass, 189-?. Pub. Toledo, OH: Libbey Glass.

Fields, Annie Adams, 1834-1915.

The Return of Persephone. A Dramatic Sketch, 1877. Pub. Boston (for the author). In her *Under the Olive* (Boston: Houghton Mifflin).

Pandora. A Festival Play, 1881. In her *Under the Olive*, as above.

Sophocles, 1881. In *Under the Olive*, as above.

Orpheus. A Masque, 1900. Pub. Boston: Houghton Mifflin.

Fields, Louisa May.
Twelve Years a Slave, 1897. Ms. Indianapolis.
Fiske, Minnie Maddern Davey, 1865-1932.
The Rose. A Comedy in One Act, 1892(?) Typescript.
A Light from St. Agnes. A Play in One Act, 1905(?) Perf. NY:
Manhattan Th., March 27, 1905. Pub. NY: C. Koch.
A Light from St. Agnes. A Lyric Tragedy in One Act, c. 1925.
Libretto. Music by W. F. Harling. Perf. Chicago: Civic Opera. Pub.
NY: Huntzinger.
Fitch, Anna Mariska.
Items. A Washington Society Play in Five Acts, c. 1874. Pub. NY: P.
McBreen.
The Loves of Paul Fenly, 1893. Pub. NY: G. Putnam.
Flewellyn, Julia Collitan, b. 1850
It Is The Law. A Drama in Five Acts, 1896(?). Pub. Lockport(?) NY.
Follen, Eliza Lee Cabot, 1787-1860.
Home Dramas for Young People, 1859. Pub. Boston: J. Monroe.
Collection of plays adapted from Barbauld, Edgeworth, and others.
Honesty the Best Policy and Other Home Dramas for Parlor Pastime,
1863. Pub. Boston: Tompkins.
Ford, Harriett, 1868-1949. (Full name: Harriet French Ford Morgan.)
The Greatest Thing in the World. A Play in Four Acts, 1899. With
Beatrice M. DeMille. Perf. NY: Wallack's Th., Oct. 8, 1900. Pub.
London, 1899.
A Gentleman of France. A Play in Two Acts, 1900. Adap. of S. J.
Weyman. Perf. NY: Wallack's Th., Oct. 7, 1900. Pub. NY: Nash, 1901.
Jacqueline, c.1909. With Caroline Duer. (Variant titles: *An
American Girl from France*; *The Silver Lady*). Pub. NY.
The Fourth Estate, 1910. With Joseph M. Patterson.
When a Feller Needs a Friend. A Play in Three Acts, 1920. With
Harvey O'Higgins. Pub. NY.
On the Hiring Line. A Comedy in Three Acts, c. 1923. With Harvey
O'Higgins. Pub. NY: S. French.
Where Julia Rules. A Comedy in Four Acts, 1923. With Caroline
Duer.
The Bride. A Comedy in One Act, 1924. Pub. NY: S. French.
The Dickey-Bird, 1925. With Harvey O'Higgins. Pub. NY: S.
French. In *One-Act Plays for Stage and Study*, 2nd ser. (NY).
The Dummy. A Detective Comedy in Four Acts, 1925. With Harvey
O'Higgins. Pub. NY: S. French.
In the Next Room. A Play in Three Acts, c.1925. With Eleanor
Robson Belmont. Pub. NY: S. French.

Mr. Lazarus. A Comedy in Four Acts, c.1926. With Harvey O'Higgins. Pub. NY: S. French.

Under Twenty. A Comedy in Three Acts, c.1926. With Leonidas Westervelt, John Clements, and Harvey O'Higgins. Pub. NY: S. French.

Youth Must Be Served. Comedy in One Act, c.1926. Pub. NY: S. French, 1927. In *One-Act Plays for Stage and Study*, 3rd ser. (NY, 1927); *Today's Literature*, ed. D. Gordon et al. (NY: c.1935).

The Argyle Case. A Drama in Four Acts, c.1927. With Harvey O'Higgins. Pub. NY: S. French.

Orphan Aggie. A Romantic Comedy, c.1927. With Harvey O'Higgins. Pub. NY: S. French.

The Happy Hoboes. A Comedy in One Act, c.1928. With Althea Sprague Tucker. Pub. NY: S. French (French's International Copyrighted Edition of the Works of the Best Authors, no. 642).

In-Laws. A Comedy in One Act, 1928. In *One-Act Plays for Stage and Study*, 4th ser. (NY).

Mr. Susan Peters. A Comedy in One Act, c.1928. Pub. NY: S. French.

Mysterious Money. A Comedy in Three Acts, c.1928. Pub. NY: S. French.

Old P.Q. A Play in Three Acts, c.1928. With Harvey O'Higgins. Pub. NY: S. French.

Wanted--Money. A Comedy in One Act, c.1928. With Althea Sprague Tucker. Pub. NY: S. French.

What Imagination Will Do. Comedy in One Act, 1928. Pub. NY: S. French.

Love in Italy. Comedy in Three Acts, 192-?. Trans. and adap. of Marivaux, with Marie L. LeVerrier. Pub. NY: S. French.

What Are Parents For? A Play in One Act, 1930. Pub. NY: S. French.

The Divine Afflatus. A Comedy in One Act, c.1931. Pub. NY: S. French.

Are Men Superior? A Farce-Comedy in One Act, 1932. Pub. in *One-Act Plays for Stage and Study*, 7th ser. (NY).

Heroic Treatment. A Comedy in One Act, c.1933. Pub. NY: S. French.

See also Duer, Caroline King.

Forepaugh, Luella.

Dr. Jekyll and Mr. Hyde; or, A Mis-Spent Life. A Drama in Four Acts, c. 1897. With George F. Fish. Adap. of Stevenson. Pub. NY: S. French (French's International Copyrighted Edition of the Works of the Best Authors, no. 15). In *Nineteenth Century Plays*, vol. 2.

Freeman, Eleanor.

When the Women Vote, 1885. Pub. Cincinnati: Standard Publishing. In On to Victory: *Propaganda Plays of the Woman Suffrage Movement*, ed. B. Friedl (Boston: Northeastern U. Press, 1987).

Freeman, Mary Eleanor Wilkins, 1852-1930.

Giles Corey, Yeoman, 1893. Pub. NY: Harper.

Frost, Sarah Annie.

See Shields, Sarah Annie Frost.

Fry, Emma Viola Sheridan.

See Sutherland, Evelyn Greenleaf Baker.

Furniss, Grace Livingston Hill, c. 1864-1938.

A Box of Monkeys. A Parlour Farce in Two Acts, 1889. First pub. Harper's *Bazaar*, 1889. Repub. Boston: W. Baker, 1890.

Second-Floor, Spoopendyke. A Farce in One Act, c. 1889. Pub. Boston: W. Baker (Baker's Edition of Plays), 1892.

A Box of Monkeys and Other Farce-Comedies, 1891. Pub. NY: Harper. Includes: *Tulu*; *The Jack Trust*; *The Veneered Savage*.

The Corner Lot, 1891. (Variant title: *A Corner-Lot Chorus*.) Perf. NY: Broadway Th., Apr. 28, 1892. Pub. Boston: W. Baker (Baker's Edition of Plays), c. 1891.

The Jack Trust, 1891. Pub. NY: Harper.

The Nyvtalops or Nyctalopia or a Nyctalops or Myctalops. In Three Acts, 1891. Pub. NY.

Tulu, 1891. Pub. NY: Harper.

The Veneered Savage, 1891. Pub. NY: Harper.

Smoldering Fires, 1894. Perf. NY: Empire Th., Oct. 11, 1894.

A Close Call, 1895. Perf. NY: Empire Th., Mar. 28, 1895.

The Flying Wedge. A Football Farce in One Act, c. 1896. Pub. Boston: W. Baker (Baker's Edition of Plays).

A Colonial Girl, 1898. With Abby Sage Richardson. Perf. NY: Lyceum Th., Oct. 31, 1898. Typescript.

Americans at Home, 1899. With Abby Sage Richardson. Perf. NY: Lyceum Th., Mar. 13, 1899.

The Pride of Jennico, 1900. With Abby Sage Richardson. Adap of novel by A. and E. Castle. Perf. NY: Criterion Th., Mar. 6, 1900.

Robert of Sicily. A Romantic Drama in Four Acts, 1900. Adap. of Longfellow. Typescript.

A Gentleman of France, 1901.

Gretna Green, 1902. Perf. NY: Madison Square Th., Jan. 5, 1903.

Mrs. Jack, 1902. Perf. NY: Wallack's Th., Sept. 2, 1902.

Honor Bright, 1906.

The Man on the Case, 1907. Perf. NY: Madison Square Th., Sept. 4, 1907. Pub. 1931.

A Dakota Widow. A Comedy in One Act, 1915. Pub. NY: S. French (French's International Copyrighted Edition of the Works of the Best Authors, no. 306).

Perhaps. A Comedy in One Act, 1915. Pub. NY: S. French (French's International Copyrighted Edition of the Works of the Best Authors, no. 317).

Father Walks Out. A Comedy in Three Acts, 1928. Pub. NY: S. French.

Captain of His Soul. A Play, n.d. Pub. London.

The Man on the Box, 1915. Adap. of novel by McGrath. Perf. NY: Madison Square Th., Oct. 31, 1905.

Gaddess, Mary L.

A Dream of Fair Women and Brave Men. Tableaux Vivantes for Any Number of Males and Females, 1891. Pub. NY: E. Werner.

The Ivy Queen, A Cantata for any Number of Girls, 1891. Pub. Boston: W. Baker (Baker's Edition of Plays).

Revels of the Queen of May and Her Fairies. A Cantata for Forty-Five Girls, 1891. Pub. Boston: W. Baker. In *Greek Costume Plays for School or Lawn Performance* (1914).

Crowning of Christmas. Musical Play, 1911. With Stanley Schell. Pub. NY: E. Werner.

Gailey, Florence Louise.

Ez-Zahra. A Tragedy of the Tenth Century, 1898. Pub. Detroit.

Gale, Rachel E. Baker.

After Taps. A Drama in Three Acts, c. 1891. Completed "from notes and unfinished manuscript of the late George M. Baker. Pub. Boston: W. Baker (Baker's Edition of Plays).

The Chaperon. A Comedy in Three Acts for Female Characters Only, c. 1891. Pub. Boston: W. Baker.

A King's Daughter. A Comedy in Three Acts for Female Characters Only, c. 1893. Pub. Boston: W. Baker.

Her Picture. A Comedy in One Act, c. 1894. Pub. Boston: W. Baker.

Mr. Bob. A Comedy in Two Acts, 1894. Pub. Boston: W. Baker (Baker's Edition of Plays).

Bachelor Hall. A Comedy in Three Acts, 1898. With Robert M. Baker. Pub. Boston: W. Baker (Baker's Edition of Plays).

No Men Wanted. A Sketch in One Act, 1903. Pub. Boston: W. Baker (Baker's Edition of Plays).

The New Crusade. A Comedy in Two Acts, c. 1908. Pub. Boston: W. Baker (Baker's Edition of Plays).

Coats and Petticoats. A Comedy in One Act, 1910. Pub. Boston: W. Baker.

The Clinging Vine. A Comedy in One Act, 1913. Pub. Boston: W. Baker.

Rebellious Jane. A Comedy, 1916. Pub. Boston: W. Baker (Baker's Royalty Plays).

Gardie, (Madame).

Foret Noire; or, Maternal Affection. A Serious Pantomime in Three Acts, 1795(?). Pub. Boston: Russell.

Gibbs, Julia DeWitt.

A False Note. A Comedy in One Act, c.1888. Pub. Boston: W. Baker (Baker's Edition of Plays).

Under a Spell. A Comedy in One Act, 1888. Adap. of Labiche and Jolly. Pub. Boston: W. Baker.

Gibbs, Julia de Wolf.

See Addison, Julia de Wolf Gibbs.

Gilman, Caroline Howard, 1794-1888.

Isadore, c.1839. In her *Tales and Ballads* (NY: S. Colman, 1839).

Ginty, Elizabeth Beall.

Werther. A Lyric Opera in Four Acts and Five Tableaux, c. 1894. Pub. NY: F. Rullman.

Sappho. A Play in Five Acts, 1895. Adap. of Daudet and Belot. Bilingual text. Pub. NY: F. Rullman.

Missouri Legend. A Comedy, 1938. Pub. NY: Random House. Acting ed. pub. NY: Dramatists Play Service, 1950.

Goodfellow, (Mrs. E. J. H.).

Vice Versa. A Comedy in Three Acts, 1892. Pub. Philadelphia: Penn Publishing, 1912.

Young Dr. Devine. A Comedietta in Two Scenes for Female Characters, 1896. Pub. Philadelphia: Penn Publishing.

Money-Making and Merry-Making Entertainments, 1903. With Elizabeth J. Rook. Pub. Philadelphia: Penn Publishing.

Easy Entertainments for Young People, 1920. Pub. Philadelphia: Penn Publishing.

Goodloe, Abbie Carter, b. 1867. (Pseud.: Carter Goodloe.)

Antinous. A Tragedy, 1891. Pub. Philadelphia: Lippincott.

To Dream Again. A Comedy in One Act, 1940. Pub. NY: S. French.

Goodrich, Elizabeth P.
  Cobwebs. A Juvenile Operetta in Three Acts, c. 1879. Pub. Boston:
  Lee & Shepard.
Gould, Elizabeth Lincoln, d. 1914.
  The Little Men Play, 1900. Adap. of Alcott. Pub. Philadelphia:
  Curtis.
  The Little Women Play, 1900. Adap. of Alcott. Pub. Philadelphia:
  Curtis.
Graham, Mary.
  Mademoiselle's Christmas Gifts, c.1899. In *A Dream of the Centuries
  and Other Entertainments for Parlor and Hall*, ed. George B. Bartlett
  (Boston: W. Baker, c. 1899).
Graves, Adelia Cleopatra Spencer, 1821-1895. (Pseud.: Aunt Alice.)
  *Jephthah's Daughter. A Drama in Five Acts. Founded on the Eleventh
  Chapter of Judges*, 1867. Pub. Memphis: South-Western Publishing.
Gregg, Helen A.
  The Little Vagrants. An Operetta in Two Acts, 1898. Pub. NY: E.
  Werner.
Griffith, Helen Sherman, b. 1873.
  A Borrowed Luncheon. A Farce, c. 1899. Pub. Chicago: T. Denison.
  The Burglar Alarm. A Comedietta in One Act, 1899. Pub.
  Philadelphia: Penn Publishing (Dramatic Library, vol., 1, no. 180).
  A Fallen Idol. A Farce in One Act, 1900. Pub. Philadelphia: Penn
  Publishing.
  A Case of Duplicity. A Farce in One Act, 1901. Pub. Philadelphia:
  Penn Publishing.
  The Sewing Society. A Drama in One Act, 1901. Pub. Chicago.
  The Dumb Waiter. A Farce in One Act, 1903. Pub. Boston: W. Baker
  (Baker's Edition of Plays).
  For Love or Money. A Comedy in Three Acts, 1903. Pub.
  Philadelphia: Penn Publishing.
  A Large Order. A Sketch in One Act, c.1903. Pub. Boston: W. Baker
  (Baker's Edition of Plays).
  *A Psychological Moment. A Farce in Two Scenes for Female Characters
  Only*, c.1903. Pub. Boston: W. Baker (Baker's Edition of Plays).
  Social Aspirations. A Comedy in Two Scenes, 1903. Pub. NY: Dick
  and Fitzgerald.
  *The Scarlet Bonnet. A Comedy in Two Acts for Female Characters
  Only*, 1904. Pub. Boston: W. Baker (Baker's Edition of Plays).
  *The Wrong Miss Mather. A Comedy in One Act for Female Characters
  Only*, 1905. Pub. Boston: W. Baker (Baker's Edition of Plays).
  The Wrong Package. A Comedy in One Act for Female Characters

Only, c.1906. Pub. Boston: W. Baker (Baker's Edition of Plays).

Maid to Order. A Farce in One Act for Female Characters Only, c.1907. Pub. Boston: W. Baker (Baker's Edition of Plays).

Help Wanted. A Comedy in Three Acts, 1908. Pub. Philadelphia: Penn Publishing, 1909.

A Man's Voice. A Comedy in Three Acts for Female Characters Only, c.1908. Pub. Boston: W. Baker (Baker's Edition of Plays).

A Merry Widow Hat. A Farce in One Act for Female Characters Only, c.1909. Pub. Boston: W. Baker (Baker's Edition of Plays).

Reflected Glory. A Farce in One Act (for Female Characters), 1909. Pub. Philadelphia: Penn Publishing.

An Alarm of Fire. A Comedy in One Act, 1911. Pub. Boston: W. Baker (Baker's Edition of Plays).

The Minister's Wife. A Farce in One Act, 1916. Pub. Philadelphia: Penn Publishing.

Getting the Range. A War Play in One Act, 1918. Pub. Boston: W. Baker (Baker's Edition of Plays).

Her Service Flag. A Play in One Act, 1918. Pub. Philadelphia: Penn Publishing.

The Knitting Club Meets; or, Just Back from France. A Comedy in One Act, 1918. Pub. Boston: W. Baker (Baker's Edition of Plays).

The Game of Old Maid. A Play for Girls in One Act, 1919. Pub. Philadelphia: Penn Publishing.

The Over-alls Club. A Farce in One Act, 1920. Pub. Boston: W. Baker (Baker's Edition of Plays).

The Ladies Strike. A Play for Girls in One Act, 1921. Pub. Philadelphia: Penn Publishing.

Guernsey, Alice Margaret, 1850-1924.

1492-1776: Five Centuries. A Centennial Drama in Five Acts, 1876. Pub. Boston: New England Publishing.

Guiney, Louise Imogen, 1861-1920.

The Martyr's Idyl, 1899. Pub. Boston: Houghton Mifflin. Dramatic poem.

Hadley, Lizzie M.

At the Court of King Winter. A Christmas Play for Schools, c. 1896. Pub. NY: E. Kellogg.

A Christmas Meeting. A Holiday Exercise for Twenty-Five Children, 1908. Music by A. Allen. Pub. Philadelphia: Penn Publishing.

Hale, Sara Josepha Buell, 1788-1879.

Ormond Grosvenor, 1839.

The Judge: A Drama of American Life, 1851. Pub. in *Godey's Magazine and Lady's Book* 42 (Philadelphia, 1851).

Hall, Louisa Jane Park, 1802-1892.

> *Miriam. A Dramatic Poem*, 1837. Pub. Boston: Hilliard, Gray. Rev. ed., 1838.
> *Hannah, the Mother of Samuel, the Prophet and Judge of Israel*, 1839. Pub. Boston: J. Munroe. Dramatic poem.
> "Miriam" and "Joanna of Naples," 1850.

Harrison, Constance Cary, 1843-1920.

> *A Russian Honeymoon*, 1883. Adap. of *La lune de miel* by E. Scribe. Perf. NY: Madison Square Th., April 9, 1883. Pub. NY: DeWitt (DeWitt's Acting Plays, no. 359), 1890.
> *Behind a Curtain. A Monologue in One Act*, 1887. Perf. NY: Madison Square Theatre, Jan. 14, 1887 (original performer, Mrs. Charles Denison). In *Short Comedies for Amateur Players*, c.1889. Also pub. separately, Chicago: Dramatic Publishing, 1892.
> *The Mousetrap. A Comedietta in One Act*, c.1889. Trans. and adap. of P. Siraudin). In *Short Comedies for Amateur Players*, c.1889. Also pub. separately, NY: DeWitt (DeWitt's Acting Plays).
> *Short Comedies for Amateur Players, as Given at the Madison Square and Lyceum Theatres, New York, by Amateurs*, 1889. Pub. NY: DeWitt; London: Griffith, Farran, Brown. Includes: *The Mouse-Trap*; *Weeping Wives* (trans. and adap. of P. Siraudin); *Behind a Curtain, Tea at Four O'Clock*, and *Two Strings to her Bow*. Pub. NY: DeWitt, 1889.
> *Tea at Four O'Clock. A Drawing-Room Comedy in One Act*, c.1889. In *Short Comedies for Amateur Players*, c.1889. Also pub. separately, Chicago: Dramatic Publishing (Sergel's Acting Drama, no. 375).
> *Two Strings to her Bow. A Comedy in Two Acts*, c. 1889. In *Short Comedies for Amateur Players*, c.1889. Also pub. separately, NY: DeWitt (DeWitt's Acting Plays, no. 376).
> *Alice in Wonderland. A Play for Children in Three Acts*, 1890. Adap. of Carroll. Pub. NY: DeWitt (DeWitt's Acting Plays).

Hatton (Variant sp.: Hattan), Ann Julia Kemble, 1764-1838. (Pseud.: Anne of Swansea.)

> *The Songs of Tammany; or, The Indian Chief. A Serious Opera*, 1794. Commissioned by the Tammany Society. Perf. NY: John Street Th., Mar. 3, 1794. Pub. NY: J. Harrison. Prologue also pub. in a volume of poems by R. B. David (NY, 1807).
> *American Brothers; or, A Visit to Charleston*, 1807. Perf. Charleston: Charleston Th., Mar. 14, 1807.

Haughwout, L. May.

> *The Princess*, 1890. Adap. Tennyson. Pub. NY: E. Werner, 1891.
> *All-Around Recitations*, 1895. Pub. NY: E. Werner.
> *Gossip Pantomime*, 1890. Pub. NY: E. Werner.

Japanese Fantastics, 1891. Pub. NY: E. Werner.
Hayes, Maud Blanche.
   The Royal Revenge. A Romantic Drama in Five Acts, c. 1898.
Typescript.
Hazard, Eleanor.
   An Old Plantation Night. A Representation of Life "in de Quarters,"
c. 1890. With Elizabeth Hazard. Musical. Pub. NY: Dick and
Fitzgerald.
Hazard, Elizabeth, 1799-1882.
   See Hazard, Eleanor.
Henley, Anne.
   Cinderella. Illustrated Play in Four Scenes for Children, 1895. Musical.
With Stanley Schell. Pub. NY: E. Werner.
   Mayanni. A Play for Children, n.d. Pub. NY: E. Werner.
Henry, Sarepta Myrenda Irish, 1839-1900.
   Victoria; or, The Triumph of Virtue, c.1865. In her *Victoria; With
Other Poems* (Cincinnati: Poe and Hitchcock, 1865).
Hentz, Caroline Lee Whiting, 1800-1856.
   Werdenberg; or, The Forest League, 1832. Perf. NY: Park Th., after it
won contest a sponsored by W. Pelby of the Boston Theatre.
   De Lara, or, The Moorish Bride, A Tragedy in Five Acts, 1831. Perf.
Philadelphia: Arch Th., Nov. 7, 1831. One source says this play won
the Pelby Prize. Pub. Tuscaloosa, AL: Woodruff and Olcott, 1843.
   Lamorah; or, The Western Wild, 1833. Perf. New Orleans: Caldwell's
Th., Jan. 1, 1833.
   *Constance of Werdenberg; or, The Heroes of Switzerland. A Dramatic
Poem*, 1850. Pub. in Georgia Newspaper Mar. 23-May 9.
Heron, Matilda Agnes, 1830-1877.
   The Belle of the Season, 1854. Perf. NY: Laura Keene's Th., Oct. 16,
1854.
   Fiaminna, 1856. Adap. of novel by Urchard. Perf. NY: Wallack's
Th., Sept. 7, 1857.
   Camille; or, The Fate of a Coquette, 1856. Adap. of Dumas *fils*. Perf.
NY: Wallack's Th., Jan. 22, 1857. Pub. Cincinnati: T. Wrightson, 1856.
   Medea, 1857. Adap of Legouve. Perf. NY: Wallack's Th., Feb. 16,
1857. Pub. NY: S. French, 1857.
   Mathilde, 1858. Perf. NY: Laura Keene's Th., June 7, 1858.
   Lesbia, 1860. Adap. of Latour. Perf. NY: Tripler Hall, Jan. 23, 1860.
   Phaedre, 1858. Adap. of Racine. Perf. NY: Laura Keene's Th., May
9, 1803. Pub. Cincinnati, 1858.
   Gamea; or, The Jewish Mother, 1863. Adap. (of Scribe?) Perf. NY:
Niblo's Gardens, Sept. 29, 1863.

Champagne; or, Step by Step, 1870. With Laura Keene. Perf. NY: Laura Keene's Chestnut St. Th., Jan. 3, 1870.

Herrick, Ada Elizabeth.
See Paul, Anne Marie.

Herring, Fanny.
Adrienne, or The Secret of a Life, 1866. Adap. of the French. Perf. NY: Bowery Th., Dec. 3, 1866.

Heywood, Delia A. (Pseud.: Polly Ann Pritchard.)
Pritchard's Choice Dialogues, 1866-1898. Series of vols. Pub. Chicago: A. Flanagan.
The Visiting Smiths. A Farce, 1920. Pub. Franklin, OH: Eldridge.

Herzog, Helene (Pseud.: H. B. Enéleh.)
One Year. A Comedy-Drama in Four Acts, c. 1884. Pub. New York: DeWitt; Chicago: Dramatic Publishing (Sergel's Acting Drama, no. 319).
Tempest Tossed. An Original Drama in Four Acts, c. 1885. Pub. NY: DeWitt (DeWitt's Acting Plays, no. 337); Chicago: Dramatic Publishing (Sergel's Acting Drama, no. 337).

Hitchcock, Martha Wolcott Hall, d. 1903.
David Harum. A Comedy in Three Acts, c. 1898. With James Ripley Hitchcock. Adap. of N. Westcott. Pub. NY: S. French, 1939.

Holbrook, Amelia Weed.
Jack, the Commodore's Grandson, c. 1893. Typescript.
The Terror, 1899. Typescript.
Friday Afternoon at the Village School. A Farcical Entertainment in One Scene, 1909. Pub. NY: S. French (French's International Copyrighted Edition of the Works of the Best Authors, no. 179).
The Rejuvenation of Miss Semaphor. A Farce Comedy in Four Acts, 192-?. Adap. of H. Godfrey. Typescript.

Holbrook, Margaret Louise.
His Heroine. A Farce in One Act, 1894. Pub. Philadelphia: Penn Publishing, 1906.

Holley, Marietta, 1836-1926. (Pseud.: Josiah Allen's Wife.)
Betsey Bobbett. A Drama, 1880. Pub. Adams, NY: W. Allen.
Josiah's Secret. A Play, 1910. Pub. Watertown, NY: Hungerford-Holbrook.

Hook, (Mrs. James), d.1805(?).
Double Disguise. A Comic Opera in Two Acts, 1784. Music by James Hook. Perf. London: Theatre Royal Drury Lane. Perf. NY: Old American Co., April 29, 1795. Pub. London.

Hope, Kate.
> *Our Utopia, Its Rise and Fall. An Aesthetic Comedietta in Two Acts*, 1882. Pub. NY: H. Roorbach (Acting Drama no. 174).

Hopkins, Pauline Elizabeth, 1859-1930.
> *Peculiar Sam, or The Underground Railroad*, 1879. (Original title: *Slaves' Escape, or The Underground Railroad*.) Musical. Perf. Boston: Oakland Garden, July, 1880. In *Roots of African American Drama: An Anthology of Early Plays*, ed. L. Hamalian and J. Hatch (1991).
> *One Scene from the Drama of Early Days*, n.d. Adap. of Blblical story of Daniel.

Horne, Mary Barnard, b. 1845.
> *The Four-Leaved Clover. An Operetta in Three Acts*, 1886. Pub. Boston: White-Smith Music.
> *A Sevres Cup; or, A Bit of Bric-a-Brac. A Comedietta in Three Acts*, 1886. Adaptation.
> *A Carnival of Days*, 1887. Pub. Boston: W. Baker.
> *The Peak Sisters. An Entertainment*, c. 1887. Pub. Boston: W. Baker.
> *The Book of Drills. A Series of Entertainments*, 1889-90. Pub. Boston: W. Baker. Includes: *A National Flag Drill; The Shepherds' Drill; The Tambourine Drill; The Mother Goose Quadrille; The Nursery Maids' Drill*.
> *Professor Baxter's Great Invention. An Unclassified Entertainment in One Act*, c. 1891. Pub. Boston: W. Baker.
> *The Last of the Peak Sisters; or, The Great Moral Dime Show. An Entertainment in One Scene*, c. 1892. Pub. Boston: W. Baker.
> *Plantation Bitters. A Colored Fantasy in Two Acts for Male Characters Only*, c. 1892. Pub. Boston: W. Baker.
> *Jolly Joe's Lady Minstrels. Selections for the "Sisters,"* 1893. With Alice M. Silsbee. Pub. Boston: W. Baker.
> *A Singing School of Ye Olden Time*, c. 1894. Pub. Boston: W. Baker. Repub. Boston: W. Baker, 1922 (Baker's Novelties).
> *Gulliver and Lilliputians Up to Date. An Entertainment in One Act*, 1896. Pub. Boston: W. Baker. Also in *Club and Lodge-Room Entertainments for Floor or Platform Use*, ed. F. E. Chase (Boston: W. Baker, 1908).
> *The Darktown Bicycle Club Scandal. A Colored Sketch in One Act for Lady Minstrels*, c. 1897. Pub. Boston: W. Baker.
> *The Ladies of Cranford. A Sketch of English Village Life Fifty Years Ago in Three Acts*, c. 1899. Adap. of Gaskell. Pub. Boston: W. Baker (Baker's Edition of Plays).
> *The Other Fellow. A Comedy in Three Acts*, 1903. Pub. Boston: W. Baker, 1904.
> See also Silsbee, Alice M.

Hosmer, Harriet.
  1975: A Prophetic Drama, 1875. Privately printed, Rome, 1875.
Howe, Julia Ward, 1819-1910.
  Leonora or the World's Own, 1857. (Variant title *Lenore*.... Also pub.
  as *The World's Own*, 1857.) Perf. NY: Wallack's Th., Mar. 16, 1857.
  Pub. Boston: Ticknor and Fields. In *Stuart's Repertory of Original
  American Plays*, no. 1 (NY: Baker and Goodwin, 1857); A. H. Quinn's
  Representative American Plays, 4th ed.
  Hyppolytus. A Tragedy in Five Acts, n.d. Perf. Boston: Tremont Th.,
  Mar. 24, 1911. In *America's Lost Plays*, vol. XVI (Princeton: 1941).
Howie, Helen Morrison.
  After the Matinee. A Comedy in One Act, 1899. Pub. Philadelphia:
  Penn Publishing (Dramatic Library, vol. 1).
  The Reformer Reformed. A Comedy Sketch, 1899. Pub. Philadelphia:
  Penn Publishing.
  His Father's Son. A Farce Comedy in One Act, 1900. Pub.
  Philadelphia: Penn Publishing.
  Those Dreadful Drews. A Comedy in One Act, 1910. Pub.
  Philadelphia: Penn Publishing.
  Too Much Bobbie. A Farce in One Act, 1914. Pub. Philadelphia:
  Penn Publishing.
Hughes, Louise Marie.
  Love's Stratagem. A Comedy in Two Acts, 1894. Pub. Philadelphia:
  Penn Publishing (Keystone Edition of Popular Plays, 1894; Dramatic
  Library, vol. 1, no. 43, 1896).
Hunt, Arzalea.
  The Menagerie in the Schoolroom, 1895. Pub. Darrowville, OH:
  School Publishing.
  A Visit from Mother Goose and Her Family. A Descriptive Pantomime,
  1895. Pub. Darrowville, OH: School Publishing.
  The Wood Fairies. An Arbor Day Entertainment, 1895. Pub. NY: H.
  Roorbach.
  Going to Meet Aunt Hattie, 189-?. Pub. Lebanon, OH: March.
  The Lost Dog. A Comic Dialogue, 189-?. Pub. Lebanon, OH: March.
  A Wedding Notice, 189-?. Pub. Lebanon, OH: March.
Huse, Carolyn Evans.
  Under the Greenwood Tree. A Christmas Operetta in One Act, c. 1895.
  Pub. NY: E. Werner.

Hyde, Elizabeth A.
> *The Engaged Girl. A Comedy,* c. 1899. Pub. Chicago: T. Denison (Amateur Series, vol. 2, no. 208).

Ingraham, Jean.
> *The Raw Recruits; or, A Day with the State National Guard. A Military Comedy-Drama in Two Acts,* 1893. Pub. Clyde, O.: Ames (Ames Series of Standard and Minor Drama, no. 322).

Ives, Alice Emma, d.1930.
> *Lorine,* 1874.
> *The Brooklyn Handicap,* 1894. Racing drama.
> *The Village Postmaster. A Domestic Drama in Four Acts,* c. 1894. With Jerome Eddy. Pub. NY: S. French (Standard Library Edition).
> *A Very New Woman,* 1896. Pub. in *The Woman's Column* 9, no. 11 (March 14, 1896). In *On to Victory: Propaganda Plays of the Woman Suffrage Movement,* ed. B. Friedl (Boston: Northeastern U. Press, 1987).

Jaquith, (Mrs. M. H.)
> *The "Deestrick Skule" of Fifty Years Ago,* c. 1888. Pub. Topeka, KS: Official Printing.
> *"Exerbition" of The Deestrick Shule of Fifty Years Ago,* c. 1890. Sequel to above. Pub. Chicago: Dramatic Publishing, 1890.
> *Ma Dusenberry and her Gearls,* c. 1896. Musical. Pub. Chicago: Dramatic Publishing.
> *Parson Poor's Donation Party. Burlesque Entertainment in Two Scenes,* c. 1896. Pub. Chicago: Dramatic Publishing (Sergel's Acting Drama, no. 441).

Jervey, Caroline Howard.
> *The Lost Children. A Musical Entertainment in Five Acts,* c. 1870. Pub. Boston: Spencer (Plays for Children, no. 1).

Johnstone, Annie Lewis.
> *On the Frontier,* 1891.

Jones, Clara Augusta (Pseuds.: Clara Augusta; Hero Strong).
> *The Matrimonial Advertisement,* c. 1877. Pub. in *Dramatic Leaflets. Comprising Original and Selected Plays* (anthology), c. 1877.

Jones, Gertrude Manly.
> *Miss Matilda's School. A Comic Operetta for Boys and Girls,* c. 1892. Pub. Boston: W. Baker (Baker's Edition of Plays).
> *Half and Hour with a Giant. A Holiday Opera for Children, Adapted to Familiar and Popular Airs,* 1892. Pub. Boston: W. Baker (Baker's Edition of Plays).

Joseph, Delissa.
The Blue-Stocking. A Comedietta in One Act, c. 1884. Pub. Chicago: Dramatic Publishing (Sergel's Acting Drama, no. 532). Also pub. with *Caught at Last* by Nomad (pseud.), NY: DeWitt (DeWitt's Acting Plays, no. 333).

Kavanaugh, (Mrs. Russell).
Kavanaugh's Juvenile Speaker, for Very Little Boys and Girls, 1877. Pub. NY: Dick and Fitzgerald.
Kavanaugh's Humorous Dramas for School Exhibitions and Private Theatricals, 1878. Pub. NY: Dick and Fitzgerald.
Kavanaugh's Exhibition Reciter for Very Little Children, 1881. Pub. NY: Dick and Fitzgerald.
Kavanaugh's New Speeches, Dialogues and Recitations for Young Children, 1884. Pub. NY: Dick and Fitzgerald.
Original Dramas, Dialogues, Declamations, and Tableaux Vivants for School Exhibitions, May-Day Celebrations, and Parlor Amusement, 1884. Pub. Louisville, KY: J. Morton.
Kavanaugh's Comic Dialogues and Pieces for Little Children, 1887. Pub. NY: Dick and Fitzgerald.

Keatinge, Ella.
The Legend of the Christmas Tree. A Play for Children in Three Acts, 1899. Pub. NY: Roxbury.
The Little Baker. A Play for Children in Two Acts, 1899. Pub. NY: Roxbury.
The Nightingale and the Lark. A Play for Children in One Act, c. 1899. Pub. Chicago: Dramatic Publishing.
The Old Trunk in the Garret. A Play for Children in Two Acts, c. 1899. Pub. NY: Roxbury.
Short Plays for Children, c. 1899. Pub. NY: Roxbury.
A White Lie. A Comedy in Two Acts for Young Ladies, c. 1899. Pub. Chicago: Dramatic Publishing (Sergel's Acting Drama, no. 455).
A Christmas Eve Adventure. A Play for Children in One Act, 190-?. Pub. Chicago: Dramatic Publishing.

Keene, Laura, 1826-1873.
Life's Troubled Tides, c. 1850.
The Macarthy; or, The Peep of Day, 1862. Adap. Perf. NY: Laura Keene's Th., Feb. 22, 1862.
Workingmen in New York, 1865. Perf. NY: Barnum's Museum, Feb. 20, 1865.
Also see Heron, Matilda Agnes.

Keene, Mattie.

Fifty Years After. One-Act Playlet, n.d. Typescript and prompt copy formerly belonging to George W. Wilson) in Harvard U. Lib.

Kellogg, Clara Louise, 1842-1916.

The Bohemian Girl. Opera in Three Acts, 1874. Music by Michael W. Balfe. Adap. of Bunn. Pub. Baltimore: Sun Printing.

Faust. Grand Opera in a Prologue and Four Acts, 1874. With Jules Barbier and Michel Carre. Music by Charles-Francis Gounod. Adap. of Goethe. Pub. Baltimore: Sun Printing.

Lucia de Lammermoor. Grand Opera in Three Acts, 1874. Adap. of Donizetti; in Eng. Pub. Baltimore: Sun Printing.

The Huguenots. Grand Opera in Five Acts by Meyerbeer, c. 1875. Trans. and adap. Pub. Baltimore: Sun Printing.

The Star of the North. Opera in Three Acts by G. Meyerbeer, c. 1876. Trans. and adap. Pub. Baltimore: Sun Printing.

Keteltas, Caroline M.

The Last of the Plantaganets. A Tragic Drama in Three Acts, 1830. Adap. of W. Heseltine. Pub. NY: R. Craighead, 1844.

Kidder, Kathryn.

The Heart of her Husband. A Domestic Drama in Three Acts and Two Scenes, 187-?. Typescript and promptbook.

Kimball, Hannah Parker, b. 1861.

Victory, 1897. In her *Victory and Other Verses* (Boston: Copeland and Day).

Merlin Revivified and the Hermit, 1900. Pub. in *Poet-Lore*, 12.4.

Kinnaman, (Mrs. C. F.)

In a Spider's Web. Musical Farce Comedy in Three Acts, c. 1900. With C. F. Kinnaman. Pub. Clyde, OH: Ames (Ames Series of Standard and Minor Drama, no. 421).

Kinney, Elizabeth Clementine Dodge Stedman, 1810-1889.

Bianca Capello. A Tragedy, 1873. Pub. NY: Hurd and Houghton.

Kitchel, (Mrs. Francis W.)

The Wager. A Comedy Duologue, 1894. Pub. NY: E. Werner.

Knapp, Lizzie Margaret.

An Afternoon Rehearsal. A Comedy in One Act for Female Characters Only, c. 1892. Pub. Hartford, CT: The United Workers and Woman's Exchange.

Lambla, Hattie Lena.

The Bewitched Closet. A Dramatic Sketch in One Act, 1872(?). Perf. Sacramento, CA: Varieties Th., Jan. 15, 1872. Pub. Clyde, OH: Ames (Ames Series of Standard and Minor Drama, no. 38).

Domestic Felicity. A Domestic Sketch in One Act, 1872(?). Pub. Clyde,

OH: Ames (Ames Series of Standard and Minor Drama, no. 42).

Obedience; or, Too Mindful by Far. A Comedietta in One Act, 1872. Perf. Sacramento, CA: Turner's Th., April 29, 1872. Pub. Clyde, OH: Ames (Ames Series of Standard and Minor Drama, no. 44).

That Mysterious Bundle. A Farce in One Act, 1872(?) Pub. Clyde, OH: Ames (Ames Series of Standard and Minor Drama, no. 40).

Lazarus, Emma, 1849-1887.

Orpheus, c.1871. In her *Admetus and Other Poems* (NY: Hurd and Houghton, 1871).

Prologue for the Theatre, c.1871. In *Admetus and Other Poems*, as above.

Scene from Faust, c.1871. In *Admetus and Other Poems*, as above.

The Spagnoletto. A Play, 1876. Priv. printing. In *The Poems of Emma Lazarus*, ed. by her sister Josephine (Boston), 1889.

The Dance to Death. A Historical Tragedy in Five Acts, 1882. In her *Songs of a Semite, The Dance to Death, and Other Poems* (New York: 1882).

Lennox, Charlotte Ramsay, 1720-1804

Angelica; or Quixote in Petticoats. A Comedy in Two Acts, 1758. Probably adap. of her popular novel, *The Female Quixote* (1752).

Philander. A Dramatic Pastoral, 1758. Pub. London: A. Miller.

The Sister. A Comedy, 1769. Adap. of her novel. Perf. London: Covent Garden Th., 1769. Pub. Dublin: P. and W. Wilson. Trans. into German, 1776 (the first play by an American-born playwright to be translated into a foreign language). Adapted by Burgoyne, John, 1722-1792, retitled *The Heiress*.

Old City Manners, 1775. Adap. of Jonson, Chapman, and Marston's *Eastward Hoe*. Perf. London: Theatre Royal Drury Lane. Pub. London: T. Becket.

Leslie, Miriam Florence Folline Squier, 1836-1919.

The "Demi-Monde." A Satire on Society, 1858. Adap. Dumas *fils*. Pub. Philadelphia: Lippincott.

Lewis, Abbie Goodwin Davies, d. 1906.

Hunt the Thimble; or, Little Nell's Surprise Party. An Original Operetta in One Act, 1884. Music by Leo Lewis. Pub. Boston: White-Smith.

Caught Napping. A One-Act Operetta for Christmas Eve, c. 1886. Music by Leo Lewis. Pub. Boston: O. Ditson.

Jingle Bells. An Original Operetta in Two Scenes for Christmas Eve, 1887. Music by Leo Lewis. Pub. Boston: O. Ditson.

Christmas at the Kerchiefs: A Musical Dialogue for Use at Christmas Tree Festivals, 1888. With Leo Lewis. Pub. Brattleboro, VT: E.

Carpenter.

The Dairymaid's Supper. A Cantata for Church and Charity Festivals, 1888. With Leo Lewis. Pub. Brattleboro, VT: E. Carpenter.

Our Easter Offering. Cantata, 1888. Music by Leo Lewis. Pub. Boston: O. Ditson.

The Rainbow Festival for Church, Sunday School, and Charity Festivals, and the Rainbow Prince, A Novel Children's Entertainment en Tableau, 1888. With Leo Lewis. Pub. Brattleboro, VT: E. Carpenter.

Programme for School Celebration of Washington's Birthday, 1894(?). Pub. Boston: Ginn.

Lewis, Eliza Gabriella.

The Outlaw. A Dramatic Sketch, c.1850. In her *Poems* (Brooklyn, NY: Shannon, 1850).

Lewis, Estelle Anna Blanche Robinson, 1824-1880. (Pseud.: Stella.)

Helémah; or, the Fall of Montezuma. A Tragedy, 1864. Pub. NY.

The King's Stratagem; or, The Pearl of Poland. A Tragedy in Five Acts, 1873. Pub. London: Truebner.

Sappho. A Tragedy in Five Acts, in Verse, 1875. Pub. London: Truebner.

Lippmann, Julie Mathilde, c. 1864-1952.

A Fool and His Money, 1894. Perf. NY: Empire Th., Mar. 8, 1894.

Cousin Faithful, 1895. Perf. NY: Empire Th., Mar. 28, 1895.

The Facts of the Case, 1896. Perf. NY: Empire Th., Mar. 26, 1896.

Facts. A Farce in One Act, 1897. Pub. Philadelphia: Penn Publishing (Dramatic Library, vol. 1, no. 88; Keystone Edition of Popular Plays).

Fool. A Comedy in Two Acts, 1901.

Cous Faith. A Comedy in One Act, 1908. Pub. Philadelphia: Penn Publishing.

Martha-By-the-Day, 1914. Adap. of her novel.

Martha. A Comedy in Three Acts, 1919. Pub. NY: S. French (French's Standard Library Edition).

Little, Sophia Louise Robbins, b. 1799.

The Branded Hand. A Dramatic Sketch, Commemorative of the Tragedies at the South in the Winter of 1844-45, 1845. Pub. Pawtucket, RI: R. Potter.

Livingston, Margaret Vere Farrington, b. 1863.

Sauce for the Goose. A Farce in One Act, 1899. Pub. Boston: W. Baker (Baker's Edition of Plays).

Locke, Belle Marshall, 1865-1933. ("Nellie M. Locke.")

Marie's Secret. A Duologue in One Scene, c. 1893. Pub. Boston: W. Baker (Baker's Edition of Plays), 1894.

The Great Catastrophe. A Comedy in Two Acts, 1895. Pub.

Philadelphia: Penn Publishing.

A Heartrending Affair. A Monologue, 1895. Pub. Philadelphia: Penn Publishing, 1911.

A Victim of Woman's Rights. A Monologue, 1896. Pub. Clyde, OH: Ames (Ames Series of Standard and Minor Drama, no. 371).

Original Monologues and Sketches, 1903. Pub. Boston: W. Baker. Includes: *A Man, A Maid, and a Dress-suit Case; How Miss Culy Took the Cake; American Beauties; Polly's Surprise Party; Uncle Ned's Ring; His Best Girl; Mrs. Follansbee's Tramp.*

Miss Fearless and Company. A Comedy in Three Acts for Female Characters Only, 1905. Pub. Boston: W. Baker (Baker's Edition of Plays).

Mr. Easyman's Niece. A Comedy in Four Acts, c.1908. Pub. Boston: W. Baker (Baker's Edition of Plays).

The Hiartville Shakespeare Club. A Farce in One Act, 1896. Pub. Philadelphia: Penn Publishing, 1913.

Breezy Point. A Comedy in Three Acts for Female Characters Only, c. 1899. Pub. Boston: W. Baker.

Logan, Olive, 1839-1909.

Eveleen, 1864. (Var. title: *The Felon's Daughter.*) Perf. NY: Wallack's Th., Aug. 22, 1864.

Armadale, 1866. Adap. Wilkie Collins. Perf. NY: Broadway Th., Dec. 3, 1866.

Surf; or, Summer Scenes at Long Branch, 1870. Perf. NY: Daly's Th., Jan. 12, 1870.

A Business Woman, 1873. Perf. NY: Union Square, Mar. 13, 1873.

L'Assomoir, 1879. Adap. of Zola. Perf. NY: Olympic Th., Apr. 30, 1879.

Newport, 1879. Adap of *Niniche.* Perf. NY: Daly's Th., Sept. 18, 1879.

La Cigale, 1879. Perf. NY: Park Th., Oct. 26, 1879.

Lord, Alice Emma Sauerwein, 1848-1908.

A Vision's Quest. A Drama in Five Acts, Representing the Hopes and Ambitions, the Love, Marriage, Pleadings, Discouragements, and Achievements of Christopher Columbus, Discoverer of America, 1899. Pub. Baltimore: Cushing.

Lovell, Maria Anne Lacy, 1803-1877.

Ingomar, the Barbarian. A Play in Five Acts, 1851. Adap. of E. Munch-Bellinghousen. Perf. Philadelphia: Chestnut St. Th., Nov. 19, 1851. Pub. NY: S. French, 1872. In *The Modern Standard Drama,* vol. 12, ed. E. Sargent (NY: J. Douglas).

The Beginning and the End. A Domestic Drama in Four Acts, 1855.

Perf. London: Haymarket Th.
Luce, Grace A.

> *Brass Buttons. A Comedy in Three Acts for Female Characters Only*, 1900. (Orig. title: *S. Sutherland Breyfogle*.) Perf. San Diego, CA: Decem Club at the St. Louis Opera House, Nov. 10, 1900. Pub. Boston: W. Baker (Baker's Edition of Plays).

Luetkenhaus, Anna May Irwin, b. 1874.

> *Master Skylark*, 1894. Adap. of John Bennett. Pub. NY: Century, c. 1896, 1914.
>
> *Plays for School Children*, 1915. Pub. NY: Century.
>
> *New Plays for School Children*, 1929. Pub. NY: Century.

Madden, Eva Annie, b. 1863.

> *A Noble Spy. An Historical Play for Boys*, 1899. Pub. NY: Kellogg.

Manning, Kathryn.

> *Francesco Carrara. A Drama in Three Acts*, c. 1899. Adap. of French original. Pub. Chicago: Dramatic Publishing (Sergel's Acting Drama, no. 550).

Marguerittes, Julie Granville (Comtesse de), 1814-1866.

> *Enoch Arden*, 1869. Adap. of Tennyson. Perf. NY: Booth's, June 21, 1869.

Marriott (Mrs.)

> *The Chimera; or, Effusions of Fancy*, 1794. Perf. Philadelphia: Southwark Th., Nov. 17, 1794. Pub. NY: T. and J. Swords, Printers, 1795.
>
> *The Death of Major Andre*, 1796. Perf. on tour in Virginia.

Mathews, Frances Aymar, c.1865-1925.

> *All for Sweet Charity. Comedy*, c.1889. Pub. NY: E. Werner (Werner Edition), 1907.
>
> *American Hearts. Comedy*, c.1889. Pub. NY: E. Werner (Werner Edition), 1907.
>
> *The Apartment. Comedy*, c.1889. Pub. NY: E. Werner (Werner Edition), 1907.
>
> *At the Grand Central. Comedy*, c.1889. Pub. NY: E. Werner (Werner Edition), 1907.
>
> *Both Sides of the Counter. Comedy*, c.1889. Pub. NY: E. Werner (Werner Edition), 1907.
>
> *Charming Conversationalist. Comedy*, c.1889. Pub. NY: E. Werner (Werner Edition), 1907.
>
> *The Courier. Comedy*, c.1889. Pub. NY: E. Werner (Werner Edition), 1907.
>
> *En Voyage. Comedy*, c.1889. Pub. NY: E. Werner (Werner Edition), 1907.

The Honeymoon: Fourth Quarter. *Comedy,* c.1889. Pub. NY: E. Werner (Werner Edition), 1907.

A Knight of the Quill. *Comedy,* c.1889. Pub. NY: E. Werner (Werner Edition), 1907.

On the Staircase. *Comedy,* c.1889. Pub. NY: E. Werner (Werner Edition), 1907.

Paying the Piper. *Comedy,* c.1889. Pub. NY: E. Werner (Werner Edition), 1907.

The Proposal. *Comedy,* c.1889. Pub. NY: E. Werner (Werner Edition), 1907.

Scapegrace. *Comedy,* c.1889. Pub. NY: E. Werner (Werner Edition), 1907.

Snowbound. *Comedy,* c.1889. Pub. NY: E. Werner (Werner Edition), 1907.

Teacups. *Comedy,* c.1889. Pub. NY: E. Werner (Werner Edition), 1907.

The Title and the Money. *Comedy,* c.1889. Pub. NY: E. Werner (Werner Edition), 1907.

War to the Knife. *Comedy,* c.1889. Pub. NY: E. Werner (Werner Edition), 1907.

The Wedding Tour. *Comedy,* c.1889. Pub. NY: E. Werner (Werner Edition), 1907.

A Woman's Forever. *Comedy,* c.1889. Pub. NY: E. Werner (Werner Edition), 1907.

A Finished Coquette. *A Comedietta in One Act,* 1895. Pub. Boston: W. Baker (Baker's Edition of Plays).

Wooing a Widow. *A Comedietta in One Act,* c.1895. Pub. Boston: W. Baker (Baker's Edition of Plays).

Cousin Frank. *A Farce in One Act for Female Characters Only,* 1896. Pub. Boston: W. Baker (Baker's Edition of Plays).

Six to One; or, The Scapegrace. *A Comedietta in One Act,* c.1887. Pub. Boston, W. Baker, c.1896.

Matthews, Edith Virginia Brander.

Six Cups of Chocolate. *A Piece of Gossip in One Act,* c. 1897. Adap. of E. Schmithof. Pub. NY: Harper.

McComb, (Mrs. D. M.)

A Conclusive Argument, c.1874. In *Beadle's Dime Dialogues,* no. 14 (1874).

McConaughy, Julia E. Loomis, b. 1834.

The Drunkard's Daughter, 1869. In *A Collection of Temperance Dialogues,* comp. S. T. Hammond (Ottawa: 1869).

McCord, Louisa Susannah Cheves, 1810-1880.

Caius Gracchus. A Tragedy in Five Acts, 1851. Pub. NY: H. Kernot.

Medina, Louisa H., 1813(?)-1838.

Kairissa; or, The Warrior of Wanachtihi, 1831. Perf. NY: Bowery Th., Sept. 11, 1834.

Wacousta; or, The Curse, 1833. Adap. of John Richardson's novel. Perf. NY: Bowery Th., Dec. 30, 1833.

Guy Rivers; or, The Gold Hunters, 1834. Adap. of W. G. Simms' novel about rural Georgia.

Outalissi; or, The Indian Council Chamber, 1834.

The Wept of Wish-ton-Wish, 1834. Adap. of Cooper novel.

The Last Days of Pompeii: A Dramatic Spectacle, 1835. Adap. of Bulwer-Lytton's novel. Perf. NY: Bowery Th., Feb. 9, 1835. Pub. NY: S. French (French's Standard Drama, no. 146), 1844. French Acting Edition, 1856. Other French editions: 1857, 1858, 1860.

O'Neil the Rebel, 1835. Perf. NY: Bowery Th., May 11, 1835.

Norman Leslie, 1836. Adap. of T.S. Fay novel. Perf. NY: Bowery Th., Jan. 11, 1836.

The Jewess, 1836. Adap. of Scribe. Perf. NY: Bowery Th., Mar. 7, 1836.

Rienzi, 1836. Adap. of Bulwer-Lytton novel. Perf. NY: Bowery Th., May 23, 1836.

Lafitte, Pirate of the Gulf, 1836. Adap. of J.H. Ingraham's novel. Perf. NY: Bowery Th., Sept. 19, 1836.

Pericles, 1837. Adap. of Shakespeare.

Giafar al Barmeki, 1837. Adap. of novel by Spring.

Il Maledetto, 1837. Adap.

Leona of Athens, 1837. Adap.

Nick of the Woods; or, Telie, the Renegade's Daughter, 1838. Adap. of R. M. Bird's novel. Perf. NY: Bowery Th., Feb. 5, 1838. [Information in first English edition: First produced at the Bowery Theatre, N.Y., Feb. 20th, 1843]. Pub. Boston (Spencer's Boston Theatre, no. LXII [prompter's copy, interleaved]), 1843; London: Dick's, n.d.; NY: French (French's Standard Drama, no. CCLXIX.), 1843.

Ernest Maltravers. A Drama in Three Acts, 1838. Adap. of Bulwer-Lytton's novel. Perf. NY: Wallack's National Th., Mar. 28, 1838. Pub. NY: French (French's Standard Drama, no CXLIII; French's Acting Edition, no. CXLIII, 1857; London: Dick's, n.d.

The Black Schooner; or, The Private Slaver Armistad, 1839. Perf. NY: Bowery Th., Sept. 1, 1839.

The Statue Fiend; or, The Curse of the Avenger, 1840. Perf. NY: Bowery Th., May 18, 1840.

The Collegians, 1842. Adap. of novel by Griffin. Perf. NY: Bowery Th., Dec. 26, 1842.

Merington, Marguerite, 1860-1951.

Captain Letterblair; or, Loves Me, Loves Me Not, 1891. Written for star actor E. H. Sothern. Perf. NY: Lyceum Th., Oct. 22, 1891. Pub. Indianapolis: Bobbs-Merrill, c. 1906.

Oh, Belinda, 1892.

Goodbye. A Story of Love and Sacrifice, 1893. Typescript in New York Pub. Lib.

A Lover's Knot, 1894. Perf. NY: Fifth Avenue Yh., Nov. 20, 1894.

An Everyday Man, 1895. Adap. of work by Sol Smith Russell. Typescript in New York Pub. Lib.

Daphne; or, The Pipes of Arcadia. Three Acts of Singing Nonsense, 1896. Pub. NY: Century.

Bonnie Prince Charlie, 1897.

Love Finds the Way, 1898. (Variant title: *The Right ot Happiness*.) Adap. of German play. Perf. NY: Fifth Avenue Th., Apr. 11, 1898.

The Gibson Play. A Two-Act Comedy Based on Mr. Charles Dana Gibson's Series of Cartoons, "A Widow and Her Friends," 1901. Pub. NY: Life Publishing.

Cranford: A Play. A Comedy in Three Acts, 1905. Adap. of E. Gaskell's novel. Pub. NY: Fox, Duffield.

Old Orchard, 1906. (Variant title: *Rose Valley*.) Perf. Chicago: Nov., 1906. Promptbook in New York Pub. Lib.

Von Rummelsberg, 1906.

The Children of Men, 1906.

The Vicar of Wakefield, 1909. Adap. of O. Goldsmith. Pub. NY: Duffield.

Holiday Plays, 1910. Pub. NY: Duffield. Includes: *Priscilla, Myles, and John; A Washington's Birthday Pageant; The First Flag; Abe Lincoln and Little A. D.; The Dulce et Decorum Club*.

Picture Plays, 1911. Pub. NY: Duffield. Includes: *The Last Sitting* (Picture, "Mona Lisa" by Da Vinci); *A Salon Carrí Fantasy* (Picture, "The Man with the Glove" by Titian); *His Mother's Face* (Picture, "Une fete champetre" by Watteau): *A Gainsborough Lady* (Picture, "The Duchess of Devonshire" by Gainsborough); *Artist-Mother and Child* (Picture, "Mme. Vigée Lebrun and her Daughter" by Mme. Vigée Lebrun); *Queen and Emperor* (Picture, "Queen Louisa" by Richter); *Millet Group* (Picture, "The Angelus" by Millet).

Festival Plays, 1913. Pub. NY: Duffield. Includes: *Father Time and His Children; Tertulla's Garden, or The Miracle of Good St. Valentine; The Seven Sleepers of Ephesos; Princess Moss Rose; The Testing of Sir Gawayne;*

A Christmas Party.

Fairy Tale Plays, 1916. Pub. NY: Duffield. Includes: *Red Riding Hood; Cinderella; Bluebeard.*

More Fairy Tale Plays, 1917. Pub. NY: Duffield. Includes: *Puss in Boots; The Three Bears; Hearts of Gold, or Lovely Mytlie; Hansel and Gretel.*

The Testing of Sir Gawayne. All Hallowe'en, c.1921. In *A Treasury of Plays for Children*, ed. M. Moses (Boston, 1921).

A Dish o' Tea Delayed. One-Act Play for High School Girls, Founded on a True Incident When the Republic USA Was Young, 1937. Pub. NY: S. French. About Benjamin Franklin.

Booth Episodes; Play in Eight Episodes, Nine Scenes, Founded on the Life of Edwin Booth, 1944. Typescript in New York Pub. Lib.

Late Dyal and Company. A Comedy in Three Acts, n.d. 19-?. Typescript in New York Pub. Lib.

At Parting. A Comedy, n.d. Adap. of sketch by A. M. Bagby. Typescript in New York Pub. Lib.

The Castaways. One-Act Sketch for Singing Quartet (Male), n.d. Typescript in New York Pub. Lib.

The Court of Ferrara. A Dialogue, n.d. Typescript in New York Pub. Lib.

Drum and Fife Parade, n.d. Typescript in New York Pub. Lib.

The Island. A Drama, n.d. Adap. of *Foul Play* by C. Reade and D. Boucicault. Typescript in New York Pub. Lib.

The Key to the House. A Play, n.d. Typescript in New York Pub. Lib.

Love Finds the Way, n.d. Typescript in New York Pub. Lib.

Kindly Light. A Modern Morality Play, n.d. Typescript in New York Pub. Lib.

The Musical Isle, n.d. Typescript in New York Pub. Lib.

One Life to Give. Verse Drama Founded on the Story of Nathan Hale, n.d. Typescript in New York Pub. Lib.

Pepilia. A Comedy, n.d. Typescript in New York Pub. Lib.

The Right Ending. One-Act Sketch in Blank Verse, n.d. Typescript in New York Pub. Lib.

Snowwhite and the Seven Dwarfs; Fairytale Play, n.d. Adap. of Goerner and the Brothers Grimm. Typescript in New York Pub. Lib.

That Little Shabby Gentleman, n.d. Typescript in New York Pub. Lib.

Meriwether, Elizabeth Avery, 1824-1917.

The Devil's Dance. A Play for the Times, 1886. Pub. St. Louis: Hallman.

The Ku Klux Klan; or, The Carpet-Bagger in New Orleans, 1877. Pub. Memphis: Southern Baptist Pub. Society.

Merriman, Effie Woodward, b. 1857.

Maud Muller. A Burlesque Entertainment in Three Acts, c. 1891. Pub. Chicago: Dramatic Publishing.

A Pair of Artists. A Comedy in Three Acts, c. 1892. Chicago: Dramatic Publishing (Sergel's Acting Drama, no. 436).

Diamonds and Hearts. A Comedy-Drama in Three Acts, c. 1897. Pub. Chicago: Dramatic Publishing.

Comedies for Children. A Collection of One-Act Plays, c. 1898. Pub. Chicago: Dramatic Publishing.

The Drunkard's Family. A Children's Play in One Act, c.1898. Pub. Chicago: Dramatic Publishing (Children's Plays).

Through a Matrimonial Bureau. A Comedietta in One Act, c. 1898. Pub. Chicago: Dramatic Publishing (Sergel's Acting Drama, no. 495).

Tompkin's Hired Man. A Drama in Three Acts, c. 1898. Pub. Chicago: Dramatic Publishing (Sergel's Acting Drama, no. 419).

What Ailed Maudie. A Children's Play in One Act, 1898. Pub. Chicago: Dramatic Publishing (Children's Plays).

Their First Meeting. A Comedietta in One Act, 1899. Pub. Chicago: Dramatic Publishing (American Acting Drama).

The Bachelor's Club, 1901. Pub. Chicago.

Deacon Jenkins' Choir Meeting, c. 1924. Pub. Franklin, OH: Eldridge (Eldridge Novel Entertainments).

Miller, Alice Duer, 1874-1942.

The Rehearsal, 1915. Typescript.

Unauthorized Interviews, 1917. In *On to Victory: Propaganda Plays of the Woman Suffrage Movement*, ed. B. Friedl (Boston: Northeastern U. Press, 1987).

The Charm School. A Comedy in Three Acts, 1922. With Robert Milton. Pub. NY: S. French.

The Springboard. A Comedy in Three Acts, 1928. Pub. NY: S. French (French's Standard Library Edition).

Also see Duer, Caroline King, 1865-1956.

Monroe, Harriett, 1860-1936.

Valeria A Tragedy in Five Acts, 1892. In *Valeria and Other Poems* (Chicago: A. McClurg).

After All, 1900. Pub. Boston: *Poet-Lore* 12.3.

The Passing Show: Five Modern Plays in Verse (Boston: 1903). Includes: *The Thunderstorm, At the Goal, After All, A Modern Minuet, It Passes By.*

Montgomery, Margaret.
>   *Per Telephone: A Farce in One Act*, c.1893. Pub. Boston: W. Baker (Baker's Edition of Plays).

Morgan, Geraldine Woods.
>   *Tannhauser and the Minstrels Tournament on the Wartburg. Grand Romantic Opera in Three Acts*, c.1891. Adap. of Wagner, with his music. Bilingual text. Pub. Berlin: 1891.

Morse, Mabel.
>   *A Foolish Investment. A Comedietta in One Act*, c.1888. Adap. of German original. Pub. NY: DeWitt (DeWitt's Acting Plays, no. 350).
>   *A Warm Reception. A Comedietta in One Act*, c. 1890. Trans. and adap. of *Im Schneegestober*, by Rudolph Jarosy. Pub. NY: DeWitt (Sergel's Acting Drama, no. 345).

Morton, Marguerite W.
>   *The Blind Girl of Castèl-Cuillè*, c. 1892. Verse play with music. Adap. of Longfellow. Pub. NY: E. Werner.
>   *Scenes from the Last Days of Pompeii*, 1894. Pub. Philadelphia: Penn Publishing (Keystone Edition of Popular Plays).
>   *The Two Roses: A Farce in Two Acts for Three Males and Two Females*, c.1894. Pub. NY: E. Werner.
>   *Poison. A Farce in One Scene for Four Females*, 1895. Adap. Pub. NY: E. Werner.
>   *The Spanish Gypsy. A Drama*, 1905. Adap. of G. Eliot. Pub. St. Paul, MN.

Morton, Martha, 1865-1925.
>   *Helene*, 1888. (Variant title: *The Refugee's Daughter.*) Perf. NY: Fifth Avenue Th., Apr. 30, 1888.
>   *The Triumph of Love; or, The Merchant*, 1890. Perf. NY: Union Square Th., June 26, 1890.
>   *The Merchant*, 1891. Probably variant of *The Triumph of Love.*
>   *Miss Prue*, 1891. Perf. NY: Lee Avenue Academy, Nov. 16, 1891.
>   *Geoffrey Middleton, Gentleman*, 1892. Perf. NY: Union Square Th., March 31, 1892.
>   *Brother John*, 1893. Perf. NY: Star Th., March 20, 1893. Typescript in New York Pub. Lib.
>   *Christmas*, 1894. Adap. of *Je Dine Chez ma Mere*. Perf. NY: Empire Th., Feb. 27, 1894.
>   *His Wife's Father*, 1895. (Variant title: *His Father's Wife.*) Adap. of A. L'Aronge. Perf. NY: Fifth Avenue Th., Feb. 25, 1895. Typescript in New York Pub. Lib.
>   *The Fool of Fortune*, 1896. Perf. NY: Fifth Avenue Th., Dec. 1, 1896. Written for star actor William H. Crane. Promptbook in New York

Pub. Lib.

A Bachelor's Romance. An Original Play in Four Acts, 1896. Perf. NY: Garden Th., Sept. 20, 1897. Written for star actor Sol Smith Russell. Promptbook in New York Pub. Lib. Pub. NY: S. French, 1912.

The Sleeping Partner, 1897.

Her Lord and Master. A Comedy in Four Acts, 1902. Perf. NY: 1902. Pub. NY: S. French (French's Standard Library Edition), 1912.

The Diplomat, 1902. Perf. NY: Madison Square Th., Mar. 20, 1902.

The Triumph of Love, 1904. Perf. NY: Criterion Th., Feb. 8, 1904.

A Four-Leaf Clover, 1905.

The Truth Tellers, 1905.

The Illusion of Beatrice, 1905.

The Movers, 1907. Perf. NY: Hackett Th., Sept. 3, 1907. Typescript in New York Pub. Lib.

On the Eve, 1909. Adap. of L. Kampf.

The Senator Keeps House. A Comedy, 1911(?). Promptbook in New York Pub. Lib.

The Three of Hearts, 1915.

Moses, Annie Jonas.

Esther. A Drama in Five Acts, 1887. Pub. Cincinnati: Bloch. Purim play.

Mowatt, Anna Cora Ogden, 1819-1870.

Gulzara, the Persian Slave, 1840. Six-act drama in blank verse. Written in Paris and first perf. in by amateurs in Flatbush, L. I., with author playing lead. Pub. by Epes Sargent in periodical *The New World*, vol. 2, no. 17 (1841).

Fashion; or, Life in New York, 1845. Perf. NY: Park Th., Mar. 24, 1845. Promptbook in New York Pub. Lib. Pub. NY: S. French (French's Standard Drama, no. CCXV), 1849. Repub. Boston: Ticknor and Fields, 1855. In *Representative American Plays*, ed. A. Quinn (NY: 1917), *American Plays*, ed. A. Halline (NY: 1935), and numerous other anthologies.

Armand; or, The Peer and the Peasant. A Play in Five Acts, 1847. Perf. NY: Park Th., Sept. 27, 1847, with author playing lead role of Blanche. Pub. NY: S. French, 1849.

Plays, 1855. Pub. Boston: Ticknor and Fields. Contents: *Armand*; *Fashion*.

Murray, Ellen.

Cain, Ancient and Modern. In *Dramatic Leaflets. Comprising Original and Selected Plays* (anthology), c. 1877.

The Crusaders. In *Dramatic Leaflets* as above.

Easu and Jacob. In *Dramatic Leaflets* as above.

Licensed Snakes. Temperance Diaolgue. In *Dramatic Leaflets* as above.

The Women of Lowenburg. A Historical Comedy in Five Acts, c.1886 [attributed]. Pub. Chicago: T. Denison (The Amateur Series).

Murray, Judith Sargent Stevens, 1751-1820. (Pseud.: Constantia.)

Virtue Triumphant, 1795. (Original title: *The Medium; or, The Happy Tea Party.*) Perf. Boston: Federal Th., March 2, 1795. Pub. in *The Gleaner,* vol. 2 (Boston: 1798).

The Traveller Returned, 1796. Perf. Boston: Federal Th., March 9, 1796. Pub. in *The Gleaner,* vol. 2 (Boston: 1798).

The Gleaner. A Miscellaneous Production, 1798. Pub. Boston: I. Thomas and E. T. Andrews, Printers. Includes essays, poems, plays.

The African, n.d.

Norton, Jessie.

Sappho. A Classical Historical Play for Girls, c.1894. Pub. NY: E. Werner.

Norton, Morilla Maria, b. 1865.

Gloria Victis, 1900. Pub. Warner, NH: Cole. About the Biblical Queen Esther.

O'Brien, Constance.

Cross Purposes. A Comedy in One Act, 189-?. Pub. NY: DeWitt (DeWitt's Acting Plays, no. 382).

The Wager. A Comedy in One Act, 189-?. Pub. NY: DeWitt (De Witt's Acting Plays, no. 383).

A Lover and a Half. A Comedy in Two Acts, 189-?. Pub. NY: DeWitt (De Witt's Acting Plays, no. 384).

Love in a Flue; or, The Sweep and the Magistrate. A Comedy in Two Acts, 189-?. Pub. NY: DeWitt (DeWitt's Acting Plays, no. 385).

Possible Plays for Private Players, 1894(?) Pub. London: G. Farran (3rd ed.). Includes: *Cross Purposes; The Wager; A Lover and a Half; The Sweep and the Magistrate.*

Oliver, Isabella.

See Sharp, Isabella Oliver.

Orne, Martha Russell.

A Black Diamond. A Comic Drama in Two Acts, 1890. Pub. Boston: W. Baker (Baker's Edition of Plays).

The Country School. An Entertainment in Two Scenes, 1890. Pub. Boston: W. Baker (Baker's Novelty List).

A Limb o' the Law. A Comedy in Two Acts, 1892. Pub. Boston: W. Baker (Baker's Edition of Plays).

Timothy Delano's Courtship. A Comedy in Two Acts, 1892. Pub. NY: H. Roorbach.

The Donation Party; or, Thanksgiving Eve at the Parsonage. A Comedy in Three Acts, 1894. Pub. Boston: W. Baker (Baker's Edition of Plays).

An Old Maid's Wooing. A Drama in Two Acts, 1899. Pub. Boston: W. Baker (Baker's Edition of Plays).

Packard, Hannah James, 1815-1831.

The Choice. A Tragedy, 1832. In *The Choice...With Other Miscellaneous Poems* (Boston: L. Bowles, 1832).

Pacheco, (Mrs. Romualdo).

Ireland; or, The Voice of the People. A Drama of Real Life in Four Acts, 1890. Pub. NY: Trow's Printing.

Incog. A Farce Comedy in Three Acts, 1892. Pub. NY: M. Witmark (Witmark Stage Publications), 1906. Later adapted by Karl Hoschna as *Three Twins*, a musical.

Tom, Dick, and Harry. A Farcical Comedy in Three Acts, 189-?. Pub. NY: S. French.

Loyal Till Death, n.d.

Nothing But Money, n.d.

Paine, Jennie E.

See Cobb, Josephine H.

Parker, Lottie Blair, 1858-1937. (Full name: Parker, Charlotte Blair.)

White Roses, 1892. Perf. NY: Frohman's Lyceum Th., Apr. 25, 1892.

Way Down East. A Drama in Four Acts, 1898. (Orig. title: *Annie Laurie*.) "Elaborated" by J. R. Grismer [This elaboration included a mechanical snowstorm in the last act]. Perf. Newport, R.I.: Aug. 28, 1897. "Elaborated" version perf. Chicago: Nov. 19, 1897; NY: Manhattan Th., Feb. 17, 1898. Was basis for Griffiths' 1920 film.

Under Southern Skies. A Play in Four Acts, 1901. Perf. NY: Republic Th., Nov. 12, 1901.

The Redemption of David Corson, 1906. Adap. of novel by Goss. Perf. NY: Majestic Th., 1906.

Parsons, Laura Matilda Stephenson, 1855-1925.

Colloquy of the Holidays. A Play for Children, 1889. Pub. Dansville, NY: Bunnell and Oberdorf.

The District School at Blueberry Corners. A Farce in Three Scenes, c. 1889. Orig. pub. Dansville, NY: Bunnell and Oberdorf. Repub. as "A Farcical Entertainment in Three Scenes," Boston: W. Baker (Baker's Edition of Plays), 1894.

Scenes in the Union Depot. A Humorous Entertainment in One Scene, c.1889. Pub. Boston: W. Baker (Baker's Edition of Plays), c.1905.

Jerusha Dow's Family Album, 1892. Pub. Boston: W. Baker (Baker's Edition of Plays).

Living Pictures of the Civil War, 1894. Pub. Boston: W. Baker (Baker's Novelties). Also in *Tableau and Pantomime Entertainments for*

School or Public Performance (Boston: W. Baker, 1914).

Scenes and Songs of Ye Olden Times. An Old Folks Entertainment, 1894. Pub. Boston: W. Baker (Baker's Novelties).

Jerusha Dow's Album No. 2: Her Friends and Neighbors, c.1899. Pub. Boston: W. Baker (Baker's Edition of Plays).

The Old Maid's Convention. An Entertainment in One Scene, c. 1899. Featured popular songs "I'm Glad I am an Old Maid" and "Priscilla at Her Spinning." Pub. Boston: W. Baker (Baker's Edition of Plays).

Aunt Jerusha's Quilting Party. A Novelty in One Scene, c.1901. Pub. Boston: W. Baker (Baker's Edition of Plays).

A Variety Contest. A Humorous Entertainment in One Scene, 1901. Pub. Boston: W. Baker (Baker's Novelties).

The New Woman's Reform Club. A Humorous Entertainment in One Act, 1902. Pub. Boston: W,. Baker (Baker's Edition of Plays).

Paul, Anne Marie.

Passe Rose, 1894. With Frances Marsh Bancroft, Susan Edmond Coyle, and Ada Elizabeth Herrick. Adap. of A. S. Hardy.

Peattie, Elia Wilkinson, 1862-1935.

The Love of a Caliban. A Romantic Opera in One Act, 1898. Pub. Wausau, WI: Van Vechten and Ellis. Adapted later by Freer, Eleanor Everest (1864-1942) as *Massimilliano, The Court Jester*, 1925.

The Wander Weed and Seven Other Little Theater Plays, 1923. Pub. Chicago: C. Sergel. Includes: *The Wander Weed*; *The Great Delusion*; *Family Reunion*; *Sunrise*; *Pity*; *Spring Cleaning*; *Spring Cleaning*; *When the Silver Bell Tree Blooms*; *Job's Tears*.

Castle, Knight, and Troubador, in an Apology and Three Tableaux, 1903. Pub. Chicago: Blue Sky Press.

Times and Manners: A Pageant, 1918. Pub. Chicago: The Chicago Women's Club.

The Great Delusion. A Drama in One Act, 1932. Pub. Chicago: Dramatic Publishing.

Peck, Elizabeth Weller.

Nathaniel Hawthorne's "Scarlet Letter" Dramatized. A Play in Five Acts, 1876. Pub. Boston: Franklin Press, 1876.

Pelham, Nettie H.

The Christmas Ship. A Christmas Entertainment, c.1888. Pub. Chicago: T. Denison (Denison's Specialties).

The Realm of Time. A Pageant for Young People and Children, 1890. Pub. Chicago: T. Denison.

The Old Fashioned Husking Bee. An Old Folks' Entertainment in One Scene, 1891. Pub. Boston: W. Baker (Baker's Edition of Plays).

The White Caps, 1891. Pub. Chicago: T. Denison. Play for children.

The Belles of Blackville. A Negro Minstrel Entertainment for Young Ladies Concluding with a Specialty Farce Entitled "Patchwork", c. 1897. Pub. NY: H. Roorbach.

Phelan, Agnes Vivien.

Margaret of Anjou. A Drama, 1888. Pub. Chicago: Donohue and Henneberry.

Phelps, Lavinia Howe.

Dramatic Stories for Home and School Entertainment, 1874. Pub. Chicago: Griggs. Includes: *The Mantle of Charity; A Picnic; Candy Pulling; A Golden Wedding; The Dandy Prince; Shenstone Society; Bringing Back the Sunshine; The Bumblebee; Am I One?; The Birch; The Gold Sunff-Box; Catnip Tea; What Makes a Man?; Morning and Night; The Bootblack; Blind Eva; The May-Basket Army; A Game of Nuts; The Kernel of Corn; The Pocket-Book; The Tangled Thread; Sorrowing Nettie; What Christmas Means; Three Ways of Keeping Christmas; A Substantial Christmas Wish; A Christmas Address.*

Phelps, Pauline.

A Cyclone for a Cent. A Farce in One Act, 1894. Pub. Boston: W. Baker (Baker's Edition of Plays).

Aunt Sarah on Bicycles. Humorous Monologue for a Woman, c.1899. Pub. NY (Pauline Phelps's Pieces).

Humorous Readings and Recitations, 1899. Pub. NY: E. Werner (Werner's Readings and Recitations, no. 20; The Reciter's Library, vol. 2, no. 5).

Minister's Black Nance, c.1899. Pub. NY (Pauline Phelps's Pieces).

A Shakespearian Conference. A Drama, c. 1899. Pub. NY: E. Werner.

Aunt Elnora's Hero. Humorous Monologue for a Woman, 1900. Pub. NY (Pauline Phelps's Pieces).

The Sweet Girl Graduate. Humorous Monologue for a Lady, 1900. Pub. NY: E. Werner.

A Telephone Romance. Humorous Monologue for a Lady, 1900. Pub. NY: E. Werner.

Rosalind's Surrender, 1901. Pub. NY: E. Werner (Pauline Phelps's Pieces).

Her Cuban Tea, 1902. Pub. NY: E. Werner (Pauline Phelps's Pieces).

Burlesque Pantomime of Shakespeare's "Seven Ages of Man," 1903. Pub. NY (Pauline Phelps's Pieces).

The Cook. Humorous Monologue in Irish Dialect for a Lady, 1903. Pub. NY: E. Werner (Pauline Phelps's Pieces).

Firetown's New Schoolhouse, 1903. Pub. NY (Pauline Phelps's Pieces).

A Jolly Brick, c.1903. Pub. NY (Pauline Phelps's Pieces).

Just Commonplace, c.1903. Pub. NY (Pauline Phelps's Pieces).

A Midnight Courtship, c.1903. Pub. NY (Pauline Phelps's Pieces).

Scorching versus Diamonds, c.1903. Pub. NY (Pauline Phelps's Pieces).

Spinster Thurber's Carpet, c.1903. Pub. NY: E. Werner (Pauline Phelps's Pieces).

A Story of Hard Times, 1903. Pub. NY: E. Werner.

A Trial Performance; or, The Stage-Struck Maiden. A One-Act Play, 1903(?). Pub. NY: E. Werner.

Deacon Slocum's Presence of Mind. Monologue for a Woman, 1904. Pub. NY: E. Werner (Pauline Phelps's Pieces).

A Family Plate. Comedy Irish-Dialect Monologue for a Woman, c.1904. Pub. NY (Pauline Phelps's Pieces).

A Millinery Melee. Comedy Monologue for a Woman, c.1904. Pub. NY (Pauline Phelps's Pieces).

The Average Boy, c.1905. Pub. NY (Pauline Phelps's Pieces).

Betsy Holden's Burglars. Comedy Monologue for a Woman, c.1906. Pub. NY (Pauline Phelps's Pieces).

A Box of Powders, c.1906. With Marion Short. Pub. NY: E. Werner (Werner's Edition).

The Confederates. Romantic Comedy, c.1906. With Marion Short. Pub. NY: E. Werner.

A Dumb-Waiter Difficulty. Monologue for a Woman, c.1906. Pub. NY (Pauline Phelps's Pieces).

The Reverend Mr. Tuffscrappen, 1906. Pub. NY (Pauline Phelps's Pieces).

Sixteen Two-Character Plays, 1906. Pub. NY: E. Werner (Werner's Readings and Recitations, no. 36).

What a Masquerade Did? Society Monologue for a Woman, 1906. Pub. NY (Pauline Phelps's Pieces).

As the Moon Rose. Dramatic Romantic Revolutionary War Recitation and Monologue, c.1907. Pub. NY (Pauline Phelps's Pieces).

Billy's Animal Show. Humorous Recitation for a Boy, c.1907. Pub. NY (Pauline Phelps's Pieces).

Daisy's Music Practice Hour, 1907. Pub. Belmar, NJ: E. Werner (Pauline Phelps's Pieces).

The Old Fifer (Dedicated to the Sons of the American Revolution), c.1907. Pub. NY (Pauline Phelps's Pieces).

Kit's Caller. Acting Humorous Monologue for a Woman, c.1908. Pub. NY (Pauline Phelps's Pieces).

Saint Cecelia. The Prize Play in One Act, 1908. Pub. NY: S. French (French's International Copyrighted Edition of the Works of the Best Authors, no. 134).

As Molly Told It, c.1909. Pub. NY: E. Werner. Published under pseud. Paul Merion.

Country Fair at Punkinville. Farce in Two Scenes, 1912. Pub. NY: E. Werner.

Courting the Widow. Romantic Comedy, c.1909. Pub. NY: E. Werner.

The Girl from Out Yonder, 1914. With Marion Short. Perf. Baltimore: Aug. 10, 1914. Pub. Chicago: T. Denison (Denison's Royalty Plays).

Jack's Brother's Sister. A Sketch in One Act, 1916. With Marion Short. Pub. Boston: W. Baker (Baker's Edition of Plays).

Cosy Corners. A Comedy in Four Acts, 1922. With Marion Short. Pub. NY: S. French (French's Standard Library Edition).

Witches' Hour and Candle Light. A One-Act Play, 1922. With Marion Short. Pub. NY: S. French (French's International Copyrighted Edition of the Works of the Best Authors, no. 442).

The Belle of Philadelphia Town. A Colonial Comedy in Four ACts, 1925. With Marion Short. Pub. NY: S. French (French's International Copyrighted Edition of the Works of the Best Authors, no. 543).

The Adolescent Young. A Satirical Farce in One Act, 1927. Pub. NY: S. French (French's International Copyrighted Edition of the Works of the Best Authors, no. 606).

The Flour Girl. A Comedy in Three Acts, 1927. (Variant title: *Hot Pancakes*.) With Marion Short. Pub. NY: S. French (French's Standard Library Edition).

Au revoir, Sallie, c.1928. Pub. Belmar, NJ.

Food Conservation Club Meeting, 1928. Pub. Belmar, NJ.

Mrs. Moneymade's Fitting, c.1928. With Marion Short. Pub. Belmar, NJ (Pauline Phelps's Pieces).

Overalls Bridget, c.1928. Pub. Belmar, NJ (Pauline Phelps's Pieces).

Pease and Beans. A One-Act Satirical Farce, 1928. Pub. NY: S. French (French's International Copyrighted Edition of the Works of the Best Authors, no. 656).

Home Sweet Home. A Comedy in One Act, 1929. Pub. NY: S. French (French's International Copyrighted Works of the Best Authors, no. 663).

A Spinster from Choice. A Comedy in One Act, 1929. Pub. NY: S. French (French's International Copyrighted Edition of the Works of the Best Authors, no. 671).

The Blue Ribbon Hat. A Play in One Act, 1930. Pub. NY: S. French (French's International Copyrighted Edition of the Works of the Best Authors, no. 681).

The Moon and the Moonstruck. A Play in One Act, 1930. Pub. NY:

S. French (French's International Copyrighted Edition of the Works of the Best Authors, no. 682).

Shavings. A Comedy in Three Acts, 1930. With Marion Short. Adap. of story by Joseph C. Lincoln. Pub. NY: S. French.

The Sprightly Widow Bartlett. A Colonial Play in One Act, 1930. Pub. NY: S. French (French's International Copyrighted Edition of the Works of the Best Authors, no. 684).

Stop! Go! A Comedy-Drama in Three Acts, 1930. With Marion Short. Pub. Chicago: T. Denison (Denison's Royalty Plays).

Black Gold. A Dramatic Comedy in Three Acts, 1932. With Marion Short. Pub. Minneapolis: Northwestern Press.

Dumb Dora. A Comedy in One Act, 1932. Pub. Minneapolis: Northwestern Press.

I Know George Washington. A One-Act Patriotic Play, c.1932. In *New Plays for Women and Girls* (NY: 1932).

The Impatience of Job. A Character Comedy in Three Acts, 1932. With Marion Short. Pub. NY: S. French.

In Washington's Day. A Play of Revolutionary Times in Three Acts, 1932. With Marion Short. Pub. NY: S. French.

The Night Club Girl, 1932. Pub. NY: S. French. Reprinted from *New Plays for Women and Girls*.

The Quilting Bee at Bascomb's. A One-Act Comedy, 1932. Pub. NY: S. French.

Shameless Sarah. A Colonial Comedy in One Act, 1932. Pub. Philadelphia: Penn Publishing.

The Wistful Widow. A Comedy in Three Acts, 1932. With Marion Short. Pub. Boston: W. Baker.

The Ryerson Mystery. A Play in Three Acts, 1933. With Marion Short. Pub. NY: S. French.

Sister Sally. A Farce Comedy in Three Acts, 1933. Pub. Boston: W. Baker (Baker's Royalty Plays).

Who Said Quit? A Comedy in Three Acts, 1933. With Marion Short. Pub. Chicago: Dramatic Publishing.

A Million Dollar Joke. A Comedy in Three Acts, 1934. Pub. Minneapolis: Northwestern Press.

The Bad Boy Comes Back. A Comedy in Three Acts, 1935. With Marion Short. Pub. NY: S. French.

Love in Bloom. A Comedy in One Act, 1935. Pub. Minneapolis: Northwestern Press.

Orchids for Marie. A Comedy in One Act, 1935. Pub. Minneapolis: Northwestern Press.

Pawnshop Granny. A Play in One Act, 1935. Pub. NY: S. French.

Uncle Peter and the D. D. S. A One-Act Farce Comedy, 1935. Pub. NY: S. French.

The Adventures of Tom Sawyer. A Dramatization of Mark Twain's Book, 1936. Pub. Sioux City, IA: Wetmore Declamation Bureau.

The Dormitory Dub, 1936. Pub. Minneapolis.

His First Shave, 1936. Pub. Minneapolis.

The Leading Lady, c.1936. Pub. Minneapolis.

Borrowed Tails. A Comedy in One Act, c.1937. Pub. Minneapolis: Northwestern Press.

Junior Buys a Car. A Comedy, 1937. Pub. Minneapolis.

The Patched Coat. A Comedy, 1937. Pub. Minneapolis.

The Christmas Rose. A Christmas Comedy in One Act, 1938. Pub. Minneapolis: Northwestern Press.

Cousin Ann. A Comedy in One Act, 1938. Pub. Minneapolis: Northwestern Press.

Glass Dishes. A Comedy in Three Acts, 1938. Pub. Minneapolis: Northwestern Press.

The Lost Letter. A Comedy in One Act, 1938. Pub. Minneapolis: Northwestern Press.

The Lost Ring. A Thanksgiving Play in One Act, 1938. Pub. Minneapolis: Northwestern Press.

Lucky Lucy. A Comedy in One Act, 1938.

Tub Trouble. A Comedy in One Act, 1938. Pub. Minneapolis: Northwestern Press.

The Bishop and the Convict. A Play in One Act, 1939. Adap. of V. Hugo's *Les Miserables*. Pub. Sioux City, IA: Wetmore Declamation Bureau.

Little Women. A Dramatization of Louisa M. Alcott's Book of the Same Name, 1939. Sioux City, IA: Wetmore Declamation Bureau.

Miss Minerva and William Green Hill. A Comedy, 1939. Adap. of Frances B. Calhoun. Pub. Sioux City, IA: Wetmore Declamation Bureau.

The Tell-Tale Heart. A Play in One Act, 1939. Adap. of Edgar Allen Poe. Pub. Sioux City, IA: Wetmore Declamation Bureau.

The Hoosier Schoolmaster. A Comedy Adapted from Edward Eggleston's Book of the Same Name, 1940. Pub. Sioux City, IA: Wetmore Declamation Bureau.

Huckleberry Finn. A Comedy Adapted from Mark Twain's Book of the Same Name, 1940. Pub. Sioux City, IA: Wetmore Declamation Bureau.

The Little Minister. A Play Based Upon J. M. Barrie's Book of the Same Name, 1940. Pub. Sioux City, IA: Wetmore Declamation Bureau.

A Merry Christmas. A One-Act Play, 1940. Scene from her

dramatization of *Little Women*. Pub. Sioux City, IA: Wetmore Declamation Bureau.

Tom Sawyer Wins Out. A One-Act Play, 1940. Adap. of Mark Twain. Pub. Sioux City, IA: Wetmore Declamation Bureau.

The Violin Maker of Cremona. A Drama in One Act, 1940. Adap. of *Fennel*, a play by Francois Coppee. Pub. Sioux City IA: Wetmore Declamation Bureau.

Jane Eyre. A Drama Adapted from Charlotte Bronte's Book of the Same Name, 1941. Pub. Sioux City, IA: Wetmore Declamation Bureau.

The Man Without a Country. A Drama in One Act, 1941. Adap. of story by Edward E. Hale. Pub. Sioux City, IA: Wetmore Declamation Bureau.

Pride and Prejudice. A Comedy Adapted from Jane Austen's Book of the Same Name, 1941. Pub. Sioux City, IA: Wetmore Declamation Bureau.

That Boy Jimmie. A Comedy in Three Acts, 1941. Pub. Syracuse, NY: W. Bigbee (Bigbee's Beacon Plays).

The Ruggleses in the Rear. A Comedy Suggested by Some of the Characters in Kate Douglas Wiggins's Story, "The Birds' Christmas Carol, 1942. (Variant title: *The Birds' Christmas Carol. A Play in One Act.*) Pub. Sioux City, IA: Wetmore Declamation Bureau.

Aunt Polly from Peru. A Comedy in Three Acts, 1947. Pub. Minneapolis (Denison's Royalty Plays).

Madame Butterfly. A Play in Two Scenes, Dramatized from John Luther Long's Story, c.1954. Sioux City, IA: Wetmore Declamation Bureau.

See also Short, Marion and Sprague, Besse Toulouse.

Phillips, Ida Orissa.

The Bright and Dark Sides of Girl-Life in India, 1891. Pub. Boston: Morning Star.

Pinckney, Maria Henrietta.

Erroneously identified as author of *Essays Religious, Moral, Dramatic, and Poetical* (1818), including *The Orphans, The Tyrant's Victims, The Young Carolinians*. See Smith, Sarah Pogson.

Plumb. Harriet Pixley.

Charlotte Temple. A Historical Drama, 1899. Adap. of Susanna Rowson's novel. Pub. Chicago: Atkinson.

Pogson, Sarah Smith.

See Smith, Sarah Pogson.

Polding, Elizabeth.

At the Fireside; or, Little Bird Blue. A Play for Children in Three Acts, c. 1898. Pub. Chicago: Dramatic Publishing.

The Dawn of Redemption; or, The Adoration of the Magi Kings. A Christmas Play in Four Acts, c. 1899. Pub. Chicago: Dramatic Publishing

(Sergel's Acting Drama, no. 576).

A Harmonious Family. Play for Children in Three Acts, c. 1899. Pub. Chicago: Dramatic Publishing (Children's Plays).

St. Elizabeth of Thuringia; or, The Miracle of the Roses. A Legendary Drama in Five Acts for Young Ladies, c. 1899. Pub. NY: Wagner.

Polson, Minnie.

Wild Mab. A Border Drama in Four Acts, c. 1891. Pub. Clyde, OH: Ames (Ames Series of Standard and Minor Drama, no. 290).

Our Kittie. A Comedy Drama in Three Acts, c. 1894. Pub. Clyde, OH: Ames (Ames Series of Standard and Minor Drama, no. 333).

Poyas, Catharine Gendron, 1813-1882.

The Convert, c.1849. In her *The Huguenot Daughters and Other Poems* (Charleston: John Russell, 1849).

The Huguenot Daughters; or, Reasons for Adherence to the Faith. In *The Huguenot Daughters* as above.

Pratt, Sarah H.

Penelope's Symposium: A Dialogue Illustrating Life in Ancient Greece, c. 1891. Pub. Chicago: T. Denison.

Provost, Mary.

Lucie d'Arville, 1863. Perf. NY: Burton's Th., Mar. 2, 1863.

Pullen, Elizabeth Jones, d. 1894.

Algernon in London. A Tragedy, 1880. Pub. Portland, ME: Portland Press.

Pulszky, Terezia Walder.

Three Christmas Plays for Children, 1858. Music by L. Jansa. Pub. London: Griffith and Farran. Includes: *The Sleeper Awakened*; *The Wonderful Bird*; *Crinolina. The Sleeper Awakened* also in *Home Dramas for Young People*, ed. Eliza Lee Cabot.

Putnam, Mary Trail Spence Lowell, 1810-1898

The Bond-Maid, 1844. Trans. and adap. of Swedish work by Frederika Bremer. Pub. Boston: J. Munroe.

Tragedy of Errors, 1861. Pub. Boston: Ticknor and Fields.

Tragedy of Success, 1862. Pub. Boston: Ticknor and Fields. Sequel to *Tragedy of Errors*.

Rand, Katharine Ellen.

New Hampshire Gold. A Comedy Drama in Three Acts, c.1897. Pub. Boston: W. Baker (Baker's Edition of Plays).

Raymond, Fannie, 1830-1890. (Full name: Ritter, Frances Malone Raymond).

Orpheus. A Grand Opera in Four Acts, c.1863. Trans. and adap. of libretto by Ranieri de' Calsabigi for Gluck's music. Bilingual text (French/English). Pub. NY: Academy of Music.

Raynor, Verna M.

The Bird Family and their Friends. A Comedy in Three Acts, c.1898. Pub. Clyde, OH: Ames (Ames' Series of Standard and Minor Drama, no. 394).

Noel Carson's Oath; or, Leonia's Repentance. A Drama in Four Acts, 1889. Pub. Clyde, OH: Ames (Ames' Series of Standard and Minor Drama, no. 408).

Read, Henriette Fanning, fl. 1848-1860.

Dramatic Poems, 1848. Pub. Boston: 1848. Includes: *Medea; Erminia; A Tale of Florence; The New World.*

Reeder, Louise.

Mary Morton; or, The Shirt Sewers, 1855. Perf. NY: Barnum's Museum, Oct. 11, 1855.

Linda the Seegar Girl, 1857. Perf. NY: Bowery Th., June 1, 1857.

Reid, Bertha Belle Westbrook, d. 1939.

The Prince of the World. The Great Christian Play, 1900. With James Halleck Reid.

As the Dance Goes On; or, Who Pays the Fiddler; or, Her Experiment; or, For Some Reason or Other, n.d. Typescript/ promptbook in New York Pub. Lib.

The Light of the World; or, The Light; or, Judith of Bethany; or (To Be Decided Upon Later), n.d. With Hal Reid. Typescript/ promptbook in New York Pub. Lib.

Reynartz, Dorothy.

Carnival; or, Mardi Gras in New Orleans. A Comedy in One Act for Young Ladies, c.1899. Adap. of French original. Pub. NY: Roxbury (Wizard Series). Repub. NY: Wagner (Sergel's Acting Drama, no. 558), 190-?.

A Cup of Coffee. Comedy in One Act for Young Ladies, c.1899. Pub. NY: Roxbury (Wizard Series) and Chicago: Dramatic Publishing (Sergel's Acting Drama, no. 526).

It Is Never Too Late to Mend. Comedy in One Act for Young Ladies, c.1899. Pub. NY: Roxbury (Wizard Series) and Chicago: Dramatic Publishing (Sergel's Acting Drama, no. 559).

A Mother's Love; or A Wreath for Our Lady. A Play in One Act for Children, c.1899. Pub. NY: Wagner (The Wizard Series).

Two Mothers. Drama in Four Acts for Young Ladies, c.1899. Pub. NY: Wagner (The Wizard Series), 191-?.

Richardson, Abby Sage McFarland, 1837-1900.

Abelard and Heloise. A Medieval Romance, with The Letters of Heloise, 1884. Adap. of Abailard. Pub. Boston: J. Osgood.

Donna Quixote. A Dramatic Idyl of the Eighteenth Century, 1890.

Pub. Cambridge.

The Prince and the Pauper, 1890. Adap. of Twain. Perf. NY: Broadway Th., Jan. 29, 1890 (Daniel Frohman production). Pub. NY: A. Seer.

Americans Abroad, 1892. Trans. and adap. of Sardou. Pub. NY: Rosenfield.

A Colonial Girl, 1898. With Grace Livingston Furniss. Perf. NY: Lyceum Th., Oct. 31, 1898.

Americans at Home, 1899. With Grace Livingston Furniss. Perf. NY: Lyceum Th., Mar. 13, 1899.

The Pride of Jennico, 1900. With Grace Livingston Furniss. Adap of novel by A. and E. Castle. Perf. NY: Criterion Th., Mar. 6, 1900.

See also Furniss, Grace Livingston Hill.

Richardson, Anna Steese Sausser, 1865-1949.

Miss Mosher of Colorado; or, A Mountain Psyche. A Comedy-Drama in Four Acts, c.1899. Pub. NY: Dick and Fitzgerald.

A Man's a Man. A Drama in Four Acts, 192-?. With Henry Leslie Fridenberg. Typescript in New York Pub. Lib.

Big-Hearted Herbert. A Comedy in Three Acts, 1934. With Sophie Kerr; adap. of story by Kerr. Pub. NY: S. French.

Let's Scrap It. A One-Act Comedy, c.1935. Pub. NY: Crowel.

Ricord, Elizabeth Stryker, 1788-1865.

Zamba; or, The Insurrection. A Dramatic Poem in Five Acts, 1842. Pub. Cambridge, MA: J. Owen. Bound with *The Christian Slave*, by Harriet Beecher Stowe.

Ringwalt, Jessie Elder.

Paul and Virginia; or, The Runaway Slave. A Play in Three Acts, 1864. Adap. of J. H. Bernardin de Saint-Pierre. Pub. Philadelphia: Ringwalt and Brown.

Ritchie, Anna Cora Ogden Mowatt, 1819-1870.

See Mowatt, Anna Cora Ogden.

Ritchie, Fannie.

Pleasant Wedding Guests. Comedy in One Act, c.1899. Pub. Chicago: Dramatic Publishing (Sergel's Acting Drama, no. 566).

Rittenhouse, Laura J.

The Milkmaids' Convention. Burlesque Entertainment, c.1898. Pub. Chicago: Dramatic Publishing. Originally *The Interstate Milkmaids Convention*, 1889; pub. Chicago: Women's Temperance Publishing.

Ritter, Lucy A.

The Fatal Mistake, c.1874. In *Beadle's Dime Dialogues*, no. 14. (1874).

Riviere, Louise.

The Little Lady, n.d. In *From Tots to Teens. A Book of Original Dialogues for Boys and Girls*, ed. Clara Janetta Fort Denton (Chicago: T. Denison, 1897).

Roberts, Elizabeth Galloway, b. 1761.

The Fortune Hunters, 1795. Philadelphia. Ms. in Cairns Collection, Univ. of Wisconsin.

Robins, Mary Ellis.

The Forerunners. A Fancy, 18-?. Pub. Woodstock, NY: Maverick Press, 1911(?).

Robinson, Harriet Jane Hanson, 1825-1911.

Captain Mary Miller, 1887(?). Pub. Boston: W. Baker (The Globe Drama).

The New Pandora. A Drama, 1889. Pub. NY: G. Putnam.

Robinson, Lucy Catlin Bull, 1861-1903.

A Child's Poems from October to October, 1870-71, 1872. Pub. Hartford: Case, Lockwood and Brainard. Includes *A Rolling Stone Gathers No Moss*; *No Use Crying for Spilt Milk*; *Victor, the King of Fairyland*.

Rohlfs, Anna Katherine Green, 1846-1935.

Risifi's Daughter. A Drama, 1887. Pub. NY: G. Putnam.

Rook, Elizabeth J.

See Goodfellow, Mrs. E. J. H.

Rosse, Jeannie Quinton.

The Egyptian Princess. A Romantic Operetta in Two Acts for Women's Voices, c.1899. Music by C. J. Vincent. Pub. Boston: Boston Music Co.

The Japanese Girl (O Hanu San). An Operetta in Two Acts for Ladies, c.1899. Music by C. J. Vincent. Pub. Boston: Boston Music Co.

Rover, Winnie.

The House on the Avenue; or, The Little Mischief-Makers. A Drama in Six Scenes, 1877. Pub. NY: Catholic Publishing Society.

Rowson, Susanna Haswell, 1762-1824.

The Female Patriot. A Farce, 1794. Perf. Philadelphia: Chestnut St. Th., June 19, 1795. Pub. Philadelphia: 1794.

Slaves in Algiers; or, A Struggle for Freedom. A Play, Interspersed with Songs, in Three Acts, 1794. Perf. Philadelphia: Chestnut St. Th., Dec. 22, 1794. Pub. Philadelphia: Wrigley and Berriman, 1794.

The Volunteers. A Farce, Founded on the Whiskey Insurrection in Pennsylvania, 1795. (Variant title: *The Volunteers. A Musical Entertainment.*) Music by Alexander Reinagle. Perf. Philadelphia: Chestnut St. Th., Jan. 21, 1795. Pub. Philadelphia: 1795.

The American Tar, 1796. Perf. Philadelphia: Chestnut St. Th., 1796.

Americans in England. A Comedy, 1796. Acted for Mrs. Rowson's benefit and farewell to the stage. Pub. Boston: 1796.

Americans in England; or, Lessons for Daughters, 1796. (Variant title: *The Columbian Daughter*.) Perf. Boston: Federal St. Th., Apr. 19, 1797.

Columbia's Daughters. A Drama, 1800. Perf. NY: Mount Vernon Gardens, Sept. 10, 1800.

Hearts of Oak, 1810. Perf. Boston: Federal St. Th., 1810-11.

Biblical Dialogues Between a Father and His Family, Comprising Sacred History. . .in Conjunction with Profane History, 1822. Pub. Boston: Richardson and Lord.

Saul, A Dramatic Sketch, n.d.

Rumsey, Eveline Hall, 1822-1900.

A St. Augustine Episode. A Drama in Three Acts, 1884. Pub. Buffalo: P. Paul, 1890(?).

Ryley, Madeleine Lucette, 1868-1934.

Christopher Junior. Comedy in Four Acts, c. 1889. Perf. NY: Empire Th., Oct. 7, 1895. Perf. London, 1896; retitled *Jedbury Junior*. Pub. NY: S. French (French's Standard Library Edition), c. 1889.

The Basoche, 1893. Adap. of Carre and Messager. Perf. NY: Casino Th., Feb. 25, 1893.

An American Citizen. An Original Comedy in Four Acts, 1895(?). Perf. NY: Knickerbocker Th., Oct. 11, 1897. Pub. NY: S. French (French's Standard Library Edition), c.1895. Later adapted by Ryley as a novel. Promptbook in New York Pub. Lib.

The Time of Strife, 1896. Perf. NY: Empire Th., Jan., 1896. Pub. NY: S. French, 1900.

The Mysterious Mr. Bugle, 1897. Perf. NY: Lyceum Th., Apr. 19, 1897.

A Coat of Many Colors, 1897. Perf. NY: Wallack's Th., Sept. 13, 1897.

My Lady Dainty, 1900. Perf. NY: Madison Square Th., Jan. 8, 1901. Promptbook in New York Pub. Lib.

Richard Savage, 1901. Perf. NY: Lyceum Th., Feb. 4, 1901.

An American Invasion, 1902. Perf. NY: Bijou Th., Oct. 20, 1902.

The Altar of Friendship. A Play in Four Acts, 1902. Perf. NY: Knickerbocker Th., Dec. 1, 1902. Typescript in New York Pub. Lib.

Mice and Men. A Romantic Comedy in Four Acts, 1902. Perf. London: Garrick Th., 1902; NY: Jan. 19, 1903. Promptbook in New York Pub. Lib.

Mrs. Grundy. A Play in Four Acts, 1905. Pub. London: The Stage Play Publishing Bureau, 1924.

The Sugar Bowl. A Comedy in Four Acts, 1904. Perf. London:

Queen's Th., Oct. 8, 1907. Promptbook in New York Pub. Lib.

Lady Jemima, n.d.

Sadlier, Mary Anne Madden, 1820-1903.

The Babbler. A Drama for Boys in One Act, 1861. Pub. NY: D. and J. Sadlier.

The Secret. A Drama Written for the Young Ladies of St. Joseph's Academy, Flushing, L.I., 1865. Pub. NY: D. and J. Sadlier, 1873.

The Invisible Hand. A Drama in Two Acts, c. 1873. Pub. NY: D. and J. Sadlier.

The Talisman. A Drama in One Act, Written for the Young Ladies of the Ursuline Academy, East Morrisania, New York, 1871. Pub. NY: D. and J. Sadlier.

Sanderson, Mary.

The Mistake on Both Sides. A Petite Comedy in One Act, 1852. Pub. NY: Baker, Goodwin. Written when author was ten years old.

Sanford, Amelia.

Maids, Modes and Manners; or, Madame Grundy's Dilemma, 1896. Pub. Philadelphia: Penn Publishing, 1911.

The Ghost of an Idea. A Comedietta in One Act and Three Scenes, 1898. Pub. Philadelphia: Penn Publishing (Keystone Edition of Popular Plays).

The Advertising Girls. A Masque of Very Fly Leaves in Two Scenes, 1900. Pub. Boston: W. Baker (Baker's Edition of Plays).

A Corner in Strait-Jackets. A Farce in One Act, 1904. Pub. Boston: W. Baker (Baker's Edition of Plays).

The Automatic Servant Girl. A Farce in One Act, 1905. Pub. Boston: W. Baker.

A Commanding Position. A Farcical Entertainment, 1909. Pub. Philadelphia: Penn Publishing (Miscellaneous Plays).

A Stew in the Studio; or, Cabbages versus Roses. An Eccentric Comedy in Three Acts, c.1910. Pub. NY: Dick and Fitzgerald.

Schmall. Alice F.

Zanetto, 18-?. Opera in one act based on *La passant* by F. Coppée.

At Sunset, 18-?. Opera in one act adapted from G. Coronaro.

Scribner, Lizzie B.

See Brewster, Emma E.

Scudder, Vida Dutton, 1861-1954.
>   *Mitsu-yu-nissi; or, The Japanese Wedding*, c.1887. With F. M. Brooks. Pub. Chicago: T. Denison (Denison's Specialties). Repub. Boston: H. Young (Young's Standard Series of Plays), 1888.

Selden, Almira.
>   *The Irish Exiles in America. A Drama*, c. 1820. In her *Effusions of the Heart, Contained in a Number of Original Poetical Pieces, on Various Subjects*, pub. Bennington, VT: D. Clark, 1820.
>
>   *Lady Jane Grey and Lord Guilford*, c.1820. In *Effusions*, as above.
>
>   *Naomi: A Sacred Drama in Three Scenes*, c.1820. In *Effusions*, as above.
>
>   *Shepherdess of the Alps*, c.1820. In *Effusions*, as above.

Seymour, Mary.
>   *Bonds, A Drama in Two Acts*, 1880(?).
>
>   *A Daughter-in-Law. A Comedy in One Act*, 1893. Pub. Chicago: Dramatic Publishing.
>
>   *Ten Years Hence. A Comedy in One Act*, 18-?. Pub. Chicago: Dramatic Publishing (The World Acting Dramas)

Sharp, Isabella Oliver 1777-1843.
>   *Frances and Mila: A Dialogue*, c.1805. In *Poems, on Various Subjects* (Carlisle[?]: A. London, 1805).
>
>   *Philander and Lucinda*, c.1805. In *Poems, on Various Subjects*, as above.

Sherman, Helen Hoyt.
>   *The Lady from Philadelphia. A Farce in One Act*, 1896. Pub. Philadelphia: Penn Publishing, 1901.

Shields, Lottie.
>   *When the Cat's Away. A Comedy in One Act for Young Ladies*, c.1890. Pub. Chicago: Dramatic Publishing (Sergel's Acting Drama, no. 454).
>
>   *Kate's Infatuation. A Comedy in One Act for Young Ladies*, c. 1899. Pub. NY: Dramatic Publishing (The Wizard Series).

Shields, Sarah Annie Frost, fl. 1859-1889. (Pseud: S. A. Frost.)
>   *Parlor Charades and Proverbs*, 1859. Pub. Philadelphia: Lippincott. Includes: "Matrimony," "Misfortune," "Stage Struck," "Marplot," "Mad-Cap," "Inconstant," "Domestic," "Purse-Proud," "Bridegroom," "Mistake," "The Hoyden."
>
>   *The Parlor Stage. A Collection of Charades and Proverbs Intended for the Drawing Room or Salon*, 1866. Pub. NY: Dick and Fitzgerald.
>
>   *Dialogues for Young Folks. A Collection of Original, Moral and Humorous Dialogues*, 1867. Pub. NY: Dick and Fitzgerald.
>
>   *Amateur Theatricals and Fairy-Tale Dramas. A Collection of Original Plays*, 1868. Pub. NY: Dick and Fitzgerald.

The Book of Tableaux and Shadow Pantomimes, 1869. Pub. NY: Dick and Fitzgerald.

Humorous and Exhibition Dialogues, 1870(?) Pub. NY: Dick and Fitzgerald.

New Book of Dialogues, 1872. Pub. NY: Dick and Fitzgerald.

The Train to Mauro. An Original Interlude in One Act, c.1870. Pub. NY: Dick and Fitzgerald.

Refinement, c.1874. In *Beadle's Dime Dialogues*, no. 14 (1874).

Dramatic Proverbs and Charades, 1876.   Pub. NY: Dick and Fitzgerald.

Parlor Acting Charades, 1876. Pub. NY: Dick and Fitzgerald.

Evening Amusements; or, Merry Hours for Merry People, 1878. With Henry T. Williams. Pub. NY: H. Williams.

The Young Amazon. A Farce Comedy in One Act, 187-?. Pub. NY: Dick and Fitzgerald (Dick's American Edition).

Aladdin; or, The Wonderful Lamp. A Fairy Tale Drama for the Little Folks, 1899. Pub. NY: Dick and Fitzgerald.

All's Well that Ends Well. A Petite Comedy in One Act, n.d. Pub. NY: Dick and Fitzgerald (Dick's American Edition), 189-?.

Beauty and the Beast, Modernized Version, n.d. Pub. NY: Dick and Fitzgerald (Dick's American Edition), 190-?.

Blue Beard. A Melodramatic Travesty, n.d. Pub. NY: Dick and Fitzgerald (Dick's American Edition), 189-?.

Bolts and Bars. A Comedy in One Act, n.d. Pub. NY: Dick and Fitzgerald (Dick's American Edition).

The Little Glass Slipper; or, Cinderella in a New Dress. An Extravaganza, n.d. Pub. NY: Dick and Fitzgerald (Dick's American Edition).

Short, Marion.

See Phelps, Pauline.

Also authored several plays alone after 1901.

Silsbee, Alice M.

Jolly Joe's Lady Minstrels. Selections for the "Sisters," c.1893. With Mary Bernard Horne. Pub. Boston: W. Baker. Includes *Jolly Joe's Lady Minstrels* and *Bells in the Kitchen*.

Smith, Adele Crafton. (Pseud.: Nomad.)

Caught at Last. A Comedietta in One Act, c.1884. Pub. NY: DeWitt (DeWitt Acting Plays, no. 333). Bound with *The Blue Stocking* by Delissa Joseph.

Smith, Elizabeth Oakes Prince, 1806-1893.

The Roman Tribute; or, Attila the Hun, 1850. Perf. Philadelphia: Arch St. Th., Nov. 11, 1850. Pub. NY.

Old New York; or, Democracy in 1689. A Tragedy in Five Acts, 1853. Perf. NY: Broadway Th., 1853. Pub. NY: Stringer and Townsend.

Smith, Lilli Huger.

A Rank Deception. A Farce in Two Acts, c.1899. Pub. Boston: W. Baker (Baker's Edition of Plays).

Daddy. A Comedy, 1912. Pub. Boston: W. Baker (Baker's Edition of Plays).

Smith, S. Jennie, d. 1904.

A Free Knowledge-ist; or, Too Much for One Head. A Comedy in Two Acts, c. 1893. Pub. Chicago: T. Denison (Amateur Series).

Doctor Cure-All. A Comedy in Two Acts, c.1894. In *Easy Entertainments for Young People* (Philadelphia: 1894).

A Perplexing Situation. A Comedy in Two Parts, 1895. Pub. Philadelphia: Penn Publishing, 1916.

Not a Man in the House. A Comedy in Two Acts, c.1897. Pub. Chicago: T. Denison (Amateur Series).

The Home Guard. An All-Female Comedy in One Act, 1904. Pub. Philadelphia: Penn Publishing.

Trying It on Beldon. A Comedy in Two Acts, 1904. Pub. Boston: W. Baker.

Smith, Sarah Pogson.

The Female Enthusiast. A Tragedy in Five Acts, 1807. Pub. Charleston: J. Hoff.

The Orphans, c.1818. In her *Essays Religious, Moral, Dramatic, and Poetical, Addressed to Youth; and Published for a Benevolent Purpose* (Charleston: A. E. Miller, 1818).

A Tyrant's Victims, c.1818. In *Essays*, as above.

The Young Carolinians, c.1818. In *Essays*, as above.

Speed, Belle Tevis.

Columbia. Drama in One Act for Thirty-One Females, 1894. Adap. of S. Rogers and J. Barlow. Pub. NY: E. Werner.

Spencer, Bella Zilfa, 1840-1867.

The Two Wives of Lynn. An Original Play in Five Acts, 1866. Pub. San Francisco: Alta California Print House.

Sprague, Achsa W., 1827-1862.

The Poet, 1865. In her *The Poet and Other Poems*, pub. Boston: White.

Sprague, Besse Toulouse, 1893.

Co-authored at least one play with Pauline Phelps after 1901.

Steiner, Olga, b. 1865. (Full name: Schlesinger, Olga Steiner.)

The Fortune-Teller. A Farce Comedy in One Act, c.1899. Pub. Chicago: Dramatic Publishing (Sergel's Acting Drama, no. 505).

The Ghost in the Boarding School. A Comedy in One Act for Young Ladies, c.1899. Pub. Chicago: Dramatic Publishing (Sergel's Acting Drama, no. 452).

Hard of Hearing. A Comedy in One Act for Young Ladies, c. 1899. Pub. Chicago: Dramatic Publishing, c. 1899 (Sergel's Acting Drama, no. 451).

Miss Nonchalance. A Comedy in One Act, c.1899. Pub. Chicago: Dramatic Publishing (Sergel's Acting Drama, no. 538).

Also wrote approx. eighteen plays in German, 1892-1921.

Stevenson, Kate Claxton Cone.

Two Orphans. A Play in Six Acts, 187-?. Adap. of A. P. Dennery and P. E. Piestre.

Stone, Mary T.

The Social Highwayman, 1895. Adap. of story by Eliza P. Train. Perf. NY: Sept. 24, 1895. Typescript in New York Pub. Lib.

House of the Wolf, n.d.

Sutherland, Evelyn Greenleaf Baker, 1855-1908.

Marsa Van, 1895. With Emma Sheridan Fry. Perf. NY: Empire Th., Jan. 25, 1895.

On the Arcady Trail, 1899. Perf. NY: Empire Th., Oct. 26, 1899.

At the Barricade. An Episode of the Commune of '71, 1899. Perf. Empire, Dec. 14, 1899. In her *Po' White Trash* (1900).

Galatea of the Toy-Shop. A Fantasy in One Act, 1899(?). In her *Po' White Trash* (1900).

A Comedie Royall, Being a Forgotten Episode of Elizabeth's Day, 1900(?). In her *Po' White Trash* (1900).

The End of the Way, c.1900 Pub. NY: H. Stone. In her *Po' White Trash* (1900).

In Far Bohemia, 1900. With Emma Sheridan Fry. Pub. Chicago. In her *Po' White Trash* (1900).

Po' White Trash and Other One-Act Dramas, 1900. With Emma Sheridan Fry and Percy W. Mackaye. Pub. Chicago: H. Stone. Repub. NY: Duffield, 1909. Includes: *Po White Trash*; *In Far Bohemia* (with Emma Sheridan Fry); *The End of the Way*; *A Comedie Royall*; *A Bit of Instruction*; *A Song at the Castle* (with Percy W. MacKaye); *Rohan the Silent*; *At the Barricade*; *Galatea of the Toy-Shop*.

Rohan the Silent. A Romantic Drama in One Act, 1900. With Emma Sheridan Fry. Pub. NY: H. Stone. Also in her *Po' White Trash* (1900),

In Office Hours and Other Sketches for Vaudeville or Private Acting, 1900. Pub. Boston: W. Baker. Includes: *In Office Hours*; *A Quilting Party in the Thirties*; *In Aunt Chloe's Cabin*; *The Story of a Famous Wedding*.

Beaucaire, 1901. With Booth Tarkington. Perf. NY: Herald Square Th., Dec. 2, 1901.

Joan of the Shoals, 1902. Perf. NY: Republic Th., Feb. 3, 1902.

In Aunt Chloe's Cabin. A Comedy in One Act, n.d. Pub. Boston: W, Baker (Baker's Novelty Plays), 1925. In her *In Office Hours* (1900). Also see Dix, Beulah Marie.

Swanwick, Catherine. (Adams, L. B., pseud.?)

Eva. A Tragic Poem. In One Scene, 1859. In *Plays and Poems of L.* Pub. NY: Delisser and Procter.

Sybelle and Other Poems, 1862. Pub. NY: G. Carleton.

Poems: Narrative and Dramatic, 1872. Pub. London: E. Whitfield.

Swayze, Kate Lucy Edwards, 1834-1862. (Pseud.: Mrs. Savage.)

Ossawattomie Brown; or, The Insurrection at Harper's Ferry. A Drama in Three Acts, 1859. Perf. NY: Bowery Th., Dec. 16, 1859. Pub. NY: S. French (French's Standard Drama, Acting Edition, no. 226), 1860(?).

Talladay, Jennie.

Aunt Hannah's Quilting Party, 1891. Pub. Auburn, NY: W. Moses.

The Little Country Store. In One Act, 1894. Pub. Auburn, NY: W. Moses.

Uncle Sam's Relation. An Original Comedy in Two Acts, 1904. Pub. NY: B. Sprague.

Stumpville Sewin' Circle. An Original Comedy in Two Acts, 1907. Pub. Auburn, NY: The Citizen Press.

Tammie, Carrie.

The Birthday Cake. A Comedy in Two Acts, c.1899. Pub. Chicago: Dramatic Publishing (Sergel's Acting Drama, no. 551).

Thayer, Ella Cheever.

Lords of Creation. Woman Suffrage Drama in Three Acts, c.1883. Pub. Boston: W. Baker (Baker's Edition of Plays). In *On to Victory: Propaganda Plays of the Woman Suffrage Movement*, ed. B. Friedl (Boston: Northeastern Univ. Press, 1987).

Thayer, Julia M.

Fighting the Rum-Fiend, n.d. In *Dramatic Leaflets* (Philadelphia: P. Garrett, 1877).

Thomas, Edith Matilda, 1854-?.

A New Year's Masque, 1885. In her *A New Years' Masque and Other Poems*, pub. Boston: Houghton Mifflin.

Thompson, Amira Carpenter.

The Lyre of Tioga, 1829. Pub. Geneva, NY: (for the author) J. Rogert.

The Trial of Atticus Before Justice, n.d.

The Tricks of the Times, n.d.

Thompson, Caroline Eunice.

Blind Margaret. A Dramatic Sketch, c.1890. Adap. of Longfellow's "Blind Girl of Castle-Cuille," a trans. of J. Jasmin. Music by G. T. Page. Pub. Chicago: T. Denison (Denison's Specialties).

Tibbets, Martie E.

Two Aunt Emilys; or, Quits. A Farce for Eight Female Characters, c.1890. Pub. Clyde, OH: Ames (Ames' Series of Standard and Minor Drama, no. 281).

Tiffany, Esther Brown, b. 1858.

That Patrick! A Comedy in One Act, c.1886. Pub. Boston: W. Baker (Baker's Boston List).

Young Mr. Pritchard. A Comedy in Two Scenes, c.1886. Pub. Boston: W. Baker (Baker's Boston List).

The Angel at the Sepulchre, 1889. Pub. Boston: L. Prang, 1890.

Anita's Trial; or, Our Girls in Camp. A Comedy in Three Acts for Female Characters, c.1889. Pub. Boston: W. Baker (Baker's Boston List).

An Autograph Letter. A Comedy in Three Acts, c.1889. Pub. Boston: Baker (Baker's Edition of Plays).

A Rice Pudding. A Comedy in Two Acts, c.1889. Pub. Boston: W. Baker (Baker's Boston List).

The Way to His Pocket. A Comedy in One Act, c.1889. Pub. Boston: W. Baker (Baker's Edition of Plays).

The Spirit of the Pine. A Christmas Masque, c.1890. Pub. Boston: L. Prang.

A Borrowed Umbrella. A Comedietta in One Act, c.1893. Pub. Boston: W. Baker (Baker's Edition of Plays).

A Model Lover. A Comedy in Two Acts, c.1893. Pub. Boston: W. Baker (Baker's Edition of Plays).

A Blind Attachment. A Comedy in One Act, 1895. Pub. Boston: W. Baker (Baker's Edition of Plays).

Apollo's Oracle. An Entertainment in One Act, 1897. Music from *Iphigenie en Tauride* by Gluck. Pub. Boston: W. Baker (Baker's Novelties).

Bachelor Maids. A Comedy in One Act for Female Characters, c.1897. Pub. Boston: W. Baker (Baker's Edition of Plays).

A Tell-Tale Eyebrow. A Comedy in Two Acts, c. 1897. Pub. Boston: W. Baker (Baker's Edition of Plays).

The Tocsin. A Drama of the Renaissance, 1900. Pub. San Francisco: P. Elder.

Club and Lodge-Room Entertainments for Floor or Platform Use, 1908. With Frank Chase. Pub. Boston: W. Baker.

A Hole in the Fence. A Farce Comedy, 1908. Pub. Boston: W. Baker.

Toler, (Mrs. H. M.)

    Thekla. A Fairy Drama in Three Acts, c.1884. Pub. Clyde, OH: Ames (Ames Series of Standard and Minor Drama, no. 144).

    Eh; What Did You Say? A Farce in Three Scenes, c.1885. Pub. Clyde, OH: Ames (Ames Series of Standard and Minor Drama, no. 148).

    Waking Him Up. A Farce in One Act, c.1885. Pub. Clyde, OH: Ames (Ames Series of Standard and Minor Drama, no. 147).

Toler, Sallie F.

    Handicapped; or, A Racing Romance. An Original Comedy in Two Acts, c.1894. Pub. NY: DeWitt (DeWitt's Acting Plays, no. 399).

    Bird's Island. A Drama in Four Acts, c.1897. Pub. Chicago: Dramatic Publishing (American Acting Drama).

Townsend, Eliza, 1788-1854.

    The Wife of Seaton; or, The Siege of Berwick. An Historic Tragedy in Five Acts, 1856. In her *Poems and Miscellanies* (Boston: [for the author] G. Rand and Avery).

Townsend, M. G.

    The Ugliest of Seven A Farce in Three Acts, 1886. Adap. of German original. Pub. Philadelphia: Penn Publishing, 1903. In *Dramatic Leaflets* (Philadelphia: P. Garrett, 1877).

Tracy, H. L.

    The Cost of a Dress, c.1874. In *Beadle's Dime Dialogues*, no. 14 (1874).

Tretbar, Helen D.

    Rustic Chivalry. Melodrama in One Act, 189-?. Adap. of G. Verga. Music by P. Mascagni. Bilingual text (English/Italian). Pub. NY: R. Saalfield.

Troubetzkoy, Amèlie Rives Chanler, 1863-1945. (Pseud.: Princess Troubetzkoy).

    Herod and Mariamne. A Tragedy, 1888. Pub. in *Lippincott's Monthly Magazine*, vol. 42 (Sept., 1888). In *A Hebrew Anthology*, ed. G. Kohut (Cincinnati: 1913).

    Athelwold. A Tragedy, 1893. Pub. NY: Harper.

    November Eve, 1923. In her *The Sea-Woman's Cloak. Two Plays* (Cincinnati: S. Kidd).

    The Sea-Woman's Cloak, 1923. In her *The Sea-Woman's Cloak. Two Plays*, as above.

    Love-in-a-Mist. A Comedy in Three Acts, 1927. With Gilbert Emery (pseud.). Pub. NY: S. French (French's Standard Library Edition).

    The Fear Market, n.d. Adapted in 1920 by Clara Berenger.

Trumbull, Annie Eliot.

See Eliot, Annie.

Tucker, Althea Sprague.
    See Ford, Harriett.
V., Mary V. (Pseud.)
    A Dialogue between a Southern Delegate and his Spouse on his Return from the Grand Continental Congress: A Fragment Inscribed to the Married Ladies of America, by their Most Sincere and Affectionate Friend and Servant, Mary V. V.. Pub. NY: J. Rivington, 1774.
    Valeria; or, Love and Blindness, n.d.
    The Village Wedding: A Drama, n.d.
Van Alstyne, Frances Jane Crosby.
    See Crosby, Fannie J.
Van Harlingen, Katherine.
    An Original Widow's Pension; or, The Fugitive Fortune. A Comedy in Four Acts, 1898. Typescript.
Varrie, Vida.
    The Coming Man; or, Fifty Years Hence, 1872. Pub. Philadelphia: E. Markley.
Victor, Frances Fuller, 1826-1902.
    Azlea, c.1851. In her *Poems* (NY: A. Barnes, 1851).
Walcot, Maria Grace.
    The Cup and the Lip. A Comedy in Five Acts, 1859. Adap. of *Le Testament de Cesar Girodot*, by M. Belot and E. Villetard. Perf. Paris: Odeon, Sept. 30, 1859; NY: Winter Garden Th., Oct. 7, 1861. Pub. NY: S. French (French's Standard Drama, no. 227), 1861.
Walker, Janet Edmondson.
    The New Governess. A Comedy in One Act, c.1899. Adap. of German original. Pub. Chicago: Dramatic Publishing (Sergel's Acting Drama, no. 537).
Wall, Annie Russell.
    Is Lying Easy? A Comedy, 1877. Adap. of Benedix. Pub. St. Louis: G. Jones.
Wallberg, Anna Cronhjelm.
    Fridthjof and Ingeborg. Opera in Three Acts, 1898. Music by Charles F. Hanson. Adap. of Tegner's *Fridthjof's Saga*. Bilingual text (English/Swedish). Pub. Worcester, MA: C. Hanson.
Walworth, Reubena Hyde.
    Where Was Elsie; or, The Saratoga Fairies. A Comedietta in One Act, 1900. Pub. NY: E. Werner.
Warren, Mercy Otis, 1728-1814.
    The Adulateur, 1773.
    The Defeat, 1773.
    The Group. As Lately Acted and Said to Be Re-Acted to the Wonder of

All Superior Intelligences, Near Headquarters at Amboyne, 1775. Pub. Boston: Edes and Gill. In *Representative Plays by American Dramatists,* ed. M. Moses (NY: 1918-25) and other anthologies.

The Blockheads; or, The Affrighted Officers, 1776 [attributed]. In *Trumpets Sounding: Propaganda Plays of the American Revolution,* ed. N. Philbrick (NY: 1972).

The Motley Assembly, 1779 [attributed]. In *Trumpets Sounding,* as above.

The Ladies of Castile, c.1790. In her *Poems, Dramatic and Miscellaneous* (Boston: Thomas and Andrews, 1790).

The Sack of Rome, c.1790. In her *Poems, Dramatic and Miscellaneous,* as above.

Wells, Anna Maria Foster, 1795?-1868

The Owl and the Swallow, c.1830. In her *Poems and Juvenile Sketches* (Boston: Hendee and Babcock, 1830).

West, A. Laurie.

The Shades of Shakespeare's Women. An Entertainment in Ten Scenes, c. 1896. Pub. NY: E. Werner (Werner's Plays).

Weston, Effie Ellsler, 1858-1942.

A Wolf in Sheep's Clothing, 18-?. Typescript/ promptbook.

Heart's Byways, 19-?. Typescript.

Her Calvary, 19-?. Promptbook in New York Pub. Lib.

His Love Story. A Play in One Act, 19-?. Typescript.

Jim and I. A Playlet in One Act, 191-?. Typescript.

As Who Shall Say. A Play, n.d. Promptbook in New York Pub. Lib.

The Flyers, n.d. Adap. of G. B. McCutcheon. Typescript.

Good Ground. An Original Play, n.d. Promptbook in New York Pub. Lib.

Hawks and Doves. An Original Play, n.d. Typescript in New York Pub. Lib.

His Official Fiancee. A Play in One Act, n.d. Adap. of novel by Berta Ruck. Promptbook in New York Pub. Lib.

His Woman, n.d. Typescript.

Honesty's Garden, n.d. Adap. of story by Paul Creswick. Typescript.

Man and the World. A Play, n.d. Typescript.

The Rosary, n.d. Adap. of story by Florence Barclay. Typescript.

Tillie, n.d. Adap. of novel by Helen Martin. Typescript.

The Turn in the Road. A Play in One Act, n.d. (Original title: *The Mills of the Gods.*) Typescript.

Wheeler, Esther Gracie Lawrence, fl. 1875-1893.
   A Cup of Tea Drawn from 1773, in Three Acts, 1875.   Pub.
Cambridge, MA: Riverside Press.
   A Doctor in Spite of Herself (Not by Moliére). Drama in One Act, n.d.
Typescript in New York Pub. Lib.
Whitaker, Lily C., b. 1850.
   Young American Progressive Hobby Club. A Farce in One Scene, 1896.
Pub. NY: E. Werner.
Wiley, Sara King, 1871-1909. (Full name Drummond, Sara King Wiley.)
   Cromwell. An Historical Play, c.1900.   In her *Poems, Lyrical and
Dramatic* (NY: G. Richmond, 1900).
Wilkins, Mary Eleanor.
   See Freeman, Mary Eleanor Wilkins.
Williams, Marie Josephine.
   A Brown Paper Parcel, c.1899.   Pub. NY: S. French (French's
International Copyrighted Edition of the Works of the Best Authors, no.
26).
   A Nice Quiet Chat, c.1899.   Pub. NY: S. French (French's
International Copyrighted Edition of the Works of the Best Authors, no.
25).
   A Helpless Couple, c.1905. Pub. NY: S. French.
Wilson, Bertha M.
   Indian Sketches. An Entertainment for Home Talent, 1894. Pub. NY:
H. Roorbach (Roorbach's American Edition of Acting Plays, no. 69).
   Playing the Society Belle; or, The Tragedy of a Slipper, c.1894.   Pub.
NY: E. Werner.
   *A Chinese Wedding. A Representation of the Wedding Ceremony in
China, Arranged as a Costume Pantomime in Seven Scenes*, 1895. Pub.
Philadelphia: Penn Publishing (Keystone Edition of Popular Plays;
Dramatic Library, vol. 1, no. 16).
   *John Brown's Ten Little Indians. A Tomahawk March and Drill for the
Male Characters*, c.1895. With music. Pub. NY: Dick and Fitzgerald.
   *The March of the Chinese Lanterns. A Spectacular Novelty Drill for
Girls*, 1895. Pub. New York: Fitzgerald.
   *Maud Muller Drill. A Pantomime Drill for Male and Female
Characters*, 1895. Pub. NY: Dick and Fitzgerald.
   *Seniors. A Three-Act Play Written for the Class of '95 of the South
Dakota State Normal School*, 1895. Pub. Spearfish, SD: Register Book
and Job Office.
   *The Show at Wilkins' Hall; or, A Leaf from the Life of Maria Jane.
Arranged for Either a Lady or a Gentleman in Female Costume*, c.1895.
Pub. NY: Dick and Fitzgerald.

Spring Garlands. A "Pose"-y Drill and March for Maids and Gallants of Ye Olden Tyme, c.1895. Pub. NY: Fitzgerald.

The Tray of Blind Margaret, 1895. Adap. of Longfellow's "Blind Girl of Castle-Cuille" (trans. of "L'aveugle de Castel-Cuiller" by Jacques B. Jasmin). Pub. Philadelphia: Penn Publishing (Keystone Edition of Popular Plays).

Wilson's Book of Drills and Marches for Young People and Small Children, 1895. Pub. NY: Dick and Fitzgerald.

Raggles' Corner. A Farce in One Scene, 1901. Pub. Philadelphia: Penn Publishing.

Mr. Spriggs' Little Trip to Europe. A Comedy in One Act, 1904. Pub. Philadelphia: Penn Publishing.

The Christmas Star. A Monologue in Two Scenes, 1911. Pub. Philadelphia: Penn Publishing.

Preciosa, the Spanish Dancer, c.1911. Adap. of Longfellow's "The Spanish Student." Pub. NY: E. Werner.

Nigger Baby. A Monologue, 1915. Pub. Philadelphia: Penn Publishing.

The Bootblack Drill. A Novelty Drill for Small Boys or Girls, n.d. Pub. New York: Fitzgerald.

Wilson, Ella Calista Handy, b. 1851.

Santa Claus at Home. A Christmas Operetta, 1883. Pub. Boston: W. Baker (Plays for Little Folks).

The Bachelor's Christmas. A Christmas Entertainment, c.1889. Pub. Boston: W. Baker (Baker's Edition of Plays).

Wilson, Jane.

Percy, 1825. Perf. New Orleans: American, Apr. 15, 1825.

Wilson, Louise Latham.

A Case of Suspension. A Comedietta in One Act, 1899. Pub. Philadelphia: Penn Publishing.

The Scientific Country School. A Farcical Entertainment, 1899. Pub. Philadelphia: Penn Publishing.

The Smith Mystery. A Comedy in One Act, c.1899. Pub. Chicago: Dramatic Publishing (Sergel's Acting Drama, no. 503).

The Trouble at Satterlee's. A Farce in One Act, 1899. Pub. Philadelphia: Penn Publishing, 1911.

Two of a Kind. A Comedy, c.1899. Pub. Chicago: T. Denison (Amateur Series).

The Wreck of Stebbins Pride. A Comedy in Two Acts, 1899. Pub. Philadelphia: Penn Publishing, 1903.

The Old Maids' Association. A Farcical Entertainment, 1900. Pub. Philadelphia: Penn Publishing.

A Little Game with Fate. A Comedy in One Act, 1901. Pub. Chicago:

Dramatic Publishing (Sergel's Acting Drama, no. 497).

A Parliament of Servants. A Comedy in One Act, 1901.   Pub. Chicago: Dramatic Publishing (American Acting Drama).

A Suit of Livery. A Farce Comedy in Two Acts, 1901.   Pub. Boston: W. Baker.

All on Account of an Actor. A Farce in One Act, 1904.   Pub. Philadelphia: Penn Publishing.

The Fortunes of War. A Farce in One Act, 1904.   Pub. Philadelphia: Penn Publishing.

Returning the Calculus. A College Comedy in One Act, 1917.   Pub. Philadelphia: Penn Publishing.

Where Is Helen? A Farce Comedy in Two Acts, 1917.   Pub. Philadelphia: Penn Publishing.

Priscilla's Room. A Farce in One Act, 1921.   Pub. Syracuse, NY: W. Bugbee (Bugbee's Popular Plays).

Wilson, Olivia Lovell.

Plays, Pantomimes, and Charades, 1857.   Pub. Boston.

The Marriage of Prince Flutterby. A Comedy for Children in One Act, 1886.   Pub. Boston: W. Baker (Baker's Edition of Plays).

The Luck of the Golden Pumpkin, c. 1887.   Pub. Boston: W. Baker. Bound with *The Old Woman Who Lived in a Shoe* [and] *Christmas* [from *Christmas Entertainments for Home and School*] by Jay Kaye.

Winn, Edith Lynwood, 1868-1933.

A Vision of Fair Women. A Dramatic Paraphrase Based on Tennyson's Dream of Fair Women, c.1891.   Pub. Boston: W. Baker (Baker's Edition of Plays; Baker's Novelty List).

Winslow, Catherine Mary Reignolds, d. 1911.

Broken Trust. A Drama in Five Acts, c.1886.

Winston, Mary A.

A Rural Ruse. A Comedy in One Act, c.1893.   Pub. Boston: W. Baker (Baker's Edition of Plays).

Winters, Elizabeth.

Columbia, the Gem of the Ocean, c.1899.   Pub. Chicago: A. Flanagan.

Japanese Fan Drill, c.1901.   In *Three Drills and a Farce by Teachers Who Have Used Them* (Chicago: c.1901).

The Green Entertainment Book: Fifty-Four Plays, Dialogs, Drills, Readings. . .for All the Grades, 1930.   With J. Barnet.   Pub. Chicago: A. Flanagan.

Wood, Juliana Westray.

The North American, 1823.   Perf. Philadelphia: Chestnut St. Th., Apr. 30, 1823.

Woodbury, Alice Gale.
  The Match-Box. An Original Comedy in Two Acts, c. 1894. Pub.
  Chicago: Dramatic Publishing (Sergel's Acting Drama, no. 400).
Woodhull, Mary Gould, b.1861.
  For Old Love's Sake. A Comedy in Two Acts, 1896. Pub.
  Philadelphia: Penn Publishing (Keystone Edition of Plays).
Woods, Virna, 1864-1903.·
  The Amazons. A Lyrical Drama, 1891. Pub. Meadville, PA: Flood
  and Vincent.
Woolson, Constance Fenimore, 1838-1894.
  Two Women: 1862. A Poem [in dramatic form], 1877. Pub. NY:
  Appleton (Reprinted from *Appleton's Journal*).
Wright, Frances, 1795-1852.
  Altorf: A Tragedy, 1819. Perf. NY: Park Th., February 19, 1819.
  Pub. Philadelphia: M. Carey.
Young, Margaret.
  Kitty. A Dramatic Sketch for Two Female Characters, 18-?. Pub.
  Chicago: Dramatic Publishing (Sergel's Acting Drama, no. 563; The
  Wizard Series). Also pub. NY: Roxbury.

Sources for Bibliography:
  Arata, Esther Spring and Nicholas John Rotoli. *Black American Playwrights, 1800-Present*. Metuchen, NJ: Scarecrow Press, 1976.
  Bergquist, G. William. *Three Centuries of English and American Plays: A Checklist*. New York: Hafner Publishing, 1963.
  Clark, Barret H., ed. *America's Lost Plays*. Princeton: Princeton University Press, 1940-49.
  Hatch, James V. and Omanii Abdullah. *Black Playwrights, 1823-1977: An Annotated Bibliography of Plays*. NY: R. R. Bowker, 1977.
  Hill, Frank P. *American Plays Printed 1714-1830*. Stanford: Stanford University Press, 1934.
  Hixon, Donald L. *Nineteenth-Century American Drama. A Finding Guide*. Metuchen, NJ: Scarecrow Press, 1977.
  Logan, Mary S. *The Part Taken by Women in American History*. New York: Arno Press, Reprint Ed., 1972. Women playwrights, pp. 789-793.
  Nichols, Kathleen, "Earlier American Women Dramatists: A Select Bibliography," *Theatre History Studies* vol. XI (1991).
  Roden, Robert F. *Later American Plays, 1831-1900*. New York: Burt Franklin, 1900.
  Three Centuries of Drama, American. Readex Micro Print.
  Wegelin, Oscar. *Early American Plays, 1714-1830*. New York: Dunlap Society, 1900.